THE HITLER ÉMIGRÉS

The Cultural Impact on Britain of Refugees from Nazism

Also by Daniel Snowman

PastMasters: The Best of History Today (ed)
Fins de Siècle (ed; with Asa Briggs)
Plácido Domingo's Tales From the Opera
*Pole Positions: the Polar Regions
and the Future of the Planet*
Beyond the Tunnel of History: the 1989 BBC Reith Lectures
(with Jacques Darras)
The World of Plácido Domingo
The Amadeus Quartet: The Men and the Music
If I Had Been . . . Ten Historical Fantasies (ed)
*Kissing Cousins: An Interpretation of British and
American Culture, 1945–1975*
Eleanor Roosevelt
USA: The Twenties to Vietnam

THE HITLER ÉMIGRÉS

The Cultural Impact on Britain of Refugees from Nazism

━━━

DANIEL SNOWMAN

Chatto & Windus
LONDON

Published by Chatto & Windus 2002

2 4 6 8 10 9 7 5 3 1

Copyright © Daniel Snowman 2002

Daniel Snowman has asserted his right under the Copyright, Designs and Patents Act 1988
to be identified as the author of this work

First published in Great Britain in 2002 by
Chatto & Windus
Random House, 20 Vauxhall Bridge Road,
London SW1V 2SA

Random House Australia (Pty) Limited
20 Alfred Street, Milsons Point, Sydney,
New South Wales 2061, Australia

Random House New Zealand Limited
18 Poland Road, Glenfield,
Auckland 10, New Zealand

Random House (Pty) Limited
Endulini, 51 Jubilee Road, Parktown 2193, South Africa

The Random House Group Limited Reg. No. 954009
www.randomhouse.co.uk

A CIP catalogue record for this book is available from the British Library

ISBN 0 7011 6880 3

Papers used by Random House are natural, recyclable products made from wood grown in
sustainable forests; the manufacturing processes conform to the environmental regulations
of the country of origin

Typeset by SX Composing DTP, Rayleigh, Essex
Printed and bound in Great Britain by
Biddles Limited, Guildford

Contents

List of Illustrations

Rudolf Bing, Fritz Busch and Carl Ebert at Glyndebourne (Glyndebourne Archives)
Fritz Busch (Royal Academy of Music/Lebrecht Music Collection)
Karl Rankl with Constance Shacklock (Lebrecht Music Collection)
Kurt Jooss and Rudolf Laban at Dartington Hall (From the Rudolf Laban Archive, National Resource Centre for Dance)
Laban drawing of moving body (From the Rudolf Laban Archive, National Resource Centre for Dance. Used with permission)
The Green Table (*above*, from the Rudolf Laban archive, National Resource Centre for Dance/ *below*, Lebrecht Music Collection)
The Penguin Pool at London Zoo
The de la Warr Pavilion (de la Warr Pavilion)
Impington Village College (The governing body at Impington Village College)

The Royal Festival Hall (Royal Festival Hall)
Cartoons by Gerard Hoffnung, published in 'The Hoffnung Symphony Orchestra' (The Hoffnung Partnership)
Martin Esslin with Samuel Beckett (Martin Esslin)
Moonraker designs by Ken Adam (Ken Adam)
The Amadeus Quartet (Milein Cosman)
Cartoon from the *Evening Standard*, London, 9 September 1969. By JAK (Atlantic Syndication)
The Red Shoes poster (AKG)
Sir Nikolaus Pevsner (Pevsner Architectural Guides: The

Sources and Acknowledgements

During the course of my work on this book, between 1997 and 2002, I recorded interviews with: Ken Adam, Felix Aprahamian, Hilde Beal (Pearton), Irene Bloomfield, Anne Bohm, Gustav Born, Norbert Brainin, Sir John Burgh, Robert W. Cahn, Milein Cosman, Martin Esslin, Alexander Goehr, Sir Ernst Gombrich, Michael Hamburger, Stephen Hearst, Eric Hobsbawm, Victor Hochhauser, Hannah Horovitz, Joseph Horovitz, Martin Isepp, Hansi Kennedy, Robert Layton, Susi Rózsa Lovett, Norbert Lynton, Thomas Maschler, Elly (Horovitz) and Harvey Miller, Lord Moser, Eva Neurath, Siegmund Nissel, Max Perutz, Dieter Pevsner, Peter Pulzer, Karel Reisz, Albi Rosenthal, Tom Rosenthal, Esther Salaman, Lionel Salter, Anne-Marie Sandler, Charles Spencer, Fritz Spiegl, Wolf Suschitzky, Marion Thorpe, John Tusa and Lord Weidenfeld. To all, my deepest thanks: their words and thoughts provide a core ingredient in the book. I would also like to thank Sarah Hutton who helped take notes on many of the interviews.

In addition, I spoke to and/or corresponded about my work with each of the following, some briefly, many at length: Audrey Ainsworth, Kitty Alexander, Martin Anderson, Alfred Bader, Sir Terence Beckett, Steven Beller, Charlotte Benton, Tony Birks, Harry Blacker, Judith Bumpus, Peter Burke, Iris Burton, Tom Bussmann, Bruce Caldwell, David Cesarani, Julia Collieu, R. M. Cooper, Hugh Courts, Yvonne Cresswell, Erica Davies, Misha Donat, David Edwards, Hella Ehlers, Ralph Elliott, Vera Elyashiv, Carl F. Flesch, Francesca Franchi, Peter Freyhan, David Goldberg, Alfred Goldstein, Gerald Goldstone, Richard Grunberger, Charles Guttmann, Michael Haas, Paul Hamburger,

Susie Harries, Kenneth Harris, Laurence Hayek, Kathy Henderson, Sue Himmelweit, Annetta Hoffnung, Gillian Hush, Lord Jakobovits, Alisa Jaffa, Ann Jungman, Eva Kammerer, Marion Kant, Liesel Kastner, Jacqueline Kearns, Frederick Kendall, Eckart Krause, Peter Kurer, Henry Kuttner, Birgit Lang, Walter Laqueur, Elbie and Norman Lebrecht, Nicholas Mann, Anna Markard, Dennis Marks, Elisabeth Maybaum, Lady Jean Medawar, Melitta Mew, Muriel Nissel, Jann Parry, Arnold Paucker, Maurice Pearton, Florence Pevsner, Daniel Pick, Malcolm Pines, Frances Pinter, Robert Ponsonby, Alan Powers, Valerie Preston-Dunlop, Frederic Raphael, Andrea Rauter, Claire Rauter, John Raybould, Sue Rose, Murray Roston, Margaret and Michael Rustin, Martin Schain, Christian Schumacher, Dorothy Scruton, Brian Sewell, Nitza and Robin Spiro, Peter Spiro, Riccardo Steiner, Geoffrey Stern, John Stopford-Pickering, Anthony Storr, Anthea Streeter, Jean Symons, Edward Timms, Shirley Toulson, Catherine Townsend, Pamela Tudor-Craig (Lady Wedgwood), Ulrike Walton-Jordan, Walter Wells, Frank Whitford, Thomas Wiseman, Sir Peter Wright and Michael Zander. To all, my grateful thanks for the practical help, advice, guidance, contacts, cautions and constructive goodwill I received.

Many of those listed above kindly helped to lead me to private sources of various sorts. In addition, sources included the works listed in the bibliography as well as all the standard reference books, journals, newspaper cuttings etc. As work progressed, I found my interests overlapping and interlinking with those of a number of institutions, among them the Association of Jewish Refugees, the Leo Baeck Institute, the Imperial War Museum and Freud Museum; the Austrian Cultural Institute (now Forum) and Goethe Institute; and several university-based institutes, notably the Research Centre for German and Austrian Exile Studies (London), the Parkes Library (Southampton) and the Centre for German-Jewish Studies (Sussex), all of which produce work from which I was able to benefit. I used several libraries, not least the local (Westminster) public library system which, despite over-worked staff and limited holdings, somehow managed to deliver an astonishing number of sources I required. I also spent time in various specialist and research libraries, notably the British

Library and (particularly for the earlier chapters of my book) the Wiener Library, and was able to benefit from several archive sources including the Sound Archives of the BBC and the Imperial War Museum and the archives of the Royal Festival Hall and Royal Opera. During the course of my researches, I visited many locations associated with the story of the 'Hitler émigrés': not only the comfortable suburbs of northwest London and elsewhere where many came to live, but also some of the cities and regions (Berlin, Hamburg, Dresden, Vienna, Prague etc.) from which they originated – and the seaside resorts on the Isle of Man that once housed several thousand of them as internees.

Throughout these intellectual and geographical peregrinations, I received consistent help and encouragement from two people on whose professional and personal goodwill I profoundly relied: my agent, Dinah Wiener, and my editor at Chatto and Windus, Penelope Hoare. It is a pleasure to record what a delight it was, from start to finish, to work with two such able and amiable colleagues.

The material in this book links the world I was introduced to by my parents with the world we learn about from our children. Special gratitude is due, therefore, to Janet, and to Ben and Anna, the other three members of our expanding little universe, who, from various fastnesses across the family firmament, continued to radiate welcome waves of warm goodwill.

The subject-matter of *The Hitler Émigrés* can arouse considerable passion. Many who read the book will doubtless feel that particular topics or personalities might warrant more (or less) attention than I have given them, or of a different kind. But I hope that, whatever the reservations about this or that tree, leaf or twig, those who read what follows will relish the immensely rich forest that I have tried to traverse.

I would like to thank the following:
- Berg Publishers: for permission to quote from Günter Berghaus (ed.), *Theatre and Film in Exile*.
- Carlton International Media Ltd: for permission to quote from the films *49th Parallel* and *The Life and Death of Colonel Blimp*.

- EON Productions: for permission to quote from the film *Moonraker*.
- Faber and Faber Ltd: for permission to quote from Kevin Macdonald, *Emeric Pressburger: The Life and Death of a Screenwriter*, and from Stephen Spender, *World Within World*.
- HarperCollins Publishers: for permission to quote from George Weidenfeld, *Remembering My Good Friends*.
- Harvill Press: for permission to quote from Fred Uhlman, *Reunion*.
- John Murray (Publishers) Ltd: for permission to quote from Kenneth Clark, *Another Part of the Wood*.
- Penguin Books: for permission to quote from George Mikes, *How To Be a Brit*.
- Phaidon Press Ltd: for permission to quote from E. H. Gombrich, *The Story of Art*.
- PFD, on behalf of Professor Arthur Marwick: for permission to quote from Arthur Marwick, *British Society Since 1945*.
- The Random House Group Ltd: for permission to quote from Christopher Isherwood, *Prater Violet*.
- Robson Books: for permission to adapt and re-present passages about the Amadeus Quartet originally published in my book *The Amadeus Quartet: The Men and the Music* (Robson Books, 1981).
- Suhrkamp Verlag: for permission to quote from Hermann Hesse, *Wanderings*.
- Yale University Press: for permission to quote from Peter Gay, *My German Question*.

If any other copyright material has been quoted, the author and publishers trust this will be brought to their attention in the hope that formal permission may be obtained and acknowledged in future editions.

Daniel Snowman, London

Introduction

London in the 1960s: the decade the press dub the 'Swinging Sixties'. Jean Shrimpton and Twiggy model provocatively short skirts, David Bailey photographs the rich and famous, EMI's Abbey Road studios provide a regular home-away-from-home for the Beatles and the latest fashion emporia are opened by Terence Conran and Mary Quant. The BBC launches a satirical decade with *That Was the Week that Was* (making stars of David Frost and Bernard Levin) and gains a second channel, while the big screen promotes the careers of Julie Christie, Terence Stamp and Michael Caine. Irreverent painters such as the playful Yorkshireman David Hockney or the more saturnine Francis Bacon produce canvases that provide new kinds of semi-licit frisson, while George Devine, Peter Brook and Peter Hall mount the latest dramatic fireballs by Edward Bond, Harold Pinter, Shelagh Delaney and Arnold Wesker, and celebrate the abolition of theatre censorship. A National Theatre, awaited for half a century, at last sets up shop, albeit in temporary premises in the Waterloo Road.

The 1960s was the decade of the contraceptive pill, of student protest, of the Campaign for Nuclear Disarmament, of a new vocabulary of political assertion, a time when people began to talk of 'Women's Liberation', of 'Sexual Politics' and of being 'Black' or 'Gay'. A popular American president was assassinated and his successor took the US into its most unpopular war. A Labour prime minister talked of the white heat of the technological revolution and financed the development of seven new universities plus a 'University of the Air' to bring education to the widest possible clientele. Throughout the western world, but especially in Britain (and even more especially in London), the young, the post-war 'baby-boomers', ascended the demographic pole and, as though determined to have a voice commensurate with their numbers, shouted louder, asserted themselves more powerfully and tried to change the world. The phrase 'Cultural Revolution' sat awkwardly on English-speaking lips, evoking images of Mao and his Little Red Book. But a cultural revolution in the broadest sense was effected by the bright new generation who took over the streets and shops, the art houses, universities and boutiques in the Swinging Sixties.

That, in outline, is the popular picture, a mythologised mantra of celebrity. But there was another cultural revolution in Britain during this period, not precisely associated with a single decade and not as noisily celebrated, perhaps, but a revolution arguably more profound.

Walter Cook had been talking of his New York Institute of Art when he said, back in the 1930s: 'Hitler is my best friend; he shakes the tree and I collect the apples.' But the sentiment was one that many in Britain came to share.

I remember thinking about this one evening in June 1965. I was at the Royal Opera House, Covent Garden, where I had managed to obtain a seat, high up and somewhat to the side but with a good view of the orchestra. Everyone had read in the papers how this production (by Peter Hall) was going to be something of a scandal, what with naked virgins and a human sacrifice. Not the sort of thing the Lord Chamberlain would normally permit on the stage, perhaps. But then this was 'high art'. In the stalls I was able to pick out Claus Moser, Berlin-born and a passionate music lover. Moser was on the faculty of the London School of Economics and would soon be appointed Director of the Central Statistical Office. He was also on the Board of the Royal Opera House and would later become its Chairman. George Weidenfeld was in the audience too. A prominent publisher and bridge between readers and the great authors of continental Europe and beyond, Weidenfeld had adored opera ever since his childhood in Vienna and would not miss an occasion like this. Present, too, was the composer and musicologist Egon Wellesz, once a protégé of tonight's composer. Wellesz had written an introductory note in the programme in which he quoted something he remembered Mahler saying in 1907. Karl Rankl, first Musical Director of this company, was there too, returning to his old house for the first time in many years and sitting hunched in near obscurity. Tonight's composer was once his professor, too.

The lights dimmed and there was a ripple of applause. Into the pit, angular elbows and shoulders pugnaciously forward, darted Georg Solti, this evening's conductor and the Royal Opera's controversial Musical Director. Sometimes too demanding for the phlegmatic English temperament, Solti was one of those Hungarians who (they would joke behind his back) enter a rotating door after you and come out ahead. Some openly disliked Solti, finding his energy excessive. Members of the chorus and orchestra would imitate his strong Hungarian accent ('But just sink how many langvages I can speak viss ziss accent!' he would riposte with a justifiable grin). On one notorious occasion the 'Get Rid of Solti' campaign led to his car being vandalised. But everybody acknowledged his formidable musicianship and his kindness to the talented young singers he constantly sought out and encouraged. Solti's ambition when he came to Covent Garden was, quite simply, to make this the finest opera house in the world. Bold words. But with Solti at the helm at Covent Garden, and especially when he was in the pit, everyone sensed that something important was going on. Especially on a night like this. Without him it would have been unthinkable for the Royal Opera to have mounted Schoenberg's *Moses and Aaron*.

Moses and Aaron was knotty, controversial, difficult to digest, uncompromisingly 'Modern'. But the production came to be recognised as one of the peaks of the Solti regime. Covent Garden in the 1960s was palpably the great international house Solti was determined to make it, able to present to the highest standards one of the most demanding works of the modern European imagination. And of the various seeds that came to flower that memorable night in London, several of the most

important had been transplanted to British soil from Hitler's
Central Europe.

Britain's artistic and intellectual life was greatly enhanced after
the Second World War by the presence of émigrés from Central
Europe, mostly refugees who had fled from Nazism and, sooner
or later, made a home in Britain. Theirs was the 'other' cultural
revolution of the 1960s.

On London's South Bank Otto Klemperer, crippled almost
to immobility by age and illness, managed to steer his way
through a series of landmark cycles of the Beethoven
symphonies and concertos, while the chamber repertoire was
regularly enriched by uplifting performances by the Amadeus
Quartet. At Glyndebourne the Festival's founding director,
Carl Ebert, returned to produce a string of memorable operatic
productions, many of them also designed, coached, rehearsed
and conducted by émigré talent. Nor was music the only
cultural activity to benefit. Ernst Gombrich, author of the
classic *The Story of Art*, was director of the Warburg Institute
during these years, while fellow art historian Nikolaus Pevsner
systematically logged and described what he considered to be
all the significant 'Buildings of England'. These were important
years, too, for publishers: George Weidenfeld had come from
Austria, André Deutsch from Hungary, and the art publishers
Phaidon and Thames & Hudson were each the creation of
Viennese immigrants. Many of Britain's leading scientists and
intellectuals, too, had been émigrés: people such as Hermann
Bondi (who became Chief Scientific Adviser to the Ministry of
Defence) and the biochemist Max Perutz, the historians
Geoffrey Elton and Eric Hobsbawm, and the philosopher Karl
Popper.

These, and many like them, had come to Britain directly or
indirectly from Germany and Austria, some from Czechoslovakia and Hungary. A few had roots further east, in Russia
and Poland. A number of the émigrés – the architect Walter
Gropius, for example – came to Britain only to move on
elsewhere, mostly to the United States. Others arrived in Britain
not before the war but afterwards. Klemperer, for instance,

spent the war years in the USA, coming to London for a glorious Indian summer as principal conductor of the Philharmonia Orchestra from 1957; Solti was in Switzerland during the war and afterwards in Germany for some years, before coming to live and work in London in 1961. Popper taught philosophy (and wrote his most important books) in New Zealand before moving to the LSE.

Many émigrés were of Jewish background, though most thought of themselves as highly assimilated, their German culture (until the advent of Hitlerism) seeming more important than their Jewishness. Some went further. Gombrich, into extreme old age, would vehemently deny that his Jewish lineage played any part in his intellectual development. A few came from highly religious backgrounds and became rabbis and teachers while there were also those to whom the politics of Judaism – Zionism – was far more enticing than its religious observance. George Weidenfeld, for example, regarded his Zionism as the Archimedean theme guiding his whole life.

We are not, of course, speaking of a single generation. Popper and Gombrich were weaned in a Vienna still feeding at the cultural table of Mahler, Klimt and Schnitzler. This was the world of Béla Horovitz, creator of Phaidon Press. But to his son, the composer Joseph Horovitz, childhood memories were of a Vienna racked by political tension while Joe's sister Hannah was a baby when she was whisked out of Vienna in 1938. The Horovitz family, like the Sigmund Freuds, were among the thousands of refugees from Nazism who left *Mitteleuropa* to settle in the UK – ten thousand of them arriving with the 'Children's Transports' in the last, desperate months before the outbreak of war.

Others made the move in less trying circumstances. Eric Hobsbawm (who had a British passport) arrived from Berlin in 1933 as a teenager when his uncle, with whom he lived, had a chance of work; Gombrich and Perutz settled in Britain in 1936, the former with a job offer and the latter to do graduate work at Cambridge. Essentially, they found themselves in Britain at a time when the situation back in *Mitteleuropa* was deteriorating to such a degree that it became preferable, then prudent, then vital, to stay. These did not come to Britain as refugees, but stayed to find refuge.

Many of the émigrés, while expressing fulsome gratitude to Britain for having rescued them from the jaws of death, also spoke of the pain of having to live in a land, language and culture not their own, the standard lament throughout the ages of people forced into exile. Some, such as the film maker Emeric Pressburger and the writer Arthur Koestler, both of whom had lived in a variety of places before putting down roots in England, felt for the rest of their lives that nowhere was really 'home'.

'Do you think we'll ever really belong anywhere?' asks the little girl in Judith Kerr's classic children's novel *When Hitler Stole Pink Rabbit* as the family travel to England.

'I suppose not,' said Papa. 'Not the way people belong who have lived in one place all their lives. But we'll belong a little in lots of places, and I think that may be just as good.'

Many refugees* retained a sense of home while in exile and some returned when it became possible for them to do so. Kurt Jooss, whose influential dance company repaid their debt to England by strenuous touring throughout the war years and beyond, went back to Germany in 1949 to become a major figure in the resuscitation of dance there after the war, while his colleague the artist Hein Heckroth (best remembered for designing such films as *The Red Shoes* and *The Tales of Hoffmann*) returned to resume his career in Germany in 1956. A few, prompted by communist convictions, left Britain after the war and went (like Brecht) to live and work in East Germany, for example the photomontage artist John Heartfield and – after a spell in prison for espionage – the atomic physicist Klaus Fuchs. More typical was the economic historian Sidney Pollard. Having become Professor of History at the University of Sheffield and a distinguished expert on the Industrial Revolution, Pollard spent his last years before retirement at the University of Bielefeld. 'Though fully at home in Britain,' he

---

* 'We don't like to be called "refugees,"' wrote the political philosopher Hannah Arendt, who fled Nazi Germany for Paris, later settling in the USA. 'We ourselves call each other "newcomers" or "immigrants". Our newspapers are papers for "Americans of German language."'

wrote, 'I never lost the feeling that I was not quite like those born here.'

Others might have been 'exiles' in the eye of the beholder, but tried not to think of themselves as such. The artist and writer Fred Uhlman, who escaped from Nazi Stuttgart to Paris, then nearly got caught up in the Spanish Civil War before finally settling in London, wrote a moving autobiography which he entitled, significantly, *The Making of an Englishman*. By the end of the book Uhlman is something of a country squire (married to the daughter of a titled British MP), living in Essex during the war before moving to London. Many refugees fought with pride in the Allied forces and recalled the experience as the melting pot that turned them into true Brits. Claus Moser's RAF commanding officer advised him to change his first name, at least for the duration, to Michael. 'Give us a tune, Mike!' called Moser's raucous messmates as Claus sneaked over to the piano hoping for a few moments of private communion with Schubert or Mozart.

A few émigrés took the adoption of a British persona to extremes, and there is a splendid but probably apocryphal story of the archetypal refugee who, having doubtless been 'more German than the Germans' before catastrophe struck, goes on to become 'more English than the English'. After innumerable obstacles, he finally receives his naturalisation papers some years after the war – and bursts into tears.

'Don't worry, old chap,' say his friends comfortingly. 'There's no longer anything to worry about.'

'I know,' blubbers the new citizen. 'But why did we have to lose India?'

Paul Tabori (who tells this tale) recounted how he could not suppress a smile when he saw a man who showed his acquired Englishness by wearing his handkerchief up his sleeve rather than in his pocket. George Mikes became famous for a series of affectionately satirical books, starting with *How To Be an Alien* (published in 1946 by his fellow Hungarian refugee André Deutsch), that observed in exquisite detail the contrasts between life on the Continent and the peculiarities of the British.

On Sundays on the Continent even the poorest person puts

on his best suit, tries to look respectable, and at the same time the life of the country becomes gay and cheerful; in England even the richest peer or motor-manufacturer dresses in some peculiar rags, does not shave, and the country becomes dull and dreary. . .

. . . On the Continent people use a fork as though a fork were a shovel; in England they turn it upside down and push everything – including peas – on top of it . . .

When people say 'England', Mikes pointed out, 'they sometimes mean Great Britain, sometimes the United Kingdom, sometimes the British Isles – but never England.'

Was Mikes an 'exile'? Yes, in a sense. But he was also proud to be an Englishman. Indeed, he rather relished his double identity. He even got used to people rhyming his name with 'bikes' instead of calling him (correctly) '*Meek*esh'. In Hungary, he said cheerily to a BBC interviewer in 1972, 'I'm the chap who became an English writer' – while in England everyone still regarded him as 'a Hungarian'.

Towards the end of his life, Mikes and two other ageing Hungarian émigrés, Arthur Koestler and Emeric Pressburger, used to get together in the heart of the East Anglian countryside where for a time each had a home. Three elderly exiles with thick Mid-European accents acting like English country gents. And what did they talk about? Pressburger's grandson and biographer Kevin Macdonald paints a touching picture of the old boys in 1982: in a re-enactment of rituals that went back to a half-remembered childhood, they set themselves up as a committee to organise a traditional Magyar 'pig-eating' orgy.

The men and women whose lives and achievements fill the pages of this book thus include the old and the young, Jewish and non-Jewish, immigrants and refugees, Rhinelanders and Danubians, patriotic British citizens and exiles homesick for *Mitteleuropa*. No single term adequately embraces them all. Nor does the word 'culture' do full justice to the range of their contributions. Half a century ago, the word 'culture' was widely understood to mean much the same as 'intellectual life' and the 'arts'. A cultured person was someone at home with the traditional canon of literature and philosophy, painting and sculpture, theatre, music and architecture. To those in the know, the word was also used in its more specialised, anthropological sense to denote the behaviour, attitudes and values of a tribe, clan or society. Thus the courtship and burial rituals of a primitive society, its divinities and devils, were deemed to be part of its 'culture'. And so, by extension, were the physical manifestations of those values and attitudes – its totem poles and bone necklaces, its axes and coffins.

By the 1960s and 1970s, clever social theorists, taking up themes from Marx, Freud and others, began to emphasise the links between these two concepts of culture and see any art or artifice as, in part, a manifestation of the values and attitudes that lay behind their production. Thus the two usages of the word 'culture' tended to converge. Today, any familiar artefact (a postage stamp, toothbrush or deckchair, a computer game, Nike trainers or the latest cooking aid or cellular phone) is liable to be included in media discussion of our 'culture', as are the latest patterns of behaviour (lap dancing, the sort of headlines our newspapers adopt, the latest home furnishings, the rhetoric of political speeches, new dating styles, whatever). All these are commonly embraced by the word 'culture' in a way that would not have been acceptable fifty years ago. The implication, of course, is that the 'art' a society produces is best understood not as a striving for creative and interpretative excellence but as a manifestation, along with all the other things we make and do, of society's wider attitudes and values.

In this book, the word culture is used in both senses. Much of what follows will consider the contribution of the 'Hitler émigrés' to the 'traditional' arts and sciences. But the attitudes and values of British society, so acutely observed by George Mikes and others, will also be brought under the microscope from time to time. Indeed, part of what is chronicled below includes changing 'cultural' attitudes towards 'high culture'.

Finally, a few words about what this book is and what it is not. It is not a catalogue of contributions from famous émigrés to

British cultural life nor, I trust, an exaggeration of their influence. I do not wish to argue that Britain had little cultural life until this particular wave of people arrived in its midst. Far from it. Britain was never a *Land ohne Musik*, much less a Land without Culture, and in the 1920s and 1930s boasted an intellectual, cultural and artistic life of high quality. It would be foolish, too, to underrate the quality and dynamism of home-grown British cultural life in the years following World War Two, which provided important opportunities for Britain's little band of exiles from Hitler, but for the most part was not created by them. Many excellent writers – cultural historians such as Bryan Appleyard and Robert Hewison as well as central players such as Noel Annan or Peter Hall – have documented the personalities and achievements of the post-war decades and the Hitler refugees get very little mention either collectively or individually.

Yet the émigrés did have an effect, as any substantial group of immigrants is bound to do, on their hosts. Earlier waves of immigration to England – the Huguenots from France after 1685, the Irish who arrived after the potato famine or the Jews from Russia and Poland who came at the end of the nineteenth century and the beginning of the twentieth – all had a profound impact upon the society in which they settled, just as subsequent waves of migrants from the Caribbean and the Indian sub-continent in the second half of the twentieth century were to do. Immigration can give rise to social tensions as two different peoples confront one another and compete for the same homes, school places and jobs. But it is also one of the ways in which a society refreshes itself and avoids the dangers of cultural stagnation. British history is undoubtedly the richer for the mix of Celts and Romans, Angles and Saxons, Normans and Huguenots, Irish and Jews, Germans and Hungarians, Indians, Africans, West Indians and Chinese who have been pushed or pulled to its shores. And the particular group featured in this book made a distinctive contribution to British cultural history. With the passage of time, it is becoming possible to see this in its proper historical perspective. The nature of that contribution, the impact of this particular stone being thrown into the lake of

British cultural life, is what this book will attempt to describe, analyse and assess.

We start with the stone and then go on to consider the lake. Who were the 'Hitler émigrés'? Where did they come from? What did they bring with them and how were they received? To answer these questions we have to go back to *Mitteleuropa*.

PART ONE

THE CULTURE THEY CARRIED

CHAPTER ONE

More German than the Germans

Under an edict of the Emperor Joseph II, Mozart's monarch, everyone of consequence in the Viennese imperial administration was required to communicate in German. German was the language of the Enlightenment, of progress, of liberal writers such as Herder, Lessing and Schiller. In the mid-nineteenth century a younger Emperor, Franz Joseph, pulled down the protective walls encircling Vienna, built a ring road round the city and brought in people from all over the Empire to construct a modern imperial capital. For the first time Jews were permitted to dwell within the city, and the Freud and Kraus families, for example, moved from the provinces to the capital during these years. Sigmund Freud, like Gustav Mahler and so many others raised in the 1870s and 1880s in the wake of German unification, were steeped in German cultural ideals, which by now also incorporated metaphysical concepts – the Will, Spirit, Transcendence – beloved of such celebrated figures as Schopenhauer, Wagner and Nietzsche. These were seductive, supra-national abstractions easily adaptable to the idea that Germany's political unity might be but the prelude to an even greater unification of all those imbued with the true German spirit. This kind of thinking was intoxicating, alluring and dangerous, like the songs of the Lorelei.

Throughout the old Habsburg Empire, which stretched from its capital Vienna north into Bohemia, eastwards to the borders of Russia and Poland and south into the Balkans, the German tongue was widely regarded as the language of culture, influence and sophistication. The Viennese critic and essayist Karl Kraus frequently wrote about the beauties of the German language and poured his satirical scorn on those (especially Jews who moved to Vienna from further east) who spoke or wrote it incorrectly. Arthur Koestler's mother, raised in Vienna but living in Budapest, felt she was living in a form of cultural exile; she never learned Hungarian properly and the only newspaper she read was the German-language *Pester Lloyd*. Martin Esslin (later the BBC's Head of Radio Drama) remembered how his grandfather was a highly respected Budapest journalist; not only that, said Esslin proudly, but he worked on one of the city's two German-language papers. 'He was the epitome of the completely emancipated Jew of that period,' he recalled, going on to describe a learned man with an enormous library who had written a book on eighteenth-century Budapest. You might be a Czech-speaking merchant in Moravia, a schoolteacher from Croatia or Romania, a wealthy Prague industrialist or Martin Esslin's grandfather in Budapest: if you had ambitions to better yourself, you needed to know German and would probably gravitate sooner or later, if you could, towards Vienna. Stephen Hearst (another refugee who later entered the higher reaches of BBC cultural programming) told me that when he applied for British naturalisation after World War Two he had to explain that, while he was born and raised in Vienna, his parents were both from Lemberg (or Lvov). Where is that? Hearst needed to elaborate: it was part of Austria-Hungary until 1918, Polish between the wars, then Russian.*

To Western sophisticates like Count Metternich, the Austrian Foreign Minister and Chancellor in the decades up to 1848, Vienna was at the easternmost edge of European civilisation ('Asia begins at the Landstrasse,' he is alleged to have said dismissively, pointing out of the window). But to many of the far-flung denizens of the Austrian Empire, Vienna represented not an end but a beginning, the entry point, the cosmopolitan capital, the epitome of progress and liberalism, a cultural bastion of the German-speaking world. 'The towns of Bohemia and Moravia were German islands in a sea of Czech peasantry,'

---

* And now Ukrainian.

writes Steven Beller, 'and the further east one went, the more did German appear to be a synonym for western progress.' Indeed, the very name 'Austria' – 'Österreich' or 'Eastern Kingdom' – suggested an outpost or a branch of the historic lands of Germany.* One day, this was the dream, the whole German world would again be one.

There was, of course, another view of German unity as observed from Habsburg Austria. It may have excited; but it also excluded. All those enticing ideas about the transcendent 'Germanness' of German art and the spiritual unity of the German-speaking peoples – these were ideals shared by many in Austria. Yet Austrians were *not* citizens of the new nation; Germany had united in 1871 without them. Could they ever be part of a greater German state? It was not impossible. The fact that Germany had united at all, albeit excluding Austria, helped whet pan-German aspirations still further. After all, reasoned the Viennese cognoscenti, for all the polite fiction of the 'dual' Austro-Hungarian monarchy (established in 1867), everybody knew that power, authority, culture resided in Vienna. And Viennese culture meant German culture, *Bildung*, a word suggesting not only book learning but also the wisdom that is acquired by the mature assimilation of all life's higher experiences. As long as the Emperor Franz Joseph was in power, German culture would continue to predominate in the Austrian Empire. And if, one day, the Habsburg monarchy should fall, then the logical step would be for Austria to become, at last, part of a greater Germany. 'As a boy in the 1920s, I grew up *wanting* Austria to become part of Germany,' recalled George Weidenfeld, little imagining the circumstances in which the dream of his childhood would become the nightmare of his adolescence.

The idea of culture – German culture – thus created a bond between people from all over the German-speaking world and beyond. This was enthusiastically shared by many of the Jewish peoples of Middle Europe. Throughout Jewish history, from

---

* In March 1938, after its annexation by Hitler, this is literally what Austria became: 'Östmark', Germany's eastern boundary land.

biblical times, great emphasis had been placed on learning. The mythologised figures in the Jewish past had been men of God, rabbis, scholars. Jacob and Daniel are praised for their devotion to their studies, Solomon for his wisdom. From the biblical Moses to Moses Maimonides in the twelfth century to Moses Mendelssohn in the eighteenth, it is the prophets and philosophers, the scribes and the scholars quite as much as the kings and generals who are the role models. In the Russian and Polish Pale, in the *Shtetl* and synagogue, the pivotal figure is the rabbi and he is not so much a preacher or prayer leader as a teacher and scholar, the person responsible for the education of the next generation, the only figure in the village capable of solving difficult questions of Jewish law. A man might climb the social scale by acquiring various practical skills. But if you really wanted to endear yourself to the parents of your betrothed, the best way was to demonstrate your devotion to Talmudic and rabbinic studies. Even those Jews who were not particularly conscious of their Jewish ancestry, or believed they had transcended or disavowed it (for instance Heine, Marx, Mahler, Schnitzler and Freud), tended to gravitate towards achievement in the intellectual and cultural worlds. Devotion to learning is a constant theme throughout the history of the Jewish people, one that was much in evidence in pre-Hitlerian Middle Europe. While Jews made up about ten per cent of the population of *fin-de-siècle* Vienna (200,000 in a population of around 2 million), they accounted for something like thirty per cent of the pupils enrolled in those elite grammar schools known as the *Gymnasium.*

It would be foolish to read too much into this admiration for learning or to apply it indiscriminately to all Jewish communities in the past. At certain times and places, it was the Jewish merchant or moneylender who became the archetype rather than the scholar or thinker. However, at least until the establishment of the state of Israel in modern times, Jews were not especially distinguished for their agricultural or military skills. But as writers and musicians, thinkers and mathematicians, people of Jewish origin and background had often been disproportionately prominent. Was this because of the age-old emphasis on the value of learning, going back (perhaps) to rabbinic and even biblical times? Maybe in part. But it arises from other influences as well.

If you were a young Jewish man in late nineteenth- or early twentieth-century Vienna or Berlin, you would have known without it being spelled out to you that the upper ranks of certain professions were, in effect, barred. You would have been unlikely to aspire towards a career in the army, politics or (obviously) the church – or, indeed, in any form of public service. 'A diplomat!' Fred Uhlman's father expostulated cruelly when his innocent son suggested the profession he thought he might enter. 'Why not a pope? Has anybody ever heard of a Jew in the diplomatic service? Who are you? A baron perhaps? Do you think I am Bismarck?'

It was partly a question of anti-Semitism; one only has to read the prose works of Wagner or the political speeches of the mayor of *fin-de-siècle* Vienna, Karl Lueger, or to recall the fate of Alfred Dreyfus, a Jew who entered the army service in France, to be reminded that anti-Semitism was not invented by Adolf Hitler. Many Jews therefore gravitated towards those fields in which Jews (with all that *Gymnasium* education behind them) tended to be more widely accepted – the law and medicine, economics and philosophy, music, literature, journalism and publishing. Steven Beller suggests that over a half of those teaching in the Medicine Faculty at the University of Vienna in 1910 and over a third of those teaching Law were of Jewish descent.

Thus the reasons why so many Jews moved into such fields included both the traditional 'pull' towards learning as well as the 'push' of exclusion from the upper reaches of the army or politics. But there is a further point. Many of the leading figures in these liberal, cultural professions may have been Jewish, but would have considered themselves no more than nominally so. Some even converted to Christianity – though Jewish converts were often uncomfortable with their adopted faith and unlikely to tempt providence by trying to 'pass' in a traditionally closed profession. After all, one of the main reasons for conversion was usually to help the proselytising family to keep out of the spotlight. Many more were neither converts nor practising Jews but, rather, thought of themselves as 'assimilated'. And assimilation presupposed almost by definition the rejection of partisan ideology, separatism, exclusivity, dogma – Jewish, or any other – and, in their place, the aspiration to embrace universal truths and the whole of humanity. These were the sentiments of the press and the academy, not of the army, church or politics. 'All Men are Brothers,' Schiller had written, a cry famously hymned by Beethoven and echoed for a century thereafter by liberal intellectuals – including many assimilated Jews who were able neatly to marry their pan-Germanism with a belief in universal values.

Pan-Germanism appealed to the emancipated Jews of *Mitteleuropa* because it seemed to embody those universalist ideals – especially, perhaps, after Germany's spectacular rise to unification and international prominence. For those on the margins of the German-speaking world, in the wider reaches of Austria-Hungary, the idea of forging stronger links with Germany also implied cutting loose from an empire that seemed inextricably tied to its eastern lands and to doctrinaire Catholicism. The liberal Jews of Middle Europe may often have had roots further east, in the villages of Poland and Russia, Hungary and Romania; but if so, they were proud of having shaken the mud from their ancestral boots, doffed their kaftans and yarmulkes, and moved upwards (and westwards) to a comfortable life of sophistication in Breslau and Berlin, Munich and Vienna. To such people, Eastern Jews (*Ostjuden*) represented the past, those who had not made it, people without culture who clung on to outmoded attitudes and rituals. Silvia Rodgers, brought up in Berlin by Polish parents, was taken on a visit to Poland in 1934 and recalled a country and a Jewish community that 'to me, brought up in Germany, did look bizarre, as if from a previous century or another world'. Germany, by contrast, stood for urban and urbane life rather than the fields and the ghetto, emancipation and enlightenment rather than atavistic obscurantism.

'To my parents,' recalled Claus Moser, 'especially my father, being German came first. He thought of himself as a German, and only then as a Jew.' It was a widespread sentiment. Moser's father was a wealthy and distinguished banker in pre-Hitlerian Berlin. He had fought in World War One and he and his wife, like so many others in their position, thought of themselves as proud and patriotic Germans. 'That's why so many of them thought – tragically wrongly – that things would be all right, that this Hitler thing would pass over and they would be OK. It wouldn't touch people like them (they thought) because, above all, they were such good Germans!'

A similar memory was shared by many other refugees from Nazism, especially those from Jewish backgrounds. 'This terrible thing cannot last,' the artist Milein Cosman's father used to announce. 'Germany is a civilised nation and these barbarians will soon be out.' Peter Fröhlich, who went on to become the American historian Peter Gay, had two uncles called Siegfried. We were the real Germans, he recalled thinking when he was a lad. 'The gangsters who had taken control of the country were not Germany – we were ... Germany, after all, was the most civilised of countries.' And here is Fred Uhlman, in his semi-autobiographical novella *Reunion* about a young Jewish boy brought up in Stuttgart in the 1930s.

> All I knew then was that this was *my* country, *my* home, without a beginning and without an end, and that to be Jewish was fundamentally no more significant than to be born with dark hair and not with red. Foremost we were Swabians, then Germans and then Jews.

The boy's father is a proud patriot and his Iron Cross, First Class, hangs over the bed alongside a picture of the Goethe-Haus in Weimar. One day a Zionist visits the family home to collect money for the cause. 'My father abhorred Zionism,' says the narrator. 'The whole idea seemed to him stark mad.' Doesn't Hitler shake your confidence? the Zionist asks. Not in the least, answers the boy's father, a popular doctor, proud of being respected by his Jewish and Gentile patients alike.

'I know my Germany. This is a temporary illness, something like measles, which will pass as soon as the economic situation improves. Do you really believe the compatriots of Goethe and Schiller, Kant and Beethoven will fall for this rubbish? How dare you insult the memory of twelve thousand Jews who died for our country? *Für unsere Heimat?*'

When the Zionist called my father a 'typical assimilant', my father answered proudly, 'Yes, I am an assimilant. What's wrong with it? I want to be identified with Germany.'

I had never seen my father ... so furious. For him, this man was a traitor to Germany, the country for which my father, twice wounded in the First World War, was quite ready to fight again.

The 'Germanness' of the German-Jewish community has been much remarked upon and sometimes derided. 'More German than the Germans' was a common sneer at people who, having thrown off the faith of their forefathers and adopted the garb of the Fatherland, naïvely assumed they were thereby immune from danger, persecution and death. And it is true that many cultured German-Jewish families felt especially betrayed when they (of all people) were turned upon by Nazi thugs.

But admiration for all things German was not confined to cultured middle- and upper-class German Jews. Throughout the nineteenth century and earlier, as we have seen, millions throughout Central Europe held aloft an ideal, a model of culture, of *Bildung*. The superior quality of German culture, boosted for many by the process of national unification, was widely asserted in all corners of the German-speaking world and beyond. This was the cultural tradition of *Mitteleuropa* that many of the Hitler émigrés imbibed as children. And this is what so many of them were to carry with them when they left their homeland.

CHAPTER TWO

Scenes from Childhood

In Central Europe as elsewhere, childhood was a time of fun, adventure, family outings and holidays, sports, films, popular songs and incipient erotic discovery. Many of the émigrés also recalled it as the period when they began to imbibe something of the German cultural tradition that they learned to regard as their proud heritage.

Music, in particular, seems to have been a powerful thread running through the early lives of many of the Hitler émigrés.* By 'music', of course, was meant 'classical' music composed and performed by Germans (and not only in the German-speaking world; in the concert halls of London, Paris and New York in the late nineteenth century and early twentieth, composers and performers with Teutonic names continued to outrank all others). Scholars tried to pin down the essence of German music, and claimed to show that certain patterns of harmony and melody and even instruments (e.g. the ancient 'lur') embodied qualities originating with the Germanic tribes or 'Volk'. A somewhat similar quest was under way elsewhere as Bartók and Kodály, Cecil Sharp and Vaughan Williams sought to capture what they thought of as a national tradition of popular music-making. But in the German world, especially after the humiliations visited upon the Wilhelmine and Habsburg Empires by World War One, this quest for the essential 'Germanness' of

---

* But not all. Freud, so responsive to the arts of classical antiquity and the Renaissance, remained largely untouched by music. Milein Cosman (whose sketches of musicians later became famous and who was to marry the musicologist and broadcaster Hans Keller), was discouraged by her father from learning to play the piano on the grounds that it might stunt her growth.

German music and its supposedly '*völkisch*' origins fed directly into the commonly felt need to reassert the virtues of a proud but embittered nation.

Many of the Hitler émigrés were thus raised in homes steeped in music. Leonie Gombrich, Ernst's mother, was an excellent pianist who was taken as a child to Johann Strauss's concerts in the Vienna Volksgarten. She later became a pupil of Bruckner (and worked the organ bellows for him) and went on to study piano with Leschetizky, Schnabel's teacher. But she never seriously contemplated a professional career ('My mother would have thought it was like wanting to become a circus rider') and instead became a teacher of piano. One of her pupils was Martin Isepp, later Head of Music Staff at Glyndebourne. The mother of the philosopher Karl Popper, too, was an excellent pianist, and the family dining room boasted a Bösendorfer concert grand and many volumes of Bach, Haydn, Mozart, Beethoven, Schubert and Brahms. Schumann's *Scenes from Childhood* was a favourite.

Popper thought seriously of becoming a professional musician. So did Claus Moser, who at an early age played piano duets with his father (who was a 'bit of a basher') and enjoyed listening to the more refined playing of his mother. Seventy years later, Moser recalled fondly his parents' *Hausmusikabende*, or musical soirées, when he was sent to bed but would creep back and crouch under the stairs so that he could listen. By the time Claus was ten or eleven, his parents had begun taking him to concerts where he heard Schnabel, Edwin Fischer, Klemperer and Furtwängler. The rule was that children had to go home at the interval – which only had the effect of making the boy want more.

'I grew up in Berlin with my father whistling *Fidelio* and my mother singing German folk songs with guitar,' recalled Hilde Beal.* When she was six, Hilde was taken to the opera to see *Hänsel und Gretel* in a production by Max Reinhardt ('the best thing that ever happened to me – I thought it had real angels!').

---

* Hilde Beal, German coach to the Royal Opera in the 1970s and 1980s, joined Covent Garden as a singer. She was one of the maidens in the *Moses and Aaron* chorus.

Gerard Hoffnung's mother spent hours playing to her son as a young child in Berlin; he later remembered her playing the full piano score of most of the popular operas, singing all the parts. Georg Solti's mother took piano lessons so that she could practise with her talented son. The cellist Anita Lasker, born and raised in Breslau (now Wroclaw), was sent at the age of thirteen to Berlin by her proud parents to study with Leo Rostal.* Several had parents whose love of music seems to have verged on the obsessive. The violinists Ida Haendel and Suzanne Rózsa, both of whom displayed precocious musical talent when young, received relentlessly attentive parental encouragement well into adulthood.

If music often came from mother, serious *Bildung* tended to emanate from father.† Ernst Gombrich remembered his father reading to the children – 'usually Homer' and German trans-lations of Indian poetry. Weidenfeld *père* believed that the language and literature of Ancient Rome were the keys to all human knowledge and once promised his son a pocket money bonus if he could write an account of a football match in Latin. Joseph Horovitz's father Béla Horovitz would come home (i.e. upstairs from the office) for lunch expatiating to his family on the latest volume he was publishing on Plato, Shakespeare, Goethe or Petrarch. Popper recalled that his father, a prominent and scholarly Viennese lawyer and exact contemporary of Freud (whose books he read on publication), loved to read history, especially in the Hellenistic period, and that he also wrote poetry and translated Greek and Latin verse into German. He had a large library, which included works by Plato, Bacon, Descartes, Spinoza, Locke, Kant, Schopenhauer, Mill, Kierkegaard, Nietzsche, Mach, Darwin, Marx and Engels, Kropotkin, Kautsky and Norman Angell. These books, Karl Popper said later, 'were part of my life before I could read them'.

While many of the future émigrés remembered early intro-

---

* Years later, in London, Leo's violinist brother Max would coach the members of what was to become the Amadeus Quartet.

† The art historian Norbert Lynton, born in Berlin, told me he remembered imbibing the great works of Goethe, Heine etc. 'more or less with my mother's milk' – which, on reflection, he corrected, in the interests of accuracy, to 'with my father's wine'.

duction to the canon of great art and literature, there was, of course, a lighter side to their cultural awakening. The historian Walter Laqueur, growing up in Breslau, would tune into the family's primitive crystal set in order to catch the latest pop tunes or *Schlager* and, like many children in the late 1920s and early 1930s, go to the cinema once a week. This was a golden age of both film and popular music in Germany, and the memory of those enriching but not especially demanding adolescent experiences stayed with Laqueur for the rest of his life. Silvia Rodgers may have been raised in the Berlin of those eerie Expressionist doctors *Caligari* and *Mabuse*, but the films she lapped up as a child were those of Shirley Temple and Dick und Dof (or Fat and Simple, as Laurel and Hardy were called in German).

Then there were books. Goethe and Thomas Mann were wonderful, of course. But for most youngsters it was probably easier to spend a leisurely evening reading Erich Kästner's *Emil and the Detectives*. Or perhaps to curl up with one of the sub-Fenimore Cooper Westerns by the German writer Karl May (who never left his native Saxony) and gasp at the adventures of a Red Indian called Winnetou and the white trapper Old Shatterhand.

Father was often too busy, or perhaps too remote, to take an active part in the children's upbringing. As for mother, her attention – at least in the more affluent homes – was distracted by the exigencies of a large household and a busy social life; *Kaffee und Kuchen* could all too easily take precedence. For the *Kinder*, serious education meant school, especially the *Gymnasium* where a thorough grounding was imparted in all the traditional subjects, including the classics. 'We started Latin at eleven and Greek at twelve, and in the last two years we added philosophy,' Martin Esslin recalled of his boyhood in Vienna. 'It was an excellent, fully rounded education.' Classes were from 8 a.m. until 1 p.m. but Martin, a quick learner, had usually done his homework by mid-afternoon and was free for the rest of the day to wander the streets and look up his friends.

Esslin's parents had moved from Budapest to Vienna around

1920 when Martin was a baby. 'Father was a typical Voltairean, Hungarian Jewish intellectual,' he recalled, 'whose heroes, or models, were people like Moses Mendelssohn and Heinrich Heine. A liberal-minded scholar-journalist, just as his father had been back in Budapest.' When Martin was nine, his mother died and his father remarried, and it was Martin's kindly and energetic stepmother who brought him up. She was from a comfortable, bookish Austrian Catholic family of Social Democrats, less cosmopolitan, perhaps, than Martin's father's family but a 'passionate Wagnerite and incredible theatre buff'. She gave the young boy a puppet theatre and, before long, her influence – not to mention the free tickets that came as perquisites of his father's job – had Martin scurrying regularly to the theatre where he absorbed the traditional German classics, as well as more recent works by Gerhart Hauptmann, Arthur Schnitzler, Ernst Toller or the young Bertolt Brecht in innovative productions by people such as Reinhardt and the politically radical Erwin Piscator.

Stephen Hearst, too, was bitten by the theatre bug as a boy. A voluminous reader from an early age, he had an inspiring English teacher who pointed him towards the great classics of British literature. By the age of sixteen, Stephen was putting on a school production of *The Importance of Being Earnest* – in English – with himself in a starring role.

In Germany, school could be oppressive. 'I remember every detail,' says the narrator in Fred Uhlman's *Reunion*, of an elite *Gymnasium* in Stuttgart in the early 1930s: '. . . the classroom with its heavy benches and tables, the sour, musty odour of forty damp winter overcoats, the puddles of melted snow, the brownish-yellow lines on the grey walls where once, before the revolution, the pictures of Kaiser Wilhelm and the King of Württemberg had hung.' The teacher was 'a sallow-faced man who . . . looked out at the world through a pince-nez on the tip of his nose with the expression of a mongrel dog in search of food.' Peter Gay describes the similarly old-fashioned Goethe Gymnasium in Berlin, which he attended as a boy:

We sat in orderly rows, each of us at an assigned desk that

was nailed to the floor, as was the chair. We knew our place and were quite literally unmovable, a situation one might read as a symbol of stability or, doubtless, more accurately, of rigidity . . . When a teacher entered the room, we rose to our feet . . . And those of us called on to recite in class wormed our way out of our tight quarters to move forward, standing just below the teacher, whose table rested on a raised platform.

Many remembered school as a place of iron discipline, the embodiment of a doctrine which (in the words of Hermann Hesse) 'makes the breaking of the will the corner-stone of education'. Hilde Beal went to a school in Berlin where girls could be caned for bad behaviour. Discipline was overdone, perhaps, by the standards of a later, more permissive age. But at the same time the system could inculcate into its young charges a cultural grounding of impressive breadth. Claus Moser, for example, appreciated the good things his *Gymnasium* had to offer. German language, literature and history were taught, of course, alongside physics, mathematics, history and geography. But music, painting and the culture of classical antiquity were there at the heart of the curriculum too. These were not considered peripheral soft options but core subjects that any educated youngster would be expected to master. Throughout the German-speaking world, nobody could be regarded as fully educated without a proper knowledge and appreciation of Bach and Beethoven, Goethe and Schiller. (Shakespeare, in the celebrated Tieck and Schlegel translation, was considered a kind of honorary German; Moser remembered being slightly surprised, on arriving as a refugee in England, that Shakespeare was known in England too.) As for the visual arts, Moser recalled that 'school outings to Berlin's museums and galleries were absolutely routine – just as much routine as playing football'.

Moser was not much of a football fan as a boy. But his fellow Berliner Peter Gay was. So were Hans Keller and Siegmund Nissel, growing up in Vienna. Sports and games were widely encouraged, and Hitler's determination to use the 1936 Berlin

Olympics as a way of displaying the superior athleticism of the German nation was, like so much else in those years, an extreme expression of a theme that long pre-dated Nazism. Had not the ancient world seen the essential links between a healthy mind and a healthy body, and between personal athleticism and communal virtue? In Italy, Mussolini consciously tried to echo the muscularity of classical Rome, while Hitler was happy to complement the Duce by evoking the manly virtues of the ancient Greeks. This atavistic belief in the moral value of strenuous team games, of the character-building camaraderie arising from shared exploits, was already a widely shared currency in the late nineteenth century, and not only in Central Europe. These were virtues espoused by Theodore Roosevelt, for example, in the USA, Robert Baden-Powell in England and by the international Olympic movement – which in 1896 succeeded in reviving the ancient ritual of the Olympic Games.* The German-speaking world espoused all this with enthusiasm; had not the miracle of national unification been achieved by precisely these virtues as epitomised in Bismarck's famous phrase about 'blood and iron'?

Sport, games and personal athleticism were often spoken of as co-operative activities contributing to the good of the community as a whole. A desire for 'wholeness' – of the individual, of the community, of society, of the nation – was a common refrain, especially in the years after World War One when so much of value appeared to have disintegrated. Popular historians and philosophers sought metaphysical links that would clasp the past to the present, thereby giving the latter new strength, while artists (invoking the spirit of Wagner) talked of creating *Gesamtkunstwerke*, which would integrate the disparate elements of their art. The new discipline of psychiatry looked for ways of integrating the separate elements in the personality, while physicists began to search for the will-o'-the-wisp that was to occupy Einstein to the end of his days: a single 'unified theory' that would unlock the ultimate secrets of the universe.

---

* The organic links between the world of Ancient Greece and the health, strength and beauty of modern athleticism were evoked with exquisite poeticism in the opening sequences of both Part I and Part 2 of Leni Riefenstahl's monumental film of the 1936 Olympic Games.

17

Physical exertion, too, was widely perceived as, literally, 'wholesome' – something that would contribute to the healthy development of the whole person. The idea of healthy personal development included, of course, the capacity to interact positively with one's fellows and virtually everyone brought up in pre-World War Two Middle Europe had memories of youth movements of various kinds. Inter-war Germany and Austria were awash with youth groups. The Hitler Youth and the *Bund Deutscher Mädel* (BDM), with their uniforms and rallies, attracted millions of youngsters in the 1930s. But there were countless small-scale groupings and bondings, too. Milein Cosman, always something of a romantic, founded a little group of 'Red Indians' among her girlfriends in Düsseldorf, complete with secret oaths, a flag and the sipping of each other's blood. Hilde Beal enjoyed going on long walks with her parents in the countryside around Berlin. At the age of seven she had been enrolled in a Communist youth group called *Fichte*. In 1933, when the Nazis came to power, all Communist organisations were outlawed and, in any case, Hilde, by now eleven, wanted to be more independent of her parents. Barred by her Jewish background from membership of the German Girl Guides, Hilde joined the BDJ, the *Bund Deutsch-Jüdischer Jugend* or League of Young German Jews, a band of non-religious Jews – proud Germans all – whose leader was Rudolph Sabor.* 'With Rudi we went on wonderful countryside hikes,' Hilde recalled, smiling as she evoked a genuinely happy memory. 'And everywhere we went we all sang together: German songs, Hebrew or Yiddish songs – everything.' In retrospect, one can see that there was no future for Jewish groups of this kind and that membership of the BDJ was playing into the cynical hands of the Nazis by drawing attention to the separate cultural identity of Germany's Jews. But for the few years it lasted, the BDJ provided a genial environment for Hilde and her comrades.

One thing that united these various youth movements and memories was the *Wandervögel*. In barest essence a craze for

---

* Sabor, then eighteen, also went on to find refuge in England where he remained a lifelong friend of Hilde Beal. He became well known after the war as a teacher and educationalist and also for his innovative writings about Wagner and his brilliant translation of the *Ring*.

long communal hikes, the *Wandervögel* was a romantic movement dating back to the end of the nineteenth century that
infused in its participants a passion to place themselves at one
with the beauties of nature (and perhaps of the fatherland), and
to share wholesome food and fellowship around the campfire.
Fred Uhlman became caught up in the *Wandervögel* and in his
autobiography recalled young men wearing sandals, short
trousers and windcheaters, playing the mandolin or the guitar
and carrying mystical novels like Hermann Hesse's *Demian*.
The girls would often wear the traditional dirndl. There were
long walks in the woods and forests. Sex, it seems, had to be
kept under iron control, the ideal relationship between a young
man and woman being a kind of confidential camaraderie as
though the noble act of walking would itself sublimate cruder
instincts. Uhlman recalls some couples putting themselves
through heroic tests – such as sleeping together but not touching
each other. Hesse, in a series of meditations he called
Wanderings, wrote that 'a good part of our wandering and
homelessness is love, eroticism'. The romanticism of wandering,
said Hesse, or at least half of it, was just an eagerness for
adventure.

> But the other half is another eagerness – an unconscious
> drive to transfigure and dissolve the erotic. We wanderers
> are very cunning – we develop those feelings which are
> impossible to fulfil; and the love which actually should
> belong to a woman, we lightly scatter among small towns
> and mountains, lakes and valleys . . .

As young people visited dramatic landscapes together, or the
homes of the heroes of history, bonds of brotherhood and
sisterhood were created, a sense of clan and comradeship further
cemented by the mysterious chemistry of communal singing. In
the words of Walter Laqueur, the *Wandervögel* was '. . . a kind
of neo-Romantic reaction against anaemic and arid intellectual-
ism; it reflected a fresh awakening to life, spontaneity, human
warmth.'

By the 1920s the idea of a healthy mind in a healthy body had become, in Germany, tied to the need for renewed individual and national assertiveness. Great sporting occasions were widely seen as opportunities for the individual and the nation to excel, outshine or vanquish. When the boxer Max Schmeling became world heavyweight champion in 1930, millions revelled in his victory and saw it as heralding a resurgence of German greatness. And when the Olympic Games came to Berlin in 1936, Hitler was keen to use the occasion to demonstrate to the world the supreme physical dedication and discipline of which Germans were capable.

In this, as in so much else, Hitler's attitude chimed closely with that of most German citizens; you did not have to be a Nazi to be excited by the possibilities of personal or patriotic prowess offered on the field of sport. Walter Laqueur, who loved swimming, remembered daring himself to dive into the pool from a higher and higher diving board. Siegmund Nissel and his father were on a touring holiday of Germany at the time of the 1936 Olympics and went to Berlin to watch some of the events. Sigi, well aware of the cynicism of the occasion, was nonetheless impressed. 'If only I could be one of them,' he recalled feeling at the time. 'It was very impressive, all that display of flags, the marching and the enthusiasm and the salutes.' Peter Gay, an avid sports fan as a lad in Berlin, was also at the Olympic stadium with *his* father, and they too watched, enthralled, constantly consulting their own stopwatch, as the world's greatest athletes competed against each other. As Jews, their dubious identity was safely diluted in a sea of patriotic Germans while, secretly, they could revel in the historic victories of non-Aryan athletes such as the black American runner Jesse Owens. As Owens won one of his gold medals, Sigi Nissel turned to look at Hitler's reaction and enjoyed observing the Führer's discomfiture.

But it was in school, perhaps, where the two-pronged attitude towards sport was most clearly exemplified – athleticism as moulding communal virtue on the one hand while also embodying and displaying individual excellence. Fred Uhlman, in *Reunion*, describes 'Muscle Max', the school gym teacher, who would call upon one of the more agile boys in his class for a demonstration of the horizontal bar, parallel bars or the vaulting horse – boys like Eisemann 'who loved showing off and anyway wanted to be a Reichswehr officer'. Schwarz, the Jewish boy, while detesting Max's 'instruments of torture', screws up his courage to show his Aryan schoolmates, especially the aristocratic young prince he is desperate to impress, that he too can excel at gymnastics.

The educationalist Kurt Hahn worked for a real prince (yet another Max – Prince Max of Baden) during World War One. After the war Prince Max, who was evidently something of an educational visionary, made a wing of his castle, Schloss Salem (orginally a Cistercian abbey), available for a school and it was here that Hahn developed his educational ideas and became a passionate and lifelong believer in the communal benefits – to body and spirit alike – of strenuous but controlled physical activity. You should aim to achieve your peak of physical strength and stamina, Hahn argued, and then channel this into team games and other forms of communal exertion. This became a central feature in the philosophy that Hahn, later a refugee in Britain, sought to embody in Gordonstoun School and the Outward Bound programme, a philosophy avowedly intent upon producing both social virtue and individual leadership. When the German theatre and opera director Carl Ebert came to work in England, it was to Hahn's Gordonstoun that he sent his son Peter to be educated.*

The pedagogical aim of integrating intellectual and physical excellence was a widely accepted aim of German education in the early decades of the twentieth century and many testified to the excellence of the *Gymnasium* education they received. But once the sinister force of Nazism began to insinuate itself into the school system, things began to deteriorate. Siegmund Nissel recalled a 'brute of a Nazi' as a teacher at his primary school in Munich. When the teacher discovered that Sigi's friend Gerhard couldn't sing, he'd deliberately call upon him – 'Moyschele, come and sing us a tune' – just to reduce him to tears. Claus

---

* Carl F. Flesch, son of the violinist, remembered attending Hahn's school in Salem (see *'Where do you come from?'*, pp.35–6, 58–9). The most famous pupil at Gordonstoun, at least in retrospect, was Prince Philip of Greece, later the Duke of Edinburgh.

Moser felt humiliated and confused when he and another Jewish boy were ordered to stay seated and silent when a teacher came into the classroom; but then, how could Jews be permitted to cry 'Heil Hitler!' and exchange the Nazi salute that had now become mandatory? Silvia Rodgers, whose parents were Communists, was ordered by her mother not to join the classroom salute; Silvia obeyed, she recalled, 'not because I was so principled and brave but because I did not dare defy my mother's strict instructions'. The poor girl, always suffering for being an outsider, finally succumbed when the whole school held an end-of-term playground rally. 'I was on the edge of the crowd, but I allowed myself to be drawn in. My hand went up for the glory of Hitler, my voice sang out to the glory of Germany.' Relief to be part of the crowd, perhaps. But Silvia's mother, standing at the school gates, saw her daughter commit this act of wickedness and laid into Silvia for her treachery.

The arrival of Hitler to power imposed burdens upon many Jewish children unaware, yet, of Nazism's profounder implications. Milein Cosman, a sporty little girl, came home one day and announced to her parents with glee that Hitler's Sports Minister, Baldur von Schirach, was coming to visit the school the next day and that she was going to be one of those awarded a medal. Her parents, who considered themselves completely emancipated Jews, nonetheless put their foot down and, sixty-five years later, Milein still remembered her sad bewilderment at this decision. Subsequently, she was fiercely upbraided when her teacher caught her drawing while the class was supposed to be reading *Mein Kampf*. In Vienna, in early 1938, Suzanne Rózsa won a violin competition. A few weeks later came the *Anschluss*, the incorporation of Austria into the Third Reich, and Susi was distraught to hear she had been denied the right to play in the prizewinner's concert.

There was honey in the belly of the beast. Hilde Beal, who had won a scholarship in 1933 to an excellent 'Middle School', was told a year later that she had to leave because she was Jewish, but recalled her teachers and fellow pupils crowding round her in a show of genuine sympathy. Walter Laqueur remembered that, although classmates were increasingly likely to turn up at school in their Hitler Youth outfits, they tried to be especially polite to him (at least until 1936) as if to make it clear that all this was of no consequence. Silvia Rodgers had a headmaster who went out of his way, when she had to leave the school, to say that he hoped the other children had not been taunting her with jibes of anti-Semitism. And Charles Spencer, a happy-go-lucky Viennese teenager at the time of the *Anschluss* in March 1938, recalled having the childish thought that Hitler was good news because the school authorities said he wasn't to attend any more. Thus, in retrospect, many gave credit to a system in which, until Nazism took over completely, they were given an excellent education by teachers of ability and integrity.

CHAPTER THREE

Dawn and Dusk

If you were born in the first decade or two of the twentieth century or late in the nineteenth, you might have carried an additional layer of experience with you into exile: that of the Middle European university. From the tankard-clanking rowdiness of Auerbach's tavern to the desperate duels and the wine, women and song, the serial jollity of German student life has been much mythologised. As with most clichés, there was a streak of truth to the myth and some of the romantic bravado continued well into the twentieth century. So did the real opportunities available to the peripatetic scholar. If you were so inclined, you might legitimately have felt yourself to be part of a seamless community of learning, free to follow any of the outstanding leaders in your chosen subject. You could, indeed, sample a variety of fields if you wished. In some, including history and literature, the curriculum and approach tended to be traditional, while in art history and physics, for example, truly pioneering work was being undertaken. A motivated student could travel from one institution to another. Thus a bright young German physicist in the 1920s might work with Max Born or James Franck in Göttingen and also gravitate towards Berlin in the hope of coming within the orbit of Planck and Einstein. A student of art history could, like Nikolaus Pevsner, work in Munich, Berlin, Frankfurt and Leipzig before gaining his doctorate on German baroque architecture. Fred Uhlman, after sampling the universities at Freiburg and Munich in the early 1920s, went off to Tübingen where he fell in love with the poetry of Hölderlin.

24

By modern standards this was a world of considerable formality. Popper regarded the men who lectured on mathematics and philosophy at the University of Vienna as demigods. 'They were infinitely beyond our reach,' he recalled later. 'There was no contact between professors and students who had not qualified for a Ph.D. dissertation. I had neither the slightest ambition to make, nor the prospect of making, their acquaintance.'

Once you began to single yourself out as a serious student, however, the demigods – or some of them – could show great kindness to their young charges. Gombrich frequently spoke with warmth about Julius von Schlosser and the friendly atmosphere in the institute he headed; students of Heisenberg would go dewy-eyed as, sixty years after the event, they would recall energetic ping-pong matches with the young master.

Student life in Middle Europe had its self-indulgent side, too. The traditional peregrinations of the *ewige Student* could, of course, encourage the sybaritic to wander from town to town in time-honoured fashion seeking the romanticised life of 'Old Heidelberg'. The student would join a club, or fraternity, an organisation that would bestow a heightened sense of camaraderie and perhaps of honour. These *Verbindungen* (literally corporations or connections) 'provided you with company, a home, colourful uniforms, useful connections for the future, romance,' recalled Fred Uhlman. 'They guaranteed to make a man, a real German, out of you: a man who knew how to fight, how to drink and how to love.' Most of these societies required their members, like young elks, to lock horns in symbolic competition. Ritual drinking bouts were common: young men would smoke, consume huge quantities of bad beer, vomit and sing obscene songs. Duelling, often over fabricated issues of 'honour', survived in many of the clubs until World War Two. The duel was fought with sabres, not guns, and not (usually) to the death – but at least to the point where victor and vanquished might proudly be able to display ritual wounds. George Weidenfeld fought a duel of honour in Vienna in 1938.

Clubs were differentiated by social or class affiliation, while many had associations with the political left or right. Politics were never far from the surface in the universities of post-1918 Germany and Austria, and no student could remain unaware of the turbulent legacy of World War One, which left every part of the German-speaking world in a state of dangerous uncertainty. With the demise of the Habsburg Empire, Austria had to adjust to the novel and unwelcome idea of being merely one small nation state among many, with Vienna no more than a somewhat bloated national capital. Other new nation states, too, were established out of the ashes of the old empire: Czechoslovakia, Yugoslavia, Hungary. Hungary lurched from an attempt at liberal democracy under Károlyi to the radical Socialism of Béla Kun. The Kun regime was itself swept away a year later and succeeded, after a few weeks of uncertainty, by the iron grip of Admiral Horthy.

Germany itself, united less than half a century before, was profoundly shaken by the magnitude of its defeat and the terms of the Versailles Treaty. Patriots spoke bitterly about being surrounded by crowing enemies. A new German Republic was instituted at Weimar, home of Goethe, while a Communist revolution, inspired by the Russian example and led by Karl Liebknecht and Rosa Luxemburg, was extinguished with extreme savagery. We tend to associate the Weimar Republic with its vivid cultural life, with the Bauhaus, the cabaret and the films. But underlying much of the creative energy of the period was a deep uncertainty, fear even, about where things were leading – exacerbated by years of economic depression.

One must avoid the dangers of historicism or hindsight. People at the time did not know that the future would hold Hitler, Auschwitz or the Second World War, and could listen to Wagner's *Götterdämmerung*, or read recent writings such as Spengler's *Decline of the West* and Karl Kraus's *The Last Days of Mankind* or watch a film like *The Cabinet of Dr Caligari* without believing the end of the world to be literally nigh. There was, nonetheless, a sense of political impermanence, of transition, throughout these years – in Germany and all the nations of Central Europe.

*

Many of those who were later to become refugees from Hitler tended as youngsters to be attracted towards the political left. Karl Popper, who became an intellectual bastion of conservative thinking in later life, confessed to having flirted with Marxism in his early youth, while the film producer Alexander Korda, to many the very personification of capitalism in the 1930s and 1940s, had worked enthusiastically as a young man in Budapest for the government of Béla Kun. Korda's fellow Hungarian Arthur Koestler was for many years a passionate undercover Marxist, travelling throughout Stalin's Soviet Union, seeing many of Communism's worst abuses, and continuing to propagate the cause until, eventually, he did a total about-face and devoted his energies to its demise.

Some people developed a political conscience early. Siegmund Nissel considered himself a committed Social Democrat by the time he was a young teenager living in pre-Nazi Vienna, and looked to the Masaryk government across the border in Czechoslovakia as his model. Silvia Rodgers and Hilde Beal were raised in Berlin by parents who were active Communists, and both girls imbibed the radicalism of their parents in the years just before (and into) the Hitler era. Silvia's mother was a particularly committed member of the KPD, the German Communist Party; she taught her daughter to despise the Social Democrats whose weakness and indecision had been responsible for the failure of the 1919 Spartacist revolution of Luxemburg and Liebknecht. Many years later Silvia was living in England and married to William Rodgers, one of the 'Gang of Four' who founded Britain's Social Democratic Party, and she noted how her commitment to the SDP in 1980s England paralleled her mother's passion *against* the Social Democrats in 1920s Germany. Hilde, too, was brought up to worship Liebknecht and Luxemburg and sang songs in their praise. She relished the memory of the red flag her mother made, which they would hang out on the balcony every year (until 1933) on the First of May. Even after the advent of the Nazis to power, Hilde's parents continued their Communist activities, albeit surreptitiously ('it was the only way we knew of opposing Hitler'), helping to distribute the by now illicit Communist paper *Die*

Rote Fahne (*The Red Flag*). At one point, Hilde's parents disappeared for some weeks to avoid possible danger, a memory that continued to haunt their daughter well into adulthood.

One young Communist who was famously to keep the faith was Eric Hobsbawm. Eric was a young adolescent in Vienna when he learned to distinguish between left and right: tenants, it seemed, were Socialists while landlords were from the right-wing side, the Christian Socials. When Eric, aged fourteen, was taken to live in Berlin in 1931, his left-wing sympathies were already well on the way to formation and he began to talk of himself as a Communist. A schoolteacher told him he was spouting nonsense and suggested he go to the library and read something: the Communist Manifesto, perhaps, and some Engels. 'Which I did. And it was a knockout!'

More typical, perhaps, was George Weidenfeld. Brought up in post-World War One Vienna, he joined the Union of Social Democratic High-School Pupils at his school at the age of twelve, relishing the uniform, the effortless camaraderie with its clenched fist salute and the communal singing of Socialist hymns such as the 'Internationale' and various menacing and melancholy old German ballads. Stephen Hearst, brought up in the apparent security of middle-class Vienna, spent the day of the *Anschluss*, when Hitler annexed Austria, cheekily placing stickers on the backs of the arriving Nazis with the provocative slogan 'Vote for Austrian Independence'. He got out of Austria the next day.

There was, of course, a large body of students whose instincts led them in the opposite direction, who shared the wounded patriotism of their parents' generation and were excited by the pageantry and promise of the reactionary right. We may take passing note, in particular, of the allure of Hitlerism. Any young boy or girl who had witnessed the anger and despair of a jobless father might have revelled in the chance to join the new Youth Movement, go on paid holidays to the coast (courtesy of Hitler's 'Strength Through Joy' movement) and share with uniformed colleagues the exhilarating sense of a nation once more on the move. Spender evoked the image of 'German youth which had been born into war, starved in the blockade, stripped in the inflation – and which now, with no money and no beliefs and an extraordinary anonymous beauty, sprang like a breed of dragon's teeth waiting for its leader, into the centre of Europe'.

Even if you were Jewish, these enticements had a superficial appeal. Claus Moser remembered the visceral excitement of watching the huge, surging crowds that would greet Hitler's public appearances. Furthermore, as Walter Laqueur pointed out, by 1933 it was commonplace to believe that democracy did not work, and that 'we were in a deep crisis, from which only an elite, or more likely a charismatic leader, could extract us'. Then, once in power, the Nazis were not only successful in restoring order and getting the unemployed off the streets; they also claimed to be doing so in the name of all that was sacred and most traditionally German. Thus, for all the brutality of their methods, the Nazis were widely popular in the early years of their power and any Jewish family proud of its German heritage might have been tempted, at least initially, to suspend judgement.

There were, however, more palatable options available to a thoughtful young German Jew. Zionism, for instance. In some ways the raising of Jewishness to a political principle might seem the polar opposite of Nazism. Yet the two movements sprang from some of the same sources. Theodore Herzl, the founder of the Zionist movement, was a non-observant Jewish journalist of Hungarian background who lived in the Vienna of Freud and Mahler. Like many of his contemporaries, Herzl was excited by the quasi-metaphysical nationalistic ideas that were common in German-speaking Europe at the time. In this he was a typical *fin-de-siècle* Viennese Jewish intellectual. Herzl's journalism had taken him to Paris where he witnessed the trial of Alfred Dreyfus, the Jewish officer falsely accused and convicted of treason. The blatant anti-Semitism of the trial aroused Herzl (as it also aroused French intellectuals such as Emile Zola) and helped stimulate him to develop the idea of a Jewish state. He did not necessarily insist that this should be in the biblical land of Palestine, but argued that there must be somewhere (Uganda was suggested at one point) where Jews might be enabled to take control of their own lives. Zionism was no revolutionary doctrine but looked back to the cultural nationalism that had shaken much of Europe back in 1848 – not least those parts of Hungary and Italy under Austrian hegemony. Many cultural, religious and linguistic groupings had demanded their own state; why not the Jews?

Herzl died in his mid-forties in 1904, but his ideas continued to gather strength. During the First World War the British Government (whose troops were leading the war effort against the crumbling Turkish Empire and about to enter Jerusalem) declared itself officially in favour of 'the establishment in Palestine of a national home for the Jewish people'. With the collapse of the Austro-Hungarian as well as the Turkish Empire at the end of the war and the creation of such newly independent states as Hungary, Czechoslovakia and Yugoslavia, the argument for a specifically Jewish state seemed even stronger. Or so it seemed to people like Arthur Koestler and, later, George Weidenfeld (both of whom were initially ignited by the fiery oratory of Vladimir Jabotinsky). Koestler's Zionism, like most of the political positions he adopted, went through various vicissitudes, including outright rejection. But to Weidenfeld Zionism became a guiding beacon throughout a long and active life.

Zionism was not for everybody. Many German Jews, as we have seen, continued to be loyal to the land of Goethe and Schiller, whatever their private feelings following the catastrophic humiliation of 1918. They did not see the need for a new national state; they already had one and their job was to help built it up again. Zionism, Fred Uhlman thought when hearing about it at university, was no doubt good for 'unhappy Russians and other Eastern Jews, but ludicrous for a German'. As far as he was concerned, he was 'a German first and a Jew only by the accident of birth'. To Eric Hobsbawm, one of the attractions of Marxism was that it seemed to provide a system of thought that flew in the opposite direction from Zionism and, indeed, transcended every form of cultural nationalism whether Jewish or German.

Even people whose life work was to be the promotion of Jewish culture were often resistant to the blandishments of

Zionism. Alfred Wiener, for example, a sophisticated Berliner and collector and creator of the Holocaust Library,* recoiled from much that he saw on a visit to Palestine in 1926. How could anybody want to live in a place like Tel Aviv, he wondered, much less a kibbutz? Wiener recognised the value of Palestine to Jews (mostly from Eastern Europe) who wished to emigrate there, but he did not see why it should be considered *his* homeland and he resented Zionism for addressing the German Jew 'as though he were in banishment'. German Jews, he argued vehemently, must remain both Germans and Jews: 'If we tear ourselves away from our German people, we will lose our Germanness and our Jewishness.' Wiener was also critical of Jewish attitudes towards the Arabs in Palestine, which he thought condescending and dangerous, a view echoed a generation later by Walter Zander, another cultured Berlin Jew who settled in England. Zander was Secretary of the Friends of the Hebrew University from 1946 until 1970, and wrote scholarly and humane works on Israel and the Middle East. Yet he never thought of living in Israel, did not consider himself a Zionist and reminded people in his gentle way that, for all the sympathy the world had for the Jewish people in the wake of the Holocaust, little would be achieved by continuing to antagonise the indigenous Arab to whom 'our return without his consent remains a forced invasion'.

Zionism was often regarded askance, too, by religiously observant Jews. Some – the more orthodox who adhered to the traditional tenets of Judaism – feared that any Jewish state that was established would almost certainly elevate secular values over spiritual ones. Immanuel Jakobovits, later Chief Rabbi of the British Commonwealth, remembered how his father, a distinguished German rabbi, felt that membership of any political grouping would have been inappropriate. 'The German-Jewish tradition of Orthodoxy in which I was raised', Jakobovits recalled, 'was distinctly lukewarm towards Jewish nationalism' and the family had never considered emigration to Palestine an option. Nor was this attitude the preserve of the traditionally

---

* From which this book has benefited.

observant. The Vienna-born, Berlin-educated Ignaz Maybaum, later a well-known scholar and Reform rabbi in England, caused considerable comment when decrying what he regarded as the politicisation of the Jewish religion.

Clearly, no single 'photofit' biography is adequate to describe the background of the Hitler émigrés. But many seem to have been from middle- or upper-middle-class German-speaking backgrounds, often Jewish, in which high value was attached to the intellectual and physical disciplines of a traditionally German education and the absorption of German culture, of *Bildung*. There was an element of social snobbery to it, no doubt, but (recalled Gombrich) 'nobody was taken seriously or accepted socially if they did not take part in this general culture, in music, literature and art'. Anyone aspiring to serious 'culture' or 'education' would thus expect to be familiar with the works of Bach and Beethoven, Goethe and Schiller.

Painting and sculpture – Gombrich's special interest – had arguably been more developed south of the Alps and west of the Rhine; there is no German movement to compare with (say) Impressionism in *fin-de-siècle* France. But any educated young German or Austrian would know something of French and Italian art and cultural history, and be familiar with the languages and artefacts of the ancient world. In Vienna, Freud could take it for granted that his readers would be acquainted with the Oedipus myth, while later generations of educated Viennese, including Gombrich, Hearst and Esslin, would expect to know about the art of the Italian Renaissance and of Ancient Rome or Greece.

But in *fin-de-siècle* Vienna, the great capital of an increasingly fossilised empire, an intellectual ferment had been taking place. As Freud worked on the interpretation of dreams and Mahler struggled over the gestation of his vast symphonies, avant-garde designers in the Viennese *Werkstätte* were experimenting with new forms and materials, and Gustav Klimt and his colleagues were 'seceding' from the salon art of their predecessors with canvases variously regarded as alluring, provocative and even shocking. The aesthetic pathways that Klimt and Otto Wagner helped to pioneer were pursued by younger artists such as Richard Gerstl, Egon Schiele and Oskar Kokoschka. While these did not form a single 'school', they shared a general credo that led them to try to express rather than repress, to reveal what lay beneath the surface, however disturbing this might be. In Germany itself, so recently united, people were more pre-occupied with industry, science and commerce. But Berlin, like Vienna, had its 'Secession', and painters of the new school such as Max Liebermann and Lovis Corinth made an impact, as did the artists of the Munich-based movement *Blaue Reiter* (Franz Marc, Kandinsky). Many centres of aesthetic orthodoxy co-existed in Wilhelmine Germany. But a sensitive student of the arts could hardly have been left untouched by the successive waves of fashion that periodically thrust themselves across the calm waters of artistic convention. And the most notable, here too, was 'Expressionism'.

This catch-all title came to denote artistic endeavour in any field that tended to reject naturalistic standards of beauty, sanity, health and harmony, and to embrace instead free-flowing conflict and artefact, the dissonant, the inchoate, the sick, the primitive, the dissolute and the destructive. Romanticism with an agonised face, if you like – something to which poets and painters, novelists and composers were drawn throughout the German-speaking world. The sculpture of Ernst Barlach, the novels of Hermann Hesse or the early scores of Arnold Schoenberg and his brother-in-law Alexander Zemlinsky all contain recognisable elements of Expressionism.

So do many of the German films of the early 1920s. Fritz Lang's *Dr Mabuse the Gambler*, for example, features a near-psychopathic criminal who is finally tracked down in his subterranean lair; Murnau's *Nosferatu* is a darkly evocative reworking of the Dracula story, while *Der Letzte Mann* is his portrait of a pathetic hotel doorman whose self-confidence erodes in a bewildering tailspin until he becomes, literally, the last man (but also has the last laugh). In the most celebrated of all Weimar-era films, *The Cabinet of Dr Caligari*, Conrad Veidt plays a sinister, somnambulating medium through whom the mad doctor commits a series of motiveless murders. Such films made pioneering use of moving cameras, extreme contrasts of light and darkness, shadow play, and sets and images that would tilt, bulge and recede – techniques designed to enhance the omnipresent sense of drift, disturbance, disequilibrium, danger, darkness and death.

Expressionism was far more than a temporary fad or fashion and too broad to have been derived from the example of any particular key figures. But there were other artistic influences, too, on the aesthetic world of pre-Nazi Germany. Like Expressionism, the *Blaue Reiter* movement also encouraged links across the arts, making overtures to Schoenberg, himself no mean painter, while establishing ties between German avant-garde art and that of France and Russia. By the early 1920s, after the shock of 1918 and partly as a reaction against the more self-indulgent grotesqueries of Expressionism, the *Neue Sachlichkeit* of Otto Dix, Max Beckmann and others briefly brought to the visual arts something of the harsh 'New Realism' or 'Objectivity' that was also becoming current in German literature at the time.

It is comfortable, and relatively simple with the benefit of hindsight, to encapsulate eras and artists under a litany of such labels. But it is important to remember that for every adherent there were as many who opposed and even more who were untouched. Siegmund Nissel was brought up in post-Expressionist Vienna. I asked him whether he soaked up the legacy of Hofmannsthal and Kraus, Schnitzler and Klimt? As a musician, did he inherit the spirit of Mahler and Schoenberg? Nissel laughed. What he most savoured from his Viennese adolescence were the girls he met and the football matches he saw.

Ernst Gombrich, ever sceptical of easy labels, spent a long life emphasising the variety of artistic achievement and experience rather than its homogeneity. Gombrich demonstrates how even the most resolutely Modernist Viennese figures looked back-wards as well as forwards: Kokoschka, for example, admired the great baroque masters and came to hate abstract art, while the architect Adolf Loos (forever associated with the phrase that 'ornament is crime') continued to argue that classical forms should be taught to architects. Artists of this stature often continued to revere the historical models they were popularly perceived as having superseded.*

Nonetheless, the last years of the Austro-Hungarian and Wilhelmine Empires saw widespread distaste for those artists who supposedly sapped the national fibre – a revulsion exacerbated by the defeat of 1918. This politico-aesthetic conservatism may have been misplaced, but it had plenty of available targets to choose from. By the 1920s and early 1930s it was easy to lambaste the free-flowing, value-free destructiveness of the Expressionist movies, or the deliberately disorientating work of playful Dadaists and collage artists such as Kurt Schwitters or John Heartfield, as contributing towards (rather than reflecting) the national unease. 'I have no country and no ideals left,' growls Hesse's 'Steppenwolf'; all that these things amount to is 'another decoration for the gentlemen who usher in the next slaughter'. The gentlemen, that is, savagely portrayed in the bitingly 'realistic' satire of George Grosz and Otto Dix. Like them, Käthe Kollwitz, the acerbic artist of hunger and death, persisted in portraying the darkest sufferings of the downtrodden. Even the famed Bauhaus, later revered as one of the great engines of architectural and industrial Modernism, was widely regarded during its heyday in the 1920s as a haven of dangerous experimentation; how could it have been otherwise, indeed, with genuine community living its principal aim, artists such as Klee and Kandinsky on the teaching staff and the Marxist Hannes Meyer its second Director? All these figures could be lumped together in reactionary circles as representing a body of Bolshevik-inspired art (*Kulturbolschewismus*) that was perceived as having systematically undermined the true values of the fatherland. 'I hope you are not *caricaturing* me,' bellowed a famous Berlin actress intimidatingly at the aspiring young artist Victor ('Vicky') Weisz.† 'Caricature is an invention of *Bolshevism!*'

Were the arts, especially the visual arts, that subversive? For

---

* The same was true among composers. Schoenberg admired Brahms, while his disciple Egon Wellesz was drawn to the musical forms of Byzantium.

† Vicky, whose savage political cartoons were among the most celebrated in Britain from the 1940s until his suicide in 1966, was clearly influenced by the work of Kollwitz.

all the mordant radicalism of Brecht and Piscator in the theatre, the satirical writings of Tucholsky and Mehring, or the biting portraiture of Grosz and Otto Dix, one might question how far art alone can ever really undermine a society. Some leading cultural figures were, indeed, surprisingly apolitical, almost to the point of naïveté. The painter Max Beckmann and the film director Fritz Lang (both later forced into exile) professed to be oblivious of the political messages some saw in their work, claiming that their creativity had nothing to do with politics.* A few, like the painter Emil Nolde, shared the dubious brand of mystical religiosity (and the anti-Semitism) of the right; he never understood why the Nazis did not welcome him more enthusiastically once they came to power. Many in the arts community during the Weimar years, even those regarding themselves as non-political, were critical of what they regarded as the philistinism of the resurgent German nationalism, and this antipathy was enthusiastically reciprocated on the right where many leading Modernist figures and movements were dismissed as dangerous and even mad. Hitler himself, ever the aesthetic traditionalist whose own architectural sketches portrayed good, old-fashioned Greek pillars and Roman arches, argued in *Mein Kampf* that the state should step in to stamp out the 'spiritual lunacy' of Modernism.

Ironically, it can be plausibly argued that the Modernist movement, far from subverting the values of extreme cultural nationalism, probably contributed, albeit inadvertently, to the eventual victory of Nazi aesthetics. The early success of German films, for example, led to the establishment at the end of World War One of a state-financed film combine, the Universum Film Aktiengesellschaft (UFA), which rapidly became the only European film-making organisation to challenge the pre-eminence of Hollywood. From 1927, UFA was run by Alfred Hugenberg, a reactionary autocrat who, on the Nazi accession

---

* Lang's vast, futuristic movie *Metropolis* features an insensitive capitalist millionaire and a vast lumpen workforce who are eaten alive by 'Moloch' and incited to revolt. Crude Marxism, one might think, and the film was lovingly restored in the (Communist) East German Democratic Republic. Yet its final reconciliation of 'head', 'heart' and 'hand' seems to condone the old economic hierarchy.

to power a few years later, was able to present them with a ready-to-use propaganda machine.*

Aesthetically, too, the tenets of Modernism were not as far from those of Nazism as both sides liked to aver. On the contrary, many of the values that lay in the main stream of German culture provided sustenance of a kind for both. The romantic and often destructive anti-rationalism of the Expressionists, the back-to-nature primitivism of the *Blaue Reiter* group, the recurrent images of personal impotence (e.g. in Lang's *Metropolis* or Murnau's *Letzte Mann*), the melancholy sense of degeneration and decline in the novels of Thomas Mann or the mystical self-destructiveness in the writing of Hermann Hesse – even the Bauhaus aspiration to feed off the inspiration of medieval masters to help bring mass-produced benefits to the ordinary people of today – all these currents flowed into the world-view of the Nazis. Hitlerism was thus not peripheral to traditional German aesthetics, a cultural aberration; rather, the Nazis picked up a ragbag of widely shared ideas and ran with them. And Hitler himself, resentful of what he regarded as the underrating of his own prowess as an artist, continued to take German aesthetic ideals seriously and merely imposed them with brutal literalness. The inspiration from ancient history, the purity of the German soil and forests, the virtues of the German family and the transcendental heroism of the *Volk* – all this was elevated into a decadent flowering of romantic nationalism, an aesthetic which, while not new, came to mean the elimination of everything (and everybody) that did not fit. Thomas Mann himself, in a wartime broadcast in the USA, acknowledged the authentic link with the past, defining National Socialism as 'German idealism gone wrong'. Thus it has been argued (notably by Siegfried Kracauer) that the birth pangs of Nazism may have been eased by that dubious midwife Dr Caligari who, like Hitler himself, hypnotised others to carry out his psychopathic, murderous will.

Once the Nazis came to power a confrontation, or at least a new

---

* Hugenberg, who played a pivotal role in helping secure Hitler the Chancellorship in 1933, was among the privileged few who accompanied the Führer to the cinema – to see a film called *Morgenrot* – '*Dawn*' – the night Hitler acceded to power.

adjustment, between the political and artistic realms became inevitable. It was not long in coming. In May 1933 a series of dramatic parades led by students in Berlin and elsewhere culminated in vast mounds of books being put to the torch. There was no mistaking the message as works by world-renowned figures were flung into a pyre in the square alongside the capital's premier opera house and opposite its leading university. 'The soul of the German people', said Goebbels, Hitler's Propaganda Minister, addressing the students so avidly doing his will, 'can again express itself. These flames not only illuminate the final end of an old era; they also light up the new.' Others, perhaps, remembered the sentiments of Heine a century earlier: 'A nation that burns its books will end by burning its people.' Today, Heine's words are engraved on a small plaque near the middle of the square. Alongside, on the ground, a discreet glass sheet – scarcely visible to busy passers-by – covers one of Berlin's most moving monuments: rows and rows of library shelves, devoid of books.

The book burnings – with their deliberate echo of Savonarola's 'bonfire of the vanities' in late-medieval Florence – had illuminated with appalling clarity the cultural predilections of the new regime. Goebbels began 'cleansing' German cultural life of Jewish and 'Bolshevik' elements, ordering the removal from the nation's museums of literally thousands of paintings by artists such as Kokoschka and Grosz, not to mention non-German modernists like Picasso or Matisse. Books by Jewish writers were removed from libraries and school curricula, the music of Mendelssohn and Mahler from the nation's concert halls. Hitler inveighed with increasing ferocity against the decadence of Cubism, Dadaism, Futurism and Expressionism which, he said, had no place in the Third Reich. At the same time (perhaps mindful of the self-consciously anachronistic buildings around the Vienna Ring that he had admired as a young man), Hitler encouraged Albert Speer and his architects and engineers to plan a series of grand edifices in a monumental, neo-classical style. Everything was to be big, impressive, permanent – preferably constructed of granite – and (of course) infused with the spirit of Germany. In addition to the great domes, sturdy columns and huge internal spaces of Berlin, the regime deemed that Hamburg was to have a suspension bridge longer than that in San Francisco, Nuremberg a stadium to dwarf all others and Munich – birthplace of Nazism and the scene of Hitler's botched but subsequently mythologised 1923 *putsch* – a monumental shrine to the arts.

In 1937, Munich played host to two exhibitions. The first was a celebration of 'Great German Art' held in the new pseudo-Hellenistic-style 'temple to the arts' that Hitler himself had had a hand in designing. With the opening of this building and exhibition, pronounced Hitler in a widely reported speech, 'has come the end of artistic lunacy and with it the artistic pollution of our people'. He did not want anybody to have false illusions, he said.

> National Socialism has set out to rid the German Reich, and our people, of all those influences which threaten its existence. And although this purge cannot be accomplished in one day, I do not want to leave a shadow of a doubt that sooner or later the hour of liquidation will strike for those phenomena which have participated in this corruption . . . From now on we will wage an unrelenting war of purification against the last element of putrefaction in our culture . . .

The next day, in a run-down gallery in the Hofgarten that could only be reached through a narrow stairway, a second exhibition was opened. This contained a selection of some of the 'degenerate' (*entartete*) art from which the good people of Germany were being rescued and by which they had evidently been in danger of corruption. Crowds came to see works by Kokoschka and Beckmann, Schlemmer and Kirchner, Grosz and Dix, Impressionists and Expressionists, Futurists and Dadaists, foreigners such as Chagall and Gauguin. Visitors outnumbered those at the exhibition of 'Great German Art' by three to one. Did they come to jeer or to cheer these forbidden icons of Modernism? Who can know? Perhaps most were merely intrigued at what would obviously be the last opportunity to see works by these notorious painters. The Nazi organisers certainly did all they could to make sure that visitors went away with the correct message. Grosz and Dix, according to the captions, had used their art as a vehicle for Marxist propaganda and portrayed German soldiers as 'idiots, sexual degenerates and drunks', while the Expressionists had seen the world as one huge whore-house. Other captions were even more grotesque. 'The Niggerizing of the Visual Arts' proclaimed one, while a further section compared the work of modern artists with that of the insane. Throughout the exhibition, 'degeneracy' was equated with the by now familiar litany of Jews, homosexuals, Bolsheviks, Negroes, gypsies, criminals and the physically and mentally sick.

The exhibition of 'degenerate' art was the latest, and most extreme, of the many measures the Nazi regime had enacted to add to the growing anxiety of all but the most acquiescent members of the cultural community. Many had already departed: Kurt Jooss, the dance director, like the artistic founders of Glyndebourne Fritz Busch and Carl Ebert, the art historian Nikolaus Pevsner and the creator of the Bauhaus Walter Gropius, had all left for England shortly after the advent to power of the Nazis.

At first, the exodus was small: a handful of shrewd people with contacts who felt the time was propitious to move out of a country undergoing what many assumed was a temporary aberration. But the Nazi regime didn't go away. On the contrary, it took increasingly firm control of all forms of intellectual and cultural endeavour, and tightened the screw relentlessly against its Jewish citizens. Thus the book-burnings of 1933 led to the Nuremberg Laws of 1935 (denying citizenship to proscribed races and forbidding sexual relationships between them and Aryans) and the exhibition of degenerate art a couple of years later. Year by year, as the fangs of Nazism embedded themselves more deeply, applications to leave Hitler's ever-expanding Reich for safer havens grew, as one family after another debated the pros and cons of emigration. 'Where can we go?' people asked. 'Where do we have friends, relatives, people who would be prepared to vouch for us, opportunities for work?'

Some Jewish families began by sending their children abroad for their education. Milein Cosman's brother was packed off to Glasgow to study metallurgy; Milein herself went as a teenager to a school in Switzerland run by a dreamy old (German) sage who had been a friend of Rabindranath Tagore, and thence to the League of Nations School in Geneva. Here she toyed with the idea of becoming an actress, taking the title role in an English-language school production of Shaw's *St Joan* (and delivering her lines, she recalled, with an accent containing streaks of Scottish, American and German).

With the easy wisdom of hindsight it is tempting to ask, incredulously, why more people, especially from Jewish families, did not leave when it was relatively easy to do so. But, of course, nobody in the mid-1930s could conceive of the mass deportations and gas chambers that are now part of history. 'We felt we were living through a period when, unfortunately, the kind of people we were and the things we valued were disregarded by a ruthless and misguided regime,' one émigré later recalled. But the regime would doubtless pass, as others had done. At Christmas time, Milein Cosman recalled, her father would say, 'By Easter this madness will be over.' At Easter it would be Whitsun, at Whitsun Christmas.

There were often practical problems, too. Perhaps the children had only two or three more years of schooling, which it would be improvident to interrupt; perhaps father spoke only German and would find it difficult getting a job abroad, while grandmother was elderly and sick. Anne Bohm's uncle, a radar specialist who was working in England and had already brought Anne over, invited her father to join them. But Anne's father, a seventy-year-old widower and retired High Court Judge, gently turned down the offer, saying he was too old to move, didn't understand the language and would feel quite lost in England. As a Prussian civil servant, he was sure no harm could come to him. In any case, he said, he didn't want to presume further on his brother's generosity. A few years later he died in Theresienstadt concentration camp.

By the end of 1938, the year that witnessed Hitler's annexation of Austria in March and the barbarity of the

Kristallnacht in November, Nazi intentions were unmistakable. Every artist and musician, dancer and designer, writer and film maker, psychologist and physicist had to confront the inescapable fact that working in the Third Reich meant, in effect, giving a degree of support to the regime. Some – and not just in Germany – saw Nazism as the ultimate fulfilment of the nihilism that much European literature and philosophy had been prophesying for a century. In Hitlerism (said Spender, who had watched its growth in Berlin and sampled responses to it all over the continent) 'the nightmares of Dostoevsky's *The Possessed*, of Nietzsche and of Wagner, were made real'. Even among Europe's most highly cultured intellectuals, he noted, there were those who 'recognized in this political movement some of their own most hidden fantasies'.

In Germany itself, some artists and intellectuals of considerable stature accepted the option of working within the system: for example, the physicist Werner Heisenberg, the painter Emil Nolde and the philosopher Martin Heidegger. A number of musicians stayed in the Reich. Some, such as the young conductor Herbert von Karajan and the pianist Walter Gieseking, and the artists engaged by Hitler's friend Winifred Wagner to perform at Bayreuth, worked as harmoniously as they felt they could with a government which, after all, offered rewards to its anointed. The choreographer and dance theorist Rudolf Laban worked for the Nazis, too, for some years. Others (Richard Strauss, Wilhelm Furtwängler), if more passive in their support, knew that their very presence offered comfort to a regime under increasing pressure to show vestiges of cultural respectability. Many went into 'internal exile', keeping their heads down and hoping the ideological clouds would lift. Musicologists, for instance, would typically turn their attention to such 'safe' academic subjects as the *völkisch* origins of German song or polyphony, or the tradition of amateur music-making, while many performers doubtless figured that theirs was in any case the art least susceptible to political interpretation or interference.

But any political trimming among the cultural community was unlikely to be condoned by a system as punctiliously in control of its culture as the Nazis. Books and paintings, compositions and concerts were, in the eyes of Goebbels and his officials, either supportive of the values of the regime or, if not, suspected of undermining it. And if the incubus of official displeasure descended, your life could be at risk. Thus, for the genuinely independent-minded intellectual or artist anywhere in the German-speaking world in the late 1930s, the idea of whether or not to leave was presenting itself as a serious option. And if you were Jewish, emigration was rapidly emerging as a question of life or death.

PART TWO

WHERE THEY CARRIED IT TO

CHAPTER FOUR

Ars Britannica (or: No Modernism Please – We're English!)

'England', to which so many refugees fled from Hitler in the 1930s, was widely believed to be a green and pleasant land whose people were blessed with a rich cultural tradition. At one with their history, the British were thought to derive strength from a past which, if imperfectly understood, continued to give them nourishment; they spoke with unselfconscious pride verging on reverence of the Anglo-Saxon race, the King and the Empire. The perception was that those at the top of the pile talked and acted as though they deserved to be there, while those lower down the pyramid supposedly 'knew their place' and showed little resentment. There had, it is true, been considerable social tension in the years immediately after the First World War, culminating in the General Strike of May 1926. But factory workers and coal miners, tempered perhaps by fear of unemployment, still doffed their caps to their bosses, while scruffy schoolchildren in the back alleys of Leeds or Birmingham might eagerly back Oxford or Cambridge in the annual boat race or pretend to uphold the honour of Eton or Harrow at Lord's. If the royal family were stuffy and the Empire and educational system anachronistic, few were prepared to say so out loud, and if a new monarch had long led what was whispered to be a 'dissolute' private life, this was scarcely even hinted at in the public press except insofar as it led towards the constitutional drama of abdication.

Across the Channel various forms of repressive authoritarianism came to power in Russia, Italy, Germany, Spain and elsewhere. But it was easy for the denizens of Britain's island redoubt to agree with the leader writers on the *Mail* or *Express* that this may have been all very upsetting for the people involved but had little to do with 'us'. Indeed, as the British stood for the National Anthem at the end of the evening's cinema presentation, tuned in to the well-oiled tones of Stuart Hibberd announcing over 'the BBC' (in 1935) that 'the King's life is drawing peacefully to a close' or revelled in Len Hutton's record-breaking innings of 364 against the Australians at the Oval in 1938, a reassuring sense of the nation-as-community became almost tangible. The English, pronounced Stephen Spender looking back, were preoccupied during the inter-war years with Empire exhibitions, royal occasions and sport, preferring to regard what happened on the Continent as 'none of their business'.

To refugees from Central Europe, the British could appear smugly self-regarding. But perhaps they had some reason to be. Britain had, after all, not only played a major part in fighting and winning the Great War and in shaping the peace settlement that followed, but had gone on to enjoy a fertile cultural efflorescence. The economy might be severely blighted by the war, the grip on empire faltering and political instability somewhat uncharacteristically the order of the day. But intellectual and artistic life were, many thought, as vibrant as ever.

London was, overwhelmingly, the cultural capital. In Hampstead and St John's Wood congregated arbiters of modern taste such as the art critic Herbert Read, the publisher Stanley Unwin and the conductor Henry Wood. A number of the dominant figures – Virginia and Leonard Woolf, Clive and Vanessa Bell, Duncan Grant, Lytton Strachey, Augustus John and his sister Gwen – all had London homes in and around Bloomsbury, where they would be joined by such Cambridge illuminati as Bertrand Russell and John Maynard Keynes and his wife, the ballerina Lydia Lopokova. Stephen Spender, admitted to their circle as a young man and one of their most acute observers, considered the Bloomsbury Group 'the most constructive and creative influence on English taste between the two wars'. They were an exclusive coterie, deliberately insulating themselves from those they considered their cultural inferiors ('the last kick of an enlightened aristocratic tradition'), putting Spender in mind of 'those friends who at the time of the Plague in Florence withdrew into the countryside and told the stories of Boccaccio'. Faintly Francophile, yet inimitably English, their cultural predilections, Spender recalled, were precisely reflected in their domestic decor: 'a fusion of Mediterranean release with a certain restraint and austerity'.

During the 1920s the trauma of the Great War ran like a deep and ineradicable striation throughout every aspect of the culture. At the heart of Virginia Woolf's *Mrs Dalloway* is a man whose life is shattered by the affliction that contemporaries euphemistically dubbed 'shell-shock'. Lady Chatterley's availability to a lover results from the incapacitating war wound of her husband. The war simply would not go away, colouring works as various as T. E. Lawrence's *Seven Pillars of Wisdom*, T. S. Eliot's bleak welcome to poetic Modernism *The Waste Land*, David Jones's epic poem *Anathemata*, the *Cookham Resurrection* of Stanley Spencer and perhaps the damp despondency of the early canvases of Matthew Smith. Even when the trenches began to retreat into history a decade or more after the conclusion of the fighting, a host of writers – Siegfried Sassoon, Edmund Blunden, R. C. Sherriff, Robert Graves – poured their wrath on the very idea of war, even while sensing (in some cases) the growing danger of something even more catastrophic.

There was nothing the mark of Cain did not touch. Not only the subject matter of art but its very form, nature, purpose, seemed different after the slaughter of the Somme. Traditional novels were still written, agreeably harmonic symphonies composed, graceful churches built, bucolic landscapes painted. But even these had to be seen through a post-war prism of modernity, less reflections of the realities of the present than yearnings for the comforts of yesteryear. If the poems of Rupert Brooke and A. E. Housman came to be revered beyond their merits, it is because the simple rustic pleasures of Grantchester or Shropshire provided reference points to a generation which, in Noel Annan's striking phrase, was 'haunted by the disappearance of rural England'. For all E. M. Forster's insistence that 'oh dear yes – the novel tells a story' and that it must respond to the laws of narrative, few could fail to recognise that the Great War was a watershed in aesthetic sensibility as in so much else.

Those with alert antennae noted a gradual shift away from coherent, integrated narrative art towards what came to be dubbed 'Modernism'. This catch-all title suggested a quest for new, non-naturalistic forms, for disjunction, disequilibrium, collage, Cubism, Surrealism, disharmony, fragmentation, atonalism, syncopation. These had seemed controversial before the war in the provocative hands of Stravinsky and Schoenberg, Braque, Picasso and Pound. But the tenets of Modernism chimed far more closely with an artistic consciousness that had experienced the violent death in battle of millions of young men and the precipitate collapse of the Russian, Turkish and Austrian Empires.

In a world that had survived the annihilation of traditional certainties, nothing could any longer be taken for granted, no state was stable, no vision unsullied, no mirror uncracked, no experience merely what it appeared. In Russia, as people struggled to adjust to the successive traumas of revolution and civil war, writers and artists tried to make sense of a situation rapidly losing cohesion. In German-speaking Central Europe, as we have seen, the post-war artistic reponse embraced every form of Expressionism, absurdity, abstraction and grotesquerie, while Modernism French-style took its cue from the punctiliously observed minutiae of Proust, the post-Impressionism of Debussy and the mystical symbolism of Claudel.

And in Britain? Britain, so deeply wounded by the war yet superficially the most immune from its effects. No English fields had been churned up to accommodate the dead and dying, no dynasties or empires overthrown, no new nations forcibly carved from its ancestral terrain. Not for English sensibilities the radical Suprematism or Constructivism of the new Soviet Union, the extremes of Dada, Expressionism, post-Impressionism or any other continental isms. Isms – ideologies, dogmas – were not generally to British tastes. If Modernism was to gain entry, it would have to be clothed in 'restraint and austerity' – and granted no more than a visitor's visa.

Or perhaps a traveller's. Several of the leading figures of 'English Modernism' either came to Britain from elsewhere (notably Eliot) or seemed to feel the need to move elsewhere for inspiration. James Joyce may have set *Ulysses* in his native Dublin. But, having named his novel after one of the ancient world's epic travellers (and his questing character after Daedalus, who flew too close to the sun), Joyce spent very little time in Ireland, preferring to work in Trieste, Zurich and Paris. D. H. Lawrence trekked even more widely, taking in not only Sardinia and France but Australia, New Mexico and Mexico on his travels.

Relatively few went to Germany. Germany was still on the cultural Grand Tour, and young men with aesthetic aspirations would journey down the Rhine, making ritual obeisance to the Lorelei, think romantic thoughts at Neuschwanstein, go on a pilgrimage to the shrines of Weimar and Bayreuth, and return refreshed by the mythic spirit of the Teutonic forests. A handful might have taken note of the *Neue Sachlichkeit*, the latest trends in German cinematography, the pioneering design ideas of the Bauhaus, the music of Schoenberg or Krenek or the alluringly decadent kitsch and cabaret of Berlin. But most modern-minded British artists and intellectuals (like their American confreres), directed their aspirations to France and made their *hajj* to Paris. This was where Jean Rhys and Ford Madox Ford came to write, where Vaughan Williams honed his harmonic gifts and where Roger Fry updated his ideas about the nature and direction of art. Stephen Spender, friend of the Bloomsbury Group but contemporary of Auden and Isherwood, spent a lot of time in Hamburg and Berlin in the early 1930s. Most of his friends found this incomprehensible. They 'deplored my spending so much time in Germany', he wrote many years later, 'and wished that I went more often to France . . . [T]o them France was still the France of Proust and the French Impressionists.'

By the 1930s the harsh realities of European politics cast their own lurid light upon the Great War. The New York Stock Market crash of October 1929 had brought down with it a whole international superstructure of aesthetic gaiety, of cultural playfulness, and helped to create a new mood of despondency exacerbated by the proliferation of harsh dictatorships in Europe. How could questions about the nature and direction of art matter in a world in which, from Madrid to Milan, Munich to Moscow, the reward for aesthetic independent-mindedness might well be the prison cell or even the execution chamber? Politics, from which many artists and intellectuals liked to consider themselves immune in the 1920s, now forced itself to the forefront of the imagination. 'The sense of political doom,' wrote Spender, 'pending in unemployment, Fascism, and the overwhelming threat of war, was by now so universal that even to ignore these things was in itself a political attitude.' He became political, he said, by the very fact of 'feeling I must choose to defend a good cause against a bad one'. Commitment was essential. But to what? To whom? To Fascism? Some (such as Wyndham Lewis) were tempted and there were undeniable attractions in the offer of efficient, uniformed leadership, British-style, offered by Oswald Mosley. Communism? Many British intellectuals visited Stalin's Russia and managed to come away believing it to be a future that worked.

But the cause that really grasped the committed *jeunesse dorée* of Britain was Spanish Republicanism. As Franco's forces took an increasingly iron grip on Spain, liberals everywhere were appalled. How could they stand by and watch while a brutal, church-obsessed, military regime, aided and abetted by Fascist Italy and Nazi Germany, plunged the land of Lorca back into obscurantist medievalism? This simplistic moral stance may have ignored excesses on the Republican side, while a variety of private motives doubtless impelled individual Republican sympathisers. But, in general, the impulse that fuelled not only the American 'Lincoln Brigade' and buccaneering Frenchmen like André Malraux but also a host of British artists and intellectuals to go to Spain and fight was not ignoble. Spender recalled contemporaries who felt passionately that, unless Fascism was halted, war was inevitable and Europe doomed. A generation of young English poets – John Cornford, Christopher Caudwell,

Julian Bell, Ralph Fox – took off for Spain, only to die there. George Orwell went to Spain to support the Republican cause. But he was seriously wounded and eventually returned disillusioned with the simple left-wing orthodoxy that had spurred him to go in the first place. Once again, it seemed, ideologies capable of arousing people across the Channel sat ill on the shoulders of sensible visitors from Britain like Orwell. The flame of continental thought may have been bright and enticing. But most of Orwell's compatriots preferred, on balance, to warm themselves from a safe distance.

Thus, Roger Fry and Herbert Read, Orwell, Spender and others acted as bridges of a sort between the somewhat circumscribed world of cultural Little Englandism and the wider aesthetic currents of Europe and beyond during the inter-war years. But British cultural life was rather like an English garden: insulated, fenced off, perhaps, from the wilder outgrowths that surrounded it, yet able to incorporate elements of the exotic and exogenous, and to superimpose upon them its own traditional structures.*

This pattern was not new. For centuries, those who governed in London had tended to eschew close links with the Continent, preferring to direct British energies towards the wider world. The trading interests of a maritime island had led to the establishment of a global empire, while tensions with European neighbours like France were preferably resolved in Canada or India rather than over the Channel. By the early twentieth century grandiose dreams might still be conceived on the playing fields of Eton; but by now it was best to put them into practice around conference tables in Wellington or Ottawa or Kingston. Imperial pageantry might play well enough in Westminster or Wembley. But it was even more impressive if reported back from the spectacular structures of Lutyens's New Delhi. 'Instead of the Grand Tour of Europe,' says the historian David Cannadine in his study of the decline of the British aristocracy, 'there was

---

* At the risk of stating the obvious, the British were not, of course, alone, or especially culpable, in their cultural insularity. 'The average German, unlike the British or French, had no experience of foreigners or foreign ideas,' writes Frederic V. Grunfeld in his book about the world of Freud, Kafka and Einstein.

the world tour of empire.' The Empire continued to provide people in Britain with cheap food and raw materials, with jobs abroad and with romantic dreams of global hegemony. And it provided boundless material, too, for imaginative reprocessing by Britain's writers and painters, musicians and film makers.

Thus youngsters with a taste for literary adventure would lap up the rollicking *Boy's Own*-style yarns of Haggard and Henty, Sapper and Saki or the novels of John Buchan, later Governor-General of Canada. Those with more sophisticated tastes might gravitate towards Forster's subtle study of mutual incomprehension, *A Passage to India*, published in 1926 or, a little later, Somerset Maugham's tales of fading glory as the imperial sun began to set over the South Seas. Sir Edward Elgar, widely acknowledged as England's finest composer in two centuries, scored one of his first popular successes with his 'Imperial March' of 1897 and his most famous with the vocal version of his Pomp and Circumstance March 'Land of Hope and Glory' arranged for the 1923 Imperial Exhibition at Wembley. Elgar himself may have shrunk from the crudity of the sentiments ('wider still and wider may thy bounds be set'), but in the minds of the masses, he had achieved apotheosis as *the* composer of Empire.

New art forms such as film, too, began to explore the possibilities presented by the Empire. By the 1930s, with the advent of the talkies and huge new budgets making location shooting possible, British film goers were offered a plethora of movies in and about the Empire,* based on the writings of Kipling, A. E. W. Mason, Edgar Wallace and others.

Links of language and history created bonds with the United States, too. Keynes became a welcome guest and guru in Franklin Roosevelt's White House, while Churchill, son of an American mother, went on lecture tours of the USA (and almost met a premature death there as a result of a road accident in 1932). D. H. Lawrence and his German wife Frieda headed for the nirvana of New Mexico, while Shaw's *The Applecart* and

---

* Such as *Sanders of the River*, *Elephant Boy*, *The Drum* and *The Four Feathers* (all, as we shall see, the products of a studio run by an émigré film maker born in Hungary).

Wells's *Things to Come* were attempts to confront the American-style political and technological future that people regarded as inevitable. As for the leading American cultural figures of the day, many felt the need to cross the Atlantic if they were to be true to their muse. England's greatest poet and sculptor, Eliot and Epstein, like the novelist Henry James and the painters Whistler and Sargent before them, were transplanted Americans, while if Stein, Pound and Hemingway wrote in Paris, they were more widely appreciated in London.

British cultural life thus took much nourishment from historical links with the wider world. But there were two limitations. First, this global view was largely portrayed as exotic and filtered through a prism of Englishness. The world tended to be perceived as acted upon by Britain rather than in its own terms. Very little of the indigenous art or music of Asia, for example, its religions, philosophy or literature, was evident in British portrayals of India, Malaya or the South Seas; it would be another half-century before the rhythm of the ragas or the gongs of the gamellan would enter the musical bloodstream of Britain. Young men with names like Nehru, Nkrumah, Menon or Kenyatta were assumed to be in London to learn about Britain and its ways, not to imbue the British with greater knowledge of the faraway places from which they had come.

Second, the British continued to display a traditional ambivalence towards continental Europe. Britain and France might have become friends and allies; as Vaughan Williams went to Ravel to learn to add 'French polish' to his orchestration and Roger Fry and Clive Bell began to act as advocates for post-Impressionism, it became fashionable to equate 'France' with 'culture'. However, as Ravel is said to have admonished his English pupil: 'I know what you will do, Mr Williams. As soon as you see the cliffs of Dover, you will forget what you have learned here, and you will think of your Sir Parry and Sir Stanford and become an Englishman again!'

As for German art and culture, this was becoming anathema to right-thinking Englishmen by the time of the First World War. Thomas Armstrong, friend and protégé of Vaughan Williams and later the Principal of the Royal Academy of Music, had a simple explanation when asked in old age about the renaissance of authentically 'English' music associated with Holst and VW. 'The thing was,' Sir Thomas expostulated, looking me in the eye, 'we had to get rid of Brahms!' The German romantic influence, he said, was overwhelming – stifling – when he was learning music and he recalled how the previous generation (Elgar, Tovey, Ethel Smyth) had all felt it necessary to receive recognition in Leipzig or Munich before being taken seriously in Britain. During the Great War, Germanophobia became widespread. People with German names, from the royal family down, felt constrained to give themselves English-sounding alternatives while credence was given increasingly to rumours of German troops raping nuns and cutting off the hands of children. Many of those who survived the trenches went on to experience the hell of emotional breakdown. In such a climate it was not surprising that politicians vied with one another over the severity of the terms that could be imposed upon the defeated Central Powers. 'Hang the Kaiser!' was the cry; and 'Squeeze the Germans until the pips squeak!'

Not everybody shared such vindictive sentiments. A dogged Teutonophile like John Christie would don his *lederhosen* and drive off in the 1920s to enjoy the opera at Munich, Bayreuth and Salzburg, while a little later Christopher Isherwood began to create his vivid literary snapshots of pre-Hitler Berlin. Back in England, privileged members of the upper classes gathering at Cliveden or writing in the pages of *The Times* would recoil from enmity towards another 'Anglo-Saxon' nation ruled until recently by the British monarch's cousin. This was a sentimental or political stance, however, rarely a genuinely cultural one. German classical music was widely played, but not 'Modern' music from the German-speaking world. The frontiers of Modernism were sometimes admired but seldom emulated. Modernism, after all, was foreign. 'Does it come off? No, not quite,' was Forster's amiable if condescending assessment of *Ulysses* in a series of lectures on 'Aspects of the Novel' that scarcely ventured beyond British shores. And Spender, a cosmopolitan figure who was at home in the Berlin of

Isherwood, regarded Modernism at first as little more than a
'popular mass-movement', the latest fashion. 'It was easy to be
advanced,' he wrote. 'You had only to take off your clothes.' As
for the colourful creations of Kandinsky or Klee, the chromatic-
ism of Schoenberg or Berg, the dark Expressionism of Fritz
Lang, the elegiac solemnity of Thomas Mann or the forceful
polemics of Brecht – these were regarded somewhat uneasily by
the sobersides of England who tended to worry, with Forster,
about ambition taken beyond easily comprehensible bounds.
Better the elegies of Housman and Brooke, the crypto-Fascism
of Wyndham Lewis, the bitter-sweet gaiety of Coward, the
stolid literary journeying of J. B. Priestley, the double negatives
of Waugh and the pseudo-medievalism of Eric Gill than the
tendentious theorising, the extremes of experimentation of
continental Europe.

Even so cultivated an aesthete as Kenneth Clark, while
struggling to perfect his German and acknowledging the
influence of thinkers like Hegel, Schopenhauer and Burckhardt
on his understanding of art, was forced to say in his patrician
way, 'I must confess that Germany is very much not my
"spiritual home".' When Sir Raymond Unwin made a speech at
the opening of a Gropius exhibition at the Royal Institute of
British Architects he pronounced, doubtless genially enough,
that

> The German people . . . loved working under a theory.
> Englishmen were not easily persuaded to a theory, were
> naturally suspicious of it and afraid of ridicule should they
> show any great devotion to any particular theory. The
> Germans on the other hand take up a theory readily, and
> follow it devotedly, so that at the first glance they might be
> blind to limitations which we are quicker to catch sight of.

And Frank Pick, the driving force behind London Transport's
innovative design ideas in the 1930s, when commissioning work
for the British Pavilion in the Paris Exhibition of 1937, baulked
at the idea of giving work to the Hungarian-born Bauhaus
émigré László Moholy-Nagy, then in exile in England. Moholy-

Nagy, said Pick, '. . . is a gentleman with a modernistic tendency who produces pastiches of photographs of a surrealistic type, and I am not at all clear that we should fall for this. It is international, or at least continental . . . Let us leave the Continent to pursue their own tricks.'

Europeans, it seemed – even to aware, innovative leaders like Unwin or Pick – had all these funny 'modern' ideas; especially, perhaps, in Central Europe (where, W. S. Gilbert had suggested in *The Mikado*, people 'listen to sermons by mystical Germans who preach from ten 'til four'). In England, so much more pragmatic and unideological, people just got on with the job. '[T]he thing really was to do what one wanted to do,' said the artist William Coldstream, founder of the Euston Road School, 'even if one was not enormously equipped to do it, rather than to follow out theories of what one ought to do.'

Thus, to the culturally aware émigré from Central Europe, British attitudes must sometimes have seemed incorrigibly insular. But how could it have been otherwise? The psychological fact of living in an offshore island had given those who lived in Britain geopolitical advantages, led them to become a global power and helped spare them from many of the conflicts that had periodically engulfed their continental neighbours. But physical insularity had also doubtless helped generate a degree of cultural insularity bordering, some European observers felt, on arrogance. The English, opined an Italian visitor as long ago as 1500, 'are great lovers of themselves, and of everything belonging to them; they think that there are no other men than themselves, and no other world but England'. And his contemporary, Erasmus, wrote that the British 'think they have a monopoly, amongst other things, of good looks, musical talent and fine food'.*

Thus, for all the German influence upon Elgar, Tovey or John Christie, the Francophilia of Roger Fry or England's historical reputation as a haven for foreign freethinkers, it seemed that a

---

*Or, in the words of the Lonely Planet phrase book (1999 edition): 'The English will go to any lengths to make other people look inferior or stupid.'

58

cosy self-image of insular 'Englishness' prevailed throughout the 'long weekend', that entr'acte between one international catastrophe and another. 'We're in the heart of England,' says one schoolmaster proudly and comfortingly to another in the first minutes of the 1939 film *Goodbye Mr Chips*, 'a heart that has a very gentle beat.' This was the England of Baldwin (or J. B. Priestley) with his pipe, Hobbs and Sutcliffe in their cricket whites, the pub for the workers and the country house for the gentry. Such was the natural order of things. Why strain oneself to understand distant rumblings that did not impinge? 'Heard melodies [wrote Keats] are sweet; but those unheard are sweeter.' This was evidently a culture that valued understatement, constraint, repression, avoidance.

'Where are you from?' Eva Neurath was asked shortly after arriving in England from the nightmare of Hitlerism.

'Berlin,' she told the lady who had enquired.

'Oh, well, never mind,'* was the kindly reply.

---

* Eva Neurath was not the first Berlin visitor to be disconcerted by this almost disdainful nonchalance. Pastor Moritz, travelling through England in 1782, wrote: 'Nothing is oftener heard than the phrase: "Never mind it!" ' – even, he noted, when someone fell down and cut his head on the pavement. In 1940, during the nightly bombing raids over London, Berta Geissmar was struck by the sang-froid of her Hampstead neighbour whose regular response was that she 'couldn't be bothered'.

CHAPTER FIVE

Early Arrivals

To many of the émigrés from Hitler, Britain was a strange land of which they knew little until they arrived, often in the last year of peace, as bewildered exiles. But several thousand made the move much earlier when it was still relatively easy to do so. These were often men and women of high principle, not necessarily threatened with anything more severe than loss of status or livelihood, at least in the immediate future, but outraged nonetheless at the barbarity of a regime that burned books. If you were an eminent architect or musician, film or theatre director, scientist or psychologist – and you had friends in Britain prepared to vouch for you – the transition could be relatively painless. Some of the earliest arrivals were also to prove among the most influential.

Carl Ebert was a highly regarded figure in the German operatic and musical world when he came to England in 1934. Tall, handsome and ambitious, Ebert had risen through the theatrical ranks to become a matinée idol during the 1920s. By the age of forty he was Intendant of the theatre in Darmstadt – not only the man in charge, but also the director of its most important theatrical and operatic productions. Indeed, since he planned to spend a good deal of his time directing, he appointed a young Viennese-born singers' agent named Rudolf Bing as his administrative assistant. He made other appointments too. Like most opera directors, Ebert could not read a full score or vocal score well enough to hear the music (and of course there were no complete recordings of operas to sample). So he asked a talented young composer/conductor called Berthold Goldschmidt to act

60

as his musical factotum. In his biography of his father, Peter Ebert recalls that Goldschmidt 'had a singular capacity for playing an opera score on the piano suggesting the moods and colours of the music, at the same time singing all the roles with the appropriate expression'. Peter Ebert described the way the two men worked together:

> While Goldschmidt performed at the piano, playing through the opera again and again, my father stretched out on a kind of psychiatrist's couch, first just listening, then making notes while following the music in the score as well as, for the first time, reading the text and, finally, questioning and arguing with Goldschmidt about the interpretation of each section.

As for the nature of the Ebert regime, Rudolf Bing recalled that

> Ebert was an extremely progressive director, both artistically and politically, and our little theatre in Darmstadt in the late 1920s was a focus for agitation in the town. As a publicly subsidized body, we were of course a regular subject of discussion in meetings of the city government. Ebert would engage controversial directors and designers to do productions at our theatre as guests, and some of the repertory was controversial, too.

Bing enjoyed his time at Darmstadt but left to try his hand in the film industry. He wasn't happy in movies and, in January 1931, returned to the operatic world as Manager of the Charlottenburg (or 'Städtische') Opera of Berlin – predecessor of today's Deutsche Oper on Bismarckstrasse. Shortly afterwards the Charlottenburg appointed a new Intendant – none other than Bing's former boss, Carl Ebert. For his opening production Ebert was expected to put on one of the great affirmations of German art – *Fidelio*, perhaps, or Wagner's *Die Meistersinger*. But in a bold move, in keeping with the uncertain times, he opted for what was at that time an almost forgotten work, which had been recommended to him by the indefatigable

Goldschmidt: Verdi's *Macbeth*. The performance, conducted by Fritz Stiedry and designed by Caspar Neher, 'was hailed as a revelation, a miracle, devastating, thanks to the fusion of music and stage which Carl Ebert had achieved'. This integration of sound and sight – something Ebert had struggled to achieve in his productions at Darmstadt – was a revelation to Berlin's audiences, accustomed as they were to the wooden routines that often passed for operatic acting at the time. Furthermore, the production proved to be one of the first and most important milestones in the worldwide revival of early works by Verdi that was to occur over the next thirty years or so.

Ebert had got off to an excellent start, but felt his theatre needed a music director. He approached Fritz Busch, then Music Director of the Dresden Opera. Busch was an outstanding conductor of Strauss, a dedicated Mozartean and one of the most respected conductors in Germany (though less famous than his violinist brother Adolf Busch, leader of the celebrated Busch Quartet). He was flattered by Ebert's invitation but reluctant to leave the security of his post in Dresden. However, he would be happy to work as a guest in Berlin and the two men decided to test the waters by collaborating on a new production at the Charlottenburg Opera in 1932. Ebert, delighted at the success of *Macbeth*, had developed the idea of a Verdi cycle and the piece he invited Busch to conduct was a new production of another piece rarely performed at the time: *Un Ballo in Maschera* (or *Ein Maskenball* as all in Berlin called it).

Busch adored the working period ('among the happiest experiences of my career'), and the result was a triumph for both Busch and Ebert. It was also the beginning of a partnership that – in the unlikely location of the Sussex Downs – was soon to set standards of operatic excellence that would be admired throughout the world.

On 9 March 1933 Carl Ebert attended a première at another of Berlin's opera houses, the State Opera on Unter den Linden, and met Busch for dinner at the Kempinski afterwards. Busch, accompanied by his wife, appeared visibly shaken and told Ebert how he had been booed by Nazi sympathisers in his Dresden theatre a couple of nights before and had had to leave the pit. Busch, like Ebert, was a high-minded man who had refused to dismiss Jewish colleagues; Ebert, a Social Democrat, gave work to people of various political persuasions, including some on the political left such as Neher. Such artistic integrity was clearly not appreciated by the new regime.

During dinner Bing appeared. He beckoned Ebert and told him that his own theatre, the Charlottenburg, had been occupied earlier that evening by the SA. The next day Ebert was summoned to see Göring, who was Prime Minister of Prussia as well as Hitler's Minister of the Interior. After an inconclusive meeting at which Ebert was subjected to a series of threats and promises, all wrapped up in Göring's notoriously oleagenous charm, Ebert resigned his post. Two days later he crossed into Switzerland hoping, perhaps, to resuscitate his career as an actor.

Busch, too, had a meeting with Göring who began by blaming the events in Dresden on a set of party men who had let things get out of hand. The Führer himself wanted Busch to return to his post. Busch said that was out of the question.

'Well, my dear friend,' said Göring, 'you know we have means at hand to compel you!'

'Just try it, Herr Minister,' Busch replied with spirit. 'A compulsory performance of *Tannhäuser* conducted by me would be no pleasure to you. You have never in your life heard anything that would be so stinkingly boring.'

Busch's son had already left Germany for Florence where he was apprenticed to Carl Ebert who was working there on the May Festival. Then, as Mrs Busch wrapped up affairs back in Germany, the conductor accompanied his daughters to England where they were to go to school, going on to Zurich where he linked up with his wife. Busch was offered an olive branch from the Nazis in the form of an invitation to conduct at Bayreuth that summer (in place of Toscanini, who had cancelled his engagement as a snub to Hitler). He turned it down with contempt. Fritz Busch was never to see Germany again.

Neither Busch nor Ebert was Jewish and neither was forced to leave Germany. But it was brutally clear to both men that everything they valued was now in jeopardy, and both felt themselves forced to seek work wherever they could obtain it. Firm friends, they kept closely in touch; they even found themselves collaborating (as joint directors of a season of German operas at the Teatro Colón in Buenos Aires). Then, in late 1933, Busch, by now based in Scandinavia, received a curious message from someone he had never heard of, in England.

It seemed that Adolf Busch, Fritz's violinist brother, had been performing in Eastbourne, on the Sussex coast. He was planning to return to London after the concert but, because of impenetrable fog, the lady who was driving him, Frances Dakyns, suggested they stay over with a cellist friend nearby. That night, talk turned to someone in Sussex who, according to a recent newspaper article, had a small theatre attached to his country estate and wanted to perform *Don Giovanni* there. Why don't they get my brother Fritz to conduct it, said Busch; he doesn't have much work lined up. Frances Dakyns arranged a meeting with the wealthy Sussex landowner, a Mr John Christie, who was serious about his opera house and talked of starting a regular opera festival. Christie wanted Adolf Busch to mastermind the whole thing, perhaps with his string quartet providing the starting point for the orchestra. That wouldn't be possible, he was told. But he might want to contact Busch's conductor brother Fritz.

Fritz Busch was startled by the enquiry, and got in touch with Ebert. The two men were hugely sceptical about John Christie and his bizarre idea. But early in 1934 Ebert stopped by in England, found his way to Christie's pile in Sussex and met the man himself. He also met Mrs Christie, the singer Audrey Mildmay, whose charm and savoir faire helped soften the edges of her ebullient and eccentric husband. 'If you're going to spend all that money,' she had said to John in words that are enshrined in Glyndebourne mythology to this day, 'for God's sake do the thing properly!'

John Christie knew little about the practicalities of opera or opera houses. He just knew what he liked and that he wanted to please his young soprano wife. How about putting on *Parsifal*, suggested the inveterate and uncritical Teutonophile? Ebert looked at the tiny theatre and replied sardonically that *Parsifal* would be fine if you put the singers and the orchestra in the auditorium and the audience on the stage. Well, then, replied Christie, undaunted, what *would* work?

'This intimate theatre simply asks for Mozart's operas.'

Christie wasn't convinced: 'English audiences don't like Mozart very much.'

'Then we must try to help them to like Mozart,' was Ebert's unanswerable riposte.

Months later, Ebert and Busch (with Rudi Bing in attendance as Contracts Manager) inaugurated the first Glyndebourne Festival. The two opening productions were Mozart's *Le Nozze di Figaro* (with Audrey Mildmay as Susanna) and *Don Giovanni*.

Walter Gropius, founding father of the Bauhaus, Germany's foremost school of industrial design and architecture, resigned the Directorship in 1928. After a period of growing frustration, he accepted an invitation from colleagues in England, where he stayed from 1934 until going on to the USA in 1937.

Born in Berlin, Gropius had developed an early interest in the links between architecture and industry. He saw no conflict between the aesthetics of fine design and its industrial mass production, and tried to bring the two together in the Bauhaus, which was established in Weimar shortly after World War One. In 1925 the Bauhaus moved to the less attractive but more congenial town of Dessau, where Gropius himself designed its main buildings: a classroom block, a workshop, a hostel with community facilities, as well as a section for Gropius's own architectural practice. The buildings were notable for their wide horizontal lines (no traditional A-frame roofs), a bridge spanning the wings and a great glass curtain wall enclosing the workshop area.

The Bauhaus style was not spectacular, but tended to emphasise clear, clean, geometric lines and honest use of materials. In the machine age, Gropius and his colleagues argued, there was no reason why the best products of a school of art and design should not be both functional and pleasing to the eye. Why not design chairs and light fittings (and entire housing estates) that the working classes could not only afford but also enjoy? Why not use the latest brick, steel and glass to create, and mass produce, the finest design? Thus the vision that inspired Gropius and his colleagues married something of the romantic medievalism of William Morris (and the English Arts and Crafts Movement) to the self-conscious Modernism of the machine age, with maybe a touch of Marxism. The school, Gropius insisted, should embody the virtues that inspired it and be, in effect, a community of like-minded artist-craftsmen. His teaching staff included such pioneers of the Modern movement as the painters Klee, Kandinsky and Lyonel Feininger, and designers Marcel Breuer and László Moholy-Nagy. They were called 'Masters', in the Hans Sachs fashion, and for a while lived on site in homes specially designed in the Bauhaus spirit – some of them by Gropius himself. The school was informed by a co-operative ethos that encouraged interchange between art, architecture and technology, and was partly financed by its own industrial mass production of goods of high-quality design.

Although the Bauhaus is principally remembered as an architectural school, it did not teach architecture at first, though students could work as apprentices in Gropius's private practice. When he left the Bauhaus in 1928, Gropius claimed that political pressures had worn him down and that he wanted to get on with his work as an architect. His successor, Hannes Meyer, was a more overt Socialist than Gropius; with the inexorable rise of the political Right, Meyer and *his* successor, Mies van der Rohe, found the position of the Bauhaus increasingly untenable. The school finally closed in 1933. Its existence had almost precisely mirrored, and coincided with, the rise and fall of the Weimar Republic.

Walter Gropius visited England in May 1934 to attend the opening of an exhibition of his work at the Royal Institute of British Architects and to meet and address (in his faltering English) the elite of English architecture. He was a celebrated figure by this time, though a good number of British architects and planners were still deeply imbued with the rural nostalgia of the Garden City ideal. Gropius's talk about mechanised production and high-density apartment blocks would have sounded alien to many. Some, however, were excited. Maxwell Fry, a leading Modernist among British architects, spoke the same aesthetic language as Gropius. So did the young men, some of them émigrés, who had formed themselves into the 'Modern Architectural Research Society' (MARS), a group devoted to bringing continental ideas to Britain. A month after this visit Gropius was writing that he was seriously thinking of looking for work in England. In October, he and his wife arrived at Victoria Station for an indefinite visit. He had been invited by the entrepreneurial designer and furniture manufacturer Jack Pritchard who offered him a home in the block which he himself had pioneered (and in which the Pritchards themselves now resided), the recently opened Isokon flats in Lawn Road in London's Belsize Park, designed by another upholder of British Modernism, the Canadian architect Wells Coates. With Gropius safely installed, Pritchard set up the Isokon Furniture Company. Gropius was its Head of Design.

Word of Gropius's arrival in London spread quickly. He and Maxwell Fry set up an architecture practice together, and Gropius found himself courted as an emissary or embodiment of continental Modernism. He was warmly welcomed by such like-minded figures as Leonard and Dorothy Elmhirst, whose arts community at Dartington was inspired by an ethos similar to that of the Bauhaus. Dorothy was an American heiress, Leonard an idealistic Englishman who had worked in India for Tagore. Together they had established an arts-and-educational community in the Devon countryside at Dartington Hall, where artists and craftsmen could live and work harmoniously and productively together. The Elmhirsts were keen to enlist Gropius's talents as they expanded Dartington and he helped adapt a small theatre for them. Other Dartington proposals, like many of his British projects, remained on the drawing board.

More fruitful for Gropius was his collaboration with Henry Morris, the Secretary to the Cambridgeshire Education Committee. Morris was excited by the educational opportunities of modern architecture and had developed the idea of what he called the 'village college' where full-time students as well as members of the local community would meet and learn. Several had been built or were in the pipeline when, on Pritchard's initiative, Gropius went to visit Morris. The result was that Morris managed (against considerable reluctance) to persuade the Education Committee to appoint Gropius and Fry as architects of a new college to be built in the village of Impington, just north of Cambridge near Histon.

Visitors to the college today look at the long, rectangular brick walls, flat roofs and window blocks, and ask what's so special about a series of structures which, to the undiscriminating eye, looks like standard school architecture. Countless educational institutions up and down Britain contain buildings along similar lines. Well, not quite. Look closer and there are many design features that arise directly from Bauhaus origins. If most of the buildings are essentially box-shaped, several of the most important lines are gently curved: the curtain wall over the main entrance of the college, the ceiling of the theatre – and, above all, the bowed corridor, reminiscent of a ship's deck, that runs the entire length of the community wing. Even the rectilinear edges of the external brickwork are curved, as though softened with a nail file. The main entry hall of the college, known as the Prom, is designed to act as a hub – a Roman forum – where people interact, meet, talk, do business and move on to the next class or activity.

Some of the teaching and staff rooms at Impington College still contain original fixtures and fittings – the clean, unembellished light fittings and wood panelling characteristic of Bauhaus industrial design. Then there are the windows, huge blocks of glass bringing abundant natural light into the classroom while enabling students to feel that they are integrally in touch with the greenery outside. Some south-facing classrooms are equipped with retracting, metal-frame hinged windows which, rather like Japanese screens, can be folded away (a feature that Berthold Lubetkin was to introduce into his High Point flats in Highgate).

But the main reason that Impington is 'special' is that these buildings date from the 1930s. Until then, much institutional architecture in England was living in the shadow of the Victorian and Edwardian legacies. Schools and hospitals, stations, hotels and government offices were still being dressed in neo-Gothic and neo-classical embellishment, while the Garden Cities, pioneered by Ebenezer Howard, were bathed in a typically English glow of rural nostalgia. Few British architects had yet embraced Modernism (Fry was the most conspicuous exception), and one can understand the hesitations of the Cambridge Education Committee before they agreed to commission the rectilinear brickwork, flat roofs and huge windows that they knew Gropius would produce.

By the time Impington College was built, Gropius had departed for the USA to become Professor of Architecture at Harvard. But he had left behind at Impington a pioneering complex that was to prove an important influence upon educational architecture and design in post-war Britain. In the 1950s, local and county councils all over the country embarked upon an unprecedented burst of school and college building. And, one after another, they opted to eschew traditional designs and instead commissioned brick-built, rectilinear buildings in the Gropius mould that would set the standards of educational architecture in Britain for a generation.

If you are walking up Hamburg's leafy Heilwigstrasse, a mile or so north of the University, look out for number 116, an arrestingly decorated building with the letters KBW prominent on its dark, perpendicular brickwork. This was, and is again, the Kulturwissenschaftliche Bibliothek Warburg, the creation of Aby Warburg, a brilliant, eccentric art-loving scion of the Jewish banking dynasty, who died in 1929. With the advent of the Nazis, the Warburg Library was transferred to London where, under the leadership of Fritz Saxl and Ernst Gombrich, the Warburg Institute revolutionised the study of art history in Britain.

Aby Warburg must have been a difficult character for his family to deal with, arousing a mixture of admiration and exasperation. Plagued since childhood by indifferent health and scarcely controllable passions, Aby was the eldest of five brothers and next in line to head the family firm. But, like many German intellectuals in the late nineteenth century, he had become besotted with the classical world and the Renaissance, and liked to make long forays to Italy to indulge his aesthetic obsession. He married a non-Jewish girl (the first Warburg to do so) and he and his bride settled for a while in Florence. Everywhere Aby went he would buy books, not just browsing among the second-hand bookshops but – with all that Warburg wealth behind him – accumulating entire job lots of valuable manuscripts and first editions. Many years before, Aby had come to an agreement with his brother Max: if Max would ensure that the family fortune would fund his book-buying habit, Aby would hand over his rights in the bank. It was a deal struck in adolescence but honoured throughout adulthood. For the rest of Aby Warburg's life he was financed by his banking brothers.

Aby Warburg not only bought books. He also aspired to write them. An inveterate note taker and scribbler, he produced countless idiosyncratic fragments and a handful of influential essays on aspects of classical antiquity and the Renaissance in which he sought organic connections between what he saw as the symbolic meaning behind works of art and the social, economic, scientific and philosophical environments within which they had been produced. His published writings may have been rare and abstruse, but Aby developed a reputation as a prodigious scholar and a compulsive communicator, an Ancient Mariner who could mesmerise his listeners. Whatever he was writing or speaking about, whether Memling or the Medici, the tapestries of Burgundy or the symbolism of Botticelli, it was the wider historical and intellectual context that he looked for. His considerable reserves of scorn were directed towards the 'connoisseurship' approach to art that encouraged people to look at a painting or a sculpture purely as a life-enhancing object of aesthetic contemplation. Kenneth Clark heard Warburg lecture and was transfixed. 'Thenceforward,' wrote the future director of London's National Gallery, 'my interest in "connoisseurship" became no more than a kind of habit, and my mind was occupied in trying to answer the kind of questions that had occupied Warburg.' Clark came to consider Aby Warburg 'the most original thinker on art history of our time', a figure who 'entirely changed the course of art-historical studies'.

Warburg was a sensitive and fastidious man driven by contradictory demons. The most assimilated member of a famous Jewish family, he nonetheless remained painfully sensitive to anti-Semitism. An aesthetic refugee from what he regarded as the crass materialism of Hamburg (and perhaps of the family firm), his entire life and work were financed by his brothers and he consistently returned, with all his booty, to the city of his birth. He once said he was 'a Jew by blood, a Hamburger at heart, a Florentine in spirit'. Like Nietzsche, one of his heroes, Warburg had a quasi-mystical love of artistic symbolism, and his collection included works on magic, astrology, numerology and the outer edges of metaphysics.

By the time of World War One this highly strung man, with his loyal wife and children, was living in a house (number 114 Heilwigstrasse) in which people had to survive in the spaces left by books. Warburg himself, deeply disturbed by the posturing nationalism and attendant horrors of the war, succumbed to severe mental instability and (like the central figure in Thomas Mann's *Magic Mountain*, written at this time) entered a sanatorium in Switzerland for an indefinite period. With Aby away, the Warburg brothers appointed his young assistant, an Austrian art historian named Fritz Saxl, to become the Library's acting director. Saxl set about rationalising and cataloguing the collection, and trying to make it available to outside scholars. It was a Herculean task, but an added stimulus came with the establishment of the University of Hamburg to which, in effect, the library became affiliated. Indeed, the Warburg Library, with the regular lectures, seminars and newsletter that Saxl organised, provided an important magnet for eminent figures whom the new university was busily luring, such as the art historian Erwin Panofsky and the philosopher Ernst Cassirer. 'This library is dangerous,' said Cassirer on his first visit, noting the unconventional but seductive range of subject matter scattered in every corner of the house. 'I shall either have to avoid it altogether or imprison myself here for years!' In the event, Cassirer researched some of his most important work in Warburg's library, including a study of the philosophy of symbolic forms, an essay on language and myth, and a major work on the philosophy of the Renaissance (which he dedicated to Aby).

While Aby was still in Switzerland, the brothers, in conjunction with Saxl and Aby's wife, talked of what to do with the Library. The family home was clogged with books and the idea arose of acquiring the next-door site, number 116 Heilwigstrasse. This was finally done when Aby returned from his sanatorium in 1924, and he was able personally to supervise the new Library's erection and design, from the *Jugendstil* lettering (KBW) on the front wall to the elliptical reading room at the back of the house. Under the supervision of Saxl and his assistant, Gertrud Bing, the collection was stacked in such a way as to link books about art and artists directly to those about their wider historical contexts, while various floors and mezzanine additions were designed to accommodate shelves and volumes of varying heights. At last this brilliant and driven man, so desperate all his life to save classical values for a civilisation in danger of losing them, had his own temple to cultural history. He had the word 'MNEMOSYNE' – the Greek for memory – inscribed on stone in large letters over the inner entrance door of the Library.

The new Library was opened in 1926. By the time Aby Warburg died, three years later, his Library and Institute provided the foremost centre for the study of art history in Germany, possibly in Europe. An astonishing achievement by any standards, it was the more remarkable for helping to bring the commercial city of Hamburg to the forefront of German intellectual and cultural life. It was perhaps fortuitous that the insatiable bibliophile who had created the Institute did not live to see the advent of a new German government in January 1933 which, by May, was publicly burning books. Before the end of that year, virtually the whole of Aby Warburg's Library of over 60,000 books had been crated up and shipped to London.

The initiative was Saxl's. He knew that a cultural institute founded by a Jew would be a prime target of the Nazis and he rapidly got in touch with contacts in Italy, the Netherlands, the United States, Britain, anywhere. People visited, were impressed and left full of goodwill. Several reported back that they might be able to accept the Library as a gift, but this would impose insuperable tax burdens. A stream of British visitors came to Hamburg and were given to understand that the Library might be theirs as a 'loan'. In July 1933 Professor W. G. Constable of the recently created Courtauld Institute of Art came to Hamburg to reconnoitre, accompanied by a colleague from Guy's Hospital. They were followed in October by Sir Denison Ross, head of the School of Oriental Languages. Back in London, Ross set up a committee under Lord Lee of Fareham. Lee, a former First Lord of the Admiralty, had been instrumental in persuading the industrialist and art collector Samuel Courtauld to found his Institute and was its Chairman.

One day Lord and Lady Lee were having dinner in Oxford with Kenneth Clark and his wife. The phone rang. It was Fritz Saxl, whom Clark had not yet met at the time.

> [Saxl] said, in guarded terms, that the time had come for the Institute to leave Germany, and wondered if there was any chance of its being established in Oxford. I knew enough about university politics to realise that this could not be done without several years of lobbying, during which time the Library would have been seized by the Nazis and the Library staff sent to concentration camps. But I said I would do what I could.

Clark returned to the table and told Lee of his conversation. Arthur Lee was one of Britain's movers and shakers, a soldier, diplomat and administrator with a wealthy American wife. In the early years of the century the Lees had filled their house in Buckinghamshire, Chequers, with art objects and then turned the home into a trust for use by future prime ministers. They went on to amass a further collection, which they intended to use as the basis for a possible teaching institution (now part of the Courtauld collection). Lee was therefore just the man to act as Saxl's good angel. He evidently acted fast. By the end of October 1933 Lee was able to send a formal letter to Max Warburg in Hamburg asking if it

> might be possible for [the] Library to be temporarily housed in London – say for a period of three years – so that the advantages and facilities it offers to all students of art

and culture might have an opportunity of continuing to be used and developed under the guidance of those who have for so long been connected with it.

Space was found in Thames House on the Embankment in London where the Library could initially be stored, and the Warburgs and Samuel Courtauld pledged money for the housing and upkeep of the collection. After some wavering, the Nazi authorities agreed to the request on condition that some 2000 books relating to World War One were retained in Hamburg and, more important, that no publicity be given to this supposedly temporary transfer. In December, as Saxl watched Aby Warburg's books, papers and pictures being packed by carefully chosen anti-Nazi workmen into 500 boxes, he reflected, 'Some scholars like Petrarch or Erasmus have always been fond of travelling, but travelling adventures are not so common in the lives of learned institutions.'

The arrival of the Warburg collection in London did not seal its permanent fate. Would the Library have to return to Germany after three years? Perhaps part of it could be transferred to the United States. In the event, initially because of the generosity of Courtauld, the Library stayed in the UK, eventually finding a permanent home adjacent to the University of London in Woburn Square.

Fritz Saxl had had his differences with Aby Warburg (including, it seems, over Gertrud Bing, who became the older man's regular travelling companion in his last years). But he was intensely loyal to his memory and within a year or so of arriving in London decided to commission someone to work through Aby's papers with a view to eventual publication. In late 1935 he offered a job to a young Viennese art historian recommended to him by the psychoanalyst Ernst Kris. His name was Ernst Gombrich.

What did 'dance' mean to the British balletomane of 1930? Essentially, Russian ballet. Even more essentially, the legacy of the Diaghilev troupe with its exotic mix of Russian fervour and discipline, and the subtle sophistication of Paris to which so many of the St Petersburg elite had fled after the Revolution. It was Diaghilev who had commissioned Bakst and Picasso to design for him, Stravinsky to create *Firebird*, *Petrushka* and *Le Sacre du Printemps* and brought Nijinsky and Karsavina to London. Massine and Pavlova had worked for him. Keynes's wife, Lydia Lopokova, had danced for him, as had Marie Rambert. So had Ninette de Valois, a young dancer who opened her own ballet school in 1926 and was shortly to found what eventually became the Royal Ballet.

But to some, 'dance' also meant something other than ballet, something less constrained by classical tradition yet equally disciplined. Isadora Duncan, an independent spirit inspired by the rhythms of nature, preached and practised a kind of 'free' dance in which mind and body were liberated from the shackles of traditional forms and techniques. Appearing not in tutu and tights but in loose costumes and bare feet, Duncan danced her way across Europe and America during the first two decades of the twentieth century. Her art (derived in part from the ideas of François Delsarte, the father of 'free dance') was intensely expressive and personal. To some, there was an element of self-indulgence to her performances. But to her admirers – and these were legion throughout Europe and America – Duncan was the very embodiment of the spiritual transcendentalism preached by her hero Walt Whitman.

Duncan was born in the United States but established herself as part of Mrs Patrick Campbell's circle in Edwardian London where she rapidly became an admired if controversial figure. She was especially popular in Germany and Austria where, it seems, the sick would attend her performances in the hope of being cured, students would carry her back in triumph to her hotel after the show and all Berlin would debate the life-enhancing principles she expounded. 'Whole columns constantly appeared in the papers,' she wrote, 'sometimes hailing me as the genius of a newly discovered Art, sometimes denouncing me as a destroyer of the real classic dance, i.e. the ballet.' Her accounts doubtless contain an element of hyperbole. But it is easy to see the appeal of a charismatic dancer whose art and life chimed so closely with the self-expressiveness advocated by the *Blaue*

Reiter artists or by Rudolf Steiner's 'anthroposophists' that were fashionable at the time (not to mention the sexual liberation being preached by Freud and his followers). To the army of her followers, Mind, Body and Soul came together in Isadora Duncan – a perception magnified by the absurd tragedy of her early death as a result of an accident, ironically involving one of the long, loose scarves she loved to wear.

Had Duncan really destroyed classical ballet? Of course not. But she had helped drive a wedge between two styles, or traditions of dance, and it is perhaps significant that her greatest impact appears to have been in those areas (Central Europe, the USA) where the classical Russo-French tradition was least ingrained. Could the two styles meet? Was it possible for modernity to meld with tradition, for the 'nature' of Duncan to coexist with the 'nurture' of Diaghilev, for 'dance' to marry 'ballet'? This was the challenge that confronted Rudolf Jean Baptiste Attila Laban de Varaljas.

Laban was born in 1879 in Bohemia in the Austro-Hungarian Empire and died in Harold Macmillan's England. The son of a wealthy and highly placed military governor, Laban was educated in Budapest and Vienna, and spent some of his formative years at his father's postings in the Balkans and Constantinople where he encountered oriental dancing, including that of the dervishes. Interested in all the arts and the relationships between them, Laban became a skilled draughtsman and painter and studied theatre production and design in Munich before going on to Paris. Here he had a thorough training in classical ballet, and got to know Diaghilev and Fokine. He also encountered the ideas of Delsarte, learning that gesture was more important than fancy footwork, and he studied for a while under one of Delsarte's pupils.

Meanwhile, Laban imbibed something of the wider artistic ferment in early-twentieth-century Paris, where Debussy and Stravinsky, Proust, Picasso and Braque were creating the artistic agenda for the new century. For a while Laban had his own painting studio in Montparnasse. Already a seeker after eternal truths, he joined the Rosicrucians during his years in Paris, was deeply impressed by Kandinsky's theories about abstraction in art and studied the latest ideas of Emile Jaques-Dalcroze, an educationalist who developed a series of gymnastic exercises to help music students build up a sense of rhythm. After further wanderings and a failed marriage, Laban – with his second wife, the singer Maja Lederer – returned to Munich, working there as a painter and illustrator, and experimenting with new forms of musical and dance notation.

In 1911 Dalcroze set up a school near Dresden. Among the people working with him were the dancers Susanne Perrotet and Marie Wiegmann (as Mary Wigman then spelled her name). Laban soon persuaded them to join him in his own enterprise: a course on the arts to be given each summer in Ascona (Switzerland) and every winter in Munich. During most of World War One, Laban and his family lived, in considerable privation, in Zurich. While in Switzerland, Laban continued to work with his chosen group of dancers (and started an affair with one of them, Dussia Bereska, which eventually led to the break-up of his second marriage), and began writing a book about his theories of dance. In Zurich, too, he encountered the early flowering of Dada, the secret seductiveness of Free-masonry (which he joined) and the virulent post-war epidemic of influenza which nearly killed him.

In the 1920s Laban's life and work finally began to take wing. He and Bereska moved to Stuttgart where he opened a school of dance and was able to put into practice his quasi-philosophical ideas. To Laban, dance was more than a picturesque art form. Dance should reveal inner motivation not exernal show; if the body moved in conjunction with the inner rhythms of the mind and spirit, dance could become the key to individual and indeed communal fulfilment. The concepts were abstract and Laban loved to express them through an impressive if arcane vocabulary ('eurhythmics', 'choreutics' and 'eukinetics'). But there was no doubting the man's conviction, his desire to bring together the best features of all kinds of dance – including the classical ballet in which he had been trained – and his determination to bring to dance the stature already enjoyed by music and theatre. If plays and symphonies could be written down, why not find a foolproof notation system for dance? In everything he did, said, wrote or choreographed, Laban preached his passionate message about the primacy of movement, of dance. In Stuttgart he created dance 'symphonies', and he experimented with speech, sound and even silence.

One of the early pupils at the Labanschule in Stuttgart was Kurt Jooss, an idealist and wanderer who had discovered the joys of folk dancing as a member of one of the German youth movements. The encounter was to prove pivotal in the lives of master and pupil alike. Jooss went on to work as theatre choreographer in Münster, taking his Laban colleague Sigurd Leeder with him, and also to Paris to study classical technique. Later, Jooss and Leeder moved to Essen where they ran their own company, a communal enterprise that included the composer Fritz Cohen and the designer Hein Heckroth. Laban, meanwhile, living a characteristically peripatetic existence, moved to Hamburg for a period, eventually taking up a post in Berlin. When Laban celebrated his fiftieth birthday in Essen in December 1929, Jooss made him a present of a new ballet.

If Laban was Germany's most famous theorist of dance, Jooss rapidly made an outstanding name for himself as a choreographer. Unafraid of tackling traditional ballets like *Coppélia* or reworking Diaghilev masterpieces like *Petrushka*, Jooss tried to incorporate some of the insights from classical ballet into the new approach to movement he had learned from Laban. For example, he eschewed the barefoot approach of Isadora Duncan and normally put his dancers into shoes. But equally, Jooss avoided the *pointe* shoes of ballet; tiptoe balance was not his aim, but expressive movement. His greatest achievement was *The Green Table*, a masked dance of death, to music by Cohen, that parodied the polite but impotent posturing of the politicians of 1914–18 whose post-war peace conference was as absurd as the war they had brought about four years earlier. In *The Green Table*, Jooss wove together the grotesque power of Expressionist drama and the passionate pacifism of *All Quiet on the Western Front*, the visual bravado of Diaghilev and the inner motivation Jooss had learned from Laban. Created for an international choreographic competition in Paris in 1932, *The Green Table* won first prize, catapulted Jooss to international fame and led to a world tour. In London he was greeted backstage by Leonard and Dorothy Elmhirst who casually invited him to visit Dartington Hall, 'a nice place in the south'.

The arrival of Hitler the following year put the entire Jooss–Leeder enterprise at risk. Several members of their company were Jewish, including Fritz Cohen. The Nazis wanted Jooss to sack Cohen or at least not to credit him as the company's composer. Then they wanted the designer Hein Heckroth removed. In 1934, Jooss and his troupe were due to visit the Netherlands. Once out of Germany, they stayed out. Shortly afterwards the entire company (and half their students) moved to Dartington where they rehearsed, performed and taught. Before long, the Jooss–Leeder school was attracting students from all over the world, while the dance company itself continued to appear not only in London and elsewhere in the UK but throughout Western Europe and North America.

Laban, by contrast, was still in Germany. Indeed, he was in Berlin, supervising dance at the State Opera. For all his penchant for quasi-mystical theorising about the relationship between mind and movement, he had proved himself highly adept at choreographing inspirational operatic spectacle. As the Nazis took control of culture, they were quick to see the value to them of talented artists like Laban. Hitler himself attended a farewell matinée at the opera for Laban who, in September 1934, took up a new post as Director of the Deutsche Tanzbühne. This appointment, falling under Goebbels's Ministry of Propaganda, essentially placed Laban in charge of dance and movement throughout Germany. At first this highly idiosyncratic artist could do no wrong in the eyes of his authoritarian masters. Laban mounted dance festivals in Berlin in 1934 and 1935 in which talented but unemployed dancers were able to work alongside established figures like Mary Wigman. He took dance to all parts of Germany, established a series of educational classes and worked on his theories of dance notation. He also began to work on various large-scale projects, including an international dance competition, planned to coincide with the Berlin Olympics of 1936.

The most ambitious of these was a vast pageant designed to

inaugurate the new open-air stage adjacent to the Olympic stadium. A thousand participants from all over Germany would laud the 'Warm Wind and the New Joy' (this was its title!) of National Socialism in a celebratory ritual of music and movement redolent of the films of Busby Berkeley or Leni Riefenstahl. At the final run-through Goebbels himself chose to be present – and promptly cancelled the entire show. He found it too intellectual, he wrote in his diary. 'I do not like it . . . It is dressed up in our clothes and has nothing whatever to do with us.' It seemed Laban had given too much rein to individual expressiveness in his choreography and insufficient to folk dance or other aspects of the party line. He was permitted to have his Olympic dance competition, after which he effectively became a nonperson in the Third Reich, denied work or recognition (officially because of his membership of the Freemasons).

Laban was crushed by this dramatic change in his fortunes. Perhaps he had been naïve to believe that an independent artist like himself, so wedded to ideas of free self-expression, could thrive for long under the Third Reich. Or perhaps some of his ideas, rooted as they were in the quasi-mystical integration of body, soul and mind, did genuinely correspond with those of Nazism. Whatever his reasons for working with the Hitler regime, the association ended painfully for Laban. In 1937 he left Germany, initially for Paris and thence for Dartington where, a tired and broken man, he was given succour by his former pupil Kurt Jooss.

In the 1920s the film capitals of the world were Los Angeles and Berlin. Hollywood boasted the vision and flair of D. W. Griffith and Cecil B. DeMille, the shrewd marriage of art and business embodied by Chaplin, Douglas Fairbanks and Mary Pickford, and the compulsive allure and bravado of Gloria Swanson and Mae West. Few in the New Babylon would have guessed that, before long, the Hollywood recipe would become even more richly spiced by the addition of directors called Preminger, Lang, Lubitsch, Czinner, Zinnemann and Wilder, and actors with names like Lamarr, Dietrich, Homolka and Jannings – and a plethora of émigré composers and technicians who would compose, conduct, light, shoot and edit a whole new generation of movies.

Many of these émigré talents emerged, directly or indirectly, from UFA, the Berlin-based leviathan, originally an amalgamation of existing companies created in 1917 to rationalise the German film industry for propaganda purposes. After the war UFA survived as a production and distribution company, and it attracted many of the best in the business from throughout Germany and beyond. Erich Pommer, the producer of *Caligari*, rose to become Head of Production. Many of the great classics of German silent cinema – *Der Letzte Mann*, *Dr Mabuse*, Lang's *Metropolis* – were UFA productions. So when the ambitious young Hungarian film maker Alexander Korda moved to Berlin in 1923, he naturally contacted his compatriot, Josef Somlo, then head of UFA's foreign division. The result was a number of UFA co-productions over the next three years, which Korda directed.

In 1926 Korda swept out of Berlin, hoping to find fame and fortune in Hollywood. As he left, another Hungarian émigré, an impoverished lad of Jewish background in his mid-twenties, arrived in the city. Imre Pressburger was born and raised near the eastern frontiers of the Austro-Hungarian Empire in December 1902. As a boy, Pressburger had showed musical talent and learned the violin, and by the age of twelve was playing in the village orchestra. He also had half a dozen languages more or less at his command. But he had no skills that he could translate into serious money.

History had not dealt Pressburger a generous hand. A postwar treaty following the disintegration of the Habsburg Empire had transferred his home region to Romania and the new authorities refused the boy's request to study in Budapest. He regarded Romania itself as a cultural backwater and therefore set off for Germany, which he considered the *fons et origo* of European culture. Arriving in Prague, his request for a visa to Germany was abruptly refused, so he enrolled in the Deutsche Technische Hochschule and stayed for a couple of years in Prague where he underwent recurrent feasts and famines of music, sex, food and football. He finally got to Germany in 1924 where he sojourned in Stuttgart, adding film and radio to his menu of enthusiasms. Returning home on the death of his father, Pressburger made and sold radio sets for a while. When the business folded and he was called into the army, he bought a one-way ticket to Berlin and slipped out of Romania – for good.

For Pressburger, as for so many other culture-hungry young-sters at the time, Berlin was an irresistible magnet. It helped if (like Stephen Spender) you were talented and well-connected. But the German capital had little pity to spare for an impecunious, unemployed East European with limited skills. Cold and hungry, Pressburger slept on park benches and in shop doorways. His violin provided temporary relief: he was booked to play in a cinema orchestra accompanying silent movies for a while – and then got himself sacked. He tried everything. A friend wrote short stories. Imre decided that he could do better and sent a selection to the Berlin newspapers. On 28 March 1928 one of his stories was published.

Pressburger was ecstatic. Emboldened by success, he bom-barded UFA with his ideas, was asked to redraft one of them for the director Robert Siodmak and – his name newly Germanised as 'Emmerich' – was assigned an office as a junior scriptwriter. Here he encountered Carl Mayer (creator of *Caligari*, *Der Letzte Mann* and much else), the poet and novelist Erich Kästner (later to become famous as the author of *Emil and the Detectives*) and another young writer called Billi Wilder.

In some ways Pressburger joined UFA at precisely the wrong moment. The heroic era of German cinema was coming to an end. Directors like Fritz Lang had persistently overspent on their artistic extravaganzas (*Metropolis* had almost bankrupted the company), while audiences were showing signs of becoming bored by poor reinventions of the old Expressionist classics. In 1927, more or less coinciding with the arrival of the talkies, UFA installed Alfred Hugenberg as its new boss. His avowed policy was to raise the entertainment quotient and lower costs. Hence-forth, UFA would steer away from projects with earnest social implications and concentrate instead on romantic comedies, musicals and dance sequences.

The UFA environment provided Pressburger with an ideal

professional apprenticeship. *Caligari* and *Mabuse* may have been no more, but their spirit lived on. The classic German tradition, in which the purely visual element took precedence, was clearly absorbed by Pressburger as he produced one highly cinematic, image-led screenplay after another in which he demanded strangely painted sets, scenes that were extravagantly lit (and shadowed), acute camera angles, dream sequences and fantasy relationships.

When the Nazis came to power in January 1933, Hugenberg enthusiastically put UFA at their disposal. All UFA employees with Jewish blood were warned that their days were numbered and in April Pressburger left Berlin for Paris. Here he soon linked up with former Berlin friends and colleagues including the directors Max Ophuls and Robert and Curt Siodmak, and the powerful and independent-minded UFA production executive Günther von Stapenhorst. Work in Paris was fitful. At times Pressburger had bursts of feverish activity (and good money) as he found himself writing a screenplay to Offenbach's *La Vie Parisienne* for Robert Siodmak or collaborating with the operetta composer Oscar Straus. But there were also months racked by inactivity and mounting debt. Less than three years after arriving in Paris, this peripatetic man – who had already lived in Hungary, Romania, Czechoslovakia, Germany and France – decided to try his luck in England.

If Pressburger had mistimed his arrival in Berlin and Paris, he came to London at precisely the right moment. Alexander Korda, having failed to impress Hollywood, was now busy establishing himself as the most successful film producer in England, the man some people were already crediting with the great revival of British film making. Korda's movie empire, based in Denham, was called London Films and its trademark (which Korda himself had chosen) was Big Ben. The irrepressible Hungarian had surrounded himself with an array of Central European talent.* Scripts came from Lajos Biro and music from Kurt Schroeder (at first) or Miklós Rózsa. Émigré

---

* It was said that the three Union Jacks flying outside Korda's studios at Denham were for the three British employees working there.

actors including Elisabeth Bergner and Conrad Veidt (of *Caligari* fame) were given starring parts, designs came from the boss's brother Vincent while a third brother, Zoltan Korda, would often direct.

London Films was basking in the critical and financial success of the 1933 movie *The Private Life of Henry VIII* and Korda, keen to expand, was actively seeking out new talent. If you wanted to work in pictures, Alex Korda was the man to know. A person of extravagant personal tastes, he could also be almost recklessly generous to others. When Winston Churchill was deep in debt and had no serious prospects of political advancement, Korda bought the rights to *Marlborough* for £10,000, even though he probably saw no serious prospect of filming it. In much the same spirit he bought a Napoleon treatment from the Berlin theatre critic Alfred Kerr who was by then living in some penury in London. The Bauhaus artist László Moholy-Nagy, briefly an émigré in London before going on to a new life and career in the USA, had a number of unlikely commissions from Korda: a nature film about lobsters, for example, and some (unused) futurological designs for the Korda movie *Things to Come*. As they said, you didn't *have* to be Hungarian to work in films. But it helped.

Pressburger – now known as 'Emeric' which may have sounded English to him but didn't fool anyone else – had been working for Stapenhorst (also by now an émigré in London) when Miklós Rózsa, with whom Pressburger played violin-piano duets, put him in touch with Zoltan Korda. Zoltan mentioned him to brother Alex. One day Pressburger's phone went. He was summoned to the presence in Denham and given a little hack work. Korda kept Pressburger on the books for a while, basically doing other people's rewrites. One particular script was causing difficulties, it seemed, because Korda needed it to contain a role for Connie Veidt. Could Pressburger oblige? He could. And at the next script conference, Korda introduced him to another of his bright young men, a tall English public schoolboy type with aspirations to direct. Name of Michael Powell. Thus began what was to blossom into one of the most creative partnerships in British film history.

CHAPTER SIX

Leaving Home

Ebert and Busch, Gropius and Moholy-Nagy, Saxl and Gombrich, Jooss and Laban, Korda and Pressburger were among the distinguished few who came to Britain from Middle Europe when it was still relatively easy to do so, their translation to a new life proving fairly painless. By the outbreak of war, Britain was to admit around 70,000 refugees from Nazi Germany, Austria and adjacent territories, the great majority of them Jews. Some re-emigrated, typically to the USA, but something over 55,000 stayed and most eventually became permanent residents.

This huge transfer paralleled a similar flow half a century before when some 100,000 Jews fled to Britain from the pogroms of Tsarist Russia. But there were important differences. Most of the earlier wave of Jewish immigrants had settled near the docks from which they disembarked in London's East End (the traditional home of England's new immigrants) or in provincial cities such as Glasgow, Leeds or Manchester, where they established traditional synagogues and kosher butchers, and found work as tailors, haberdashers or watchmakers. As with previous (and subsequent) waves of immigration, British generosity was tinged with resentment. By 1900 anti-Semitism was inflated by a general fear of 'the foreign', fuelled by the Boer War and the political isolation that accompanied it. 'Aliens' – including Jews – came to be commonly regarded with suspicion, and migration into Britain was severely restricted in the early twentieth century by the Aliens Act of 1905, which empowered immigration officers to keep out anyone they considered 'undesirable'.

The onset of war in 1914 saw a renewed surge of xenophobia and the Aliens Restriction Act, passed through all its stages in a single day in August 1914, required aliens to register with the police and entitled the authorities to deport without appeal. Well over half of the 60,000 Germans and Austrians resident in Britain were interned and there were even demands to strip distinguished (and wholly loyal) émigrés such as Sir Ernest Cassel and Sir Edgar Speyer of their knighthoods. As popular hysteria called for the banning of the music of Germans like Beethoven, many people (including the royal family) anglicised what had been German family names for fear of popular reprisals. After the war the government passed the Aliens Restriction (Amendment) Act 1919; this, and the Aliens Order of the following year, gave immigration officers the power to refuse admission, except temporarily, to anybody who did not have a labour permit or visible means of support.

This was the basic legislative framework confronting Gropius, Ebert, Busch, Saxl and Jooss when they applied to enter Britain. A foreigner could visit the UK, as teacher or tourist, performer or producer, actor or academic, so long as the visit was temporary and papers were in order. You had to show that you would not be a burden to the state. And, of course, it helped if you had a well-connected sponsor like John Christie, Jack Pritchard, Arthur Lee or Leonard Elmhirst to vouch for you.

With Hitler in power in Germany, the British government came under pressure to reconsider the mechanisms under which Jews from Germany might enter the UK. Sheer humanity suggested that Britain ought to provide a generous haven for refugees from political oppression, just as it had for the French Huguenots after 1685, the liberal revolutionaries of Europe after 1848, or the Emperor Napoleon III and his wife. On the other hand Britain, like much of Europe and America, was undergoing severe economic depression and high unemployment – not a good time in which to admit thousands of foreigners, even on a temporary basis. Inevitably, some would seek jobs, or be perceived as doing so, and that might lead to further anti-Semitism. Indeed, might not the admissions of large numbers of Jews at such a time exacerbate the problems of anti-Semitism, rather as it had done in the 1890s?

This idea – that the best way of defeating anti-Semitism was to impose strict limits upon Jewish immigration – struck some as a singularly perverse way of conniving at the cruelties of the Nazis.* Several of the leaders of Anglo-Jewry got together and promised the government that, if immigration restrictions could be eased for Jewish refugees from Nazism, any resulting financial burden would be borne by the existing community 'without ultimate charge to the State'. Neither they, nor the government which accepted this pledge, had any conception of the scale the immigration would reach by the last years of the decade.

Initially, numbers were small. During Hitler's first fifteen months in power, Britain (having refused very few applicants) took about 2000 refugees from Nazi Germany. Far more chose to go to the adjacent territories: France (21,000), Poland (8000) and Czechoslovakia (3500). About 10,000 German Jews left for Palestine. The overwhelming majority of German Jews simply kept their heads down and hoped the whole nightmare would soon pass.

As the Nazis put further pressure on Jews and dissidents, however, more of them thought seriously about getting out. But where to go? When Hitler marched into the Rhineland to his west and cast an acquisitive eye towards the Czech and Polish borderlands to his east, the options narrowed. Palestine began to close its doors.† What about more distant corners of the British Empire – Australia and Canada, Kenya and Rhodesia, India and Ceylon, Trinidad and Jamaica? All were considered, but none provided realistic opportunities for large-scale migration. The most attractive destination for many was the USA. Rather as in Britain, you needed an 'affidavit' – someone to vouch for you so that you would not be a financial burden on

---

* It was to be paralleled thirty years later by politicians who argued that the best way to improve race relations in Britain was to keep as low as possible the number of blacks allowed into the country.

† A serious Arab rebellion against British rule in 1936 led the authorities in Palestine to restrict Jewish migration; the last thing they wanted was increased tension between Jews and Arabs.

the state. But the Americans operated a strict quota system, and the limited number of immigrants permitted from Germany was permanently oversubscribed.*

It was to Britain, therefore, that more and more would-be emigrants looked, if only as a temporary refuge before moving elsewhere. 'My father had been talking about leaving for years,' Claus Moser recalled, 'and when his bank was expropriated he and my mother decided the time had come.' The hope was to go to America. For Claus, who had been learning English, the prospect of emigration was quite an adventure. There was already something of an exodus. Several of Claus's friends and relatives – including an aunt and her family – had left. 'Now it was our turn.' And Britain was clearly the place to make for. A liberal democracy with a tradition of tolerance, it seemed to be outside the range of Hitler's ambitions, yet nearer (and therefore cheaper to reach) than North America.

Departure was not without its excitements as the family tried to take as much of their worldly wealth as they could while not drawing attention to themselves. 'My father explained that we would travel separately; he with my brother, me with my mother.' Thus the Moser family came to London in 1936. They didn't move on to America but settled in Putney.

Numbers were still small and manageable. Then, in 1938, the trickle became a flood. In March Hitler annexed Austria. The *Anschluss* – when Hitler incorporated Austria into Greater Germany – was sometimes portrayed (especially in post-war Austria) as a forced annexation. That is not how George Clare remembered it. Later an émigré living in Britain, Clare (he was Georg Klaar then) witnessed at first hand the Nazis' ecstatic reception in Vienna. The entire city, he wrote, 'behaved like an aroused woman, vibrating, writhing, moaning and sighing

---

* Peter Gay recounts how, because his father was born in Poland, his chances of obtaining a visa for the USA were reduced to insignificance because the Polish immigration quota was lower than that for people born in Germany or Austria. The family only survived because entry to certain Latin American countries could be bought, at a price, and an uncle in America paid for them to have visas to Cuba. In Havana they joined a Jewish refugee community of over 3000 people (eventually entering the USA in January 1941).

lustfully for orgasm and release. This is not purple writing. It is an exact description of what Vienna was and felt like on Monday, 14 March 1938, as Hitler entered her.' Overnight, every Austrian became a German citizen, every Austrian Jew subject to the laws of the Third Reich.

Who could know for sure where Hitler might strike next? Suddenly Czechoslovakia and Poland looked a lot less secure. No German with an independent mind – certainly no Jew anywhere in the expanded Third Reich – was safe. People wrote to long-lost cousins for help. Karl Schwander (later Charles Spencer) went with his father to the American embassy in Vienna where they scoured the New York and Chicago telephone books and wrote to anyone they found with a similar name. Perhaps you are distant relatives of ours? If so, I wonder whether you would be prepared to sign an 'affidavit' on our account?

The queue for exit papers, and the odds against obtaining them, lengthened. So did the numbers of desperate people waiting in line for entry visas outside the besieged foreign embassies in Vienna and Berlin, above all those of the United States and Britain. But you were unlikely to obtain either set of permissions, exit or entry, without already having obtained and paid for guaranteed passage to a defined destination. Applicants met resistance at every stage and were often fleeced by unscrupulous travel companies. A lucky few obtained all the requisite papers and managed to leave.

The Anglo-Jewish community was no longer able to under-write the cost of what became a rapidly rising wave of refugees and turned for help to the British government. The authorities were in a dilemma. Entry visas were still normally on a temporary or 'transit' basis. But those who had been admitted tended to ask for their stay to be extended and, in practice, there was often nowhere else they could go. So the government resorted to what amounted to a rationing system. Entry might be granted to 'distinguished persons, i.e. those of international repute in the field of science, medicine, research or art' along with certain 'industrialists with a well-established business'. But small shopkeepers, artisans, minor musicians, commercial artists and rank-and-file lawyers, doctors and dentists were consigned to the back of the queue. Britain already had a lot of these.

It was hard to believe that things would get worse. But they did. In September 1938 Hitler annexed the Czech Sudeten lands, an act of international piracy swallowed by Germany's western neighbours, Britain and France, who were desperate to believe that these acquisitions would represent the Führer's final outrage. On the contrary, Hitler felt emboldened. When a Nazi official was assassinated at the German embassy in Paris in early November, the Hitler regime unleashed a pogrom known euphemistically to history as *Kristallnacht*. Throughout the Reich, shops owned by Jews were vandalised and looted, and synagogues put to the torch while the Nazi police looked on and the crowds bayed. The next day Jews whose property had been destroyed were forced to their knees to clean up the mess. A lot of glass was broken on *Kristallnacht*; but so were people's heads. Men 'disappeared'. Jewish families remaining in the Third Reich panicked. People tried to sneak illegally over borders, stow away on international trains, go on holidays to Sweden or Switzerland, Norway or the Netherlands, France, Spain or Britain with the firm intention of never returning.

British immigration policy during the 1930s has been subjected to fierce scrutiny in the decades since. Some historians have criticised it as having been cynical and selfish, essentially condemning people to die in order not to inconvenience the surface comforts of the English. Others argue that, given the political realities of the time, British policy was probably as generous as was realistically possible and a great deal more so than that of most other nations.

Controversy has raged, too, over the role of the Anglo-Jewish community already living in Britain. Would more refugees have been saved had the leaders of Anglo-Jewry put greater pressure on the British authorities? Most of Anglo-Jewry (apart from a handful of Sephardi Jews of ancient lineage) was of East European origin, the legacy of the Jews who had come to Britain from Tsarist territories following the pogroms of the early 1880s, and they tended to resent what they saw as the airs and graces of the educated and largely assimilated Jews of Germany. It was not that they did not feel sympathy for the plight of their German co-religionists. But even the more sophisticated leaders of Anglo-Jewry (some of whom, such as the redoubtable Otto Schiff, were themselves of German background) sensed that too large a wave of Central European refugees could prove hard to manage and lead to intracommunal tensions.

Then, at the end of 1938, a minor miracle occurred – major to those whose lives were saved by it. The British authorities agreed to accept shiploads of minors from Germany-Austria (in part by way of compensation for the immigration clampdown they had imposed in Palestine). The Children's Transports, which began in December 1938 and continued until the eve of war nine months later, saved the lives of nearly 10,000 youngsters, three-quarters of them Jewish. Charles Spencer, then aged fourteen, was one of them. He had been working as a messenger boy at the Jewish organisation in Vienna where they processed the young applicants. 'You've got to get yourself on to those lists,' his mother told the boy. One day Charles spotted a sheet of paper in a typewriter: it was a catalogue of names. It was still there when everyone went home for the night. The boy stayed on to clear up – and typed in his own name: Karl Schwander. He probably owed his life to this piece of youthful bravado.

A few weeks later his mother took him to Vienna's West Station and embraced him. 'Learn languages,' she told him, then added, with emphasis that the boy did not fully appreciate at the time, 'That's something they can't take away from you.'

Fritz Spiegl, too, remembered the scene at the station. It was packed with anxious parents and excited children, each of whom carried a suitcase and wore a number round the neck. Few children could have begun to comprehend what their parents were doing: saying goodbye, in most cases for ever, in the desperate hope of consigning their beloved youngsters to a safer, better life elsewhere. There was much kissing and crying, after which the children boarded the train. 'Handkerchiefs were waved and then it seemed as if the town of Vienna was moving backwards,' wrote Spiegl in his newly acquired schoolboy

English a few months later. 'I supposed that children would weep or something like that. But luckily no-one did. Mostly I stood by the window and looked at the country, which was lovely anyhow. I did not sleep at all . . . After one and a half days we came to the German–Dutch frontier.'

At the border the German guards would do a final check, relieving the children of anything of value that they were carrying. Then, finally, the train would pass into Holland where the children were typically showered with goodwill. 'At the first Dutch station', one recalled years later, 'a large number of people were on the platform and as our train drew in they waved and cheered – they actually cheered. We were momentarily stunned and then returned the cheers and waved frantically.'

Up to now, many of the children had tended to be subdued and reflective. 'But from this point onwards we were a noisy, boisterous bunch.' The kindly Dutch were, of course, making a political point. But they also purveyed tangible signs of goodwill. Spiegl remembered the hot lemonade and buns, Spencer the sandwiches with banana and chocolate. 'I doubt if any of us was really hungry,' said another, recalling the orgy of milk, sweets and chocolates. 'But this first meal on foreign soil, on free soil, I ate with genuine gratitude and thanksgiving. This touching reception intoxicated us. The milk might as well have been brandy.' What did it matter if some of the fare was regurgitated into the North Sea a few hours later?

Arriving by overnight ship at Harwich, children without a specific contact or place to go were given temporary accommodation (at Dovercourt or other East Anglia holiday camps) before being assigned to families and schools. Some were taken by train to London's Liverpool Street Station for processing. Attempts were made to match the children to appropriate families, but for some – particularly those from orthodox Jewish backgrounds – this proved difficult. From April 1939, only those with prearranged guarantors in England (who had to pay £50 for the privilege) were admitted and numbers dropped back.

Many of those who owed their lives to the Children's Transports have spoken of what they experienced. Most had nothing but praise for the strange English people who decided their fate. The film director Karel Reisz recalled the Quaker boarding school in Reading to which he was sent and the kind headmaster who gave him a bicycle. Some, however, found the adjustment difficult as they were made to live with new families, speak a foreign language, suffer from the cold of poorly insulated English houses, sleep in beds covered with thin blankets and obey an unfamiliar set of customs and courtesies. 'Remember to lower your voice when in public,' the children were told, 'and don't let the English hear you speaking German.' Many missed traditional European cooking: they were given porridge and kippers for breakfast and greasy mutton for lunch (with hot English mustard), washed down with tea with milk. Some were billeted with earnestly Christian families who, no doubt from the purest motives, took their young wards to church and tried to indoctrinate them into their faith. Not surprisingly, many of the children went through phases of acute homesickness, some becoming surly and resentful as they saw their host families as mini-dictatorships imposing unreasonable demands upon unwilling captives.

Hans Schidlof's experience was typical. Born and raised in a small village in rural Austria, not far from the Czech border, Hans (later Peter Schidlof of the Amadeus Quartet) learned to play the violin from the local blacksmith and – like many Jewish children from the Austrian provinces (e.g. Fritz Spiegl) – had been sent for his education to a Catholic school. But the Schidlofs were Jewish, and to Hans's parents the *Anschluss* meant only one thing: the children had to get out. Hans and his sister were on one of the first transports. Shortly after their arrival in Harwich, they were assigned to a boarding school in East Anglia, St Felix's in Southwold, Suffolk. Here, Hans played his violin in a school concert where he was heard by Stephanie Hess, the sister of the music teacher at St Felix's and herself an accomplished violinist. She managed to get the gifted youngster transferred on a special music scholarship to Blundell's School at Tiverton in Devon.

The long, slow, mid-winter train journey across England to Devon imprinted itself upon Schidlof's impressionable young mind. England looked interminable and dreary – but at least it seemed relatively safe from Hitler. This melancholy mood was modified, Schidlof recalled, by the kindness he experienced from the people at Blundell's. Mr French, his generous-spirited Housemaster, introduced the boy as gently as he could to the rigours and routines of public school life – early-morning runs, stiff white collars, straw hats, games of rugger in which people seemed to be licensed to kick you in the stomach so long as they then said 'sorry'. 'I have seldom met a boy with a greater charm of manner,' wrote Mr French at the time, adding that Schidlof was 'extremely popular with the other boys on account of his obvious sincerity and admired for his talent in music which absorbs most of his thoughts'.

The Classics Master, Mr Hall, loved music and literature, and did his best to lift the spirits of the bewildered newcomer. It was from Mr Hall's record collection that Schidlof first became acquainted with Elizabethan music and the wonders of Purcell. The Headmaster, Mr Gorton (who later became Bishop of Coventry), was equally encouraging, even to the point of permitting the talented young musician to practise his fiddle instead of attending classes. One master offered to house the boy's mother and father on his farm if a way could be found to bring them over. Alas, this did not prove possible and both Schidlof's parents were later to perish in concentration camps.

Schidlof's Amadeus Quartet colleague Siegmund Nissel also owed his life to the Children's Transports. Born in Munich in 1922 and taken by his widowed father at the age of nine to Vienna, Nissel, too, was a talented violinist. One of his teachers was Max Weissgärber, who had his own string quartet and was a member of the Vienna Philharmonic Orchestra. When the Nazi troops entered Vienna in March 1938, they marched along the Linzerstrasse right past the Nissel home on the western out-skirts of the city. Like George Clare, Sigi watched with horror and incredulity as the stolid burghers of Vienna welcomed the Nazis as 'liberators'.

Nissel's best friend in Vienna, a boy called Fritz ('Freddie') Fleischer, was already in England and he had persuaded the family he was staying with, the Klinkarts, to be guarantors for

Sigi. Sixty years later Sigi still recalled saying goodbye to his father at the station, conscious that this could be the last time.

The train took Sigi right across Germany to the Dutch border where he knew he was safe. Then came the boat journey from the Hook of Holland across the North Sea to England and reunion with Fritz in the home of the Klinkart family in the London suburb of Richmond. Here Sigi was soon knocking on doors, trying to find someone prepared to act as guarantor for his father. A kind Anglican family called Farrer who lived in Twickenham – complete strangers – agreed to do so. As a result, Nissel *père* came to England on a temporary basis on what proved to be the last possible train, at the end of August 1939. A week later war broke out. All temporary visas were immediately suspended and the Nissels, father and son, were redesignated as 'friendly enemy aliens'.

By now, Sigi had little time for music and in any case loved science and wanted to become a chemist. During the early years of the war he did air raid precaution (ARP) work in and around Richmond. Whenever he could, however, he brought out his violin and practised. Once he was invited to play to Bronislaw Huberman, founder of the Palestine (later Israel) Philharmonic Orchestra, who was visiting London, but nothing came of the encounter. Huberman apparently lay down flat on the floor under the piano and Sigi was not sure whether he was listening or sleeping. When the great man surfaced he was very flattering and told the boy he should go to Palestine, neither a feasible nor an enticing suggestion at the time. It was not until he was interned on the Isle of Man that Sigi had the leisure to pick up the violin properly again. The results were greatly to enrich the musical life of Britain and the wider world for the next half-century.

CHAPTER SEVEN

In a Strange Land

'London was grim, a dirty, smelly city,' recalled the Vienna-born Ernst Gombrich, who arrived in December 1935 and found digs in Ebury Street near Victoria Station. 'It was freezing cold. My landlady lit a tiny fire which was so weak that it didn't warm the room at all. I had very little money – a grant of £250 per year – which was very little, and usually ate in those Lyons or Express Dairy cafés which seemed very dirty and smelled of old fat.'

It was not only the icy bedrooms and the greasy food and tea with milk that upset the new arrivals. More disturbing was the incomprehension with which they felt themselves regarded by their new hosts: the understatement, the double negative, the kind but controlled concern, tinged, perhaps, with a streak of muted xenophobia, all masking unawareness of the true nature and scale of the brutality from which the exiles had fled. 'I was astonished at the sheer phlegm of the English,' said the painter Oskar Kokoschka, 'who remained heedless of the war, while on the Continent people were letting the Führer drive them over the edge of the abyss like panic-stricken sheep.' George Clare's desperate attempts to explain to his hosts what the *Kristallnacht* had really been like were rewarded with a concerned frown ('It must have been quite, quite terrible for you') and then, as he ended a sentence: 'Do have another piece of cake, George, please do. And some more tea?' George Weidenfeld encountered a society hostess who turned to him over tea and said, 'I hear you come from Germany. Did you know the Görings?' To which Weidenfeld managed to splutter that he had lived in Vienna while the Görings were busy in Berlin.

Stephen Hearst fled Vienna the day after the *Anschluss*. After a sojourn in Trieste and Zurich, he arrived in England in the late summer and immediately bought a paper to find out what was going on back home. But it was Len Hutton's Test Match score against Australia that filled the front page and he had to hunt to find, in small print, the fact that Hitler's troops were massing on the borders of the Sudetenland. As for the writer and erstwhile Communist activist Arthur Koestler, recently jailed in Spain by Franco and then in occupied France as a suspicious foreigner, he flew from neutral Portugal to Bristol in November 1940 and was promptly transferred (by an apparently amiable police escort) to London and placed in Pentonville prison until friends in high places obtained his release.

Incomprehension, incredulity, ignorance – these can go both ways, of course. Many of the refugees were as ill-informed about the British as their new hosts were about them. 'If it had been China I could not have known less about the country which is now my second home,' confessed Fred Uhlman. 'I had some nebulous notion of an endless, flat, park-like landscape, mostly green and pleasant but rather dull, with horses and cattle everywhere – except where the grim industrial towns lay under their palls of black smoke.' Although an artist, Uhlman scarcely knew what a Gainsborough or a Reynolds looked like and had heard in Paris that England had not produced a first-class painter since someone he called *Turnère*. He prided himself in being fairly well read, not only in German literature but among the French and Russian classics as well. But, apart from Shakespeare and a handful of other British greats, he confessed to having been profoundly ignorant of English literature. Why? 'One reason has to do with England's cultural isolation from the Continent,' Uhlman wrote later. The details of British history, let alone of its artistic life, had been somewhat peripheral to a youngster learning about the Greeks and Romans, the history of the Hohenstaufens, local state history and something of the history and culture of Germany's looming neighbours Russia and France.

Silvia Rodgers, an anxious adolescent when she arrived, found England 'rich with pastures for its aboriginals but for me alarming and unsettling'. Everything was disconcerting. Not only the language, which everybody spoke so quickly, but the light switches that had to be flicked up and down instead of turned, the bulbs that did not screw but had to be clicked into place, the traffic that drove on the wrong side of the street, the top-heavy double-decker buses. For Silvia, as for so many, food and drink featured among her earliest impressions. She liked the bananas and oranges ('spoils of Empire') and the white bread and butter, but was shocked to see people preparing meals out of tins. She knew nothing of British history or literature, however, and found solace in reading Greek myths (in German) which 'were more comprehensible to me than the society I had landed in'.

Many had little English when they came. The Polish-born nuclear physicist and Nobel Peace Prize winner Joseph Rotblat came to Liverpool University on a one-year Fellowship in the late 1930s to work with James Chadwick (discoverer of the neutron). 'I thought that, because I could understand a scientific paper in the journal *Nature*, I understood English,' Rotblat recalled. 'And I thought I knew all about the English people because I had read Polish translations of P. G. Wodehouse!' Silvia Rodgers was quick to learn that to say 'I don't think so' was more polite than a straight 'No'. But she was always conscious of talking louder, more demonstratively than the English, 'of asking questions English people never ask, and referring to things English people ignore'. When Fred Uhlman had a show and someone asked how it had gone, he had to learn to answer 'Not too badly' (those double negatives again); it was evidently thought conceited to say – however truthfully – that it had gone really rather well. The philosopher Karl Popper (who settled in England in 1945 after spending the war years in New Zealand) was a man of forceful opinions; but when one of his students went on about a continental philosopher then in vogue of whom Popper disapproved (Sartre perhaps?), Popper restrained himself and said that this was not his cup of tea and that the English tradition was 'not so bad'.

The social mores were never spelled out in so many words, but the ignorant alien who contravened them was made to pay for his sins. Walter Laqueur, who had spent the war years in Palestine and witnessed the birth of Israel, arrived in Britain in the early 1950s and called upon an Oxford academic he knew, unannounced, rather as one might have done in Tel Aviv or Haifa. His reception was (as the English would have said) less than enthusiastic and within one minute Laqueur found himself back in the street. The don, though having spent many years abroad, 'had no wish to make concessions to foreign habits'.

Many of the new arrivals, like generations of immigrants before and since, tended to congregate together. As Otto Schiff and others had anticipated, the Hitler refugees did not settle in the traditional Jewish enclaves in the East End of London but gravitated towards more affluent parts of London like St John's Wood and Hampstead. A new synagogue was established in Swiss Cottage (later the Belsize Square Synagogue), with the help of Lily Montagu and the Liberal Jewish establishment, to accommodate the spiritual needs of the refugee community. Home life, while uprooted by the trauma of exile, was lovingly transplanted into its new soil. The poet Michael Hamburger recalled the family home in St John's Wood, with its beautiful dark furnishings, including a desk and table designed by Ernst Freud. Hamburger senior was a paediatrician whose patients in Berlin had included the Freud children; Ernst Freud had designed his consulting room. Now, in St John's Wood (where Dr Hamburger's patients included the offspring of the Kordas and Marlene Dietrich), the Freud and Hamburger families found themselves friends and neighbours once again. In the evenings, Michael Hamburger recalled, his parents would hold music evenings at which Feuermann, Max Rostal, Lili Kraus and Szymon Goldberg would play. A ghetto? Yes, in a way. But those who formed it would have disavowed the name and simply regarded themselves as reproducing the style and quality of life they had been forced to abandon.

The exiles not only lived and worked alongside each other. They also gave each other a helping hand whenever they could. Scientists tried to make spaces in their labs for fellow exiles, recently arrived orchestral players talked up the merits of other émigré musicians. Fritz Saxl at the Warburg Institute offered jobs to fellow Austrians including Gombrich and Albi Rosenthal, while Kurt Jooss, already installed with his dance company at Dartington, helped give refuge to Rudolf Laban. Alexander Korda, who had been in England since the winter of 1931–2, gave work and succour to a host of refugees; his compatriot, chief scriptwriter and becalming influence Lajos Biro, was a distant cousin of Martin Esslin and helped the lad along with a little money. Max Rostal taught Norbert Brainin, Siegmund Nissel and Peter Schidlof, and refused to charge for the lessons. Children and younger-generation refugees were catered for, too. Anna Essinger, a German Quaker of Jewish background, had run a progressive, co-educational boarding school at Herrlingen in the Swabian Jura district. In October 1933, with help and advice from the British Quaker community, she transported the school to Bunce Court, Otterden, Kent (and later to Shropshire) where it was run by and for refugees; Bunce Court pupils included Gerhard (later Gerard) Hoffnung, the artist Frank Auerbach and the immunologist Professor Leslie Brent (formerly Lothar Baruch).

If many refugees created something of a German-speaking fortress around themselves, this did not stop them – especially the younger arrivals – from reaching out to clasp the hand offered by the wider British (and Jewish) community. There are countless stories of the great generosity of hosts (like Sigi Nissel's Klinkart and Farrer families) to people they scarcely knew. Michael Maybaum, son of the Berlin rabbi Ignaz Maybaum, stayed for some six months with over a dozen other refugee children under the wing of a wealthy paediatrician called Bernard Schlesinger (father of the film director John Schlesinger), a kindly figure who kept in touch with his 'children' and their subsequent progress for the rest of his days. Older people, even those already well established, needed help, too. The publisher Stanley Unwin befriended his Viennese colleague Béla Horovitz, founder of Phaidon Press, and invited him to use Unwin's London premises as the distribution base for Phaidon – thereby not only bringing an important publishing house to Britain but also helping to save the lives of Horovitz and his family.

Every contact was useful. For those furnished with the right addresses and phone numbers, and the ability to push themselves forward in not too arrogant a fashion, there were succulent fruits to pick. The day Stephen Hearst arrived in England an international student service sent him to the home of a man who they said might be able to help him. Three hours later his new friend offered him a flat (vacated by the actor Robert Donat who thought a basement apartment was aggravating his asthma) – and took him to the Savile Club where he was introduced to H. G. Wells. George Weidenfeld found himself staying with a family of Plymouth Brethren in north London and learned to relish picnics at which fifty or sixty people – half of them fellow refugees! – would sing hymns together, eat cucumber sandwiches and bask in the glow of interfaith companionship. At the Refugee Committee Weidenfeld was interviewed by a lady who wrote on his behalf to a man who was working for the president of the World Zionist Organisation, Chaim Weizmann – a contact that led to Weidenfeld becoming secretary to the founding President of the state of Israel a few years later.

Among the scientific community there were similarly uplifting stories. Talented young scientists, indeed, were especially well catered for thanks to the devoted efforts of an organisation known initially as the Academic Assistance Council (from 1936 the Society for the Protection of Science and Learning). The AAC arose initially from the angst and energy of the Hungarian physicist Leo Szilard. Szilard, brilliant but eccentric, had been working in Berlin with Einstein but left as soon as the Nazis took over – warning his colleagues, especially those with Jewish backgrounds, to do the same. Visiting Vienna, he was introduced to Esther (Tess) Simpson, a young Englishwoman with several languages, a love of music and a powerful social conscience. Simpson was working for the Director of the World Alliance of YMCAs in Geneva at the time, and Szilard put to her his idea of an émigré university, maybe in Switzerland. This was not feasible. Among those visiting the same hotel in Vienna was William Beveridge, Director of the London School of Economics (and future father of Britain's Welfare State) who listened sympathetically to what Szilard had to say.

Around the same time, Beveridge's LSE colleague Lionel Robbins and the Austrian economist Ludwig von Mises spent an evening with Beveridge in Vienna. Von Mises arrived, agitated, with an evening paper announcing the first academic dismissals in Germany by the new Nazi government. The report included some prominent names, among them Moritz Bonn, Hermann Kantorowicz and one of the great founding figures of modern sociology, Karl Mannheim. Surely it was possible to make some provision in Britain for the relief of such victims?

> This was one of Beveridge's great moments [Robbins recalled later], his finest hour . . . All his best instincts, his sympathy with the unfortunate, his sense of civilized values, his administrative vision and inventiveness were quickened by this question. Slumped in a chair, with his great head characteristically cupped in his fists, thinking aloud, he then and there outlined the basic plan.

Beveridge acted fast.* A letter appeared in *The Times* in May 1933, signed by some of the most powerful figures in British scientific and intellectual life, proposing the establishment of a body to be called the Academic Assistance Council, which would help salvage the lives and careers of displaced academics in the sciences. Two months later Tess Simpson had left her lucrative job in Geneva and returned to London to run the AAC's tiny office: a couple of rooms at the top of Burlington House above the Royal Society. Simpson found Szilard already installed and in August they were joined by Walter Adams (a London University lecturer with an interest in the history of science and later Director of the LSE) as General Secretary. Adams promptly went off on a reconnaissance trip to Germany to spread the word.

---

* Beveridge was evidently a man of generous impulses. At one time he was on the point of giving refuge at the LSE to the entire body of the Frankfurt Institute for Social Research when he was dissuaded at the last moment by Robbins. One wonders what the consequences might have been had Beveridge gone ahead, and whether the presence in England rather than America of Frankfurt refugees such as Marcuse, Adorno and Horkheimer – all of them subsequent heroes of the New Left – might not have sharpened British radicalism and/or blunted that of the USA.

In London, holding the fort, the level-headed Tess Simpson was anxious that the AAC should not appear to promise more than could realistically be delivered. The Council was not a charity; it had some funds, but no academic jobs to offer. Furthermore, nobody with a foreign passport would be granted long-term entry into Britain without private money or reasonable hope of employment. 'What we did was find out about the scholar's situation from colleagues; we got his German referees, of course, and the opinion of British colleagues to confirm that he was likely to become absorbed, not necessarily in this country, in academic work.'

Simpson and her colleagues made a systematic record of applicants (colour-coded according to discipline), assessed their chances and, if appropriate, offered them a small grant to help tide them over and (if necessary) learn passable English. Grants were only given to those with a reasonable chance of obtaining an academic post. 'What we told the others was that there was plenty of opportunity in teaching and also in industry, for instance for chemists and physicists. Those that went into industry were often much better off than those that went into academic work.'

At first the flow of applicants was more or less manageable. But as the Nazis tightened their grip ever more intensely on German intellectual life, the flow became a flood and threatened to become a deluge. Clearly, the displacement of refugee scholars was no short-term emergency requiring temporary 'academic assistance' but a problem likely to be semi-permanent. Beveridge suggested the AAC be renamed to reflect this and in 1936 it became the 'Society for the Protection of Science and Learning'.

The newly-constituted SPSL was unable to find academic posts for all its qualified applicants. 'The difficulty', recalled Tess Simpson, 'was that we had done our best to place the first lot and so there was very little room left at our universities. We are a very small country.' The United States, on the other hand, was a very big country which, up to then, had not taken many refugees except the most famous. So Simpson worked to develop better links with American academic institutions – not just the big Ivy League schools but also many less famous universities in the Midwest and elsewhere which, often enough, felt it a matter of prestige to bag an academic from the Continent. Many an émigré physicist or chemist would embark on a US lecture tour or semester-long internship, with travel and maintenance costs underwritten by the SPSL. In virtually every case, Simpson recalled, 'they came back with a job in their pocket'.

In order to deal with the growing workload, the SPSL had to move into larger premises – initially in an annexe of the LSE and then, in 1937, into Gordon Square (and during the war to Cambridge). With the *Anschluss* in March 1938, and the horrors of *Kristallnacht* eight months later, a torrent of desperate requests for help poured into its offices. Simpson, ever the hard-headed realist, found herself forced to point many applicants to the USA, Latin America and the British Dominions. Szilard himself went off to the States (where he was instrumental in persuading Einstein to write to President Roosevelt alerting FDR to the possibility of an atomic bomb). A number of distinguished scientists were admitted – such as the physicist Max Born, who was soon snapped up by the University of Edinburgh. But the medical profession, for instance, was particularly resistant to the admission of what it presumably saw as rivals from abroad. Tess Simpson, a former resident of Vienna herself, acknowledged being 'bitterly disappointed that in 1938 this country did not take the opportunity of inviting the Viennese medical school to come here en bloc'.

Over the decades, the SPSL helped refugee scholars fleeing not only from Hitler and Mussolini but also from Franco and Salazar, from Stalin's Russia, from Hungary in 1956 and Czechoslovakia in 1968. But its finest hour, or decade, was undoubtedly its first when it was responsible for helping to save the lives, and work, of many scientists who might otherwise have perished. In Britain alone, by 1992, seventy-four displaced Central European scholars or their children had become Fellows of the Royal Society and thirty-four Fellows of the British Academy. Sixteen were Nobel laureates and eighteen were knighted.

Many of the refugee scientists, particularly, perhaps, the

younger among them, were at first somewhat bewildered by what they found in their adopted country. British colleagues were almost too welcoming, and a lecturer accustomed to the hierarchy of university life in Berlin or Vienna could be disconcerted by a professor wearing scruffy flannels and using first names. The nuclear physicist Rudolf Peierls recalled bumping into Lord Rutherford a few days after taking up a post in Cambridge in 1935. Rutherford asked how things were settling down and whether Peierls's first pay cheque had arrived yet. Peierls said he expected it would come at the end of the month, at which Rutherford immediately asked solicitously if he'd be able to last until then. The biologist Hans Krebs, who came (like Max Perutz) to work under Sir Frederick Gowland Hopkins at Cambridge, was touched by the warm informality he encountered. He spoke for many when he recalled how refreshing he found it that people would 'argue without quarrelling, quarrel without suspecting, suspect without abusing, criticise without vilifying or ridiculing, and praise without flattering'.

Hitler had been prepared to destroy German science; but one direct result of his policies was to export some of its finest minds to Britain and the wider world.

Britain declared war on Germany on 3 September 1939. Immigration was abruptly halted and all temporary visas granted to people from enemy territories invalidated. Anyone with dreams of re-emigrating to the USA had to put such fantasies on hold. A handful of Nazi sympathisers, such as Hitler's former friend and Press Secretary Putzi Hanfstängl, were interned. The great majority of Germans or Austrians in Britain, bona fide refugees, were now trapped, stateless, in a country not quite sure how to treat them. Maybe (hinted a jingoistic press and some nervous politicians) some among them were spies for the Third Reich, cleverly planted in Britain as a Nazi 'fifth column'. To the Home Office this seemed unlikely, but with the onset of war the authorities were in no mood, mind or mode to check the detailed life histories of every exile in their midst. Government attitudes were wonderfully caught in the new classification assigned to the refugees: 'friendly enemy aliens', an oxymoronic construct that accurately reflected the ambivalence of the British press and officialdom. During the autumn of 1939 tribunals were set up to assign every refugee to a security category: 'A' for those deemed high risk (who were immediately interned),* 'B' for those whose loyalty was probably not in question but who needed monitoring, and 'C' (the overwhelming majority) about whom the tribunals were completely satisfied. Thus, during the so-called 'phoney war' or 'Bore War' of 1939–40, some 50,000 category 'C' refugees lived in a sort of quiet limbo, wondering with apprehension what would happen next.

What in fact happened next was the *blitzkrieg* of spring 1940, the rapid Nazi advance through much of north-western Europe. By April, with the fall of Holland and Belgium and the evacuation of Britain's demoralised troops from Dunkirk, it was obviously only a matter of time before Hitler would bring the war to England. As Churchill became Prime Minister and invasion seemed a real possibility, drastic action was required. The whole of the south and east of England was to be off limits to aliens from enemy countries. And the best way to guarantee *that* was to intern the lot.

'You can't do that. He's practically an Englishman!' Albi Rosenthal's caretaker remonstrated with the policeman on the stairs, but to no avail. It did not help that Albi, a young antiquarian book expert who had been in Britain since 1936, had a big map of Europe in his room on which he had been following the German progress. Most internees retained vivid memories of their arrest. 'The policeman who came to arrest me said that I would be gone for only a few days,' recalled Max Perutz, as he was removed from Cambridge for processing to Bury St Edmunds, thence to the Liverpool area and on to the Isle of Man. A quiet and conscientious biologist, Perutz – evidently far too dangerous to keep anywhere in Britain – was subsequently deported to Canada.

---

* Absurd mistakes were made. Among category 'A' prisoners was the writer Sebastian Haffner, whose anti-Nazi credentials were clearly laid out in his book *Germany: Jekyll and Hyde*, published while he was interned. Haffner later became a stalwart of the resolutely liberal Sunday *Observer*.

The police tried to be as decent as possible in carrying out their duties. They certainly knew where to look. There are stories of cops peering Keystone-like into the public libraries of north-west London, confident that, at any given time, several of their potential quarry would be present. Stephen Hearst was taking an exam at the University of Reading when two police-men arrived – literally in the examination room. 'They escorted me back to my hall of residence,' he recalled, still incredulous, 'and looked over my room.' His books at the time included the Everyman edition of Marx's *Das Kapital* and Mussolini on Fascism (which Stephen hoped might cancel each other out). The police confiscated both and took the miscreant off to Reading Gaol, where he blithely declaimed Oscar Wilde to his bewildered minders before being removed, like so many other internees, to the north-west.

Claus Moser had taken a girl to see the opera *Aida* the night before he was taken. To Hans Schidlof, internment was some-thing of an adventure. 'Don't forget your tennis racket,' the policeman called, trying to carry out his distasteful duty in as friendly a fashion as possible. In fact, Hans took his violin, as did Sigi Nissel. And so did another young internee, a Billy Bunter figure from Vienna called Norbert Brainin whose musical talent had already led him to become a pupil of the most celebrated of all violin teachers (whom Nissel had also played for), Carl Flesch – himself a refugee from Nazism.

Many of the leading figures in post-war British musical life spent time in internment: composers and musicologists like Hans Gál, Egon Wellesz, Franz Reizenstein and Hans Keller, while performers included the popular pianists Rawicz and Landauer and three-quarters of what was to become the Amadeus Quartet. Kurt Jooss was interned, as were his choreographer Sigurd Leeder and designer Hein Heckroth. Internees included a future editor of the *Financial Times* (Fredy Fisher), a future Controller of Radio Three (Stephen Hearst), the journalist Sebastian Haffner, the Dada artist Kurt Schwitters, economists, sociol-ogists, publishers, psychologists, photographers, physicians, classicists, cartographers and a critical mass of top scientists.

Nobody relished being interned. To Claus Moser it was an

insult but to his father it was a humiliation. How could they imprison us, the 'friendly enemy aliens' asked each other, we who, more than anyone, had nailed our anti-Hitler colours to the mast? Worse, many feared that by congregating so many refugees together behind barbed wire, the authorities had guaranteed the internees' fate in the event of a successful German invasion. 'The British have done the Nazis' work for them,' moaned Stephen Hearst's tent-mate, Hans Heilbronn (later Professor of Mathematics at the University of Bristol), while Siegmund Nissel remembered thinking 'we'll be handed to them on a plate!' as rumours of the imminent Nazi invasion of Britain swept through the camps. Nor were the internees reassured by the apparent naïveté of their officers, most of whom had little real understanding of the conditions from which their charges had fled. 'I didn't know there were so many Jews among the Nazis,' said the commander at Huyton internment camp genially as he watched a new batch of inmates arriving.*

Yet for all the absurdity and indignity involved, most internees understood why the British authorities had decided to act as they did and resolved to make the best of a bad job. It was certainly better to be imprisoned by the British than by the Germans, they reflected. In some ways it was actually rather fun. In the Isle of Man most people were placed in seaside guest houses that had been requisitioned for the duration, wired off from the local population perhaps, but not over-officiously so. Everybody had something to contribute. 'A man who'd been a banker set up a camp bank,' one former internee told me. 'I remember it clearly. I remember queuing for money. But I don't remember what on earth we could do with the money. There was nothing to buy!'

Many former internees (particularly those housed around Hutchinson Square in Douglas and in nearby Onchan) would look back almost with nostalgia at the quasi-university

---

* The Hungarian-born André Deutsch recalled receiving friendly treatment from an Isle of Man camp commander who turned out to be not only half Hungarian but the son of the Baroness Orczy, creator of the Scarlet Pimpernel. This revelation did not, apparently, inspire Deutsch to try to escape.

atmosphere that soon established itself. 'Apart from a huge number of English, six French and four Spanish courses,' one recalled, 'it was also possible to learn Latin, Greek, Russian and Japanese, and there were lectures on the history of art as well as English and German literature.' Kurt Schwitters would draw portraits of his fellow prisoners, while Nissel and others would give concerts. 'There was lots of music in camp; I played string quartets with Max Jekel and remember playing the Bach E major concerto with Reizenstein at the piano.' It was in camp that Nissel met Peter Schidlof and afterwards Norbert Brainin. 'Later, some kind person in the camp wrote to Max Rostal,' Nissel recalled, 'saying there were these talented young musicians and would he consider taking them on as his pupils. And that's how the Amadeus really got started.' Claus Moser, later Harold Wilson's personal choice as Head of the Government Statistical Office, had similar memories. 'One bloke who was a mathematician set up a camp statistical office – I suppose, for something to do. Anyway, he asked me to be his assistant. And that was the first time I had ever done anything like that.' Moser not only learned to became a statistician in camp but also put on weight. 'We used to go to the café every afternoon,' he told me, 'and our officers, who were meant to be guarding us, would take iced coffee and whipped cream and cakes with us. God knows where all that came from – I suppose from all those gourmet chefs who were in camp with us.' Nissel still smiled with contentment over sixty years later at the memory of the cordon bleu dinners he consumed in his Isle of Man guest house when one of 'His Majesty's Most Loyal Enemy Aliens'.

Thus, for some, internment had its benefits and even joys. Others, especially older people accustomed to a life of affluence, dignity and domestic servants, found it degrading. Some 10,000 internees suffered the further indignity of being transported, in the most primitive and dangerous conditions, to Canada or Australia, like colonial convicts. Max Perutz never forgot the resentment with which he regarded his involuntary exodus to Quebec.

To have been arrested, interned, and deported as an enemy alien by the English, whom I regarded as my friends, made me more bitter than to have lost freedom itself. Having first been rejected as a Jew by my native Austria, which I loved, I now found myself rejected as a German by my adopted country.

Internment was a bitter pill. But as Walter Zander put it:

The most interesting point . . . is not how much the interned have had to suffer – for suffering is general all over the world at present – but how far they have been able to stand up, spiritually, to their trial, and to transform their adversities into productive experience.

And it is true that the internment camps, hotbeds of frustrated mid-European talent, tended to turn into mini-universities. 'Well, there was nothing else to do,' Perutz told me wryly. Perutz, in his memoir of internment, recalled how Hermann Bondi, like himself exiled to Canada, 'taught a brilliant course in vector analysis. His towering forehead topped by battlements of curly black hair, he arrived at his lectures without any notes and yet solved all his complex examples on the blackboard.'

At one Isle of Man camp a typical week's worth of activities in October 1940 included, *inter alia*, history lectures on Metternich, the Rise of English Democracy, Church history, Medieval Culture and the British Empire; science lectures on bacteriology, physical chemistry, mathematics and aspects of nutrition; a philosophy series on the Ancient Greeks; lectures on French and German literature, and various literary and musical recitals. What could one do, Fred Uhlman wrote later, 'if Professor William Cohn's talk on Chinese Theatre coincided with Egon Wellesz's Introduction to Byzantine Music? Or Professor Jacobsthal's talk on Greek Literature with Professor Goldmann's on the Etruscan Language? Perhaps one felt more inclined to hear Zunz on the *Odyssey* or Friedenthal on the Shakespearean stage.'

At Hay in Australia, the musician Peter Stadlen organised

choral performances of Handel's *Messiah* (with orthodox Jews singing 'la-la' whenever the name of God or Jesus occurred in the text). Science lectures at Hay covered Group Theory, Matrices, Tensors, Vector Analyis, Projective Geometry, Differential Equations, Optics, Theoretical Physics, Radio Engineering and Electronic Gauges. At the women's camp on the Isle of Man, at Rushen,* there were so many disputes about who had the right to give lectures that the camp commander had to adjudicate. Everywhere there were camp newspapers and journals, readings and recitals, concerts and cabarets. One Isle of Man revue was directed by G. M. Hoellering, a former colleague of Brecht who, after the war, ran the Academy Cinema in London's Oxford Street; the music was by Hans Gál† and the writers included the social theorist Norbert Elias and Otto Erich Deutsch who later achieved fame as the man who catalogued the works of Schubert.‡

Was internment romanticised in retrospect, infused with a roseate glow of camaraderie by those who experienced it together? Perhaps by some. It must have been exhilarating for the refugees to have crowded round the camp wireless in the autumn of 1940 cheering on the successes of the British air force. But most were desperate to get out and do whatever they could to help the war effort. They had escaped to Britain because they valued the very freedom that Britain was fighting for. The policy of locking up friendly refugees, they felt sure, would surely soon be reversed.

Several figures who had earlier taken up their cause (notably the Bishop of Chichester George Bell and MPs Eleanor Rathbone and Josiah Wedgwood) had complained from the start that internment was a violation of civil liberties. They were

---

* Much of Port St Mary and Port Erin, on the Rushen peninsula in the south-western tip of the island, became designated the area where some 4000 women were interned. Here local homeowners were permitted to stay put and take in women internees as residents.

† Hans Gál described the review in some detail in his interview for the Imperial War Museum Oral History Archives.

‡ Word reached Max Perutz, transported to Canada, that his sixty-three-year-old father was interned on the Isle of Man and that he was sharing this fate with Otto Deutsch, 'a frail meticulous old Viennese with sensitively cut features who was distraught at having his life's work interrupted for a second time'.

not always rewarded for their pains. When the Bishop visited the camps, the *Isle of Man Examiner* labelled him a 'self-appointed champion of captive Nazis and Fascists' (and there were some Nazi sympathisers interned on the island, mostly at Peel). But as accurate information gradually seeped out of the camps into public consciousness, the civil liberties argument increasingly took hold. Internment was not only unfair and an absurdly blunt instrument; it was also expensive. And it was clearly contrary to the national interest to intern healthy young men, most of whom were evidently keen to enlist.

In early July 1940 the *Arandora Star*, a troopship transporting internees to Canada, was torpedoed in the North Atlantic with much loss of life.* Many of those on board were Italian chefs and waiters who had worked in Britain for years and had no interest in politics. Clearly, the undiscriminating internment of all aliens from all enemy territories was too heavy-handed. 'Why not lock up General de Gaulle?' asked Michael Foot ironically in a prominent *Evening Standard* feature article published shortly after the occupation of France by the Nazis.

Release from internment came early for some. Claus Moser, a youth who clearly posed no security threat, was let out after just a few weeks (far earlier than his father and elder brother) and went to study at the LSE. Sigi Nissel went before a board chaired by the kindly Ralph Vaughan Williams and found himself released with a batch of other 'persons of eminent distinction who have made outstanding contributions to Art'.

The quickest way for most refugees to quit (or avoid) internment was to volunteer for the Auxiliary Military Pioneer Corps, a kind of Foreign Legion sans guns or glamour. The irony was not lost on the internees. 'There I was,' Stephen Hearst recalled, 'swearing allegiance and agreeing to fight for King and country – while still imprisoned *behind* barbed wire!' Thus, learned refugee lawyers and professors packed away their brains and harnessed their brawn to the war effort, digging ditches and latrines for the Pioneer Corps. All wanted to do

---

* One of those to survive was Guido Pontecorvo, later Professor of Genetics at Glasgow University (and brother of the film maker Gillo and of the nuclear physicist Bruno who later defected to the USSR).

something more worthwhile. Arthur Koestler (who had recently been a member of the real Foreign Legion) managed to move from the Pioneer Corps into educational and intelligence work. Some (Julius Carlebach, Helmut Koenigsberger) graduated from the Pioneer Corps to the Royal Navy. Ken Adam became a fighter pilot but his experience was exceptional. More typical was Claus Moser. Moser had collected the best LSE degree of his year, wanted to do his bit towards the defeat of Hitler and marched into the RAF office in London's Euston Road in the middle of the war. A formidable recruiting officer asked him about his background and education. Got a top degree at LSE, did you? Yes, sir. And you want to be a fighter pilot? Yes, sir. Well, if you want to join the RAF you can be a flight mechanic. So Claus, who could scarcely change a light bulb, spent three years in the RAF fixing and repairing the instruments in planes he himself was not allowed to fly.

Many, especially women and younger refugees, did civilian work. Lucie Rie, the potter and ceramicist, became a fire watcher, and worked in a button factory and later an optical industries factory. Anne Bohm worked as a secretary at the London School of Economics (exiled to Peterhouse College, Cambridge, during the war). Hilde Beal spent the war in Shropshire as a market gardener while her mother did domestic work in Surbiton (complete with white cap and apron). There were gardeners among the men, too – and urban labourers. Nikolaus Pevsner, desperate to get back to his studies on the history of architecture, wielded pick and shovel, and helped clear bomb damage. John Burgh (later Director-General of the British Council) left school at fifteen-and-a-half and worked in a factory in west London making plastic hoods for aircraft. Norbert Brainin took a job as an unskilled machine tool fitter ('so unskilled', he recalled years later, 'that it's a wonder we didn't lose the war!'), Sigi Nissel worked in a metal factory in the East End making brass and gun metal out of scrap while Hans Schidlof trained as a dental mechanic. It is a minor miracle of musical history that the hands and fingers of these three future members of the Amadeus Quartet emerged from the war intact.

Digging ditches, cleaning houses, removing debris or making gun metal were all very well. But what most refugees wanted was to be able to use their brains. Some were allowed to do so. Rudolf Peierls, Klaus Fuchs and Joseph Rotblat went to work on the Manhattan Project at Los Alamos. Ernst Gombrich, Martin Esslin and George Weidenfeld were recruited by the BBC Monitoring Service and, using their languages, helped keep the British authorities up to date with the latest Axis pronouncements and speeches. Max Perutz, less than three years after returning from the humiliation of transportation to Canada, recrossed the Atlantic as part of a top-secret British delegation whose mission was to check with the Canadian and US authorities the feasibility of building a series of floating Arctic air bases built of reinforced ice. Many refugees – Stephen Hearst, Charles Spencer, the historian Peter Hennock – were able to use their linguistic skills to interrogate prisoners of war. And Claus Moser, after three years as an RAF mechanic (rising to the dizzy rank of sergeant), was finally able to use more sophisticated skills, investigating and assessing the actual damage caused by bombing raids – a task that called upon his German, his statistical prowess and no doubt considerable diplomatic finesse.

For many refugees the war years involved a succession of humiliations. Young men raised in middle- and upper-middle-class homes back in Germany and Austria found themselves consigned to menial jobs and working-class lifestyles. Women accustomed to giving orders had to learn to receive them. 'Ah, a piano! It's a Bechstein, no?' exclaimed one former Viennese *hausfrau* as she was shown the drawing room she was expected to clean. 'You must come in and play some time,' came the icy response, 'when everyone is out.' It was hard to retain one's dignity in such circumstances and some undoubtedly suffered from what they regarded as the degradation they were made to undergo. But at least they were alive and this was cause enough for celebration.

More than that, the Hitler émigrés were living in a society that was even then being stimulated by the most terrible and destructive war in its history to rethink the nature and quality of life in peacetime. 'We are fighting not to win, but to win *something*,' said an educational pamphlet issued by the Army Bureau of Current Affairs (ABCA) in 1942, 'and the more we clear our minds here and now about the world we want after the war, the more likely we are to attain it.' Heady stuff. Just as Pericles had spoken at the height of the Peloponnesian Wars about the quality of Athenian life he was sworn to defend, there were those in Britain prepared to think beyond the need for military victory towards the better world they hoped would follow. While the war was still being fought, opinions were expressed, initiatives drafted, soundings taken, meetings held, committees formed and finances benchmarked that would help prepare the way towards a rich cultural flowering in decades to come. And as we shall see, many of the Hitler émigrés found themselves – to their own surprise – present at the creation.

PART THREE

CULTURE AT WAR

CHAPTER EIGHT

The Commissars Close Ranks

'What people need is reassurance!'

The doughty pianist Myra Hess, with her rolling gait and no-nonsense approach, had approached the Director of London's National Gallery, Kenneth Clark, a fortnight after the outbreak of war in September 1939 suggesting a series of concerts in the Gallery. Bach, Beethoven and Brahms. That kind of thing. Once a week.

Clark, whose first priority was to remove the great collection of paintings to safety outside London, liked the idea of filling his domed gallery at lunchtime with concert goers. But why only once a week? he asked – and pronounced that they should give one every day. Myra Hess 'recovered rapidly from the shock', Clark recalled, and got down to work. The first concert was announced for Tuesday, 10 October 1939, three weeks later. Hess herself would play 'in case the whole thing is a flop'. She need not have worried. On the day, queues formed halfway round Trafalgar Square and the Gallery doors had to be closed after over a thousand people had been crowded into a venue officially licensed to hold 200.

The National Gallery concerts ran throughout the war, continuing even during the height of the bombing of London when they were relocated from the upstairs gallery to an underground shelter. Hess herself attended most days and often played twice in a week. The series was finally concluded, after an astonishing 1698 concerts (and total audiences of over 800,000 people), on 10 April 1946.

*

During the dour, doleful days of war, many people clearly hungered for the fine arts. The success of the National Gallery concerts provided abundant evidence of this. But everyone's priority, of course, was to win the war, and most pianists and painters, no less than plumbers and postmen, had to down tools and join the forces. Cricket and football grounds grew to seed or were commandeered for military training. Civic parklands were converted into market gardens with families given allotments on which to grow fruit and vegetables. John Christie's estate at Glyndebourne, strategically sited near the south-east coast, would probably have become a military encampment had it not already been converted to a refuge for children evacuated from London; Rudolf Bing recalled going to Woolworth's in Lewes to place a large order for chamber pots. Sadler's Wells Theatre, home of Lilian Baylis's opera and ballet company, was taken over by the Borough of Finsbury as a rest centre for people rendered homeless by the blitz. As for the nation's premier opera house, Covent Garden, this was leased to Mecca Cafés Ltd as a *palais de danse* for the delectation of troops home on leave. How could you put on grand opera, its former patrons asked one another sadly, when most of the leading artists of recent years were either German or Italian, and had therefore suddenly become Britain's mortal enemies?

What is remarkable about wartime Britain is not, however, the abandonment of Verdi and Wagner at Covent Garden or of Test Matches at Lord's. On the contrary, it is the resilience of the arts at a time when so much physical and mental energy had to be devoted elsewhere. Myra Hess's National Gallery concerts may have been emblematic, but they were far from unique. For opera, ballet and the theatre, these were formative years as, under the leadership of Tyrone Guthrie and Joan Cross, Kurt Jooss and Ninette de Valois, they reached out to new audiences throughout the land. In Manchester and Liverpool, moribund local orchestras were dramatically revivified, while some of Britain's most talented graphic artists reached out to capture images of wartime life. Film, too, saw something of a golden age as Powell and Pressburger launched one of the most creative partnerships in the history of British cinema and producers such as Korda, Balcon and Rank strove to marry propaganda to art.

It would be foolish to pretend that every Hess concert, Jooss ballet performance, Piper painting or Pressburger movie was of the highest quality. All the normal artistic resources – rehearsal rooms, musical instruments, paints and paper, cameras and costumes – were in short supply and many of the finest talents absent on military duties. But it was widely recognised from the outset that 'public taste was serious', as the theatre director Tyrone Guthrie put it, and that, if serious artistic endeavours were to survive, 'they must be financially "encouraged" and enabled to disperse their services wherever at a given moment they might be most useful'. The authorities acknowledged a responsibility to give leadership and financial support to the nation's artistic and intellectual life. This novel principle provided one of the foundations of a new cultural climate in which many of the most talented of Britain's recent refugees were to flourish during the decades following the war.

The idea of state patronage of the arts was not, however, delivered fresh-faced and perfectly formed. On the contrary, it was born 'in a very English, informal, unostentatious way', in the understated words of one of its most influential midwives, Lord Keynes, Chairman of the Council for the Encouragement of Music and the Arts (CEMA) and of its successor the Arts Council. Its very conception was muddled and its parenthood disputed; many men – and one woman (Mary Glasgow, CEMA's powerful Secretary) – might be said to have been its principal progenitor. In a deeper sense, however, CEMA and the Arts Council were symptoms of a growing belief in the value of government planning, a concept that received a powerful fillip from the exigencies of war and came to be embodied in what history calls the Welfare State.

Everybody in Britain remembered where he or she was at 11.15 a.m. on 3 September 1939 when Prime Minister Neville Chamberlain announced over the wireless that 'this country is at war with Germany'. The cast and crew of Alexander Korda's latest movie extravaganza, a remake of *The Thief of Bagdad*, crowded into a coal bunker at Denham before trooping back to work. Harold and Vita Nicolson, with their sons Ben and Nigel, were at their home, Sissinghurst; Nigel, who had been insouciant enough to join Nazi torchlight parades when on holiday in Göttingen a couple of years earlier, recalled being immensely exhilarated by Chamberlain's 'funereal announcement'. Kenneth Clark heard Chamberlain's 'tired old voice' in a café in the Charing Cross Road, after which he went wandering aimlessly through the streets of central London until his reverie was interrupted by an air raid warden checking that he was carrying his regulation gas mask. Ralph Vaughan Williams was booked to be in Hereford on 3 September for the opening of the Three Choirs Festival but was at home in Dorking glued, like millions of others, to the radio. Ninette de Valois was in Liverpool where the Vic-Wells ballet had performed the night before. Some people were further away from home when the announcement came. David Webster, music lover and General Manager of the Bon Marché store in Liverpool, would normally have attended the visiting ballet, but in fact was in mid-Atlantic, sailing home from New York when war was declared (as was John Reith, who had been the founding Director-General of the BBC). The publisher Stanley Unwin and his family were caught in Zurich, having met up with their eldest son who had been doing a summer job in Budapest.

From that day on, everything was subordinated to the requirement of war. It did not matter if you were Len Hutton or Denis Compton, Alec James or Malcolm Campbell, Laurence Olivier or Ralph Richardson, or a prince of the royal blood. Every able-bodied young man was required to join the forces or contribute in some way to the war effort. Women were recruited into war work too, some of them in the fighting services, many more putting on factory overalls. Some found themselves making munitions in what, until the war, had been the music publisher Ralph Hawkes's wind instrument factory in Edgware. Anyone too old, too young or too sick to work directly for the war could contribute in other ways. There were ambulances and fire engines to drive and staff (Stephen Spender joined the Auxiliary Fire Service, having been rejected by the army), roads and railways to maintain, food and vegetables to grow and distribute.

In addition, there was something called 'morale' to maintain. Broadcasters and journalists, artists and entertainers – all were required to play a part. Gone were the days when an aesthete like Virginia Woolf could decry political commitment as being beneath the serious artist. Whether you were a singer or actor, whether you ran an art gallery, a ballet company or a publishing firm, previous plans went into abeyance as everything became filtered through the prism of the war.

That much was common ground. But little else. When the war started, the BBC introduced regular news programmes in which it supposedly told the truth and nothing but (but often not the whole truth), and went on to achieve legendary popularity with 'morale-boosting' entertainment programmes like Tommy Handley's *ITMA* ('It's That Man Again!'), *Workers' Playtime* and popular music programmes featuring upbeat artists such as Vera Lynn and the Crazy Gang. Much of what we might regard as the censorship to which the Corporation bowed was cheerfully self-imposed. Yet even a docile BBC became embroiled in disputes with government about such mildly controversial broadcasters as J. B. Priestley, whose bluff Yorkshire populism did not sit easily with the strong-arm *dirigisme* of Churchill. Nor were broadcasters the only butt of governmental ire. Fleet Street, too, periodically came into Churchill's sights. In early 1941 the government banned the Communist newspaper, the *Daily Worker* (reinstating it after the Nazi attack on Stalin, which suddenly rendered the USSR an ally). More significantly, they also moved to close down the mass-circulation *Daily Mirror* (a left-leaning paper that believed it was supporting the war effort by pointing out what it regarded as blunders by the government), but were prevented from doing so by the support the *Mirror* received from the rest of the press.

What were the legitimate obligations to art and truth in time of war? What were the outer limits of free speech and of artistic expression? Most accepted that the overall priority was to win the war, or at least to maintain the morale of those on the front line. In this, as in so much else, Churchill took the lead. From the moment he became prime minister in May 1940, his forceful personality and growly voice embodied the unwavering determination that became standard issue during the war. Everybody lined up loyally behind the 'Man with the Big Cigar' and it rapidly became unthinkable – or at least unsayable in public – that Britain might lose. 'Who do you think you are kidding, Mr Hitler,' sang the Crazy Gang at their cheeky, defiant best, 'if you think Old England's done?'

> We are the boys who will stop your little game,
> We are the boys who will make you think again!

But there were as many paths towards such worthy objectives as there were people pursuing them.

'I was fortunate in that I had an immediate, unquestionable duty.' Kenneth Clark, Director of the National Gallery, knew as soon as war clouds began to gather that he had to ensure that the nation's greatest collection of pictures was removed from London to safety. The larger paintings were at first evacuated to a castle in north Wales and the smaller ones to the National Library of Wales at Aberystwyth, home at the time of Clark's friend the émigré art historian Johannes Wilde,* formerly of the Kunsthistorisches Museum of Vienna (and Director of Vienna's Albertina Museum). Clark relished the memory of Wilde in post-*Anschluss* Vienna replying to the obligatory '*Heil Hitler!*' of his professional colleagues with a carefully calculated '*Grüss Gott!*' Aberystwyth must have seemed a welcome haven to Wilde, the more so for the unexpected deposit there of some of Britain's greatest art treasures. Wilde's friend and colleague, Sebastian Isepp, the chief restorer from the Vienna Museum, had also found refuge in Britain and he, too, made Aberystwyth his professional base for the duration, commuting each week from Shrewsbury to help look after Clark's paintings. Then, as Hitler thrust his way through western Europe and threatened Britain, both men were interned as 'enemy aliens', Wilde deported to Canada.

---

* Johannes Wilde later became Professor of Art History at London University and Deputy Director of the Courtauld Institute.

The proximity of Hitler and the beginning of the air raids over Britain forced Kenneth Clark to think again about how best to secure the National Gallery's art collection. North Wales may have been safer than central London, but the region could easily collect bombs intended for Liverpool or the West Midlands. At first the idea was mooted that the paintings should be sent abroad for safety. Canada was suggested. Clark was reluctant to send them through U-boat-infested seas. A member of his staff discovered an abandoned slate quarry containing a vast cave in one of the most inaccessible parts of North Wales. Maybe this was where the nation's Titians and Caravaggios should be consigned. Churchill was consulted. The old patriot replied by return: 'Bury them in the bowels of the earth, but not a picture shall leave this island. WSC.'

Easier said than done. Pathways had to be dug, tunnels hollowed out, air-conditioning installed and the entire National Gallery collection transferred. At one point the truck carrying the Gallery's tallest picture, Van Dyck's *Charles I on Horseback*, approached a bridge which was fractionally too low and got through only by the ruse of letting the air out of the tyres.

Kenneth Clark had been appointed Director of the National Gallery at the age of thirty and was not a man to let a war, or the interment of his entire picture collection, interfere with a starry career as an arts administrator. In addition to the National Gallery concerts, Clark also set up a scheme that helped finance artists of the calibre of Paul Nash, John Piper and Graham Sutherland to create memorable images of planes, bombs and bomb damage. Henry Moore's vivid depictions of the crowds huddling for shelter in the London Underground stations were to become among the most evocative images of the war. Few of Clark's artists were of this stature and the War Artists Committee was criticised for the humdrum level of much of the work it generated. But the project helped give employment, and travelling exhibitions, to scores of artists who were thereby contributing to the war in the way they knew best. And it gave Clark a renewed sense of the sheer glory of artistic patronage. Did he think of himself as a latter-day Sforza, Borgia or Medici? Hardly. But he did begin to think how wonderful it would be if government provided serious money for the arts on a regular basis, money which he, Kenneth Clark, had to administer.

For a while, this 'incurable aesthete' (his self-description) was recruited into the Ministry of Information, a beehive of bureaucrats holed up in London's Senate House supposedly responsible for censorship and propaganda in time of war. If the MinInf was to become the model for Orwell's Ministry of Truth, the reality fell endearingly short. Clark learned with some bemusement that he was to be the director of the Film Division. The Hugenberg of British film, perhaps? The Maecenas of movies? No more than he was a Borgia. Clark had no qualifications for the film job and could only attribute his appointment to his reputation for knowing about 'pictures'. At the time he took up his post he did not even know the difference between producers, distributors and exhibitors. But he was not alone in his ignorance. The figure at the apex of the MinInf was a pleasantly indolent Scottish judge called Lord Macmillan, who was soon replaced as Minister by a compatriot far more driven but equally ineffective: John Reith.

Clark did his best to learn about film and consider how it could be harnessed to the war effort. He met industry leaders, helped enlist the talents of Graham Greene and Noël Coward, prepared a film about minesweepers and planned a big feature about Anglo-French collaboration against the Germans (starring Leslie Howard and Danielle Darrieux), which was abruptly aborted when France fell. Some of the work required of this patrician propagandist was faintly embarrassing – such as the time Clark had to borrow three tanks from another Ministry in order 'to show our great tank force grinding round Parliament Square, the number plates and drivers being changed for each circuit'. Goebbels's minions doubtless had access to more impressive props.

Like everybody else, Clark succumbed to the charm of Alex Korda, wondering how a poor boy raised on a farm in provincial Hungary could have achieved 'a considerable culture, perfect manners and all the *allure* of a man of the world'. Korda, for all his cosmopolitanism and the array of European talent on his books, had displayed his new-found patriotism in the 1930s with a string of popular films evoking the glories of British imperial history. At the outset of the war he produced a propaganda film called *The Lion Has Wings*, proclaiming the invincibility of the RAF.* Clark found Korda 'irresistible' and was impressed by his suggestion that the Division should make films so short (like the TV ads of a later age) that distributors would easily incorporate them into their programmes – a policy the Division adopted.

During Kenneth Clark's tenure at the Ministry of Information much of his time consisted of meetings with film producers, writers and directors keen on obtaining MoI money. 'What's your proposal?' Clark would ask, summoning up a welcoming grimace for one petitioner after another. Early on, when everyone in Britain was wondering how to get the Americans to join in, Clark received a visit from Michael Powell and Emeric Pressburger. Pressburger, a refugee from Nazism, was consumed with the desire to devote all his talents as a screenwriter to the cause. The visit to Clark was, perhaps, a little premature. Quizzed about their storyline, the two film makers could only respond by saying something about it concerning the American-Canadian border but that they would not be able to give details until they had been on a research visit to Canada.

Powell and Pressburger must have made a persuasive pair, for it was agreed to fund their trip. It was (according to Pressburger's biographer) 'the first and only time that the government directly financed a feature film'. As he sailed gingerly across the Atlantic, Pressburger began to develop his ideas: a U-boat is torpedoed and the survivors crawl ashore in a remote part of Canada. Gradually, as they come into contact with some of the variegated denizens of Canada's great spaces, including Eskimos and Hutterites, the contrast is drawn between the cruel authoritarianism of the society from which the Germans have come and the natural democracy of the

---

* Later in the war Korda, never a man to do things by halves, was thought by some to be carrying out secret intelligence work, possibly at the personal behest of Churchill – which may or may not help explain why, from June 1940, Korda 'deserted' Britain and spent three of the war years in the relative safety of the USA.

North-American frontier. On the way back, Pressburger completed the treatment of what became *49th Parallel* – and on his arrival in Britain was saved from internment and/or deportation as an 'enemy alien' only by the direct intervention of the MoI.

By the time Kenneth Clark left the Ministry he had become 'Controller of Home Publicity' and chairman of the 'Home Morale Emergency Committee'. Notwithstanding the grand titles, he was never much of a civil servant. He felt he was 'head of the waste-paper basket department', spending too much of his time turning down crack-brained schemes for winning the war and saving the world. An unreconstructed patrician, Clark was more at home cavorting discreetly with top people in the world of the arts and film. And – as Myra Hess and Henry Moore, Michael Powell and Emeric Pressburger had all been lucky enough to discover – Clark was happier saying 'yes' than 'no'. He loved the arts and he loved running things. Maybe the arts themselves needed running.

A number of others had been having similar thoughts. From the Fabians and early Socialists on the left of the political spectrum to Britain's incipient Fascists on the right, many had been demanding that the nation's artistic life be better planned and run. The Soviet commissars may not have been quite the model for England, nor Goebbels's Ministry of Propaganda, both of which assessed art and artists by crudely political criteria. But Germany's cultural life continued to benefit from a tradition of subsidised theatres, orchestras and opera companies, while UFA still trailed distant clouds of glory for the early films it had helped generate. There were mild parallels in Britain: the British Film Institute and the British Council, for example, were both created in the 1930s. More important, there was the British Broadcasting Corporation. The BBC, established in the 1920s and financed by a licence fee, had quickly established itself under the doggedly committed leadership of Reith as an admired arbiter of national taste – a kind of halfway house between the unbridled control of culture by those alternative evils, government or commerce, and the prototype of the much-vaunted 'arm's-length principle' from government that would later underpin the creation of the Arts Council. With the establishment of the BBC Symphony Orchestra in 1930 under its conductor Adrian Boult, the Corporation proclaimed itself a proactive arbiter in the musical world. What Boult and the BBC chose to play, the nation would hear.

The idea of cultural planning (with the BBC and perhaps the German opera houses as background models) came to appeal to more and more of the nation's movers and shakers in the 1930s – people like Dr Thomas Jones, a consummate political manoeuvrer and long-term confidant of Lloyd George, who was Secretary of the Anglo-American philanthropic foundation the Pilgrim Trust. Something of an appeaser in the mid-1930s and openly impressed by Hitler's informed interest in the arts, Jones felt that a degree of centralised planning and financing, albeit less wholeheartedly espoused than in Berlin, would help bring culture and education to the working classes of Britain.

John Christie, on the other hand, did not care overmuch for either the BBC or the working classes. But the growing success of Glyndebourne (and maybe his vestigial love of things German) fed Christie's vanity, and gave him a taste for command and control. Since he obviously knew better than anyone else how to run a complex arts organisation, the nation would surely benefit, Christie sensed, if he and people like him were to form a 'Council of Power' or 'National Council' for Music and the Arts, and to be entrusted with running them all. Christie particularly had his sights on the Royal Opera House, Covent Garden, a receiving house that had no permanent opera or ballet company.

In March 1938 he hosted a conference at Glyndebourne to consider how to advance his 'National Council'. Several of the nation's top musical figures were present, among them the conductor Malcolm Sargent and Britain's senior composer Ralph Vaughan Williams. A leading figure in the rediscovery of the folk roots of English music, Vaughan Williams was an aesthetic traditionalist taking his inspiration from the English countryside and seascape, and the legacy of Tudor music, rather than from the jagged musical modernism of post-Mahlerian *Mitteleuropa*.

But in his desire to bring 'ordinary' people to appreciate art and culture – and, indeed, to produce it – VW was a fervent radical. What he wanted, he said, was 'to make opera popular and the thing that everyone wants to go to, from the richest to the poorest. We may have to leave out perfection to get popularity.' Christie, by contrast, expressed his alarm that artistic control of his new Council might be exerted by the poor (who had no taste). Nor did he want subsidy, which in general he was against, to fall into the hands of the already rich.

The wealthy personage Christie had in mind was probably the conductor and impresario Sir Thomas Beecham. Beecham had spent nearly thirty years trying to establish opera on a regular basis at Covent Garden and had led recurrent international seasons at the Royal Opera House. He was also the creator and conductor of the London Philharmonic Orchestra. Wilful and notoriously independent-minded, Beecham was capable of breathtaking generosity verging on bravado. When Berta Geissmar, the part-Jewish secretary of the great German conductor Wilhelm Furtwängler, fled Nazi Germany, Beecham took her on as his own assistant and doubled her asking salary; one of the first jobs he assigned to her, in 1936, was to organise an LPO tour of Germany which, with all Beecham's confidence and prestige behind her, required Geissmar to revisit her homeland in comfort and security. But the elegant, conceited Beecham, with his silk pyjamas and large cigar, also had a waspish side to him and many of his contemporaries were badly stung. When John Christie, another prickly and self-centred English eccentric, wrote to Beecham asking him to conduct at Glyndebourne, Beecham did not even deign to reply.

While Christie and Beecham treated each other with haughty disdain, both largely disregarded what proved to be arguably the most important development in the performing arts at the time. Lilian Baylis was the antipode of these men of money. A poor girl scornful of airs and graces, Miss Baylis had aided and then succeeded her aunt, Emma Cons, as good fairy to the working people of south London. As the Salvation Army or Toynbee Hall were to the homeless, so Miss Baylis perceived her Old Vic Theatre in the Waterloo Road: a beacon of light, succour for the hungry, an elevation of the spirit. With her droopy face, spinstery bun and unfashionably uneducated accent, Baylis spoke with the conviction of a missionary about the working people who would flock to see good theatre, opera and ballet, if only it were made available to them. 'Don't worry, God will provide,' she would promise, as young actors like Sybil Thorndike or Ralph Richardson or singers like Joan Cross or Heddle Nash anxiously enquired about the costumes they needed for the next night's performance. And, miraculously, He usually did.

He also provided Baylis with her audiences. So much so that she bought and refurbished a second theatre: Sadler's Wells in the (then) only marginally more salubrious district of Islington. North Londoners, too, would be given food for the soul. From 1934, Baylis divided the 'Vic-Wells' company into two: the drama troupe would henceforth perform exclusively at the Old Vic, while opera and ballet would be based at Sadler's Wells. Standards might not always be as high as elsewhere. Shakespeare at Stratford was sometimes deemed better than Shakespeare in the Waterloo Road, while the Vic-Wells ballet, run by the energetic and ambitious Ninette de Valois and starring home-grown talent, could hardly measure up to the great days of the Ballets Russes. The Vic-Wells opera, too, suffered from international comparisons and could scarcely compete with the pricey festivals mounted by Christie and Beecham. But John Christie, an indomitable patriot for all his snobbery, sometimes found himself wanting to engage Sadler's Wells stars for Glyndebourne. He was usually slapped down by his team. The Glyndebourne audience, Rudolf Bing reminded him, 'has . . . been spoilt at Covent Garden and all over the world by international celebrities and doesn't care a bit what nationality singers are [and] will refuse to pay £2 to hear artists they can normally hear for 6 shillings at Sadler's Wells.'

If there was little love lost between Christie and Beecham, there was open hostility between Christie and John Maynard Keynes. The animosity between the two is said to have gone back to their school days at Eton, but one can see how the bull-headed, homophobic Sussex landowner and the sophisticated, bisexual Cambridge economist, forceful egotists both, would have acted like negative magnets upon each other. Both loved opera. But Keynes loved ballet even more and was married to Lydia Lopokova, a former Diaghilev ballerina. In 1930 Keynes helped his wife and others (including Ninette de Valois) create the 'Camargo Society', a dance company which only survived a few years but, along with de Valois's Sadler's Wells ballet, provided the ground base for the eventual establishment of year-round subsidised ballet in Britain. A few years later Keynes set up, and found partnership money for, the Arts Theatre in Cambridge. He, too, was developing a taste for cultural entrepreneurship.

While nobody doubted Keynes's commitment to the arts, he was primarily famous as an economist, the high priest of deficit spending – the idea that governments, especially at times of economic downturn, should be prepared to prime the pump and thus spend their way out of recession. If government was pre-pared to spend money (so went the theory), more people would be gainfully employed, society at large would benefit and more revenue would be generated to help replenish the government's coffers. The Keynesian approach had had an important influence upon the New Deal policies of President Franklin D. Roosevelt in the USA, where not only foresters and road builders but also painters and playwrights benefited from government largesse.

In Britain, a rising chorus was thus becoming audible, not necessarily crying out for substantial government funding of the arts but at least for some degree of overall planning and help. Composers such as Bliss and Vaughan Williams joined the chorus. As in any choir, there were discordant voices, a few would-be soloists and the odd frustrated conductor. Harmony among Britain's cultural commissars was not to be achieved easily. Yet for all the mutual animosities and jealousies, there were also important links between several of the most promi-nent members and all sang more or less the same tune.

One day, soon after the outbreak of war, a delegation that included Tom Jones, Lord Macmillan and Kenneth Clark went to see the President of the Board of Education, Lord de la

Warr.* Their proposal was that, in the novel situation of wartime, the Pilgrim Trust and the Department of Education put up matching funds to help ordinary people to enjoy music and drama, and learn from otherwise idle artists. What could be better for morale, all agreed, than for government to demonstrate that it cares about the cultural life of the nation? At a preliminary informal meeting, Jones and the two Ministers, Macmillan and de la Warr, had agreed that a one-off sum of £5000 from each side might be reasonable. At the formal meeting the Pilgrim delegates upped their proposal to £25,000, initially from the Pilgrim Trust and then matched by the Education Department. De la Warr, reluctant to dispute publicly with a fellow Minister, agreed and the meeting went on to establish a Committee (later a Council) for the Encouragement of Music and the Arts. CEMA, initially an ad hoc response to an emergency, proved to be the beginning of state subsidy of the arts. Its first Chairman was Lord Macmillan.

---

* Stephen Hearst stayed on the de la Warr estate soon after his arrival in England in 1938. His job was to clear out the stables. One day His Lordship wandered by and asked the lad what he thought of the way things were going. Stephen, who had recently seen the *Anschluss* at first hand, said he thought there'd be a war. Nonsense, my dear young man, came the reassuring reply. 'He, being a member of the government, had more information than I did,' Hearst acknowledges. 'But I had one advantage over him. I had read *Mein Kampf* and Chamberlain's Minister of Education had not!' In the 1950s de la Warr became Postmaster General, the Minister responsible for the establishment of Independent Television.

CHAPTER NINE

By the Waters of Isis and Cam

On 1 April 1940 a busy Adolf Hitler took time off between his conquests of Denmark and Norway to deliver a speech that was broadcast on the BBC. The Führer reminded his listeners that Columbus had discovered America with the help of German science and technology. This gave Germany the legitimate right 'to have some part in the achievement which this voyage of discovery was to result in'. Hitler claimed to have no more territorial demands in Europe. But, he added ominously:

> there are in America national minorities closely connected by race and tradition with the German Reich. In Chicago alone there are 324,000 Czechs, and those Czechs keep asking themselves, 'Why can't we come under the Protectorate?' In . . . New York, there are 476,000 Poles . . . They have a right to be protected by Germany and I shall enforce that right, not only theoretically but also practically.

A chilling speech – and one that led the CBS network to contact the BBC in something of a panic to ask where the Corporation had picked up the broadcast.

A glance at the date might have sown seeds of suspicion, though Martin Miller's impersonation of Hitler was almost faultless, and the cheers and 'heils' utterly authentic. 'The Führer Speaks' was one of the star turns performed by Miller (born Müller) at the *Laterndl*.* This was an Austrian theatre-in-exile that established itself (after an initial sojourn at the Austria Centre in Westbourne Terrace) in the refugee heartland of Swiss Cottage between Hampstead and St John's Wood.

The *Laterndl* was one of several organisations that tried to feed the flickering flames of culture among the refugee community while providing a social centre and regular home-away-from-home entertainment. The Blue Danube Club, initially a breakaway from the *Laterndl*, tended to concentrate on hard-edged cabaret evenings and revues. The German exiles, meanwhile, set up the *Freier Deutscher Kulturbund* ('Free German League of Culture'), an ambitious umbrella organisation (initially much infiltrated by the political left) with five sub-sections for artists, musicians, actors, writers and scientists. Thanks to the efforts of the Bishop of Chichester, the FDKB acquired premises (including library and coffee room) in Hampstead. The FDKB was ambitious, radical and star-studded; its founding members included Stefan Zweig, the film director Berthold Viertel and Fred Uhlman at whose home it was created. Its first chairman was Berlin's most famous theatre critic, Alfred Kerr, recently arrived in England via Paris. Kerr was succeeded in 1941 by the painter Oskar Kokoschka. Kokoschka's international fame, not to mention his Austrian birth, German career and Czech citizenship, gave him the authority to speak on behalf of the entire refugee community (although, disliking organisational or administrative work, he regarded his FDKB title as largely nominal).

The primary function of the *Laterndl*, Blue Danube Club and the various branches of the FDKB was probably social: they provided members with a reassuring echo of the life they had recently had to forgo. Here you were off duty. For a few hours you did not have to worry about how others regarded you – your accent, the fur or feather in your clothing, the way you spoke with your hands, how you held your knife and fork. Here

---

* The *Laterndl* (Lantern) was said to have been named as a homage to *Die Fackel* (*The Torch*), the satirical Viennese journal edited and distributed for over thirty years by Karl Kraus, who had recently died.

you could talk (and be entertained in) German, consume *Strudel* and strong coffee, hear news of precious people and places, learn about a flat or a job, laugh at jokes the English wouldn't understand – laugh at the English, indeed. You attended the *Bund* to bond.

But these institutions also acquired wider cultural significance and *réclame*. Cabaret and satire, for example, were scarcely known in England where the 'well-made play' and the 'West End comedy' with traditional decor and production standards still largely prevailed. To those more attuned to the meaty radicalism of Brecht or Tucholsky than the herbivorous good manners of Ivor Novello, Somerset Maugham or Noël Coward, the little clubs of Hampstead were to provide much-needed nourishment. In addition, as many mainstream theatres closed down or faced an uncertain future, refugee productions began to attract occasional visitors from the wider theatrical world, including the more adventurous critics, eager to experience the efforts of the exiles. Some had supported them from the outset. 'We have no form of theatre so intimate, so direct as this,' wrote Goronwy Rees approvingly in his review of the opening production at the *Laterndl* (still in Westbourne Terrace) published in the *Spectator* in July 1939. 'It has all the charm of amateur theatricals without the amateurishness. Anyone who saw the skill with which the actors used their tiny stage last week realised how much art there was in their spontaneity.'

Sympathetic British theatrical celebrities agreed to lend their support to the various refugee clubs. Sybil Thorndike was a patron of the FDKB and made a point of attending some of its productions. When in 1944 the FDKB mounted a German-language production of J. B. Priestley's play *They Came to a City*, Thorndike wrote to say what a deep impression it had made on her, how it 'got the bare bones of the play . . . in a way that I felt was missed in the West-end performance. The sincerity, the vigour – the brilliant characterisations were so clear and true – and what was done with that tiny little stage is a tribute to any producer.'

Few productions elicited so generous a bouquet from so distinguished a source, however. Generally speaking, the refugee productions remained a closed shop to the wider theatre-going public. Most productions, particularly in the earlier years, were in German. Styles of acting and direction, too, were almost as alien in a country that had so far picked up little of the innovative stagecraft of Piscator or Brecht and liked its sets to be 'realistic'. A few émigré actors went on to make stage, screen and radio careers in their accented English.* But most found it difficult to adjust to what they saw as the milk-and-water styles expected by British (and American) audiences.

Fritz Kortner, for example, 'always striving to achieve the utmost expressiveness', found to his dismay that he had to renounce the style that had made him famous in Germany and learn instead to be 'casual' and 'nonchalant'. In Britain, actors were expected to 'underplay'. This 'anaemia of expression', Kortner felt, 'had diminished, and was in turn influenced by, the actual power of imagination of the English. Thus the theatre became paler and paler.' Frederick Valk, who played Othello and Shylock for the Old Vic company during the war (in productions directed by another refugee, Julius Gellner), was similarly damning:

> Shakespeare's tragedies are born in hell and an actor, who dares to play them, must make a trip to hell . . . But most of the actors don't go down to hell. Either they don't know the way or they don't want to go at all. They prefer a temperate ante-room where one can sit and behave like a gentleman, delivering a declamation beautifully, with legs nicely crossed, in well-pressed trousers. Surely they will deliver the poetry – not a word will be lost – but it will be a dehydrated poetry and you will not hear the voices of Macbeth, Lear or Othello – baked in hell.

One place that *did* welcome people with Middle European accents and acting styles was that archetypal British institution the BBC. 'Anyone who, like me, had burst in from an alien scene

---

* Among them Martin Miller, Agnes Bernelle, Anton Walbrook, Fritz Kortner, Frederick Valk, Conrad Veidt, Lilli Palmer, Herbert Lom, Elisabeth Bergner and Oscar Homolka, all of whom spent time as refugees in England.

came to identify the BBC with Britain,' wrote George Weidenfeld, one of the refugees it snapped up at the outbreak of the war. For the BBC, as for so much else in British life, the war proved pivotal. 'Public Morale' became a key concern as the broadcasters, albeit working closely with the Ministry of Information, struggled to retain their editorial independence. Output expanded rapidly as the Corporation, for the first time in its history, undertook to broadcast regular news bulletins. Staff numbers grew from 4000 to 11,000 as actors, announcers and news analysts shared premises with producers and personnel officers, secretaries, engineers and an army of maintenance staff. All were 'boffins', fighting the same war as the soldiers and Spitfire pilots, but in their own way – and equally unrecognisable by the general public. Or even by their own colleagues. 'I knew directly or indirectly most of the senior staff up to the outbreak of war,' said one old-timer. 'Now,' he said, looking back at the end of the war, 'I shared lifts with complete strangers.'

The BBC offered a variety of opportunities to talented and ambitious refugees. Some of the most prominent, such as Arthur Koestler, were periodically invited to write and read scripts, while Thomas Mann recorded a number of talks in Los Angeles, which were broadcast by the BBC. These figures would reflect on the war, its progress and the humane values of the Allies: stirring messages somewhat impeded by the stilted and accented delivery. Mischa Spoliansky, the film composer from Berlin, wrote music for Geraldo and his orchestra to broadcast. His songs were sung on the air by the refugee actress Lucie Mannheim. There were BBC programmes beamed to the domestic audience (the 'Home Service'), programmes to the troops (the 'Forces Programme'), foreign language broadcasts – and propaganda, including 'black' propaganda purporting to come from within Germany, under the leadership of the brilliant and mercurial Richard Crossman.

All attracted refugee talent, but none more so than the BBC's German Service, aimed overtly at the populations of Central Europe. Martin Esslin first made his name producing programmes for the wartime BBC German Service. Much of its output consisted of news programmes and popular music. But it also produced a lot of drama – serious productions of important plays, as well as a variety of innovative and amusing sketches. The Script Editor and Head of Features was the actor Marius Goring* (Lucie Mannheim's husband) and many of the *Laterndl* and FDKB actors were called in to contribute. Did their efforts help induce love of Britain among their surreptitious listeners and increase resentment of their Nazi rulers? Probably not. If you were courageous or foolhardy enough to listen to the BBC in Nazi-occupied Europe you were already, *ipso facto*, a resister. But people in post-war Germany, perhaps anxious to display their credentials, would regale British visitors with accounts of their favourite BBC programmes. Especially popular, it seems, was a fast-moving, Berlin-style dialogue called *Kurt and Willi* – and a programme called *Der Gefreite Hirnschal*, which was said to have been greatly enjoyed by Konrad Adenauer.

Early in the war the Corporation built up a series of provincial centres, partly for reasons of security. One improbable BBC location was a mansion called Wood Norton near Evesham in the West Country. Here, amid the groves and orchards of rural England, the BBC set up a quasi-secret department whose members, many of them highly cultured refugees from Central Europe, spent eight-hour shifts monitoring Axis broadcasts in a variety of languages and dictating summaries for a 'BBC Digest' that was sent to selected government departments. Speeches by Hitler, Mussolini and their henchmen were recorded in London and sent to Wood Norton for translation and analysis. Excerpts from both recent and earlier speeches were used in news digest programmes and in features outlining the history of Fascism and the Third Reich.

George Weidenfeld and Martin Esslin were initially recruited by the BBC as monitors, as were the art historians Ernst Gombrich and Ernst Buschbeck. Thus a number of refugees, still technically 'enemy aliens' in some cases, were required to abide by curfew restrictions – yet deemed to be doing work vital to the

---

* Its overall head, Hugh Carleton Greene, brother of the novelist Graham Greene, later became the BBC's Director-General.

war effort and therefore exempt from internment. If officialdom regarded this exotic platoon of beret-and-borscht boffins with some ambivalence, so did the local families with whom they were billeted, most of whom had scarcely encountered a foreigner before, let alone a forceful Austro-Jewish intellectual. The resulting culture shock was often bewildering if (let us hope) mutually enlightening. The locals could, for example, be quite upset by the frequency with which their foreign guests insisted on having a bath ('they must be very dirty if they want to bath that often'). Gombrich, working late shifts, had to endure the disapproval of his host for the apparently disreputable habit of returning home at 2 or 3 a.m. and sleeping on until ten in the morning.

For all their preternatural conspicuousness, however, it did not take long for the refugee monitors to become adjusted to their new surroundings. Esslin learned to read the *Spectator* and enjoy cricket, Weidenfeld to cycle through the English country-side to work, waving as he arrived to the solemn, pipe-smoking figures whose shift had just ended. As the BBC continued to expand, furthermore, and the blitz made London ever more vulnerable, other BBC departments, including its Drama Repertory Company and part of its Music Department, were relocated to Evesham. A natural sense of camaraderie soon developed among the variegated BBC personnel, a self-sustaining intellectual biosphere. Weidenfeld found it all-absorbing: 'I felt that the world outside the Corporation was but an enlarged model of the BBC universe.'

Listening to German or Italian broadcasts for eight hours at a time was rather like monitoring the baggage X-ray at an airport: hugely important but – almost all the time – perilously tedious. Gombrich, deprived of his books and art works, spent some of his spare time penning whatever he could remember of the history of art (for a book later destined to become the most famous ever published on the subject). He soon rose to become a supervisor; henceforth, his job was to monitor the monitors. But when in April 1945 he heard the German radio play a movement from a Bruckner symphony written to commemorate the death of Wagner, Gombrich himself listened intently. Shortly afterwards, a solemn announcement came over the airwaves that 'Our Führer has fallen in the struggle against Bolshevism'. Gombrich immediately arranged for the news of Hitler's death to be telephoned to Churchill.

Weidenfeld's BBC career, meanwhile, had taken on less orthodox contours. A cheeky talent for mimicry led him to develop a party turn in which he imitated not only his colleagues and bosses but also the world figures he had to spend all day listening to. One day a BBC recording of a Hitler speech failed to turn up at Wood Norton in time for a programme in which it was to be used. That night, Weidenfeld made his broadcasting debut as the Führer. Unlike Martin Miller, Weidenfeld did not go on to have a distinguished career as an actor; but he did make something of a name for himself in a regular BBC feature broadcast to the Italian forces in which he played the part of a blustering German businessman who spoke Italian with a strong German accent. He found himself fascinated by the nature of mass communication and mass psychology. He moved from monitoring to news analysis and was soon transferred to London where he came to the attention of the team under Richard Crossman responsible for propaganda broadcasts. At the BBC's premises at 200 Oxford Street, where Weidenfeld's colleagues included George Orwell, Edmund Blunden, William Empson and Norman Collins, he delivered (in his own voice and name!)* regular commentaries to the wider world.

As 'our European correspondent', Weidenfeld needed to woo the most important émigrés from the Third Reich as well as all the London-based governments-in-exile. This required great bouts of socialising with not only de Gaulle and the Free French, but also the Czechs, Poles, Dutch, Norwegians and the rest. He also befriended the first emissaries from Tito's Yugoslavia (a contact that was to prove of inestimable value to Weidenfeld a few years later). Somehow, he had sufficient residual energy for

---

* His real name was Arthur Weidenfeld, but his programme director told him bluntly that his surname was too long and that Arthur didn't transmit well on short wave. 'Do you have a middle name?' 'Georg.' 'Drop the Arthur, drop the feld.' So for the rest of the war he broadcast as George Weiden. Afterwards he reverted to his full surname, but by then so many people knew him as George that he stuck to it.

his BBC work. Indeed, he also wrote a weekly column in the *News Chronicle*, a liberal newspaper edited by Gerald Barry, and a book dissecting Nazi propaganda techniques in which one of his principal sources was the émigré critic Alfred Kerr. Weidenfeld, it would be fair to say, had a 'good war', during which he tasted the elixir of intellectual entrepreneurship. As the war ended and the older denizens of Broadcasting House and Fleet Street returned from the front to their old desks, he was seized with a new ambition. 'I yearned to start something myself and turn my condition of being with the English but not of the English into an advantage.'

'With the English, but not of the English': it was a phrase that would resonate with many of the Hitler émigrés as they gradually came to embrace their new homeland. They were not in Britain from choice. Most mourned the land and language they had been forced to quit and a few dreamed of going back when the dust of war had settled. Many more harboured dreams of re-emigrating to North America. For example, Helene Isepp's mother and sisters both lived in the USA (one was married to Herbert Lehman, the American banker and Governor of New York) and Sebastian and Helene and their children expected to follow in due course. But it didn't happen; their son Martin therefore grew up feeling himself to be a young Englishman and still reflects wryly on the fact that he might have been an American but for what he calls a tiny twist of fate.

Martin Isepp must have been developing into a very English young Englishman when, after school in Bognor Regis and a couple of years living in Shrewsbury, he and his parents moved to Oxford. The Isepps had a number of friends in Oxford. Gertie and Raimund von Hofmannsthal, respectively the widow and son of the poet and librettist, were living there, as were Rudolf Bing and his wife. Bing commuted daily from Oxford to and from his wartime job at the Peter Jones store in London's Sloane Square. Another Oxford resident was the composer and musicologist Egon Wellesz, an early baton carrier in Britain for the serialism of the Second Vienna School; it was Wellesz who had first introduced Sebastian and Helene Isepp to each other. A further reason for going to Oxford was that it was the home of Martin's piano teacher, Leonie Gombrich (mother of Ernst). But the main reason Sebastian Isepp took his family there was that he had become friendly with the director of Oxford's Ashmolean Museum, who offered him a job.

During the war years, as people and institutions (and art objects) were evacuated from London, Oxford became a centre for what, in retrospect, one might dub 'refugee culture'. A number of émigré philosophers taught at the university, among them Wolfgang von Leyden and Heinz Cassirer (whose students included Iris Murdoch). Arnaldo Momigliano, a leading authority on the world of the Greeks and Romans and an exile from Italian Fascism, found refuge there during the war, before going on to become Professor of Ancient History at the University of London. Nicolai Rubinstein, Berlin-born and Florence-trained, lived in Oxford during the early years of the war, lecturing on Renaissance history, before taking a post at the University of Southampton. Wartime Oxford also boasted a clutch of top scientists (Francis Simon, Nicholas Kurti, Heinrich Kuhn, Ernst Chain and the physicist Rudi Koempfner), some of them brought to the university en bloc as a result of a 'shopping' trip across Germany in 1933 by the then Head of the Clarendon Laboratory, Frederick Lindemann.

In addition, wartime Oxford was enriched by the presence of a number of influential exiles later to make their names in the arts world. Béla Horovitz and Ludwig Goldscheider, the founders of the art publishing house Phaidon Press, moved to Oxford during the war. You can still find the occasional early edition in second-hand bookshops with the imprint 'Phaidon, 14 St Giles, Oxford'. When the Ashmolean became home for the evacuated Slade School of Art, which moved to Oxford under the auspices of the Ruskin School, one of its part-time students was Béla's son, the future composer Joseph Horovitz. An undergraduate at New College, Joe's artistic ambition at that time outran his promise as a musician. Another Slade student was Milein Cosman; she had followed the school from Gower Street to Oxford where she lived a happy, 'gilded-cage existence and felt both guilty and grateful'. Milein remembered a town full of budding poets and translators, among them Franz Steiner and Michael Hamburger.*

Albi Rosenthal, later the doyen dealer in ancient books and manuscripts, was another who moved to Oxford during the war. The son of a leading antiquarian bookseller in Munich, and a passionate and talented amateur musician, Albi was nineteen when he first visited Britain in October 1933 to stay with a family friend, Dr Robin Flower, Deputy Keeper of Manuscripts at the British Museum. Flower got Albi a reader's ticket and awakened the lad's interest in medieval books by placing the museum's illuminated manuscripts at his disposal. Some weeks later Albi's father was in London and took him to meet his friend Fritz Saxl at the newly arrived Warburg Library. 'You look as though you need an assistant,' said the proud father. 'If so, my son here is good at languages and he knows art history.' The kindly Saxl offered Albi a job on the spot. Albi was flabbergasted; what could he contribute? Don't worry, said Rosenthal senior. You'll swim!

He did. For several years, Albi was assistant to Rudolf Wittkower, whom he helped with his scholarly work and with the organisation of the department of reproductions. In time, Albi began to research articles of his own; his first, on Dürer, was published in the *Burlington Magazine*. Rosenthal loved his work at the renascent Warburg; colleagues such as Saxl, Gertrud Bing (the Deputy Director), Wittkower, Gombrich, Otto Kurz and Hugo Buchthal (with whom Albi shared a flat for a while) provided what Rosenthal thought was 'the nearest approximation in the modern world to an ancient Greek academy'. Like the original Olympians, these transplanted German and Austrian scholars were thoroughly at home with the culture and history of the ancient world, and understood its links to the Renaissance and beyond. Talking to each other and to their students in a kind of Germano-English (with liberal doses of Italian), they formed a tiny bubble of Central European

---

* If, instead of following the Slade to Oxford, Milein Cosman had gone with the Royal College of Art to its wartime location in the Lake District, she might have come across another young refugee who spent some time there playing string quartets and whom she was later to marry. His name was Hans Keller.

scholarship, a quasi-private club whose insights were, as yet, scarcely known to the wider world.

In 1936 Albi, still only twenty-two, founded his own firm, A. Rosenthal Ltd, and embarked upon a career as an antiquarian bookseller that would last into the twenty-first century. As the business grew, he left the Warburg (in 1938) and he and his books moved into a house in Curzon Street, in London's Mayfair. One night in November 1940 the house was bombed. Miraculously, neither Albi nor the books were touched, but it was clearly becoming urgent to leave London. Albi was engaged and his fiancée lived in Oxford. In addition, he urgently needed to compile a new catalogue for his rapidly expanding business and his normal source of archive information, the British Museum Library, had been evacuated; the only available library of equivalent quality was the Bodleian. So in January 1941, for two good reasons, Albi Rosenthal moved to Oxford.

Albi combined a love of music with his professional interest in antiquarian books, and soon began dealing in historic musical manuscripts. In Oxford he met Egon Wellesz and became firm friends with the older man. Wellesz was a Fellow of Lincoln College and the university's leading historian of music. For all his formidable accomplishments as both a prolific (and performed) composer and a distinguished academic musicologist, Wellesz, a Catholic convert, was a kindly, sociable man, a natural magnet for the émigré community. 'To enter the Wellesz home in the Woodstock Road was like sniffing the air of old Vienna,' one of them recalled. You worked your way past walls and glass cases packed with musical memorabilia (not to mention a plethora of Byzantine icons, crucifixes and altar pieces) and there was always a welcome supply of coffee and cakes, and some of the most stimulating company in Oxford. Books were piled high in the copious bookcases and double-stacked so that, in order to dig out the one he was looking for, Wellesz was often sidetracked by the ones he first had to remove.

Wellesz was a man of wide cultural and musical interests and tastes. A pupil (and biographer) of Schoenberg, Wellesz had a number of stage works to his name, many of them based on

ancient Greeks sources, and had also been an early champion on
the Continent of the music of the new generation of English
composers such as Holst, Vaughan Williams and Bliss. In 1932
Wellesz, following in the footsteps of Haydn, was given an
honorary degree at Oxford. Six years later, in March 1938,
Wellesz was in Amsterdam for a performance of one of his
works under Bruno Walter when news came through of the
Anschluss. Wellesz knew he could not return safely to Vienna
and, on the advice of friends, crossed to England where he soon
settled in Oxford. At first the trauma of exile and war seemed to
dam the creative juices. But in 1943 he began composing again,
setting some poems by Hopkins and starting work on a string
quartet, and he went on to enjoy a long and vigorous old age as
composer (of nine symphonies), scholar (of baroque and
Byzantine music and musicology) and, above all, as an influential bridge between the English musical tradition and that of
Viennese serialism. Robert Layton, who read Music at Oxford
after the war and used to visit Wellesz's home for tutorials,
remembered him as an inspiring teacher, a living link to Mahler
and Bartók, a man of immense charm who, whether or not he
actually taught you what he was supposed to teach you, always
left you with a warm glow of accomplishment. When Wellesz
wanted you to leave, Layton recalled, he would fix you with his
warm smile, extend a hand and say gently, '*Gut* . . .'

The presence of so much refugee talent helped give wartime
Oxford a particularly cosmopolitan buzz. Many of the British-
born men and women who would normally have taught or
studied at the university had been called away by the war; their
return in 1945–6 would transform the university and town once
again. But during the war itself, the city of dreaming spires and
lost causes also became an important enclave of Central
European cultural ideas and values.

So, in its own way, did Cambridge. Cambridge in the 1930s, like
Oxford, became home, at least initially, to a number of émigré
scientists (Peierls, Krebs, Perutz, Blaschko). Several went on to
carve out careers of great distinction, in Cambridge and
elsewhere; all continued to speak warmly of the welcome they

had received. 'Everyone was away,' Perutz recalled, 'except a handful of former refugees who weren't wanted for anything else!' Many of the émigré scientists in Cambridge had been helped by Tess Simpson and the Society for the Protection of Science and Learning which, when war broke out, moved out of London to the relative safety of Cambridge.

So did the entire LSE. Cambridge (unlike Oxford) had a worldwide reputation for economics, economic theory and what were coming to be known as the social sciences. It had been home to the leading economic theorist at the beginning of the century, Alfred Marshall, while the most influential economist of the 1930s and 1940s, John Maynard Keynes, was born in Cambridge and based at King's. Thus, when great London-based institutions evacuated the war-torn capital and the Slade School of Art went to Oxford, it was fitting that the London School of Economics and Political Science should find temporary accommodation in and around Peterhouse College, Cambridge. The LSE was founded in 1895 by Fabian Socialists concerned to harness economic theory to the greater benefit of the people, and soon established itself as the leading academic institution in Britain not only in its core fields of economics and politics but also in such related disciplines as law, history, philosophy, sociology and anthropology. It was a broad church, though something of the social conscience of its founders continued to drive the School in the years when Beveridge was Director and its stars included the Socialist Professor of Politics, Harold Laski. Nothing quite like the LSE existed anywhere else. Those who were lucky enough to benefit from its wartime evacuation to Cambridge tend to remember the experience with a roseate glow. Asa Briggs, the brilliant young scholarship boy doing a History degree at Sidney Sussex College, was intrigued by the additional presence in town of the LSE and attended lectures by many of its transplanted stars.* Among them, the most formidable was the Vienna-born Friedrich von Hayek.

The Hayek family, ennobled by the Emperor Joseph II back in

---

* Briggs took an external London University degree, concurrently with his Cambridge degree, and famously got a First in both.

Mozart's day, had produced strings of scientists and civil servants by the time Friedrich was born in 1899. His father was a doctor and botanist who had published works on the flora of the Austrian Alps, while his mother's family boasted a number of prominent Austrian jurists and civil servants. Friedrich's brothers Erich and Heinz became Professors of (respectively) Chemistry and Anatomy. His distant cousin, Ludwig Wittgenstein, was a philosopher of seminal importance who had moved to Cambridge University in 1911 and, after a break during and after the First World War, had been there much of the time since. When Friedrich von Hayek himself moved to Cambridge with the LSE, he already had a reputation as a rigorous and highly original economic thinker.

Hayek fought in the last year of World War One, a witness to the carnage in the battlefields and to the defeat and dismemberment of Austria-Hungary. His experiences in northern Italy brought home to the sensitive young man not only the staggering human catastrophe of the Great War but also something of the mismanagement that had helped lead to it. The much-vaunted multinational, multilingual nature of the Austro-Hungarian empire, for example, did not impress Hayek, who witnessed for himself the very fragility that helped accelerate the empire's dissolution. 'I served in a battle in which eleven different languages were spoken,' he recalled many years later. 'It's bound to draw your attention to the problems of political organisation. It was during the war service in Italy that I more or less decided to do economics.'

In the month of the Armistice, November 1918, Hayek entered the University of Vienna. A 'mild Socialist' at the time, he achieved doctorates in both Law and Political Economy. At the university he encountered Ludwig von Mises, a charismatic public administrator and economist who had recently published a damning critique of Socialism. Mises had been put in charge of an Austrian government office set up to sort out the war debts of the newly established nation. Hayek, deeply impressed by Mises, was rapidly weaned of his Fabianism. State intervention of whatever kind, he became convinced, always had deleterious consequences.

Mises offered the younger man a job as his legal consultant. Hayek and his new master watched, aghast, as the Great Inflation of 1923 spilled over into Austria and washed away people's homes, jobs and dreams. The very first economic duty of any government, Hayek felt, must be to stabilise prices and, thereby, the value of people's lifetime savings. Thereafter, the state should leave individuals to make their own economic decisions.

After a period in the USA, during which he encountered the latest techniques of statistical research, Hayek returned to his job in Vienna and attended Mises's informal fortnightly seminars exploring the principles of economics. In 1927 he and Mises set up a research institute devoted to the study of the business cycle. Hayek was also offered a teaching post by the University of Vienna in 1929, the year in which he published his book *Monetary Theory and the Trade Cycle*. Already, at thirty, a celebrated economist of a markedly conservative hue, Hayek was becoming a well-known figure on the international circuit.

Hayek soon acquired admirers and advocates in Britain. Lionel Robbins, the precocious and thrusting star of the LSE Economics Department, had just been given a chair by Beveridge, the School's Director. Keen to recruit like-minded colleagues, Robbins had heard good things about Hayek and, with Beveridge's approval, invited him over in 1931 to deliver a series of lectures. Later that year Hayek was appointed Tooke Professor of Economic Science and Statistics at the University of London. His appointment was initially for a year; he was to stay for nearly twenty.

Throughout the rest of the 1930s, Hayek and his wife and young family lived comfortably in Hampstead Garden Suburb. Robbins was a neighbour and became a close friend. At the LSE the two men soon formed an axis of economic conservatism, favouring the microeconomic, anti-interventionist approach Hayek had imbibed in Vienna and arguing the benefits of free market economics, of capital and interest, savings and retrenchment. As successive governments tried to come to grips with the problems of slump and unemployment, international debt and increasingly militant European Fascism, Robbins and Hayek invited many of the leading British, European and American thinkers to visit the LSE, thus helping to place the School, and its seminars on economics, at the fulcrum of international debate. John Kenneth Galbraith recalled these seminars as 'possibly the most aggressively vocal gathering in all the history of economic instruction' – but also noted that Hayek himself was 'one of the gentlest in manner, most scholarly and generally most agreeable men' Galbraith had ever encountered. Aubrey Jones, who attended Hayek's lectures as an undergraduate, remembered that he 'wore a perpetually benevolent smile, a trait which did not belie his nature' – but that one had to sit near the front in order to follow what he was saying. To know economics in those days, Jones sensed, one had to know German. To Robbins, Hayek 'lived at the frontiers of speculation'.

Opposed to the Robbins–Hayek axis was the liberal tendency, gravitating around the august figure of Keynes and his disciples, who proclaimed the merits of macroeconomics – of state-planned investment and deficit spending. In 1936 Keynes published his *General Theory of Employment, Interest and Money*, a highly influential book which, to the intense dismay of Hayek, caught the collectivist mood of the times and (though Keynes himself was no Socialist) provided succour to the left.

Intellectual conflict lay at the very root of the relationship between Keynes and Hayek – the brilliant, arrogant English advocate of state interventionism and the courtly, conservative Austrian to whom the primary (and almost only) economic duty of governments was to protect a private sphere of interest in which individuals could be left to make their own decisions. Early in his English career Hayek was invited to Cambridge to expound his theories to an audience of Keynesians (though not the great man himself, who was unavoidably absent). Robert Skidelsky, Keynes's biographer, reports that the lecture was met with stony silence. Richard Kahn decided to break the ice. 'Is it your view', he asked Hayek, 'that if I went out tomorrow and bought a new overcoat, that would increase unemployment?'

'Yes,' replied Hayek, turning to a blackboard full of triangles, 'but it would take a very long mathematical argument to explain why.'

Skidelsky contrasts not only Hayek's views but also his penchant for relentless methodological precision with the genius for communication displayed by Keynes who, that same month, argued in a broadcast that 'Whenever you save five shillings you put a man out of work for a day'.

Yet for all the contrasts of style and content, a genuine friendship seems to have blossomed between the two men. Hayek had first met Keynes at a conference in London in 1929 when the Cambridge economist apparently '[tried] to go like a steamroller over the young man' but was gracious when Hayek stood up to him with serious argument. Throughout the years of the intellectual prizefight between the LSE and Cambridge – a magnificent spectator sport for those not personally bruised by it – Hayek and Keynes corresponded with one another, treated each other's writings with seriousness and respect, if thoroughly disagreeing with each other, and remained on courteous personal terms. 'Hayek has been here for the weekend,' Keynes wrote to his wife Lydia in 1933. 'We get on very well in private life. But what rubbish his theory is.' Hayek, for his part, admired 'the magnetism of the brilliant conversationalist with his wide range of interests and bewitching voice'. When the LSE moved en bloc to Cambridge, Keynes welcomed Hayek and helped him find rooms at his own college, King's. In 1944 Keynes proposed Hayek for a Fellowship of the British Academy. And it was in wartime Cambridge that Hayek, drawing upon his continental roots and experience and allying them to what he had learned since his arrival in England, was to write the book that caused his name to be both revered and reviled throughout the intellectual and political world for more than a generation.

Anne Bohm remembered Hayek wearing riding boots in Cambridge. He was one of the relatively few LSE professors actually to live there during the war and riding was one of the few traditional off-duty pleasures readily available to the émigré Austrian aristocrat. Anne joined the LSE in 1941. A cousin of hers had been looking through the job ads in the *Cambridge Evening News*. One of them seemed made for Anne; it appeared that someone needed an applicant who spoke German, understood academic research and could type. The advertiser was the LSE historian and Dean of Postgraduate Students L. G. Robinson, who was based at Peterhouse. Robinson needed an administrative assistant to help him run courses on European history that he had been asked to set up for officers in the armed services. Anne applied and got the job, and discovered Robinson to be a charming but prolix academic who would dictate long memos for her to type. She soon found this onerous and offered to draft letters and memos for him. Like many refugees who had studied English academically, she savoured the language and its nuances. Before long, Robinson achieved a new measure of respect around the LSE for the precision and economy of his correspondence – and Anne became indispensable to him and, indeed, to the School. In due course Anne gave up the role of Research Assistant and helped Robinson run the Postgraduate Department in Cambridge, effectively taking over the job when the School returned to London. Here, she became the guiding light and mother confessor to generations of LSE postgraduate students and intimate friend to many of its most illustrious professors. In an LSE career spanning forty-five years (and, informally, close on sixty), Anne Bohm became a one-woman, single-span bridge linking the modern LSE to the historic legacy of Laski and Hayek.

As Hayek went striding across Cambridge in his riding boots during the war years, I wonder whether his path crossed with that of a bright-eyed, dark-haired girl from Berlin. Hilde Litthauer had been sent to England for part of her schooling as an adolescent, so perhaps it was not too strange for her to enrol as an undergraduate at Newnham during the war. Hilde (who married Fred Himmelweit in 1940) went on to obtain a Double First, studying Modern Languages and then moving to psychology. One of her first jobs was as an assistant to the behavioural psychologist Hans Eysenck, himself a refugee. Eysenck recalled that Hilde, who became his first Ph.D. student, had 'all the advantages and all the disadvantages of a Cambridge training – a good experimental background, together with an appreciation of theory, but a curious lack of knowledge in the psychometric field – in fact, when she joined me she couldn't even calculate a correlation!' Eysenck, later famous (or infamous) for his controversial measurements of intelligence, doubtless put her right. After some years as a clinical psychologist, Hilde Himmelweit joined the staff at the LSE in 1949 becoming, over the next thirty years, one of Britain's most forceful and best-known social psychologists. Her seminal work on the impact of television on young minds also made her one of the most influential.*

Another young figure scurrying across Cambridge during the war years – as different from Hilde Himmelweit as it was possible to be – was Walter Ullmann, a conservative-minded Austrian Catholic who had trained as a lawyer. Ullmann, initially a beneficiary of Tess Simpson's Society for the Protection of Science and Learning, took a job as a teacher in a Leicestershire boarding school during the war. But he spent as much time as he could in Cambridge ('only about 150 kilometres from the school') pursuing his studies on medieval ecclesiastical and common law, a field virtually unknown in Britain at that time. A few years after the war Ullmann, to his own surprise, was plucked from virtual obscurity and offered a Chair of History at Cambridge where, for over twenty-five years, he was a uniquely persuasive advocate of the pivotal importance to modern European history of the medieval papacy. With his beaky appearance, the arms of his professorial gown flapping expressively like the wings of a bat, Ullmann would mesmerise student audiences and, by the sheer exuberance of his own enthusiasm, induce otherwise incorrigible modernists (like myself) to enjoy delving among arcane medieval manuscripts.

The wartime experience of Oxford and Cambridge was reproduced, with local variations, throughout the schools, colleges

---

* Hilde Himmelweit was related to Max Perutz's wife Gisela who, at one time, had worked for Tess Simpson and then for L. G. Robinson. Tess Simpson wanted Gisela back; hence the newspaper ad that was answered by Anne Bohm. Another close relative was Gabriele Ullstein who later married the young Cambridge don Noel Annan. Eysenck's second wife was Sybil Rostal, daughter of Max Rostal, teacher of the Amadeus Quartet's Norbert Brainin, Siegmund Nissel and Peter Schidlof.

and universities of non-metropolitan Britain. Young men and women marched off to war, resources were reallocated and entire institutions relocated. Just as the paintings of the National Gallery were taken off to North Wales and the BBC Symphony Orchestra to Bristol and Bedford, so most of the constituent colleges of London University had their buildings expropriated by government departments and were made to leave the capital. Thus parts of University College, London, were sent to North Wales, King's to Bristol and Glasgow, and the Institute of Education to Nottingham. Students from the Royal College of Art, expecting the rigours of London, were evacuated to the Lake District. Some from Bedford and Queen Mary Colleges were sent to Cambridge, where they found themselves sharing facilities with, *inter alia*, medical students from Guy's and St Bartholomew's Hospitals as well as the young seminarians from Chichester Theological College.

Up and down the country the appointment of refugee scholars filled some of the gaps caused by the war and played an important part in sustaining the nation's educational institutions. Many of these émigrés went on to introduce fresh perspectives and sometimes completely new strands of scholarship to British intellectual and cultural life. It was a story that would continue to unfold in the decades after the war as a younger generation of Middle European émigrés began to make its mark. On the books at the LSE, for example, were Claus Moser, John Burgh, Ralph Milliband, Ernest Gellner, Peter Bauer, Hilde Himmelweit, Bram Oppenheim and Michael Zander. As the years passed, these and others gradually emerged into prominence, revelling – like the prisoners in *Fidelio* – in the freedom and security so improbably bestowed upon them, determined to make the most of their extraordinary good fortune.

CHAPTER TEN

The Freedom of the Foreigner

Emeric Pressburger was always arriving just as Alexander Korda was leaving. As we have seen, Pressburger had spent half his life wandering – from Hungary and Romania to Prague, Stuttgart, Berlin, Paris and London. By 1939, in London, he was at last settling down. He had just enjoyed his first British success: *The Spy in Black*, starring Conrad Veidt, which Korda had called him in to rewrite, and the one through which he first met his sparring partner and alter ego Michael Powell. When war broke out Pressburger felt, maybe for the first time since childhood, that he was no longer a foreigner. 'Suddenly I had something in common with everyone I met,' he recalled later, and went on to write one film after another that evoked the spirit and values of his new homeland.

Alex Korda shared the sense of exhilaration as the rumbling threat of war finally burst into reality. London Films had undergone a series of crises and Korda himself had lost executive control of Denham. In a sense he needed the war; the 'sharing of danger' gave him a sense of putting down roots, of belonging. His country's enemies were *his* enemies – a point he was quick to demonstrate. On 2 September 1939, the day after Hitler invaded Poland (and the day *before* Chamberlain's declaration of war), Korda summoned his colleagues and told them that, despite all the time and money still required to complete his latest epic, a remake of *The Thief of Bagdad*, London Films was going into the propaganda business. He promptly redirected major resources – and money out of his own pocket – into a film lauding the virtues of the Royal Air

Force. *The Lion Has Wings*, a mixture of documentary and dramatised feature, was completed in six weeks and released to an admiring public before the end of October. With *The Lion Has Wings*, not to mention the decisive speed with which it had been undertaken, Korda once again proclaimed his British patriotism. Six months later, in June 1940 – at the very nadir of the war – Korda left England for the USA.

From the mid-1930s onwards, in the canteen at Denham, the lobby of the Cumberland Hotel or the restaurants of Soho and the cafés of Hampstead and Swiss Cottage, the film community in exile would laugh, quaff and quarrel, share contacts and experiences with newcomers and chew over the worsening international situation. Conversation, like the bill of fare, tended to be full of colour, highly spiced and not always easy to digest. Producers and directors including Stapenhorst, Gabriel Pascal, the Italian Filippo del Giudice ('Del'), Berthold Viertel, Ludwig Berger and the Brazilian-born Alberto Cavalcanti, writers such as Carl Mayer, Carl Zuckmayer and Lajos Biro, the actors Bergner, Homolka, Veidt and Walbrook, musicians like Rózsa, Goehr, Spoliansky and Allan Gray (born Josef Zmigrod* in Poland), art directors such as Heckroth or Alfred Junge – all found themselves grounded in England, deposited by the vicissitudes of recent history.

London was not where they would necessarily have expected, or wanted, to be. To most, Hollywood was the mecca of movie making and several moved on to the USA. The world remembers Homolka for *War and Peace* rather than *Rhodes of Africa*, Rózsa for a plethora of Hollywood scores (*Lust for Life, Ben Hur, El Cid, The Green Berets*) rather than for *The Four Feathers* or *The Spy in Black*. But England was home, at least temporarily. And, as most acknowledged with eyebrows raised and hands outstretched, things could have been worse. They could indeed. Throughout Central Europe, as in Stalin's Soviet Union and Mussolini's Italy, film was now a branch of politics. In Germany itself, where UFA had lost its Jewish personnel and

---

*On display in the new Jewish Museum in Berlin is an attendance list for Schoenberg's composition class for 1927–8 showing the names of both Walter Goehr and Josef Zmigrod.

much of its creative impulse, film, like every cultural manifestation, was subordinated to the demands of Goebbels's
Ministry of Propaganda. Authoritarian regimes can produce
great art; Leni Riefenstahl worked to the dictates of Hitler as
Eisenstein worked under Stalin. But Germany never regained the
imaginative urgency that had catapulted it to the forefront of the
film world in the 1920s.

Berlin's loss was London's gain. In Britain, film making did
not achieve the early prominence with which it had been
endowed in Moscow, Berlin and Hollywood. But by the mid-
1930s, as the bulk of the émigrés began to arrive, two important
trends in British film making were emerging. The first was the
documentary movement associated with John Grierson, Edgar
Anstey, Basil Wright, Humphrey Jennings and others. In an era
of high unemployment and mounting international tension,
Grierson had been greatly impressed by the social concern, as
well as the editing techniques, of Soviet directors such as
Eisenstein, and he strove to apply the juxtaposition or montage
of powerful, symbolic images (as in *Battleship Potemkin*) to
films documenting the state of contemporary Britain. Documentary film, he and his colleagues believed, had the potential
to educate and improve society. For several years, Grierson was
in charge of the GPO Film Unit; the Unit's *Night Mail* (words by
Auden, music by Britten, directed by Basil Wright) is a little
masterpiece of technique, skilful cross-cutting and the integration of vision and sound. Such documentaries can look
politically anodyne today, with their patronising attempt to
elevate the dignity of the ordinary worker. But the political
culture of Britain in the 1930s was a great deal more decorous
than in later years (and one should remember that the GPO Unit
was financed, no less than the work of Eisenstein or Riefenstahl,
by an agency of government). The importance of the British
documentary movement lay less in the message than in the
medium – and in the subsequent influence of some of the people
it employed.

Many refugees gravitated towards documentary film.
Wolfgang Suschitzky was a Viennese-trained photographer who
had originally wanted to study zoology. After a brief period (and

a failed marriage) in Holland, Wolf came to London where his sister, a Bauhaus-trained architect,* was married to an Englishman. Wolf met Basil Wright who put him in touch with another leading figure in the documentary movement, Paul Rotha. Rotha liked Wolf's photography and attached him to a team that was making a series of films with the biologist Julian Huxley, then Secretary of the Zoological Society of London. While thus learning the art of cinematography, Wolf continued to work as a freelance photographer, publishing regularly in Stefan Lorant's new magazine *Picture Post*. During the war he rejoined Paul Rotha Productions and shot documentaries for the Ministry of Information (which, incidentally, exempted him from internment), working again after the war with Huxley on a book about mammals brought out by the fledgling publishers Thames and Hudson. Wolf Suschitzky went on to become a celebrated photographer and cinematographer whose screen credits were to include *Ring of Bright Water*, *Get Carter* and *Living Free*.

Julian Huxley was evidently the most entrepreneurial of zoologists. Later famous as a participant in the BBC's *Brains Trust* programmes, he teamed up in 1934 with the unlikeliest, yet most obvious, collaborator in order to produce a documentary film: Alexander Korda. Korda, throughout his life vulnerable to the charge of vulgar showmanship, commissioned Grierson (and Osmond Borradaile) to film a fifteen-minuter called *The Private Life of the Gannets* – which went on to win an Academy Award. Korda, 'striving always not to be second-rate' (according to Muir Matheson), later told Paul Rotha that, of all his films, this was the one for which he would most like to be remembered.

If the documentary movement was a trifle earnest, socially committed and penny-pinching, the same could hardly be said of London Films, the house of Korda. A byword for extravagance and show by the time he settled in England, Korda liked to spend money he didn't have, stay in homes he couldn't afford and embark upon projects that had limited prospects of completion. Yet he also produced a string of immensely popular

* Edith Tudor-Hart who, like her brother, became a highly successful photographer.

masterpieces of mass entertainment. A man of prodigious charm and energy who found it difficult to delegate, Korda was frequently on set, itching to get behind the cameras himself. The fact that he did, in fact, direct two of his most successful British films, *The Private Life of Henry VIII* (1933) and *Rembrandt* (1936), both starring Charles Laughton, only increased Korda's confidence in himself and his team. Both films had been carefully designed by Vincent Korda, with elaborate touches of authentic Tudor and Dutch detail, while the scripts (Biro had a big hand in each) nicely projected the wit and impulsiveness of Henry and the poignancy of the ageing Rembrandt.

In the mid-1930s Korda bestrode English film making like a colossus. Denham became his Xanadu, Chaplin and Fairbanks his US business partners, Prudential Assurance his financiers. The glory days didn't last as Korda, and then the entire British film industry, went through a period of severe financial crisis. But Korda whistled bravely into the wind, and audiences, probably oblivious of his volatile fortunes, poured into the cinemas to enjoy his latest extravaganzas, from *Sanders of the River* and *The Ghost Goes West* (both 1935) and the futurological *Things to Come* (1936) to that further trio of imperial adventures *Elephant Boy* (1937), *The Drum* (1938) and *The Four Feathers* (1939). In these and many other Korda movies it was often the costumes and sets that stayed in the mind rather than the subtlety of individual performances. Designs were usually by Alex's brother Vincent; both loved spectacle. By 1939, when Alex was producing the remake of *The Thief of Bagdad*, he was forever on set, countermanding the instructions of his chosen director, Ludwig Berger, bringing in others (including Michael Powell) to shoot scenes and constantly ordering wide shots at the expense of close-up and character.

Korda was not alone in the 1930s in thinking of film as spectacle. These were the great days of producers like David O. Selznick and Sam Goldwyn, of Cecil B. DeMille and Busby Berkeley – and of Riefenstahl's *Triumph of the Will* and *Olympia*. But it was Korda who brought these values to British film production, Korda who gave the British industry the confidence to undertake international films, movies that would stand up by comparison with those produced anywhere else in the world. And it was Korda who gave work and creative opportunities to a generation of exiled artists whose influence upon British film and television would be felt for a generation and beyond.

The Thief of Bagdad was running over time and over budget. Korda needed to raise money for this and other projects and, once Britain was at war (and filming in Egypt and Arabia now out of the question), he considered transferring production of *The Thief* to the USA. In February 1940 he went to America. In April Michael Powell and Emeric Pressburger sailed to Canada on the research grant they had obtained from Kenneth Clark. In May both parties returned to Britain. Korda had secured multi-million dollar loans from banks in New York and Los Angeles, and promptly went back to the USA for an extended stay. Pressburger, meanwhile, had written the outline of *49th Parallel*, a film that he and Powell (not to mention the Ministry of Information) hoped might help convince the Americans they should join the war.

It was not the first Powell and Pressburger production. After meeting on *The Spy in Black*, the pair had made *Contraband*, a comedy thriller (a vehicle for Conrad Veidt) in which the blackout background lent itself to the sharp shadow play so characteristic of earlier Expressionist film. But the film with which the pair announced themselves as a major new force was *49th Parallel*, with its contrast between the tightly structured community of stranded Germans and the (literal) great openness of Canadian democracy. Edited by the young David Lean, with a score by Vaughan Williams, it reached its climax in a speech delivered to the Nazis by the leader of the Hutterites. Anton Walbrook spoke Pressburger's lines with deep conviction:

You call us Germans – you call us Brothers. Yes, we are Germans, we older people. Our names are German, our tongue is German . . . But we are not your brothers. Our Germany is dead today . . . Our children grow up against new backgrounds, new horizons . . .

You talk of the New Order in Europe! ... You and your Führer are like the microbes of some filthy disease filled with a longing to multiply yourselves by thousands of millions until you destroy everything healthy in the world.

49th Parallel was a popular triumph, not only in Britain and Canada but also in the USA, and Powell and Pressburger soon developed the idea of creating their own production company, 'The Archers', which for the next decade came up with a stream of memorable collaborations 'Written, Produced and Directed by Michael Powell and Emeric Pressburger'. Pressburger, the Hungarian charmer bursting with visual imagination, provided plot and screenplay, while Powell, the mercurial English public schoolboy, would direct. But both men were involved in every stage of the process, arguing over casting, budgets, locations, script, shots, edits and titles. Yin and yang, animus and anima: from the dialectic of opposites something emerged that was bigger than either could have produced alone. The Archers were a marriage of complementary talents in which the squabbles were always superseded by agreed solutions. The results provided an aesthetic document of British tastes and values throughout the war and after.

Watch some of the major wartime British films, not just those of The Archers, and one theme tends to stand out above all others. Britain might be class-ridden; officers speak with a cut-glass accent while the lower ranks tend to sound cockney. But the demands of war have thrown all ranks and classes together. In Britain (as opposed to Germany) war is the great leveller, a force for democracy. Nor was this new camaraderie restricted to depictions of the fighting services. Whether a film was portraying men trapped on a holed ship, a neighbourhood united in the face of bomb damage, villagers plotting against an occupying platoon of disguised Germans or King Henry V moving anonymously among his troops before Agincourt, the message was similar: what unites us is more significant than what divides us.

This was common currency. It is there in documentaries produced by the armed services and by Humphrey Jennings for the Crown Film Unit (successor to the GPO Unit), in highly wrought features by Noël Coward (*In Which We Serve*), Alberto Cavalcanti (*Went the Day Well?*) or Carol Reed (*The Way Ahead*) and in the films of Powell and Pressburger. But there was something especially moving, perhaps, in watching a disparate cast of characters united in adversity in films like *One of Our Aircraft Is Missing* (1942) or *A Canterbury Tale* (1944) that had been created by the fertile imagination of a grateful refugee.

The most ambitious, the most successful and in many ways the most characteristic of The Archers' wartime films was *The Life and Death of Colonel Blimp*. Blimp was the name the cartoonist David Low had given to his apoplectic retired colonel, a red-faced, pot-bellied, moustachioed old boy given to spouting outdated imperialist, xenophobic and racist platitudes. Easy to make fun of. Yet Pressburger recognised that the caricature embodied some of the virtues of the British as well as their prejudices. He also knew that every intolerant veteran had once been a flaming radical and fell to wondering how the crusty old Blimp of 1942 had come to be that way. The theme had been crystallised in a line Pressburger had originally written into an earlier script where an older man reflects to a young colleague: 'I was just like you thirty years ago and you'll be just like me thirty years from now.'

Pressburger's Blimp-like character is called Clive Candy, and the film starts and ends with his humiliation during World War Two at the hands of a bunch of brash and prankish young soldiers. In between, we learn from a series of vignettes how a courageous and honourable gentleman born in High Victorian England might have developed through the intervening decades. Candy (a role written for Olivier but eventually taken by Roger Livesey) is a thoroughly likeable, clubbable innocent who believes that wars should be conducted, like sport, according to agreed rules. Those who fight fairly will win. 'The Germans have shelled hospitals, bombed open towns, sunk neutral ships, used poison gas – and *we won*!' he says exultantly when the war ends in 1918. Candy apparently gained the Victoria Cross for extreme gallantry in the Boer War. But, like Don Giovanni who never actually succeeds with any of the women he pursues, Candy is portrayed as a somewhat quixotic character who recurrently charges at evasive targets, is serially unlucky in love and wins no more than token rewards. The walls of his house are crammed with stuffed animal heads, a growing tally of trophies later augmented by a portrait of his dead wife.

There are two constants in Candy's life. The first is that (like Hoffmann, and in some ways like Pressburger himself) he keeps falling in love with the same woman. The girl he meets in Berlin in 1902, the wife he marries in 1919 and his young ATS driver in 1942 are all played by the same actress (the twenty-two-year-old Deborah Kerr). And he develops a profound friendship with a 'good' German, Theo, whose presence at pivotal moments in his life becomes the film's central leitmotif. In the 1902 sequence Candy and Theo (played by Anton Walbrook) fight a pointless duel, injure each other and find themselves recovering in the same convalescent home. Theo falls in love with an English girl whom he meets through Candy. In 1919 Theo is a prisoner of war in England; at first he spurns Candy's offer of friendship but the bond is eventually renewed when he joins him at a gentlemen's dinner party. Twenty years later Theo is a refugee from Hitler, seeking clearance from the sceptical British authorities.

It was provocative, to say the least, writing a 'good German' into a British film script in 1942, and *Blimp* ran into serious political trouble. Churchill himself wanted it stopped. Perhaps he sensed himself in some of the Blimpery he assumed it made fun of. In the event, government disapproval merely helped boost the film's public reputation and ensure its success. The first colour movie produced by The Archers, *Blimp* was designed by Alfred Junge (like Pressburger, a product of UFA) and looked ravishing. The musical score by Allan Gray was constantly upbeat and gave the proceedings a cheeky lilt that belied its 163 minutes and prevented it from ever becoming solemn. The great historical set pieces – the Berlin music café and duel in 1902,* the gentlemen's

---

* The build-up to the duel scene greatly impressed the young Martin Scorsese. It had, he wrote, 'an almost religious quality in the way it shows the ritual, and it had a direct influence on the way I showed very little of the actual fights in *Raging Bull*'.

dinner party in 1919 – were impeccably researched, written and shot. The cast all gained critical plaudits, especially Roger Livesey for his virtuoso portrayal (comparable to that of Robert Donat in *Goodbye Mr Chips* or Orson Welles in *Citizen Kane*) of an ambitious young man whom we see ageing scene by scene.

But the spine of the film was the friendship between the Blimp character and the 'good' German. As in *49th Parallel*, it was given to Walbrook to deliver the most memorable and moving lines in the film. It is November 1939 and Theo is having to undergo interrogation. He explains that he left Germany in 1934. 'Most refugees left Germany early in 1933,' says his British interlocutor, 'when Hitler came to power.'

Theo answers that he thought he had nothing to fear from Hitler. 'It took me eight months to find out I was wrong.'

'Rather a long time,' says the British agent. Silence from Theo. 'Don't you think so?'

'Please, I mean no offence – but you in England took five years.'

So why did Theo come to Britain? He says he is a tired old man who has come here because he is homesick. He explains to his uncomprehending interrogator that his wife was English and that she died in 1933. Their two sons went over to the Nazis and did not even attend her funeral. Theo then recalls his friendship with Candy, the convalescent home they shared forty years earlier, the dinner party in 1919 when 'a party of distinguished men tried their utmost to comfort me when the defeat of my country seemed to me unbearable' – and 'the countryside, the gardens, the green lawns, the weedy rivers and the trees' of England that his wife loved so much.

The speech was delivered in the restrained and dignified tones of Anton Walbrook. But the voice behind the voice was surely that of Pressburger himself – admiring, deferential, sceptical – and, through him, of every refugee from Nazism.

Pressburger's wartime movies evoke a quirky but welcoming Britain in which petty differences are subordinated to the common cause. But they often had other trademarks as well, hints of an emerging Archers' style that would go on to stamp itself on post-war film production. There was usually a playful touch to a Pressburger script, a streak of filmic bravado designed to add wonderment and mystery. Several Archers productions begin with a visual coup: a pilotless plane (*Aircraft*), a hawk that turns into a plane (*Canterbury Tale*) or a plane on fire which is about to crash (*A Matter of Life and Death*). The opening credits of *Blimp* acknowledge David Low, 'creator of the mortal Blimp' – at which some leaves fall from a tree to turn the adjective into 'immortal'. Sometimes the credits are ingeniously built into the storyline (the ending of *Aircraft*, the opening of *I Know Where I'm Going*). Often Pressburger would place gently alienating devices in mid-film, too. There is an extravagant dream sequence aboard an overnight train in *I Know Where I'm Going* in which top hats become steam engine funnels. In *A Matter of Life and Death*, where heaven is portrayed in monochrome and life on earth in colour (the two are connected by a giant escalator), Marius Goring comes down to earth to collect the supposedly dead David Niven, smiles to the camera and says wearily how 'one is starved for technicolour up there!'

The visual impact of The Archers' early productions was powerful yet understated. Eschewing the flamboyance of the Korda brothers, Powell and Pressburger leaned towards the subtler talents of Alfred Junge or, later, Hein Heckroth. Not that The Archers avoided making a big statement when the occasion required. The giant stairway to heaven or the great 'trial' that takes place there between the historic values of Britain and America in *A Matter of Life and Death*, for example – such images pack symbolic content, like the class-ridden skyscraper in Fritz Lang's *Metropolis*, while Pressburger's UFA baptism is surely also evident in the fantasmagorical decor of later films like *The Red Shoes* and *The Tales of Hoffmann*.

It may seem odd, almost perverse, that the person who actually wrote the screenplay to such films was a man to whom English was merely his fourth or fifth language. But some émigrés became more expert in their adopted language than many who were born to it. Karl Popper, who struggled to present complex philosophical thoughts into acceptable English, noted that 'English standards of writing were utterly different, and far higher than German standards. For example, no German reader minds polysyllables. In English, one has to learn to be repelled by them.' Pressburger became a connoisseur of language, a voracious consumer of reference books, punctilious in his search for the *mot juste* and (in the felicitous phrase of his biographer) 'immune to cliché'. He sweated over his screenplays, paring away padding, entering the spirit of the characters he created. His daughter remembered him as a man of insatiable curiosity.

> He was always studying how people went about their everyday business – tradesmen who came to the house, taxi drivers, clerks, shopkeepers . . . Tradesmen all loved him because he took such an interest. He always used to invite the dustmen in for a beer and chat to them for a quarter of an hour . . . I remember going to the butcher as a young girl and he would stand for what seemed like hours, discussing the various cuts of meat, the names for them in English, how they should be cooked – and how that compared to how they were cooked in Hungary or Italy – all in tremendous detail. He loved detail.

In his novel *Prater Violet*, Christopher Isherwood portrays a refugee film maker. Isherwood's principal model is Berthold Viertel (who proved he was as English as the next man by directing *Rhodes of Africa* – before going on to the USA) and the personality Isherwood sketches is of a deeply pessimistic Central European in the 1930s anticipating war. But parts of Isherwood's affectionate caricature might have applied to Pressburger, as seen, perhaps, by a young English assistant.

> During those first weeks our working day steadily increased in length, until I had to make a stand, and insist on going home to supper. He seemed determined to possess me utterly. He pursued me with questions about my friends, my interests, my habits, my love-life. The week-ends, especially, were the objects of his endless, jealous curiosity. What did I do? Whom did I see? Did I live like a monk? 'Is it Mr. W. H. you seek, or the Dark Lady of the Sonnets?' . . .

And (like Pressburger):

> . . . [He] talked to taxi-drivers, to medical students in bars, to elderly colonels returning from their clubs, to clergymen, to Piccadilly tarts, to the boys who hung around the medallion of W. S. Gilbert on the Embankment. Nobody seemed to mind, or even to misunderstand his intentions. I envied him his freedom: the freedom of a foreigner.

'The freedom of a foreigner.' Maybe Pressburger remained a foreigner after all. But perhaps that was not such a bad thing to be. One is reminded once again of the positive answer the father of the refugee family gives in the Judith Kerr novel when his daughter asks if they'll ever really belong anywhere. 'I suppose not,' said Papa. 'Not the way people belong who have lived in one place all their lives. But we'll belong a little in lots of places, and I think that may be just as good.' It was a philosophy that would have appealed to Emeric Pressburger. He knew where he was going.

CHAPTER ELEVEN

'Somewhere in England'

The war had two opposing effects on British cultural life. On the one hand things became decentralised as never before. Many of the nation's historic and artistic treasures were removed from London for safety (just as thousands of children left London and the Home Counties to live with families in less vulnerable parts of the country). A number of the great cultural institutions, too, were evacuated from the capital. But for all the 'de-metropolitanisation' of British cultural life – BBC outposts in Bristol, Bedford or Evesham, or the temporary dismemberment of London University and the re-establishment of its colleges up and down the country – a contrary trend was becoming perceptible. The exigencies of war produced the most *dirigiste* government in modern British history. Everything had to be ordained from headquarters. The politics might have been democratic, but attitudes became quasi-military. No ifs, no buts, people said. Don't you know there's a war on? Civilian organisations developed chains of command, with ranks and grades known by initials and nicknames. If government needed to expropriate a building, such as London University's Senate House or the LSE site, it would do so. If Ralph Hawkes's wind instrument factory in Edgware had to be converted to munitions production or part of Korda's Denham studios become a sugar store, so be it. There was nothing sinister about this. Or not much. By and large, people accepted the principle, if not every individual instance. The war had to be won and everything was subordinated to that effort. The result, however, was an unprecedented degree of government involvement in the nation's intellectual and cultural activities.

In the garden at Glyndebourne (1936): Rudolf Bing, general manager; Fritz Busch, conductor and artistic director; and Carl Ebert, producer and artistic director.

Fritz Busch in rehearsal.

Karl Rankl with Constance Shacklock
(October 1948), working on the score of
Der Rosenkavalier. Shacklock was one of
the many young British singers whom
Rankl encouraged when he was musical
director at Covent Garden.

(*Below*) Kurt Jooss and Rudolf Laban
at Dartington Hall (1939).

(*Above and below right*) Jooss's most famous ballet, *The Green Table*.

Drawing by Laban, showing how the body is capable of moving in most spatial directions.

Berthold Lubetkin's Penguin Pool at London Zoo (*top*, 1934) was one of the earliest and most striking examples of architectural modernism in Britain – as was the de la Warr Pavilion at Bexhill-on-Sea (*above* and *right*, 1934-5) by Eric Mendelsohn and Serge Chermayeff.

THIS
PLATE WAS LAID BY
THE MAYOR OF BEXHILL
THE RIGHT HONOURABLE
EARL DE LA WAR
ON 6TH MAY
1935
ERICH MENDELSOHN
SERGE CHERMAYEFF
F.R.I.B.A. CHERMAYEFF

The Royal Festival Hall was the first major public building erected in Britain after the
Second World War (and the only permanent feature of the 1951 Festival of Britain).
The architect placed in charge of its detailed design was the German-born Peter Moro.

Impington Village College, Histon, Cambridgeshire (1936-9) by Walter Gropius and Maxwell Fry. *Above*: architects' model; *below*: bay windows.

'The Horn' and 'The Wagner Tuba', cartoons by
Gerard Hoffnung dating from the mid-1950s.

Martin Esslin (*right*)
with Samuel Beckett
at a rehearsal of
Beckett's *Krapp's
Last Tape*.

Did this mean that art became confused with propaganda? Yes, sometimes. But all art reflects the values of its creators. If some of Powell and Pressburger's wartime films, Kokoschka's paintings or Koestler's broadcasts were harnessed to the war effort, who can say that the results were thereby compromised?

These two trends, the diffusion around the country of aspects of the nation's cultural life counterpointed by increasingly centralised decision making, were to cast long shadows in the decades to follow. Indeed, the uneasy coexistence between them was a recurrent theme in the cultural history of Britain throughout the second half of the twentieth century. The two tendencies – the forces of centrifugality and those of centripetality – were to provide the framework within which the émigrés from Middle Europe sought to provide a distinctive voice in their new land.

Some, a fortunate few, established themselves early. Hayek, Wellesz and Kokoschka, for example, were already well-known figures before the war, while Gombrich, Esslin and Weidenfeld rapidly became highly respected in the BBC and beyond. Anne Bohm found good work at the LSE in Cambridge, as did Sebastian Isepp in Aberystwyth and then at the Ashmolean in Oxford. But for many, including some of the most talented, the war years were a period of alternating frustration and fulfilment, idleness and overwork.

When the war broke out, theatres closed, publishers succumbed to the twin forces of censorship and paper rationing, and the BBC scheduled nothing but news and lightweight theatre organ recitals. Or so it seemed to some of the exiles,* huddling in chilly bedsits wondering what was to happen to them. Internment was a nadir for many, especially the older among the refugees; their emergence, like that of any prisoner allowed out of captivity, did not always provide the opportunities freedom had seemed to promise.

Some never fully recovered the élan of their earlier lives. Claus Moser's parents, accustomed to the dazzling world of wealthy

---

* Not only to the exiles. Kenneth Clark noted: 'For some mysterious patriotic reason the BBC provided no serious music, but endless programmes of "Sandy Macpherson at the Organ".'

and cultured Berlin, settled stoically in their semi-detached house in Putney. The painters Ludwig Meidner and Kurt Schwitters never felt at home or adequately appreciated in Britain and neither ever fully recovered from the experience of having to go into exile. Alfred Kerr, whose incisive critical pronouncements had illuminated the inter-war renaissance of the German theatre, lost his public voice and thereby his authority, once he had lost his language.* Elias Canetti railed against what he regarded as the philistinism and insouciance of his new countrymen. His apocalyptic German-language novel *Die Blendung* was translated into English by C. V. Wedgwood as *Auto-da-Fé* and hailed by the young Iris Murdoch as 'one of the few great novels of the century', while *Crowds and Power* was a virtuoso cross-disciplinary analysis and evocation of the dangers of populist Fascism. Canetti went on to receive the Nobel Prize for Literature for 'writings marked by a broad outlook, a wealth of ideas and artistic power'. But he never felt that he and his work were fully appreciated in Britain.

For others, however, especially younger émigrés with portable, adaptable skills, life in Britain gradually began to create new opportunities. For a while, blackout enveloped the land and places of entertainment were ordered to close their doors. Then, like the palace guards in *The Sleeping Beauty* or the toys in *The Nutcracker*, an eye blinked open here, a limb stirred there, a light went on – and a semblance of London's normal artistic life, particularly its musical life, returned. Myra Hess began her National Gallery concerts. The London Philharmonic Orchestra played every Sunday at the Queen's Hall and the Proms were promised for 1940. Chamber ensembles emerged out of nowhere; in 1941 Karl Haas founded what was to become (in 1943) the London Baroque Ensemble, precursor of the post-war

---

* One is reminded of the speech by Thomas Mowbray, Duke of Norfolk, on his banishment in *Richard II*:

> The language I have learn'd these forty years
> . . . now I must forgo:
> And now my tongue's use is to me no more
> Than an unstrung viol or a harp . . .

George Steiner recounts that, as a young German-speaking boy, raised in Paris, this was the first Shakespeare speech he was made to learn by heart.

baroque revival. String quartets and singers took up where they had left off – at the Wigmore Hall and a variety of smaller venues such as Friends' House in Euston. The Royal Academy and Royal College of Music continued to train their young charges while, at Morley College, Michael Tippett gathered around him an impressive array of teaching and performing musicians, many of them refugees. Among these were the soprano Ilse Wolf, young violinists like Maria Lidka and Norbert Brainin, that early advocate of baroque music in general and the recorder in particular, Walter Bergmann and the composer and musicologist Mátyás Seiber. They were an entrepreneurial lot and most did other work. Seiber helped Francis Chagrin to found the Committee (later the Society) for the Promotion of New Music. Bergmann worked for the music publishers Schott (whose rivals, Boosey and Hawkes, snapped up a clutch of refugees from Vienna: Alfred Kalmus, Ernst Roth and Erwin Stein).

Among the musicians at Morley College, the one who was probably closest to Tippett was Walter Goehr, a Berliner who had studied with Schoenberg. Goehr had come to England in the early 1930s to a job at the Gramophone Company (where he shared offices at one time with Walter Legge). Here, in the infant recording industry, Goehr thrived, turning his multivalent musical facility to whatever was required. He coached, arranged, orchestrated, accompanied, conducted. He loved it, and was soon in demand at the BBC where (as conductor of the Orchestre Raymonde) he rearranged large scores for the fifteen players at his disposal (a skill he had acquired in his Schoenberg days) and conducted regular broadcasts of light classics. During the war, Goehr moved his wife and young son Alexander to the safety of Amersham, while he himself, a jobbing musician of enormous versatility and preternaturally a big city man, spent as much time as he could in London. He positively revelled in the work and play available in the wartime capital, arranging and conducting BBC concerts and film scores* and putting his own

---

* Goehr conducted and/or helped arrange the musical scores of several Powell and Pressburger films, and composed the music for David Lean's 1946 masterpiece *Great Expectations*.

money into the 'Walter Goehr Orchestra' that performed at the Wigmore Hall. Morley College was a natural magnet to a man of Goehr's background and talents, and many of the refugee musicians who worked there had their first performing experiences under Goehr's baton. He pioneered the first performances in modern times of a work that was then virtually unknown and has gone on to become almost standard repertory: Monteverdi's *Vespers*. In 1944 Goehr conducted the world première of Tippett's oratorio *A Child of Our Time*, a searing work inspired by the tragic event that had precipitated the pogrom of *Kristallnacht*.

Alexander Goehr remembers that it was at the BBC that his father felt most at home – especially once he had found a special niche as, effectively, composer-in-residence to the BBC's celebrated Features Department. If you wanted to compose, arrange, play or conduct, the BBC was the place to apply and many refugee musicians found a temporary home there. Few, however, were as fortunate, or became as established, as Walter Goehr. As the BBC, like so many other London-based institutions, removed some of its departments to safer parts of the country, the people you needed to see were often scattered. Sir Adrian Boult's BBC Symphony Orchestra was evacuated to Bristol and, when that city became vulnerable to the blitz, to Bedford, which nobody imagined even Hitler would want to bomb. Just in case he did, broadcast concerts were announced as coming to you from 'somewhere in England'.

What was most characteristic of these years, in fact, was the dissemination of music and the other performing arts throughout the country. Many London theatres, like Covent Garden and Sadler's Wells, were converted to wartime functions or else simply closed their doors* (an additional reason why private theatre companies like the *Laterndl* were so highly valued). The destruction by a bomb of London's premier concert venue, the Queen's Hall, close to the BBC's London headquarters, in mid-

---

* A notable exception being the Windmill Theatre where the vaudeville girls continued to strip throughout the worst of the blitz, thereby acquiring the famous slogan: 'We never closed!'

May 1941 was thus an emblematic as well as a literal loss.* Major musical events, including the Proms, were eventually moved to the Royal Albert Hall in South Kensington, while empty theatres like the Cambridge and the Stoll† were pressed into service as temporary concert venues. But never again would London dominate the nation's musical life quite so completely as it had done hitherto. The London Philharmonic Orchestra, the band that had played the final Queen's Hall concert (and lost many of its instruments in the bombing), took to the road. Berta Geissmar, charged with administering the LPO's affairs, recognised that touring was the route to survival. She was robbed of her greatest attraction, for the orchestra's founder-conductor, Sir Thomas Beecham, was in Australia. But one of the men to whom the LPO handed the baton on its provincial tours was to prove just as big a draw (and no mean conductor): the popular Viennese tenor – and himself another refugee from Hitler – Richard Tauber.

London's loss proved the provinces' gain, and not just in music. With the encouragement of the newly formed CEMA, Lewis Casson and his wife Sybil Thorndike took a company of Old Vic actors on a tour of the mining towns of South Wales, while another Old Vic company played *King John* to capacity audiences all over Lancashire. Ninette de Valois led the Sadler's Wells ballet across the nation and beyond (including to the Netherlands in May 1940, where they were nearly stranded by the German invasion and only managed to return to England in the most dramatic circumstances). Joan Cross, meanwhile, took a tiny Vic-Wells operatic troupe, with no more than a couple of props and a piano, to perform *Traviata* and *Figaro* to enthusiastic audiences in Oldham, Accrington, Stockport and Burnley. Burnley, in fact, became the headquarters of the Vic-Wells in exile for a couple of years. From here they toured throughout the north and north-west, returning for short seasons, and then more or less permanently, to the New Theatre (now the Albery) in St Martin's Lane, London. This was the

---

* The same massive raid destroyed the chamber of the House of Commons.
† The Stoll, just south of Holborn tube station, closed in 1957 and was demolished.

theatre from which the three Vic-Wells companies – drama, opera and (especially) de Valois's ballet – began to position themselves for possible independence after the war. When the opera company arrived at the New Theatre in 1942 it marked its return to the capital with a brand-new production of Mozart's *The Magic Flute*. The producer was Kurt Jooss.

Since arriving in England in 1934, Jooss and his dance company, from their base at Dartington Hall, had spent at least half of each year touring. To a British public inured to frilly tutus and dying swans, the Ballets Jooss must have provided something of a shock, with their angular 'free dance' movements and expressionist choreography. A number of new Jooss productions appeared during the 1930s, which the company also included on their tours of Western Europe and North and South America. Most were designed by Hein Heckroth with music by Fritz Cohen – though the score to *Chronica* (1939), a Renaissance-era parable about the evils that flow from dictatorship, was by another refugee composer whom we last encountered working with Carl Ebert in Darmstadt: Berthold Goldschmidt.

In 1940 'enemy aliens' were ordered away from the southern coasts, and Jooss and his colleagues had to leave Dartington. Several, including Jooss himself, were interned, while the remnants of the company toured America (and had difficulty returning); Heckroth was temporarily transported to Australia. For a while it seemed inconceivable that the Ballets Jooss – much less the Jooss–Leeder school – could ever be revived. But Jooss re-established operations, this time in Cambridge with Keynes's Arts Theatre as home base. While the company regrouped, Jooss was invited by another peripatetic company, the Vic-Wells opera, to undertake a couple of its productions.

'The danger of importing a producer for opera from another sphere of theatrical art', pontificated the influential critic Edwin Evans on Jooss's production of *Figaro*, 'is that, whereas musicians would trust the music to hold the attention, they are inclined to put insufficient faith in it and impart too much movement.' The secret, he believed, lay in drawing the line between animation and fussiness. Did Jooss succeed? He did.

But only just. According to Evans, Jooss 'carried vivacity to a point where a little more might have become irritating'. Fortunately, 'he succeeded in keeping on the right side of that decisive line'. From this distance it is impossible to judge how far and to what effect Jooss's production of *Figaro* (or his *Magic Flute*) benefited from having a producer who was in essence a choreographer. But there is a wonderful photograph of a scene from Jooss's *Figaro* showing the bewigged and tricorned men bowing deeply to curtseying ladies, and the whole thing suggests a rare sense of sweep and movement.

Jooss, reunited with Leeder and Heckroth, picked up the threads of his company and launched, once more, into a round of tours, while refreshing his repertoire when time allowed. The wartime pace was frenetic and performances inevitably showed the strain. The arresting originality of *The Green Table* was unlikely to be reproduced at its umpteenth performance in yet another draughty provincial hall a dozen years after its première. But a new Jooss ballet like *Pandora* was an event of artistic importance. Designed by Heckroth with music by Roberto Gerhard,* *Pandora* was first performed at the Cambridge Arts Theatre in 1944. Inside the box of gifts offered by the beautiful Pandora are all the evils and miseries of mankind – eagerly grabbed by materialist characters like the Go-Getter. Pandora is contrasted with the ethereal and virtuous figure of Psyche. In Heckroth's striking designs, Pandora was clad in crimson, white and purple, and wore a headdress of snakes. The elemental struggle between the forces of Good and Evil, between spiritual and material values, may seem over-blown today. But the message of *Pandora*, as well as the visual extravagance of its treatment, must have had strong appeal for audiences in 1944.

Jooss was one of many artists whose wartime work was financed, in part or whole, by CEMA. The initial creation of CEMA would have meant little or nothing to most of Britain's

---

* Gerhard, born in Spain in 1896, studied in Germany and attended the Schoenberg class, going on to become the leading avant-garde composer in Spain, before fleeing from Franco and settling in England. Based in Cambridge, Gerhard continued to compose, achieving widespread recognition by the 1960s.

Hitler émigrés in 1940. Most had come from countries where government routinely subsidised film and art galleries, theatres and orchestras, and now controlled them; that kind of thing, they sensed, didn't happen in Britain where culture, if starved of funds, was at least able to remain independent of politics. In any case, few of the refugees had much interest in the politics of artistic finance and administration in their new country at this moment in their lives for they had more pressing things to think about. But to many, CEMA would soon become a lifeline as Tom Jones's idea bore fruit, Pilgrim Trust money was replaced by Treasury money and, for the first time in Britain's history, the principle was established of regular government funding for the arts. Not just the Ballets Jooss and Vic-Wells ballet but the Ballet Rambert, too, benefited from CEMA funding during the war; not just the Vic-Wells opera but the doyen of touring companies, the Carl Rosa Opera (whose music director during the pivotal period 1943–5 was the Czech-born conductor Walter Susskind). All toured the country with help from CEMA, as did chamber ensembles such as the Blech Quartet, while a young Lancastrian contralto called Kathleen Ferrier learned her trade on 'CEMA safaris'. The refugee violinist Ida Haendel, a Polish-born teenager accustomed to being chaperoned everywhere by her father, was whisked off in a jeep for a CEMA recital in a military mess room ('about one and a half hours from London') packed with American bomber pilots and crews. The men were weary but appreciative and Ida, who got back to her concerned parents at two in the morning, went on to give dozens of CEMA concerts up and down the country.

Shortly after CEMA came into existence, a parallel organisation, soon to become a rival, was launched. This was the Entertainments National Service Association, headquartered in the Drury Lane Theatre. ENSA was initially intended to complement the activities of CEMA: where CEMA would disseminate the work of serious artists, ENSA would concentrate on mass popular entertainment. CEMA believed its job was to subsidise touring art exhibitions, symphony orchestras, string quartets, Shakespearean theatre companies and the like while ENSA, presumably, was there to send comedians and light entertainers such as George Formby around the factory, workshop and garrison canteens of Britain and beyond. But the distinction between these two roles soon became blurred. Fundamentally, the clash between the subsidising bodies prefigured a philosophical issue that was to cloud post-war arts policy for the rest of the century: the nature of 'art' as opposed to 'entertainment'. But it was also a matter of politics and personalities. ENSA was run by the theatrical producer Basil Dean, not a person predisposed to limit his ambitions. And as his music supremo, Dean engaged a man who was rapidly emerging as perhaps the most forceful musical impresario in the country: Walter Legge.

Legge was the leading record producer at HMV (and part-time music critic for the *Manchester Guardian*). Beecham had invited him to act as his Assistant Artistic Director at Covent Garden for the two seasons before the outbreak of war and put him in charge of casting. By the time he came to ENSA, therefore, Legge (who could speak German like a native) was on intimate terms with the world's greatest classical musicians. He enjoyed planning their artistic peregrinations and, like a military general or movie mogul, issuing orders from his centre of command and control. A man with a taste for power and controversy, Legge could be stubborn beyond endurance, insisting against the conventional wisdom of colleagues on recording this piece or using that singer. But the worst of it was that he was usually right. When Legge called, you came. This had worked at HMV and at Covent Garden. It was how he intended to conduct business at ENSA.

In keeping with the spirit of the times, Legge saw his job as taking culture out of London to the troops and workers – sometimes out of Britain – but retaining control of every detail. A tug on a string here and the Sadler's Wells ballet would pirouette off for another forces' tour. A tweak there and to the Mediterranean front went the pianist Solomon to perform on whatever pianos were available. Orchestras in desperate need of funds would be given a series of concerts. The Liverpool orchestra, recently established on a permanent basis by David Webster, benefited from Legge's munificence, as did Manchester's Hallé Orchestra under its new conductor John

Barbirolli. Berta Geissmar described the exhausted members of the LPO travelling from one draughty venue to the next, missing a concert because of fog, losing their instruments because a railway van was misdirected and sleeping in ARP blankets on the floor of the local town hall after a performance.

Orchestras, like theatrical troupes and university departments, were often hard put to produce a full complement and had to be manned (and womanned) by whoever was available – in other words, people who, for whatever reason, were not doing war work. On the outbreak of war the BBC Symphony Orchestra lost some thirty of its youngest players. When Barbirolli arrived in Manchester in 1943 and realised he had scarcely the bare bones of an orchestra at his disposal, he rapidly set up auditions, joking grimly that the Hallé would take anybody, whatever was wrong with them, so long as they could play their instrument. This meant the disabled, the too old, the too young – and the refugees. Indeed, every orchestra in the country turned to the refugee community to boost its depleted ranks.

The presence in Britain of such a pleiade of musical talent from Central Europe created something of a problem for the Establishment. Nobody resented the brilliance of Susskind, Stein and Stadlen, Haas, Haendel and Hamburger, Goehr, Gál, Gellhorn and Goldschmidt. All were welcomed and encouraged for the glittering contribution they could make. But their very presence tended to reinforce the Central European dominance of musical life from which a generation of British composers and practitioners had been trying to wean themselves. It was not that Holst, Vaughan Williams, Bax, Ireland or Walton disdained the talents of Bach, Beethoven and Brahms, or that Beecham or Henry Wood did not admire the outstanding continental singers and instrumentalists they regularly engaged. On the contrary. Their challenge was to find the confidence to shake off the continental shackles, to move beyond Brahms, to find a characteristically British, or English, musical voice, to listen to Myra Hess as well as to Schnabel, to Sammons as to Kreisler, to the harmonies of the Tudors or the cadences of folk song as much as the art of fugue or the lilt of the ländler.

Nobody had done more to re-establish English music and music-making than Vaughan Williams. Profoundly, proudly English yet never insular, VW explored the idea of national character in his writings, used folk song in his compositions, and touched something of the pulse of traditional England in works such as the 'Greensleeves' and Tallis Fantasias, *On Wenlock Edge*, *The Lark Ascending* and the *London* and *Pastoral* symphonies. A patriot keen to pull his weight at a time of crisis, VW was 'desperate for useful work' as the clouds of war began to darken. Now in his late sixties, he had a vision of the kind of society Britain ought to be and of the civilised values he felt it should be fighting for. We have already encountered him arguing (with John Christie) that opera should be made accessible to a wider public, helping create CEMA and composing music for patriotic films (among them, *49th Parallel*, *Coastal Command*, *The Flemish Farm*); he was also on the committee that helped Myra Hess establish the National Gallery concerts. From his home in Dorking, south of London, VW started a series of lecture recitals, organised the local collection of salvage – and wrote streams of letters to the great and good throughout Britain and North America and beyond on behalf of refugees who needed work, money or a home.

Vaughan Williams's work for the Dorking Refugee Committee was paralleled on a national level when he was appointed Chairman of the Home Office Committee for the Release of Interned Alien Musicians. Many of the refugees who were later to enrich the wider musical world owed a debt of gratitude to Vaughan Williams. Yet, as this kindly man frankly acknowledged (in *National Music and Other Essays*):

> The problem of home-grown music has lately become acute owing to the friendly invasion of these shores by an army of distinguished German and Austrian musicians. [They] have great musical traditions behind them. In some ways they are more musically developed than we are and therein lies the danger.

One of the refugees found himself engaged in a fascinating

correspondence with Vaughan Williams. Ferdinand Rauter was an Austrian pianist and folk song collector (best known as accompanist to the Icelandic singer Engel Lund). In 1942 he invited Vaughan Williams to become Patron of the newly formed Anglo-Austrian Music Society. VW wrote back saying that the invitation had presented him with an acute dilemma.

> The great thing which frightens me in the late peaceful invasion of this country by Austria is that it will entirely devour the tender little flower of our English culture. The Austrians have a great musical tradition, and they are apt to think that it is the only musical tradition and that . . .they have a mission to impose their culture wherever they go as being the only one worth having.
>
> Now this seems to me to be all wrong.
>
> We cannot swallow the strong meat of your culture (even if we wished to) our stomachs are not strong enough – indigestion and finally artistic putrefaction would result. To try and make England, musically, a dependency of Austria could kill all the musical initiative in this country – destroy all that is vital and substitute a mechanical imita-tion of your great art – which will have no vitality, no roots in the soil and no power to grow to full stature.
>
> What do I suggest therefore? – We want your art and we want your help – Become Englishmen – try to assimilate our artistic ideals and then strengthen and fertilize them from your own incomparable art.

There is a tendency among the English, VW went on, to assume that if you are called Schmidt you are musical but not if you are called Smith. And he concluded with an appeal to Rauter and his fellow Austrians to 'help Smith to realise that he is musical, help him to discover where his artistic nature lies hidden and help it to grow to a full flower'.

It was a moving and revealing insight into the ambivalence felt by Vaughan Williams, and many other British musicians of his generation, towards the musical hegemony of Central Europe. Rauter, in his reply, pointed out with equal frankness and courtesy that, for their part, Austrian refugees like himself had not had much exposure to English music. But they were now trying 'to root themselves in British soil' and were beginning to understand 'that the musicality of the British people was existent too, even to an astonishing degree, but different'.

It was typical of Vaughan Williams (who of course agreed to become Patron of the Anglo-Austrian Music Society) to express not only a problem but also a possible solution. How far the refugee musicians took his advice and tried to assimilate, strengthen and fertilise British artistic ideals and (at least in their music) to 'become Englishmen' – this, as we shall see, is a rondo theme recurring throughout much British music and music-making over the half-century that followed.

During the war, many artistic enterprises thus benefited from two factors that had scarcely registered beforehand: the fountain of talent, especially musical, newly available from the refugee community, and the fillip provided by funding from CEMA and ENSA. Those in government pulling the strings were primarily concerned with retaining morale in wartime rather than with artistic policy, while the artists merely wanted the chance to work at what they did best and earn a little money. In the event, all were beneficiaries. Many refugee artists and entertainers were able to ply their trade and hone their skills, and to feel that, by so doing, they were playing a legitimate part in the overall project of winning the war. Conditions were challenging. Yet in those dark, chilly town halls and cinemas, on those endless bus trips to outlying factories and canteens, the seeds were sown for a new way of organising the arts in Britain, one that would attempt to steer between the Scylla of inadequate funding and the Charybdis of state control. Berta Geissmar had seen both extremes. Her old orchestra, the heavily subsidised Berlin Philharmonic, was now a tool of the Nazi state while the LPO, deprived of a wealthy peacetime clientele that was in any case a precarious basis for survival, lived off CEMA grants and slept on the floor under ARP blankets. 'Perhaps England will create a new way to support the arts,' she reflected towards the end of her autobiography, published in 1944, 'which will avoid the evil of governmental dictatorship on the one hand, and financial want . . . on the other.'

Her hopes were prescient. After the war, Britain was to embark upon precisely this path. But the journey was to be dogged by two further dichotomies which were also prefigured by the experience of wartime. The first we have already noted: the desire by the authorities to distribute cultural provision throughout the country while at the same time retaining centralised decision making. The second was the conflicting claims made on behalf of 'art' and 'entertainment' – another conflict of priorities that was to stalk the corridors of policy making for the rest of the century.

PART FOUR

CULTURE AT PEACE

CHAPTER TWELVE

Three Wise Men

It is spring 1936. Friedrich von Hayek has invited a fellow Austrian to deliver a paper to his seminar at the LSE, a philosopher named Karl Popper. Popper has recently made his name with the publication, in German, of a book on the logic of scientific discovery that picks up some of the topics of the famed 'Vienna Circle'. For his LSE presentation Popper chooses as his subject what 'he calls 'The Poverty of Historicism'. His appearance at Hayek's seminar attracts the big guns – Lionel Robbins and other LSE illuminati are present. So is another Vienna-born intellectual recently arrived in Britain: the art historian Ernst Gombrich. Over the next fifty years this trio – Hayek, Popper and Gombrich – will have a profound impact upon intellectual and cultural life in Britain, the wider English-speaking world and beyond.

Each was prodigiously learned, if a little earnest for pragmatic British or American tastes – in some ways the very archetype of the professor from *Mitteleuropa*. All three were to display throughout a long life the intellectual tenacity and self-discipline of pre-Hitlerian Europe at its finest. Complex arguments were consistently illustrated by fact, example and analogy, while contrary arguments would routinely be presented and rebutted. Above all, each of these three Austrian exiles, having seen the abyss to which transcendental, ideological thinking had led, was to mount a lifelong crusade against precisely the kind of metaphysical system building associated with some of their intellectual predecessors. Hayek, the economic theorist, turned his big guns against the idea of 'planning', while Popper, the philosopher, railed against Hegel and refused to acknowledge such empty abstractions as the 'spirit of the age'. And Gombrich, the art historian, when asked how he approached his task of explaining the development of art, replied, 'I just want common sense! This is my only method.'

As the fortunes of war turned and people in Britain gradually permitted themselves to imagine post-war society, every kind of Utopia seemed possible: a world where war was outlawed, nobody would go hungry or homeless, education and the arts would be available for all. Many talked enthusiastically of 'planning' and even of the 'nationalisation' of Britain's principal resources and services. Nor was this surprising in a country where victory had only seemed achievable by dint of the most rigorous central planning anyone could remember. Some more radical spirits (perhaps unaware yet of the full brutality of Stalinism) liked to point to Britain's ally, the Soviet Union, so recently feudal, which had industrialised in a mere generation or so with a series of Five Year Plans to the point that it was now capable of defeating the German war machine. Back home, by contrast, the absence of planning was said to have left Britain on the eve of war with an underproductive economy and a population that was class-ridden, much of it ill-educated, unemployed and/or sick.

The idea of planning appealed more to those of the left than of the right, and you were more likely to read about its virtues in volumes issued by the Left Book Club than in the pages of *The Times* or *Daily Express*. But traditional partisan politics had largely been in abeyance for the duration of the war, and planning appealed across a broad spectrum. When Sir William Beveridge wrote, in his 1942 report, of the importance of a co-ordinated scheme of social security and of the role of the state in vanquishing the five 'giants' (Want, Disease, Ignorance, Squalor and Idleness), he received widespread approval, his supporters including – initially – a host of Conservatives proud to display their social conscience. Bipartisanship in wartime extended to educational planning, too, culminating in the Education Act of 1944, which aimed to provide appropriate education, free of charge, to the entire school-age population. This was steered through the House of Commons in 1944 by R. A. Butler, son-in-law of Samuel Courtauld and later a Conservative Deputy Prime Minister.

The truth is that centralised state planning had become a habit of mind on right and left during the war, widely accepted as desirable for both pragmatic and ideological reasons. Without planning, most people in Britain felt, we would never have been in a position to win the war. And if we were to enjoy the fruits of victory and enable everyone to inhabit the better world for which we had all been fighting, that, too, could require planning. It was a view from which, by the last years of the war, few dissented. Thus, in the first general election for a decade, an elated but war-weary public went to the polls in July 1945 and elected a Labour government under Clement Attlee with a mandate to nationalise the coal mines and steel mills, the railways and shipyards, the gas and electricity industries and to centralise and co-ordinate the nation's health and social services. Everywhere, planning was the buzzword. Those who opposed the new orthodoxy (the mine owners, the British Medical Association, economists like Hayek, politicians like Churchill and the Tory right) might cry out in pain or indignation and prise the occasional concession from the nation's new political masters. But they were powerless to staunch what many regarded as the flow of history. Planning, in the words of Angus Calder, 'became a kind of universal craze'.

Everyone was at it, including some of the nation's most powerful cultural tsars. The BBC's Director-General, William Haley, reorganised the Corporation's radio networks, introducing new 'Home' and 'Light' Services, and creating a cultural network to be called the 'Third Programme'. Keynes, guru to the victorious powers as they established the post-war economic system, somehow found time to preside over the transformation of CEMA into the Arts Council of Great Britain and also to chair its largest beneficiary, the newly established Royal Opera House Board.

Post-war planning, if comprehensive, was not total. Thus, while the state might help look after you from cradle to grave, a pragmatic government retained private schools and private doctors for those who wished (and could afford) to use them. Culture and the arts, similarly, were never expropriated by the state as they had been under Stalin or Hitler, but benefited instead from the 'arm's-length principle'. Public finance might be directed into the coffers of the BBC or the Arts Council; but those who decided how to distribute it were supposedly independent-minded experts to whom genuine cultural provision was paramount.

To the Hitler émigrés, the final years of war brought mixed emotions. All were overjoyed at the growing prospect of Allied victory, to which many had contributed. But they experienced mounting horror and incredulity as they heard of Berlin and Dresden being reduced to rubble and ash and learned of the Nazi death camps. Who knew, who would ever know, what had happened to mother, father, sister, brother, uncle, aunt, lover, neighbour, school friend? The lesson was unambiguous: once the war was over, the world should be planned in such a way as to ensure that nothing remotely comparable could ever happen again.

There were others, however, to whom the lesson was the opposite: the belief in centralised planning (something advocated by influential German economists back in the days of the Kaiser) had contributed to the suspension of Germany's fragile experiment with democracy and thereby helped produce the monstrous tyranny of Nazism in which government planning had led to government control and thence to the worst abuses of authoritarianism. To Friedrich von Hayek, a man with personal memories of the demise of the Austro-Hungarian Empire and of the extremes of hope and disillusionment that followed, the pipe-puffing planners in Britain's Labour Party thus displayed alarming parallels with the disingenuous optimists of Germany's short-lived Weimar Republic who had paved the way for Hitler. In the USSR, too, the obsession with planning had led directly to the mass deportations and labour camps. Any form of socialistic planning, Hayek was convinced, was the gateway to the loss of individual liberty, whether in the form of Communism,

'National Socialism' or the ostensibly democratic Socialism of his LSE colleague Harold Laski. When people like Laski argued that the nation's resources and services should be placed in the hands of the state, Hayek maintained, they were in danger of pushing Britain down exactly the road that had led to the gulag and the concentration camp.

Hayek penned his thoughts during the war years for a volume he entitled *The Road to Serfdom*, first published in 1944. Provocative and overstated, the book was to become an iconic text of the rearguard right in Britain and (especially) America for forty years, a passionate *cri de coeur* from a mild-mannered man who felt forced to don the mantle of Jeremiah. Hayek regarded *The Road to Serfdom* as a 'warning to the socialist intelligentsia of England' and the writing of it 'a duty which I must not evade'. It was, he says, 'the product of an experience as near as possible to twice living through the same period – or at least twice watching a very similar evolution of ideas'. And just in case any reader in 1944 could have misunderstood his message, he announced starkly, 'It is Germany whose fate we are in some danger of repeating.'

The Road to Serfdom is written by an intellectual convinced that ideas (and intellectuals) can have a crucial impact upon history. There is no point in merely hating Germans, says Hayek; the point is to understand the ideas that have led them to their present state and to ensure that we do not follow the same ideological path. And the principal idea on which Hayek vents his wrath is that of economic planning (a term he uses more or less interchangeably with Socialism, Communism or collectivism). However well-intentioned – and he acknowledges that many early Socialists might have had genuinely altruistic aims – planning cannot but create circumstances within which, sooner or later, individual liberty will be snuffed out. Collectivism in all its guises – Fascist, Nazi or Socialist – is antithetical to freedom, says Hayek, asserting that nothing is more fatal than 'the present fashion among intellectual leaders in extolling security at the expense of freedom'.

Hayek is better on what (and whom) he is against than on what he is for. The liberty he advocates is little more than a loosely defined market economy free from the shackles of state planning though constrained by the rule of law – the kind of thing he first learned back in Vienna in the 1920s and had written and spoken about many times before. He is far more memorable when taking a swipe at writers (including Laski) he disapproves of. This normally gentle academic even allows himself a dig at 'socialist refugees' who, clinging to their beliefs, are inadvertently leading Britain down the same road as the one from which they themselves have so recently escaped. There is scarcely a leaf out of Hitler's book, Hayek says angrily, which somebody or other in England or America has not recommended us to take and use for our own purposes.

> This applies particularly to many people who are undoubtedly Hitler's mortal enemies because of one special feature in his system. We should never forget that the anti-Semitism of Hitler has driven from his country, or turned into his enemies, many people who in every respect are confirmed totalitarians of the German type.

Such a passage must have rendered apoplectic any Jewish refugee with Socialist leanings, and much of the book is equally outspoken. Hayek was aware of sailing out of the harbour of economic theory and into the rougher waters of political propaganda. Hence, perhaps, the occasional extravagance of his rhetoric, the straw men he sets up in order to demolish them and the tendency towards overstatement and repetition. He himself continued to stand by the book, his only reservation in later years being that, perhaps because of the wartime alliance with the USSR, he had somewhat restrained his hatred for the Soviet system and poured most of his vitriol against the Nazis. That he believed in his overall thesis there can be no doubt. *The Road to Serfdom* blazes with the sincerity of one who has already seen the evil he fears could recur.

The book had a mixed reception, arousing admiration and criticism of equal fervour – and going straight into the first of many reprints. Widely admired for the courage of his convictions, Hayek was nonetheless profoundly out of step with intellectual fashion in post-war Britain. In 1950, partly for personal reasons, he moved to the USA where, despite the achievement of cult status among conservative libertarians, he found himself eclipsed in the 1960s by the ascendant radicalism of the left.

Hayek lived long enough to see his ideas regain favour, winning the Nobel Prize for Economics in 1974. In Britain his writings (and occasional presence) provided inspiration for the Institute of Economic Affairs, a conservative think-tank that fed into the resurgence of strictly monetarist, anti-inflation, free-market policies in the 1970s and was embraced by Margaret Thatcher. In 1979, when Hayek was eighty, Thatcher became British Prime Minister and immediately set about trying to unravel much of the Welfare State in order (she said) to maximise individual liberty. There was no such thing as society, she was quoted as saying. Or, at least, society was really a collection of individuals. As for planning, this was to be relegated to the scrap heap of history. Throughout her premiership Thatcher (like the advisers to President Reagan) took guidance from the ideas of Hayek. A decade after her arrival in Downing Street, in May 1989, Thatcher – still Prime Minister of Britain – wrote to congratulate the old sage on his ninetieth birthday. None of her achievements, she said in a fulsome letter, 'would have been possible without the values and beliefs to set us on the right road and provide the right sense of direction. The leadership and inspiration that your work and thinking gave us were absolutely crucial.' The road to serfdom, she felt (and one hopes he did too), had been avoided.

While Hayek was writing *The Road to Serfdom*, another Austrian refugee, destined to become equally celebrated and arguably equally influential, was busy honing his ideas, and his capacity to express them in English, some twelve thousand miles away.

Karl Popper, like Hayek, had been appalled at the wholesale destruction and suffering caused by the First World War. Sixteen when the war concluded, Popper witnessed 'the breakdown of the Austrian Empire, the famine, the hunger riots in

Vienna, and the runaway inflation' which 'destroyed the world in which I had grown up'. Popper was close enough to hear the bullets whistle when, on the occasion of the Declaration of the Austrian Republic, soldiers started shooting at members of the Provisional Government assembled on the steps leading to the Parliament building. For a brief time Popper was attracted to Marxism, or what his friends called 'scientific Socialism'. This appeared to advocate the adoption of any methods in order to ensure a somewhat distant end and Popper was soon disillusioned. Not only did the cool subordination of means to ends involve further suffering and destruction, but he began to question how such a creed could properly be called a 'science'. How, indeed, could any overarching system that claimed to have answers to everything be demonstrably true? Popper's adolescent flirtation with Marxism made him conscious for the first time of the difference between what he thought of as 'dogmatic' as opposed to 'critical' thinking.

By the time he was seventeen, Popper was a student at the University of Vienna where he began to encounter other overarching theories such as those of Freud. He learned about Einstein and attended a lecture when the great man came to visit but was so mesmerised by the presence that he took in very little of what was said. What did impress him, then and later, was Einstein's acknowledgement that he would regard his theories as untenable if they failed certain tests. Einstein's theories, in other words, were susceptible to verification by other scientists in a way that those of Marx or Freud were not. If a scientific theory could in principle be proved wrong, Popper began to think, it could be regarded as correct until and unless falsified; if it could not in principle be refuted, or falsified, it was not science.

A serious young man with a strong moral conscience and a philosophical bent of mind, Popper gravitated towards the study of mathematics and theoretical physics. Food and clothing were scarce, and Popper, whose sympathies with the Viennese proletariat outlived his brief infatuation with Marxism, worked for a while at various manual jobs, including a stint as a cabinet-maker, and he also did social work. His one luxury during these years was the occasional concert ticket.

Popper's first love (like Gombrich's) was music. A crusty conservative ('Schubert was the last of the really great composers'), Popper couldn't abide what he thought to be the romantic lushness of the late nineteenth century and early twentieth, and he tried but failed to understand contemporaries such as Schoenberg.* Wagner, in particular, Popper abhorred, not only for what he regarded as the overblown nature of his art (he thought the libretto of the *Ring* ludicrous) but also for 'having sponsored the uncritical and almost hysterical idea of the unappreciated genius' who is 'ahead of his time'. Wagner attracted Popper's particular odium for having introduced into music an idea of progress, of the inevitable triumph of the music of the future – precisely the thinking that Popper was later to label and lambaste as 'historicism'. Popper's natural musical habitat was much earlier; he felt most at home in the fugues of Bach. A great work of music was, to Popper, like a great scientific theory: 'a cosmos imposed upon chaos'. From the contrasting works and personalities of Bach and Beethoven, he developed a theory of what he entitled the 'objective' and 'subjective' approaches to art.

Many strands were coming together in Popper's mind as, working initially as a schoolteacher, he began to make his name in Viennese intellectual circles in the late 1920s. This was the time and place, legendary in philosophical history, of the famed 'Vienna Circle', a group of thinkers (Moritz Schlick, Rudolf Carnap, Herbert Feigl, Victor Kraft, Otto Neurath) whose ruminations were to have profound international influence. One of the philosophers granted access to the Vienna Circle was the young English scholar A. J. Ayer, later the leading British proponent of what became known as 'logical positivism', the argument that no empirical statement that cannot be logically tested can be said to have meaning. Popper, always a slightly distanced figure – a music lover who studied science and mathematics, a scientist who was interested in philosophy – was in close touch with the Vienna Circle and attracted to what he

---

* At one time Popper worked with Schoenberg's pupil Erwin Stein, helping with rehearsals of the *Chamber Symphony* and *Pierrot Lunaire*.

saw as their rationalism. In later life he liked to emphasise his differences with them, his early fears that their ruthless pre-occupation with the logical demonstrability of all propositions would lead to a new, narrow-minded scholasticism. Be that as it may, Popper's first book, *Logik der Forschung* (published in Vienna in 1934), was a theory of knowledge that confronted many of the epistemological issues that preoccupied the Circle.

In particular, Popper tackled the problem of induction. Scientists, it had commonly been said (since the time of Bacon), first observe the data available to them and then – and only then – build up an appropriate hypothesis, which must remain adaptable in the face of further evidence. This is the process of 'induction', of argument from facts to theories, from specifics to the general. The alternative model was 'deduction', beloved of the Medievals who started with a theory and then looked for individual data to validate it. Popper's argument was, in effect, a refutation of both models. It is impossible, he said, for a scientist (or any human being) to take account of data 'out there' without already having some organising hypothesis. Rather, Popper posited a world in which we perceive facts through the filter of pre-existing hypotheses, which we and others can then proceed to adapt or falsify, verify or strengthen according to the availability of new evidence. If you start with no hypothesis at all, the facts you observe can have no meaning. But if your initial hypothesis is too inflexible, greater dangers arise: those of subordinating evidence to dogma.

Popper's view was widely admired, not least by scientists themselves. The biologist and Nobel laureate Sir Peter Medawar thought that Popper had produced a paradigm that corres-ponded precisely to both the principles of scientific discovery and to the day-to-day experience at the workbench. While making due obeisance to the genius of Bacon, Medawar opined (in 1972) that Popper, 'is incomparably the greatest philosopher of science there has ever been'.

Popper's assault on dogmatic, closed systems was even more ferocious than his demolition of Baconian 'induction'. In *The Poverty of Historicism* and *The Open Society and Its Enemies*, Popper launched a sustained attack on those, notably Marxists, who believed that the whole of previous human development had proceeded according to scientific laws which had now been identified and which could be used to predict its next stages. This belief in the inevitability of future development according to the 'laws' of history was what Popper called 'historicism'. He was not sparing in his identification and criticisms of those he considered the enemies of the open society – not only Marx but also such giants as Plato and Hegel.

The ideas in *The Poverty of Historicism* were first aired in Brussels, then in London in 1936 at Hayek's LSE seminar. During his stay in England Popper also visited Oxford (where he met Schrödinger, later to make a hair-raising escape from the Nazis before settling in Dublin) and Cambridge, where Russell ('perhaps the greatest philosopher since Kant') gave a paper on the limits of induction. Ayer, who was present at the Cambridge meeting, encouraged Popper to speak. Brilliant and provocative, Popper tried in his halting English to argue that there was no such thing as induction, that what we call 'scientific knowledge' was never true, only hypothetical. The audience, who apparently took this for a joke, or a paradox, laughed and clapped politely. Looking back at his lukewarm reception in Cambridge, Popper (like the young Disraeli, who said with some bitterness that one day the House of Commons would listen to him) later wrote: 'I wonder whether there was anybody there who suspected that not only did I seriously hold these views, but that, in due course, they would be regarded as commonplace.'

As Nazism sunk its claws into Germany and threatened Austria, Popper was anxious to quit Vienna. During his visit to England he was introduced to Esther Simpson and Walter Adams of the Academic Assistance Council, and offered academic hospitality at Cambridge. But a firm job offer turned up from Canterbury University College in Christchurch, New Zealand, and it was here that Popper spent the war years, contemplating the global conflict from the greatest possible distance.*

---

* A. J. Ayer tells of a dinner party in Oxford where he and Isaiah Berlin were talking about Vienna. Ayer mentioned that 'poor Popper has had to take refuge in New Zealand' – at which a fellow diner leaned over and said to Ayer, 'I never knew your father was an Austrian.'

It was while in New Zealand that Popper developed his ideas into the two works by which he is best known. Popper regarded *The Poverty* and its elaboration in the two volumes of *The Open Society* as his 'war effort': 'I thought that freedom might become a central problem again, especially under the renewed influence of Marxism and the idea of large-scale "planning" (or *"dirigism"*); and so these books were meant as a defence of freedom against totalitarian and authoritarian ideas.' They are books of philosophy, sternly moralistic in tone and not easy to absorb; Popper himself came to regard *The Poverty of Historicism* as 'one of my stodgiest pieces of writing'. Handicapped by the limited resources available to him in New Zealand, Popper found himself struggling to make his own translations of Plato (with the help of a school grammar he had brought from Austria) and drifting from pure philosophy into political and historical speculation. He sent his work off to possible publishers but was rejected. Nor did he receive encouragement from the university authorities who told him that trying to publish books took him away from the teaching duties for which he was being paid. It was a low point in his life.

Then, by chance, Popper obtained the English address of Gombrich, with whom he had lost touch. He wrote to Gombrich sending him a copy of his work, asking him to read it and, if he liked it, to pass it on to Hayek, which he did. Both wrote back encouragingly. Hayek managed to get *The Poverty* published in 1945 by *Economica* (of which he was acting editor), and gave the manuscript of *The Open Society* to Herbert Read, who worked for Routledge, where it was published in that same year. Popper's gratitude and relief were immense. He felt that Gombrich and Hayek had saved his life.

Hayek did more than help Popper get published. He managed to get him invited to a tenured post at the LSE. In due course, Popper and his wife arrived back in England (where they were met off the boat by Gombrich). Popper was to stay at the LSE for nearly twenty-five years. Just as Hayek and Robbins had given the LSE international pre-eminence in economics before the war, Popper's presence bestowed upon the School great philosophical distinction and renown. John Watkins, later

Popper's successor as Professor of Philosophy at the LSE, attended his lectures as an undergraduate and remembered him speaking 'uncluttered by notes or other paraphernalia, with a peculiar intensity and urgency, his words falling so exactly into place that one seemed to be hearing the ideas themselves'. Never an easy man to work with, Popper could not abide what he regarded as intellectual sloppiness and could be inordinately sensitive when crossed or criticised. Another future LSE professor, Kenneth Minogue, went along to some of Popper's seminars and admired the precision with which Popper argued, but gained the impression of one 'who so loved the world that he could not forbear to put it right'. People joked that Popper's most famous work should have been called 'The Open Society by One of Its Enemies'.

Popper's curmudgeonly streak came out forcefully soon after his arrival at the LSE when he was invited to give another paper in Cambridge. Popper decided to argue for the existence of genuine philosophical problems. This was deliberately provocative since he knew Wittgenstein would be present. Wittgenstein, another notoriously prickly customer, was the original inspiration behind logical positivism and contended that there were no genuine problems in philosophy, only linguistic puzzles. Predictably, Wittgenstein, who was sitting near the fireplace, kept interrupting Popper and started playing with the poker. Popper mentioned the idea of moral rules, which Wittgenstein denied were the province of philosophy. He challenged Popper: 'Give me an example of a moral rule.' To which Popper replied, 'Not to threaten visiting lecturers with pokers.' Wittgenstein stormed out and the incident rapidly assumed legendary status.

One can see why Hayek had been so keen to help his fellow Austrian. Quite apart from the natural sympathy of one émigré for another, Hayek, fresh from his labours on *The Road to Serfdom*, sensed in Popper's work a fellow spirit in the struggle for freedom. What Hayek called planning and Popper historicism approximated to the same thing: the abdication to the all-knowing state of individual liberty. As the evils of Nazism were finally defeated, both these mid-European professors were appalled to see members of the supposedly liberal-minded intelligentsia in the victorious English-speaking world drifting towards the social system of the Soviet Union. Stalin might have been our ally in the war; but to Popper, as to Hayek, Soviet Marxism was as much an abrogation of individual liberty as Nazism and Fascism. What the Allies had been fighting for was the defence of freedom, not the opportunity to hand it over to the state. It was a campaign both men were to continue to the end of their very long lives.

Ernst Gombrich was to remain a close friend of Popper until the latter's death in 1994. When Popper and his wife arrived in England after the war they stayed at first with the Gombrichs, and Gombrich sat in on Popper's LSE lecture course on logic.

Although the two men scarcely knew each other in Vienna, they shared a similar background, a love of music, a rigorously rational intelligence and a predilection for seeking connections between ostensibly unconnected disciplines. Profoundly committed to intellectual bridge building between the sciences and humanities, both prided themselves on their sceptical, critical approach to problems, eschewing anything that smacked of the mystical or transcendental. 'I was very happy', said Gombrich of *The Poverty of Historicism*, 'to see that [Popper] too had so many objections to the idea of the "spirit of the age".' Both men were fascinated by the genius of Plato – and disturbed by the ideological uses and abuses to which his concepts were subjected by latter-day Platonists. Gombrich's oeuvre is peppered with admiring references to his friend's work and is clearly imbued with Popper's methodological principle, that you can refute a theory but can never prove one.

Just as Hayek's most famous book, *The Road to Serfdom*, is a popular deviation from his theoretical work, Gombrich, too, is best known for a book that he regarded as subsidiary to his main career. Back in Vienna in 1934–5, he had been commissioned by the publisher Walter Neurath (soon to become a refugee in Britain himself) to write a history of the world for children. He had done this at great speed, and had then begun to pen a few sample chapters for a possible follow-up volume on the history of the world's art. During the war, while Gombrich was working for the BBC's Monitoring Service, he was approached by another publisher, Béla Horovitz of the Phaidon Press, who, like Gombrich's parents, was part of the refugee community in nearby Oxford. Horovitz wondered whether Gombrich had any book ideas to offer.

> I said to Dr Horovitz: 'I have a few chapters of a history of art for young people. I don't know whether that would interest you.' And he answered: 'Give it to me, I'll show it to my daughter [Elly], who is sixteen.' Well, the daughter read it and said: 'Yes, I think you should publish this.'

Horovitz gave Gombrich a contract for fifty pounds and told him to start writing properly. Gombrich was at first too busy with his BBC job to get on with the book. Each time he visited his parents in Oxford he seemed to bump into Horovitz who would ask him how he was getting on. Eventually Gombrich owned up to the truth and offered to return his advance. But Horovitz persisted. 'I don't want your fifty pounds, I want your manuscript.'

After the war, Gombrich returned to the Warburg Institute (by now part of the University of London) where Saxl expected him to undertake serious academic work and not fritter away his time writing a popular book. But there was that little matter of Gombrich's contract with Phaidon. Eventually he arranged for a typist to come in three times a week, dictated the text more or less from the material in his head and chose illustrations from the books he had at home. First published in 1950, *The Story of Art* was still in print over fifty years later, with worldwide sales to date of over 6 million copies in thirty languages.

From the outset, *The Story of Art* announces a fresh intelligence, a robust stylist, a writer in love with art but unimpressed by the pretensions of the art world. In words that, to the art lover, became as celebrated as the opening of *Pride and Prejudice* or *A Tale of Two Cities*, Gombrich wrote:

> There is really no such thing as art. There are only artists. Once these were men who took coloured earth and roughed

out the forms of a bison on the wall of a cave; today some buy their paints, and design posters for hoardings; they did and do many other things. There is no harm in calling all these activities art as long as we keep in mind that such a word may mean very different things in different times and places, and as long as we realize that Art with a capital A has no existence. For Art with a capital A has come to be something of a bogey and a fetish. You may crush the artist by telling him that what he has just done may be quite good in its own way, only it is not 'Art'. And you may confound anyone enjoying a picture by declaring that what he liked in it was not the Art but something different.

Is it idle to detect in this brilliantly arresting opening the craft of a man whose linguistic and presentation skills had just been honed by five years spent monitoring and translating propaganda broadcasts?

In a world starved of art and books, *The Story of Art* propelled Gombrich to instant celebrity. Soon he was appointed Slade Professor of the History of Art at Oxford and thence to other visiting professorships, in the USA and elsewhere, 'because of the reputation of that book'. But for all the popularity of 'that book', Gombrich remained based at the Warburg Institute. Like Aby Warburg, Gombrich's intellectual centre of gravity was the art of the Quattrocento Renaissance, though he was to venture widely into other places, periods and styles. Much of his scholarly work addresses fundamental questions: *why* did Leonardo or Botticelli (or whoever) paint these particular images in this particular way? Not for Gombrich the narrow questions of provenance and connoisseurship. 'My ambition', he said, 'is to explain', and in a torrent of lectures, articles and books of immense erudition, he tried to uncover the intentions of the artist. In order to do so he interested himself in psychology, sociology, biology, ethology – any area of study that might aid his quest. Like Popper, Gombrich is supremely sceptical of 'spirit of the age' explanations, which he finds evasive, always preferring to concentrate on the individual artist. 'It is not a collective consciousness which creates a style,' he wrote, adding sharply that if somebody had not invented a new style it would not have come about. Whether considering the arrival of Gothic architecture or the figures Michelangelo chose to portray on the Sistine Chapel ceiling, Gombrich refuses to hide behind mystical or symbolic explanations.* 'There is no reason to believe that the Sistine ceiling has more meanings than what we see.' Even Freud, whose insights Gombrich uses admiringly when appropriate, comes in for typically tart demystification when, for example, he claims that Leonardo painted St Anne because he had two mothers. To Gombrich, always keen to puncture what he sees as pretension, it is far more likely that Leonardo painted St Anne for the more humdrum reason that she was the patron saint of Florence and that he had been commissioned to paint her.

Our perceptions of art are a different matter. Here again, the influence of Popper is evident. When we look at a painting, says Gombrich, we bring to bear all sorts of personal and cultural baggage that might have nothing to do with the original intentions of the artist. 'Whether we know it or not, we always approach the past with some preconceived ideas, with a rudimentary theory we wish to test.' There is no point in denying this, he says. If you tell me that a picture is by your twelve-year-old son or daughter, and that another is by Albrecht Dürer, I will inevitably look at the two of them differently. Just as Popper argued that there is no such thing as induction, that scientists could not derive their theories from the objective observation of facts 'out there', Gombrich denied that we could ever look at a work of art with an 'innocent eye'. We look at art, or anything else we encounter, through a set of hypotheses which we then test or modify in the light of what we think we perceive. The principal difference between the methodologies of the sciences and the humanities is that the hypotheses of science, unlike those in the arts, are verified (or falsified) by the extent to which they lead to accurate prediction. A scientific hypothesis about gravi-

---

* Gombrich tells, with maybe a touch of mischievous glee, how his friend and senior colleague, Erwin Panofsky, used to dread coming across scholarly articles that parodied his own inclination to find symbols behind even the most straightforward works of art.

tational pull is verified each time an object is dropped and falls to earth. The hypotheses of the historian, including the art historian, make no such claims and are more concerned with individual instances – but can be similarly verified or falsified according to the availability of further evidence.

Gombrich, like Hayek, had something of a double career. Serious contributions to theoretical scholarship were eclipsed in the popular mind by the dazzling fame of a single work. Celebrated worldwide for *The Story of Art*, Gombrich sensed that his colleagues at the Warburg had never read the book. But they did read his papers on Poussin and Leonardo, his book on the psychology of art (*Art and Illusion*) and his pioneering work on decoration (*The Sense of Order*).

In 1959 Gombrich was made Director of the Warburg Institute, a post he held until his retirement in 1976. He was knighted in 1972. The most famous art historian since Kenneth Clark, and far more prolific, Gombrich always considered himself a product of the Vienna school of art history and bearer of the mantle of Aby Warburg.* This meant that the study of art history should be systematic, professional, interdisciplinary – and intellectually rigorous. It meant treating topics such as Mannerism seriously, and asking what had brought it about, what it meant to people at the time, rather than dismissing it as merely the decadent art of the late Renaissance. It meant seeing art in its widest context, and examining the continuing tradition of the art of ancient Greece and Rome through the Renaissance to the world of today. In Britain, when he first arrived, Gombrich found too much preoccupation with detail, with minutiae, with the provenance and value of paintings. His approach, by contrast, was to ask broader philosophical questions, to encourage a wider discourse than can possibly be available to mere connoisseurship. The greater the range of your examples, the more persuasive your explanatory hypotheses.

---

* Gombrich's last public lecture, delivered in his precise, accented English to a huge and admiring audience in the University of London's Logan Hall in October 1999, was an assessment of aspects of the work and methodology of Aby Warburg. Gombrich died in November 2001.

Gombrich, like many of the Hitler émigrés, was a man with a moral mission. Like all of them, he had seen centuries of civilisation come close to annihilation. Throughout his life in Britain Gombrich regarded himself as fighting to maintain the values represented by the highest achievements of the past. It was a crusade he shared with Hayek and Popper. And the role of the art historian in particular? '[We] are the spokesmen of our civilization: we want to know more about our Olympus.'

CHAPTER THIRTEEN

The Wolf Gang

Hayek, Popper and Gombrich were not the only ones aspiring towards Olympus. During the war, people all over Britain had revealed a hunger for culture that had initially surprised the mandarins responsible for providing it. Now that men were returning from the services and normal life could resume, many wished to make permanent the structures which aimed at the raising of cultural standards. Thus, as the nation's health, social security and transportation systems were being planned, so were important segments of its artistic life. By the end of 1946 the Royal Opera House had reopened, CEMA was transformed into the Arts Council of Great Britain, complete with Royal Charter, and the BBC inaugurated its 'Third Programme'. In 1946, too, a year in which some 30 million people were regular cinema goers, Powell and Pressburger released *A Matter of Life and Death* in which heaven is portrayed in monochrome but life on earth in rich colours.

If the British were forced to endure the grey austerity imposed by a shattered economy (and to suffer the coldest winter in living memory in 1946–7), there was nothing to stop them dreaming in colour. Why not celebrate the cricketing feats of Edrich and Compton, flaunt the 'New Look' and imagine a time without rationing? As Britain's young actors and musicians, poets and painters crawled out of their overalls and uniforms, and got used to their demob suits and jobs, they could scarcely believe their luck. For refugees who had escaped from the hell of Hitlerism the ecstasy of peace was often tempered by the contemplation of what – and whom – they had lost. But as they gradually mastered English, looked for work, began to earn and spend money, and bought their first homes, many learned to flourish in the new, frankly optimistic cultural environment that was emerging.

On 20 February 1946, in the presence of the King, the Queen and the two Princesses, the Royal Opera House, Covent Garden, reopened with a new production of *The Sleeping Beauty*, starring the young Margot Fonteyn, before an audience sporting whatever tiaras and evening dresses war-torn London could muster for the occasion. Ninette de Valois darted back and forth, a stern note for a dancer here, a courteous smile for a visiting dignitary there. Covent Garden's General Administrator, David Webster, beaming and rubicund, was ubiquitous. Ballet was established; opera would follow.

Yet the evening really belonged, in a sense, to Keynes who had used his access across the overlapping worlds of finance, politics and the arts to brilliant effect. Indeed, as first Chairman of the Arts Council *and* of the Royal Opera House Board (a dual role not perceived in those innocent days as involving conflict of interest), Keynes had played a key role in guaranteeing proper funding for Covent Garden, thereby helping to enshrine a major new principle in British public life: that the state should help fund the arts on a regular basis. If any one person might be said to have embodied the hopes and aspirations riding on that gala *Sleeping Beauty* it was Keynes.

As the audience settled into the house, he readied himself for the arrival of the royal party – and suffered a minor heart attack. His wife summoned Webster, who duly did the honours and ensured that the wicked fairy failed to douse the party spirits. Two months later Keynes was dead.

The establishment of the Royal Opera House as the permanent home for both a ballet and an opera company came about as a result of determined planning. The men who did the planning back in bleak, war-weary 1944 were inspired by the same desire to raise the quality of life in post-war Britain as drove the Beveridges, Butlers and Bevans. Opera and ballet may not have involved as many people or required as much money as the nation's educational or health systems, but the problems the planners needed to overcome must at times have seemed almost equally fearsome. In the end their labours bore fruit and Covent Garden became home to what grew into the Royal Ballet and the Royal Opera. For many in the refugee community the Royal Opera House also became, for much of the next half-century, a major showcase and substantial beneficiary.

The Mecca lease on Covent Garden was due to expire in December 1944, with an option to renew unless someone else could be found who would use the theatre for opera and ballet. But who? Philip Hill, the Chairman of the proprietors, asked the impresario Harold Holt whether he might be interested in applying and Holt, who had his hands full, passed on the idea to two of his directors, the music publishers Leslie Boosey and Ralph Hawkes. Mecca were pressing for an early decision. So Boosey and Hawkes took out a five-year lease on the theatre (permitting Mecca to use it as a dance hall until September 1945) and set up a consultative committee, headed by Keynes, that included many of the great figures in music and the arts such as William Walton, Kenneth Clark and Steuart Wilson. Their brief, outlined by Boosey and Hawkes in what would nowadays be called a mission statement, was to establish Covent Garden as an international opera house on the traditional continental model, financed – as never before in British history – by a regular, guaranteed government subsidy with no strings attached.

The first thing the committee had to do was to appoint someone to be in charge of their theatre. There were several strong contenders. Names popularly assumed to be in the ring included those of Sir Thomas Beecham, who had periodically leased the house before the war and produced and conducted opera there, the record producer and ENSA boss Walter Legge, and the Viennese émigré Rudolf Bing who had run Glyndebourne for its founder, John Christie. Christie himself was an obvious candidate in many people's minds (evidently including his own). The problem was that all these were regarded as wilful, slightly eccentric figures, none of them quite the safe pair of hands sought by Boosey and Hawkes, Keynes and Clark. Instead, the choice fell upon a relative unknown (in London, at least): David Webster. Webster had been Manager of Liverpool's Bon Marché store and then of Lewis's, the city's prominent department store. He was also Chairman of the Liverpool Philharmonic Orchestra and responsible, against considerable opposition, for having retained quality music-making on Merseyside throughout the war. Webster's enthusiastic understanding of music and the arts was beyond question, as were his superb administrative skills. Hawkes met him over lunch at the Ritz Grill and was enchanted. Here was just the man to whom the delicate tasks ahead could safely be entrusted.

Webster was charged with the Sisyphean task of establishing, from nothing, permanent opera and ballet companies of the highest quality. The ballet came first for the simple reason that Ninette de Valois's troupe, by now ready for major exposure in a large theatre, was transferred en bloc from the Sadler's Wells company to Covent Garden. It took longer for the resurgent 'Royal Opera House' to live up to its name and house an opera company. Joan Cross, the driving force behind the Vic-Wells opera company, was a great singer and powerful personality. But she was a contentious spirit, her company had none of the glamour or international aspiration of their balletic counterparts, and eventually she, Peter Pears and Eric Crozier, buoyed up by the success of Benjamin Britten's latest opera, *Peter Grimes*, seceded from the Sadler's Wells opera company altogether to set up what was to become the English Opera Group.

As Webster and his colleagues contemplated the task of setting up their own opera company they had hard decisions to make. The first, and most crucial, was whom to choose as Musical Director. As with Webster's own appointment there were, on the face of it, a number of possible contenders. Beecham, again, of course, though his recurrent supercilious sniping ruled him *hors de combat*. Another prominent name was that of John Barbirolli who had returned to England in 1943 after seven years at the helm of the New York Philharmonic to take over Manchester's Hallé Orchestra. Webster, with his Liverpool background, was well acquainted with Barbirolli's gifts and lunched him periodically. But Barbirolli was disinclined, after his New York years, to assume another similarly high-profile post and was profoundly committed to the Hallé.

There were two conductors whom Webster approached with a serious offer: Eugene Goossens, who had worked with Beecham at Covent Garden in the 1930s, and Bruno Walter, one of the great conductors in pre-Hitlerian Germany and Austria, and by now equally celebrated in his adopted country, the United States. Both men fired a lot of questions in Webster's direction. How much time would the Musical Director have to spend at Covent Garden, how long would the initial contract last? Goossens wanted to know if Webster was inflexibly committed to performing all operas in English, and expressed doubts over the wisdom of alternating opera and ballet evenings. Walter said he would insist on knowing who were the singers, chorus master, director and designer in any production he was to conduct. Couldn't Carl Ebert come and work with him at Covent Garden, he wanted to know – and Rudolf Bing? Webster, unable to answer some of these reservations, and dilatory by nature, lost Goossens and then Walter. Perhaps he was relieved. People like Beecham or Walter were giants, potentially overmighty subjects whom Webster – still struggling with his new job – might have found it difficult to rule.

In the event, his choice fell upon a less stellar figure. Karl Rankl had studied with Schoenberg and worked as coach and chorus master under Weingartner at the Vienna Volksoper in the 1920s. Later he assisted Klemperer at the Kroll Opera in Berlin, and went on to hold senior posts in Wiesbaden, Graz and Prague. With the advent of Hitler, Rankl returned to his native Austria, directing opera in Graz, then moved on to Prague, before escaping to England in 1939 where, the following year, he was interned.

When Rankl was invited to become Musical Director at Covent Garden he did not regale Webster with haughty questions about time, money and artistic power. A refugee grateful for the offer of an important job, Rankl was a practical man of the musical theatre, a competent composer-conductor who knew the business and would, Webster sensed, get the show on the road. If that makes the new job sound humdrum, it certainly did not seem so at the time. Like a chef with a large kitchen, a series of feasts to prepare and no ingredients, Rankl had to create his operatic fare from nothing. There were no productions to build on, no costumes or sets, no music staff, no chorus, not much of an orchestra.* More celebrated figures had turned down the job. Goossens had expressed alarm at having to make 'bricks without straw'. Beecham, who had not been asked, sneered contemptuously at the appointment of a foreigner. All this Rankl knew as he contemplated the steep gradient before him.

The Rankl appointment was announced in June 1946 – along with a statement that the curtain would go up on the new opera company in November with a production of Purcell's *Fairy Queen* (the visiting San Carlo Opera of Naples helped plug the intervening gap). If Purcell was not exactly standard operatic fare, at least he was an English composer, while *The Fairy Queen* was composed to an English-language text and was loosely based on Shakespeare. Although it was more of a masque than a proper opera, it was nevertheless just the kind of work that could benefit from discreet help from the ballet company. Thus Covent Garden's initial offering was conducted not by its Musical Director but by Constant Lambert.

The real debut of the opera company, and Rankl's debut in the pit, was in *Carmen* in January 1947. This was the culmination of six months' work during which Rankl had engaged a chorus and chorus master, enlarged and trained the orchestra, auditioned countless solo singers in Britain and abroad, and busied himself with every aspect of his new company. He had also taken the lead in planning the gradual build-up of operatic repertoire the house would need. As the Musical Director took his place for the first night of *Carmen* – *his* first night in his own house – he might have reflected with some satisfaction on the exacting journey on which he and his company had embarked and which was about to pass its first milestone.

---

* Rankl later recalled (*Opera*, July 1968) that 'only a third of the orchestra had ever played a whole opera'.

The evening was not the sensational success for which Rankl and Webster had hoped. The chorus was praised, the production and principals less so. Rankl himself was adjudged by the critic Philip Hope-Wallace to have 'handled this adorable score with, at best, a sort of cavalier efficiency'.

The heights of Olympus were not to be scaled easily. Perhaps the Covent Garden audience (and critics) had been spoiled by hearing singers of the calibre of Gigli and del Monaco with the visiting Naples troupe in 1946 while, a year later, they were exposed to the Vienna State Opera, whose casts and conductors (Clemens Krauss and Josef Krips) Covent Garden could not hope to rival. For vintage opera goers a new production of *Der Rosenkavalier* with mostly British singers conducted by Rankl could hardly rate alongside the memory of Lehmann and Schumann under the baton of Bruno Walter (all of them by now exiles in the USA).

It took some years before the ingredients that Webster and Rankl required began to come together. Money, at least, was reasonably secure. The cosy links between Covent Garden, government and the Arts Council that Keynes had established were strengthened by his successor as chairman of the Board, Lord Waverley.* Singers of the calibre of Flagstad, Hotter and Schwarzkopf were persuaded to sing in the house and agreed to learn their roles in English. The young Peter Brook and the eccentric Salvador Dali collaborated on a sensational production of *Salome*, which split the critics (and which Rankl, who conducted, detested).

The trouble was that Rankl's critics wanted to have it both ways. Soon after his appointment, the Incorporated Society of Musicians publicly inveighed against the choice of a foreign Musical Director and demanded that this should never be permitted to happen again. To some it was humiliating that the best opera at Covent Garden in the immediate post-war period had come not from the home team but from – of all places – Italy and Austria. Yet many also pounced upon the supposed inade-

---

* The ennobled Sir John Anderson who, as Home Secretary, had charge of Britain's internal security and immigration policies in the pivotal years of 1939–40, and had been Chancellor of the Exchequer in 1943–5.

quacies of British artists whom Rankl thought it his job to promote, arguing that, by casting Kenneth Neate or Edgar Evans instead of Anton Dermota or Luigi Infantino, Rankl was guaranteeing lower standards.

Things got worse before they got better. In June 1948, at a highly-publicised Foyle's Literary Luncheon, Beecham chose to denounce English singers as having 'pleasant but woolly voices that cannot carry beyond the fourth row of the stalls'. He seemed to be arguing, in his peculiarly acerbic way, for a revival of the glamorous international seasons over which he had presided before the war: the best artists from all over the world – but under home-grown management. 'The Italians, the French, the Germans, and other countries', he went on to his audience, 'would not dare to put a foreigner in charge of a national institution.' By choosing Rankl as Musical Director, said Beecham witheringly, '[w]e proclaimed to the world that we could not govern our own musical institutions. Covent Garden is the laughing stock of the world!' A few months later, at the annual conference of the ISM, Beecham thundered against the 'nitwits' who had appointed Rankl; the choice of this alien was, he said, like a bad dream. And he poured scorn on a national opera 'established and controlled by a body from which the leaders of the musical profession in England have been carefully excluded'. By which everybody understood him to mean himself.

Heading a two-month festival of Italian or German opera was one thing. What Rankl was trying to do was far more ambitious, something for which Beecham, with his penchant for the limelight, would have been utterly unsuited. 'My aim', Rankl wrote later, 'was to form a company and an ensemble which could perform at short notice . . . any one of the 40-odd operas which are the standard repertory.' During his five years as Musical Director, Covent Garden did indeed produce thirty operas of which Rankl rehearsed, prepared and conducted twenty-four. Yet he would have been less than human had he not been ground down by the attacks from Beecham and others.

Ironically, it was Rankl's very success that led to his eventual departure. By 1950 the opera company, if not as widely known and admired as the ballet, was well established, with a number of excellent productions to its credit. Artists such as Constance Shacklock, Sylvia Fisher and Geraint Evans were turning in first-class performances, singing comfortably alongside colleagues with international reputations. The policy of performing everything in English began to be breached (notably when Boris Christoff insisted on singing *Boris Godunov* in Russian), and leading directors and designers from abroad expressed interest in working with the company. Covent Garden was gradually becoming what Webster and Rankl had always wanted it to be: a home of international-quality opera.

If Covent Garden was the nation's premier showcase for opera, it was not the only one. There was opera, too, at Sadler's Wells, while at the Cambridge Theatre Jay Pomeroy put on short seasons of opera, casting celebrated singers in some roles. Outside London there was opera at the Edinburgh Festival from 1947, primarily performed by the Glyndebourne company whose own Festival resumed in 1950. Meanwhile Benjamin Britten's English Opera Group appeared in a variety of venues, including Glyndebourne and (from 1948) Aldeburgh. If Covent Garden was to be the undisputed leader, the criterion of taste and quality, it required one further ingredient: guest conductors capable of inspiring a good orchestra to greatness.

When Webster wrote a careful letter to his Musical Director proposing the engagement of Erich Kleiber, he affected surprise when Rankl bridled. But Kleiber's presence in the house over the winter of 1950–1 led everyone to enthuse about the orchestral standards he achieved, particularly in *Rosenkavalier* and *Wozzeck*. 'We must do everything in our power to keep [Kleiber],' wrote Kenneth Clark to Webster. But he added, significantly, that, 'when all had been said, he couldn't have used the instrument unless Rankl had created it'.

Perhaps. But Rankl was deeply hurt. Strauss and Berg were *his* repertoire, he felt, and he resented the plaudits that Kleiber received. Rankl rankled was not a pretty sight, especially if you were David Webster. But as Webster's own confidence grew, he ran roughshod over his Musical Director, persuading Beecham (of all people) to return to his old house, planning a *Tristan* with

Clemens Krauss conducting four out of five performances (Rankl got to conduct the fifth) and inviting Barbirolli to Covent Garden as guest conductor. In May 1951, the month the Festival of Britain opened, Rankl announced his resignation.*

Rankl had never been completely at east at Covent Garden. His tragedy was that the company he created outgrew him. Critics were inclined to be indulgent when, early on, a clearly overworked Musical Director conducted an occasional lack-lustre performance. But as the opera company began to poke its nose above the parapet of mediocrity and sniff the intoxicating elixir of excellence, Rankl's limitations became liabilities. He was a monochrome maestro in a world beginning to dream again in colour, a workhorse criticised for not being a thorough-bred. He became understandably bitter, describing himself to Kenneth Clark in 1953 as 'the man who, unaided by anybody and hampered by antagonism on all sides, nevertheless suc-ceeded in building up from scratch an opera company that still exists.' Looking back in 1968 from the perspective of the Solti era, Rankl, shortly before his death, allowed himself the very English thought that his own 'five years of very hard work were not entirely wasted'. Indeed they were not. For the Solti years would never have been possible without the Rankl years.

> I would want the Light Programme to play the waltz from *Der Rosenkavalier*. Then about a week or ten days later I would hope the Home Service would play one act . . . And within a month the Third Programme would do the whole work [from beginning to end, dialogue and all].

The BBC's Director-General, William Haley, a Jersey-born journalist with no university education, had propelled himself into the upper echelons by sheer ability. A man of serious moral convictions Haley, like many of his contemporaries, believed that Britain, like every civilised nation, was a pyramid, socially as well as intellectually, 'with a lamentably broad base and a

---

* From 1952 to 1957 Rankl was in charge of the Scottish National Orchestra. He went on to accept a post in Australia in anticipation of the opening of the Sydney Opera House.

lamentably narrow tip'. The aim of those in a position to plan such things was to help raise people up a stratum or two. Accordingly, Haley set up three radio networks: the Light and the Home in 1945 and, in September 1946, the BBC's new cultural network, the Third Programme. The aim was for these to be separate but complementary.

It did not quite pan out that way, as Haley was ruefully to admit in retrospect. Individual programme heads had considerable autonomy and did not work together as closely as Haley had hoped, and the Third Programme often found itself struggling for want of available talent. People with long memories were later to speak of legendary highlights: a series of Schnabel concerts (relayed from Central Hall, Westminster), literary features by Louis MacNeice or the debate between Bertrand Russell and Father Copleston about the existence of God. But such a standard could hardly be maintained on a daily basis. One critic complained that the speech on the Third was dominated by 'third-rate poets, Bloomsbury intellectuals and BBC producers who should have been schoolmasters', while those planning the network's huge musical output sometimes had to resort to the second-rate. After one of the Schnabel concerts, a Third Programme mandarin noted ruefully that 'such a standard [has] not been heard in an English concert hall since 1939'. The BBC Symphony Orchestra, exhausted by war work, was in urgent need of new blood and when the Head of the Third Programme proposed broadcasting two chamber concerts a week his Director of Music was frankly sceptical. 'There are not many good Chamber Music combinations in this country,' he wrote, 'and extremely few of outstanding quality.'

It was all too true. The war had caused a serious hiatus in musical life, as in so much else. There had been, as we have seen, a great deal of musical activity up and down the country, much of it performed by people who were the wrong age, sex or nationality to fight. But standards were patchy. Furthermore, the spring was not being replenished. For all the efforts of Myra Hess and John Barbirolli, Tippett and Tauber, CEMA and ENSA, music-making during the war largely lived off existing capital. Then, as cultural life began to emerge from the rubble of war, it became clear that many of the great international musicians of the 1930s were either dead or no longer available for (or perhaps capable of) performances of pre-war quality. Many younger British musicians of promise, moreover, had just spent six years in uniform in conditions not exactly conducive to the highest standards of artistic excellence. Visiting artists such as Josef Szigeti, Artur Schnabel, Elisabeth Schumann and Yehudi Menuhin, accustomed to appearing in the Queen's Hall, returned to London but had to perform in the Wigmore Hall, which was too small, or the Royal Albert Hall, which was too large. If a young British musician – a Kathleen Ferrier, say, or a Dennis Brain – was seen to reach the highest international standards, this was regarded as exceptional, an occasion for rare self-congratulation.

The chamber music world was a particularly untended wilderness. There were plenty of good instrumentalists around and, since chamber music was cheap and therefore attractive to promote, many of the best players had been heard around the country during and after the war. But the bad mingled with the good and frequently drove it out, halls were often half filled, acoustically poor and draughty, and the highest standards of professional ensemble playing were hard to find. The Busch Quartet's days were drawing to a close and its appearances in Britain rare. The Grillers were about to move to the United States, thus depriving Britain of one of its best home-grown ensembles. There was a thirst for good chamber music, but a paucity of groups capable of providing it.

The BBC, the record companies, audiences – all were hungry for new talent just at a time when a number of able people in the refugee community were ready to help provide it. Virtually all the Hitler émigrés had made the practical and emotional decision to stay in Britain after the war, most of them going on to acquire naturalisation when, in theory, they might have returned to the countries from which they had come. But if they were British by conviction, many also became increasingly conscious of providing a bridge between the cultural traditions of their former and present homelands. In addition, some seemed keen to link past, present and future; several refugee musicians experimented with repertoire and styles from before and after the mainstream symphonic and operatic repertoire (rather as Weidenfeld first made his name by publishing historical memoirs). For such bridge builders the Third Programme provided a perfect platform. Walter Goehr, who had worked regularly for the BBC during the war, conducted Monteverdi's *Vespers* on the Third Programme in 1947; Norbert Brainin was one of the instrumentalists coached by Arnold Goldsborough in 'period style' for concerts of Handel and Rameau. Egon Wellesz spoke on the Third about 'Early Christian Music', while Mátyás Seiber broadcast about Bartók, and Peter Stadlen about Schoenberg. Stadlen's illustrated musical exegeses of twentieth-century music were punctuated by enormous enthusiasm and he once overran by twelve minutes, thus delaying the relay of a live concert.

Seiber and Wellesz were among contemporary composers who had their own music performed periodically on the Third, though the planners worried, even from earliest days, about alienating their already small audiences and were probably happier scheduling Vaughan Williams and Tippett, or at least Lennox Berkeley and Rubbra. After a concert that included Seiber's second string quartet, the composer wrote to the BBC to ask if they might repeat the performance on the Third. 'Quite frankly,' came the reply, 'we are able to broadcast only a very little of music so radical as this. The audience to whom it would appeal is, as you know, extremely small.' Seiber wrote back that this was 'a rather sad state of affairs'. All over the Continent, he said, 'the Third has a tremendous reputation because it can fearlessly and without making any compromise broadcast music of any school and style, including the most extreme . . . It would be a pity if this courageous policy would be given up.' What the mandarins at the Third most yearned for was traditional, classical 'high culture' given to the highest standards.

Rudolf Bing felt the same way. We last met Bing at Glyndebourne where he had been John Christie's General Manager, and in Oxford during the war whence Bing commuted to his temporary job as a division manager in the London department store Peter Jones.* Bing dreamed of getting operatic production going again as soon as the war was over. Glyndebourne itself was not yet equipped for a proper Festival and became temporary home for, among others, Benjamin Britten's English Opera Group. Britten's *Rape of Lucretia* had its debut at Glyndebourne and the EOG then took it on tour to Manchester, Liverpool, Edinburgh, Glasgow, and back to Oxford and London. The tour was no great success, but it reinforced an idea that Bing had had earlier: that fully-fledged Glyndebourne productions might be mounted elsewhere. Britten and his colleagues went on to perform in Holland and at the Lucerne Festival (where Pears suggested they should start their own Festival, in Aldeburgh). Bing, meanwhile, was pushing ahead with his idea of Glyndebourne-away-from-Glyndebourne. The ideal setting, he thought, would be 'an international festival in which the other nations of the world could join in paying tribute to Britain's courage and sacrifice in the struggle against Hitler'.

The model that Bing, an Austrian refugee, had in mind was the Salzburg Festival. England, he noted, had no cities like Salzburg. But Scotland did. 'My mind kept returning to the sight of the castle, on the cliff at Edinburgh.' Bing had been struck by the beauty of Edinburgh, and its similarities to Salzburg, during the first weeks of the war when he and Audrey Mildmay were wandering through town late at night after a performance there of *The Beggar's Opera* by the touring Glyndebourne company. In 1944, we find him lunching with Henry Harvey Wood, the British Council's man in Edinburgh, discussing the possibilities of a festival. Bing said he was 'convinced that musical and operatic festivals on anything like pre-war scale were unlikely to be held in any of the shattered and impoverished centres for many years to come' and that he was therefore anxious to try to build up something in the UK. He persuaded Harvey Wood that 'such an enterprise, successfully conducted, might at this moment of European time, be of more than temporary significance and might establish in Britain a centre of world

---

* It is an odd coincidence that the Managing Directors of two of the world's most prominent opera houses – David Webster of Covent Garden and Rudolf Bing of the New York Metropolitan – had previously worked in English department stores.

resort for lovers of music, drama, ballet and the graphic arts'. Harvey Wood recommended Edinburgh and promised to make initial investigations.

Edinburgh was a magnificent city with its own proud history and culture, adequate hotels, theatres and concert halls (though no proper opera house), and good rail connections. Its university had a strong musical tradition. Sir Donald Tovey – composer and critic, pianist, professor and musicologist *extraordinaire* – had acted as a magnet to many of the great figures in the 1920s and 1930s, a role that came to be filled from 1945 by the multi-talented émigré musician Hans Gál; the Scottish Orchestra, whose previous conductors included Barbirolli and Szell, were led from 1946 by Walter Susskind (until Rankl took over in 1952).

In 1947 Bing inaugurated the first Edinburgh International Festival. In a world still licking the divisive wounds of war, Bing's Edinburgh was able to herald the re-emergence of a truly international culture. True to his initial intention of providing a temporary showcase for Glyndebourne, Bing's first Festival featured the Glyndebourne productions of Mozart's *Figaro* (conducted by Susskind) and Verdi's *Macbeth*. Performances were in the cramped King's Theatre. The *Macbeth* was directed by Carl Ebert, conducted by Berthold Goldschmidt and used the designs of Caspar Neher – a conscious echo of the teamwork that had produced this opera, under Bing's managerial eye, in Berlin in 1931.* The walk-on part of Fleance, Banquo's son, was played by the twelve-year-old George Christie.

In addition to the two Glyndebourne operas, the opening Festival also featured chamber music played by a multinational collection of stellar performers whose countries of birth had so recently been at war: Arthur Schnabel, Josef Szigeti, Pierre Fournier and Scotland's own William Primrose.† But the

---

* Bing had originally engaged Szell to conduct both works. But Szell ('a nasty man, God rest his soul') had evidently left Bing in the lurch and Bing had therefore engaged Susskind and Goldschmidt to step into the breach.

† There was very little avowedly Scottish presence at the first Edinburgh Festival and the press, while full of praise, wondered why the Festival did not feature a play by James Bridie or James Barrie, or the poetry of Hugh MacDiarmid or Edwin Muir. It was a legitimate criticism. But Bing's purpose had been to create an international Festival, not a Scottish one.

presence that sealed the Edinburgh Festival was that of Bruno Walter, directing the Vienna Philharmonic Orchestra. The VPO was trying to emerge from the incubus of the Nazi years. Many in Britain regarded Austria as a nation on parole whose people had willingly collaborated with their compatriot, Hitler. Walter had had to flee Central Europe for his life. That he now led the VPO at Edinburgh was thus of immense symbolic value.* Just as great, however, was the quality of the music-making. It was at Edinburgh that Walter conducted performances, later captured on record, of Mahler's *Song of the Earth* in which the contralto soloist was Kathleen Ferrier. Walter was so taken by Ferrier (whom Bing had introduced him to a year earlier) that he also agreed to accompany her at the piano in a recital at that first Edinburgh Festival.

Until Edinburgh, Bing had always been somebody's assistant. Here, for the first time, he was in charge – and he loved it. The Festival was a great success, the prototype of a plethora of artistic festivals that were to spring up all over Europe, America and beyond in the decades that followed.

To mark the twenty-fifth Edinburgh Festival in 1971, Rudolf Bing, by then far better known as General Manager of the Metropolitan Opera, New York, was given a knighthood. Sir Rudolf had to explain to an uncomprehending press that, yes, he was still a British citizen and, yes, it was he who had founded the Edinburgh Festival.

On 10 January 1948 a long queue of voluble enthusiasts snaked round the corner from the entrance to London's Wigmore Hall, eager to be admitted. The performance that afternoon was not by Schnabel or Cortot, or any of the other established lions of the concert circuit, but by four cub musicians presenting their debut recital. For once the cliché 'long-awaited' was appropriate, for the Hampstead hotline and the Golders Green grapevine had spread word that *this* was the big one. The Amadeus Quartet started, appropriately, with one of the most

---

*Immediately after Edinburgh, the VPO players went to London to join forces with their sister organisation, the Vienna State Opera, in what proved a triumphant visit to Covent Garden.

powerful works by Mozart: the D minor, K 421. They followed this with the Verdi, the performance of which difficult work 'placed this quartet right at the top of the tree technically, intellectually and musically', according to the critic of *The Scotsman* (John Amis). And they brought the proceedings to a triumphant close with Beethoven's *Razumovsky* No. 3, which even the sober *Times* had to acknowledge was played 'robustly [but] without roughness or neglect of minutiae'. In addition to all the usual critics, the BBC were there, talent scouts for the Third Programme, and they immediately approached the Quartet with broadcasting offers.

Norbert Brainin, Siegmund Nissel and Hans Schidlof had become increasingly friendly during the war, talented refugee violinists of similar age and background. Brainin lived with relatives in Hampstead Garden Suburb; Nissel and Schidlof roomed together in Streatham and Upper Norwood for a while, but were forever gravitating towards north-west London. Here, people like Dr Edward May, an enthusiastic amateur cellist who lived in Highgate, or Martin Cahn of St John's Wood, would organise informal musical soirées to which talented members of the émigré community would be invited. It was at the homes of such people as May and Cahn, and at music evenings arranged by the FDKB and Ferdinand Rauter's Anglo-Austrian Music Society, that a sense of common purpose first developed as Brainin, Schidlof, Nissel, Susi Rózsa and her friend the cellist Martin Lovett and others played together in various ad hoc permutations. A further bond was provided by the fact that Brainin, Nissel and Schidlof were all students of Max Rostal.

The debt the three were to owe Rostal was incalculable. Without his generous help (he never took a penny from Nissel and Schidlof whom he knew to be living off meagre resources), they simply would not have been equipped to launch themselves upon the joint career that was soon to follow. Rostal took the three of them right back to the fundamentals of string playing and gave them a thorough grounding in their art. Himself a refugee and a protégé of Carl Flesch, he retained vivid memories of those lessons. Norbert was always bubbling over with new ideas, experiments, questions, doubts and confusions, not just about music but about everything else in life. His basic musical gifts were obviously of the highest order and the questing, almost impulsive quality that Rostal sometimes detected in the relatively immature approach of those days was gradually applied, under careful tutelage, to excellent account. Sigi, by contrast, was a more accommodating pupil, less inclined to ask awkward questions, using time profitably and digesting rapidly what he was told. Hans Schidlof was the most exuberant player of the three, wild even. 'He played everything with fantastic temperament,' Rostal recalled. 'He nearly cut the violin in half, overpressed madly, and played with tremendous intensity.' Schidlof was the most difficult of the three for Rostal to 'tame' (quite a contrast to the beautifully controlled, almost restrained viola player the world would soon know).

Rostal ran a chamber ensemble and he used this to extend the experience of his more promising pupils. The set-up varied from one concert to the next. Sometimes Norbert or Hans would be asked to play the viola part. The first time Schidlof played the viola in public was in a Rostal Chamber Orchestra performance of the Bach Brandenburg Concerto No. 3; he could not even read the viola clef when they first rehearsed the piece.

The three young men were not sufficiently established to be invited on to the CEMA or ENSA circuits, and their music-making had to be fitted in around mundane war work. Every now and then an engagement materialised – sonatas at the National Gallery, perhaps, or a concert in Leeds with the pianist Fanny Waterman 'in aid of Mrs Churchill's Fund for Russia'. When the war came to an end, all three were caught up in the general euphoria and optimism. From now on music had to come first.

In October 1946 Norbert Brainin, brimming with that impulsive confidence Rostal had tried to canalise, went in for the Carl Flesch Gold Medal Award, named in memory of the teacher whom both had revered and who had died two years earlier. By way of preparation, Brainin spent much of 1946 perfecting his technique and agonising over the ineffable depths of the Bach C minor Sonata (the very work Nissel had played to Flesch seven years earlier) and the bravura of the Brahms

Concerto. During the summer Imogen Holst invited him down to Dartington Hall, where she was Music Director. An admiring colleague noted in her diary:

> Norbert is dynamite – electrified everyone, including audience . . . Does everything with whole of himself – eating, playing and laughing . . . Everything he does, and is, is Gargantuan. Quartets for two hours and then reduced us to jellies of laughter with his 'funny anecdotes' . . . Extra-ordinary playing – intense, burning, but very controlled . . . In that hall, with a few listeners, it was one of those occasions that sear into one's system.

Brainin won the 1946 Flesch prize and was overcome; his victory, as only he really knew, represented an extraordinary feat of mind over body. But the strain of competitive music-making had depressed him and he vowed never again to subject himself to that sort of pressure. His greatest fulfilment came from chamber work and for a while he played trios with Edmund Rubbra on the piano and the cellist William Pleeth. He took up again with the Rostal Chamber Orchestra and tried his hand at the viola from time to time – sharing this double act with Schidlof (by now known as Peter). Sigi Nissel was a regular partner. One day Peter Schidlof had a call from fellow Rostal student Suzanne Rózsa. She had to withdraw from a Wigmore Hall concert at which she and Martin Lovett were due to give the first performance in England of the violin and cello duo by Honegger. Could Peter stand in for her and do the violin part? Peter knew Martin well; they had last played together in the orchestra at Glyndebourne for the world première of Britten's *Rape of Lucretia*. He told Susi he would be happy to oblige. Thus the two young men, who were destined to share so much of their lives, gave their first joint chamber concert.

Norbert, Sigi, Peter and Martin all knew and appreciated each other's playing. Equally important, each was coming to realise that what he did best and enjoyed most was chamber music. It is unclear who first suggested they should get together as a quartet, though once the decision had been reached there was total dedication from all four, a powerful communal impulse that led them to rehearse together for six hours a day. Norbert and Peter both played the viola as well as the violin and at first there was some talk of the two sharing violin and viola duties. But as the foursome got down to serious rehearsals in early 1947 it became clear that, if they were to achieve a high standard of musicianship, this sort of chopping and changing was not possible and Peter agreed to subordinate his principal instrument to the less familiar one.

Nobody knew what direction the new working partnership would take. They didn't even have a name. Imogen Holst invited them down to give a concert in the Banqueting Hall at Dartington in the summer of 1947 and they performed as the 'Brainin String Quartet'. When Imogen mentioned to the Elmhirsts that Brainin's Amati violin was borrowed for the occasion, they sent him off to W. E. Hill's, the violin dealers, where he chose a Pietro Guarneri of Venice for which they paid (a bill of £1250). Imogen herself, a person of great generosity though without the resources of the Elmhirsts, was sufficiently impressed by the quartet to offer to underwrite, out of her own pocket, their professional debut. They were to book the Wigmore Hall and she would put down the then not inconsiderable sum of £100 to cover basic expenses.

A fortnight before the posters and leaflets were due to be prepared the foursome had still not decided what to call themselves. Brainin was not yet a well-known figure comparable to Adolf Busch or Sidney Griller with their eponymous quartets, and in any case the habit of adopting an impersonal name – the Aeolian or Pro Arte, for example – seemed more in tune with the times. Geographical names were popular (though these could be misleading: all four members of the Budapest Quartet were Russian) and for a while they thought of themselves as the 'London–Vienna Quartet'. 'Sounds like a railway timetable,' snorted one and the idea was dropped.

Nissel proposed the name 'Amadeus'. It sounded nice, embraced the ideas of love and God, and was Mozart's middle name. 'Ridiculous!' came the inevitable first reactions. 'They'll think all we can play is Mozart'* Other names were tried and discarded, but Amadeus kept resurfacing, like an insistent rondo theme. The posters had to be printed and a name chosen. 'OK,' they agreed, 'let's be the Amadeus String Quartet and the hell with it!' Friends soon dubbed them the 'Wolf Gang'.

A full programme, a packed house, favourable reviews in all the right places and offers to broadcast on the BBC – no young group could have hoped for a more successful debut. Why, in addition to the basic fact that they obviously played well, did things go quite so unerringly their way? Why, indeed, were so many people eager to get into the Wigmore Hall in January 1948 to hear a group with no record of public achievement? Part of the answer lies in the *esprit de corps* of the refugee community. There was an almost parental pride among many who saw the posters that sprouted in and around London at the end of 1947. 'Do you remember those talented boys whom we heard playing at Eddie May's and Martin Cahn's and at Anglo-Austrian musical evenings?' people said. 'Well, it seems they've formed themselves into a professional quartet. We really ought to go along and help launch them.' A further explanation of the extraordinary impact of the Amadeus is suggested by the comment, in one review, that 'we must welcome their appearance warmly for the shortage of good quartets is acute' (a view the cultural commissars at the BBC obviously shared).

If the Amadeus Quartet had been able to time their emergence on the scene they could hardly have chosen a better moment. A London-based ensemble who played the classics with irresistible authority, they rapidly reached a huge audience with their recordings, tours and broadcasts. Once successfully established they decided, after considerable heart-searching, to take their message back to the land of their musical and (for three of them, personal) origins. Their first tour of Germany (in 1950) was a tremendous success; a year later they signed up with a German record company (Deutsche Grammophon). They were particu-

---

*A problem that was to dog quartets such as the Borodin, Berg, Smetana and Bartók.

larly gratified, and moved, by the enthusiasm with which they were later received in Austria.*

There was doubtless an element of Mid-European guilt in the welcome accorded to such musicians and other visiting artists and intellectuals from Britain in the land of their former enemies and erstwhile compatriots. But the visitors had more than sentiment to offer. British cultural life, for all its continued insularity, was beginning to display early signs of a panache, a confidence, a bravura which gave succour to continental artists and audiences only just emerging from the ashes of Hitlerism. Thus the Third Programme rapidly built a reputation not only at home but also among intellectuals and cultural leaders in war-torn Europe, even if most of these could not actually hear it. Not only Seiber and Wellesz but such European giants as Barth, Jung, Croce and Maritain were entertained as potential broadcasters.

As early as 1947 – the year Rankl launched the Covent Garden Opera and Bing the Edinburgh Festival – the music critic William Glock was sent by the BBC on a tour of Central Europe to seek out talent for the Third and came back with news of his encounters with the composers Boris Blacher and Karl Amadeus Hartmann, and the conductors Hans Rosbaud and Georg Solti. Shortly afterwards Glock became Director of the influential Bryanston summer school of music, soon relocated at Darting-ton. Here he would invite distinguished émigré composers such as Hindemith and Blacher – and, year after year, the Amadeus Quartet.†

---

* 'Only a Vienna quartet could play Schubert like that!' gushed one critic in the Austrian capital in the early 1950s. He went on to explain to his readers that three of the quartet were local boys but that one had been born in England – Norbert Brainin.

† In 1959 Glock joined the BBC as Controller of Music where, for nearly a decade and a half, he presided over an era in which the legatees of English romanticism were firmly displaced by the spirit of Stravinsky and Schoenberg.

CHAPTER FOURTEEN

Bruised Veterans of the Totalitarian Age

London was possibly the most cosmopolitan city in the world in the last years of war and the first of peace, playing host to a veritable caravanserai of exotic global travellers. The pubs and dance halls in and around Soho and Fitzrovia were packed with peripatetic pleasure seekers: fancy-free secretaries eager to learn intimate instruction in various European languages, GIs proffering candy bars and stronger enticements, languid aesthetes looking for each other, demob-happy troops from the Antipodes drinking away the hours before the long voyage home, would-be painters seeking models, actors chatting up producers, poets publishers. Francis Bacon, Lucian Freud and Feliks Topolski were habitués of the watering holes of Soho, Fitzrovia and nearby Bloomsbury; here, a talented young poet like Michael Hamburger (who had known Lucian Freud since their Berlin childhood) could be confident of encountering the influential Ceylonese editor Tambimuttu or the habitually inebriated Dylan Thomas. As the colleges and libraries returned to London and the political pendulum swung from the constrictions of wartime to the radical reforms of Socialism, firebrands of colonial freedom from Africa and India reiterated the arguments for national liberation, sensing that their time would soon come. Over in Mayfair and Knightsbridge, George Weidenfeld spent the twilight years of the war cultivating the allied governments in exile, tasting Yugoslav slivovitz, Czech brandy, Norwegian aquavit, Dutch kümmel and varieties of French wines – all in the pursuit of his BBC duties, of course.

Most of the exiles would soon return whence they had come.

De Gaulle and the Free French went back to France, Jan Masaryk to Czechoslovakia, Queen Wilhelmina to the Netherlands, Kwame Nkrumah to Africa. But most of the German-speaking refugees stayed; the world in which they had been raised had been utterly obliterated. Not that those undertaking the regeneration of normal life in Oslo, Paris, Amsterdam or Warsaw were to have an easy task, for the scars of Nazi occupation would take generations to heal. But none of these was returning to a country in which millions had been systematically enslaved, weakened and put to death with the willing connivance of their compatriots. To an exiled Frenchman, Norwegian, Dane, Czech or Pole, the end of the war appeared to offer promise of return to a liberated homeland. To those from German-speaking Central Europe, the homeland itself had been the heart of darkness. Virtually every one of the Hitler émigrés learned, sooner or (more often) later, of friends and relatives lost in the anonymous barbarity of the death camps. How could they return to live in a country in which a genuinely popular government had wished to murder them?

So they stayed – and tried to reproduce something of the world they had lost. Thus the denizens of north-west London's 'Little Vienna' would set out in their berets and furs to hear Wagner at Covent Garden and chamber concerts at the Wigmore Hall, or to Georg Hoellering's Academy Cinema in Oxford Street to catch the latest art film from the Continent and then, perhaps, make for a good meal of 'heimische' food at Schmidt's restaurant in Charlotte Street. You wanted the latest German-language book? The best person to go to was probably Fritz Homeyer in the foreign department at Bumpus, or you might try Joseph Suschitzky's* bookshop or Mrs Waterhouse's second-hand emporium, both at the Swiss Cottage end of what genial bus conductors called 'Finchleystrasse'. You could then spend all day reading it over a single cup of coffee, or consuming *Schnitzel* and *Strudel* with fellow refugees at the always welcoming Cosmo. 'Have you heard Hitler's final territorial demands?' someone would ask the assembled company in a

---

* Run by cousins of the photographer and cinematographer Wolf Suschitzky.

voice of some urgency. 'No? Hampstead and Swiss Cottage!' – and everyone would collapse in gales of laughter.

When the war was finally over, many found it hard to comprehend at first that Hitler was really dead and Nazism defeated. The initial ecstasy was authentic enough but, as the appalling truths of what had been going on began to seep out, it was tempered by feelings of grief, horror, even guilt. A further ripple of refugees, with numbers branded on to their arms, flowed into Little Vienna and its satellite and sister colonies around the country, and émigrés old and new would weep, embrace and seek comfort, even strength, from the tragedies they shared. They would debate long into the night whether they would, or should, ever revisit their old homeland, whether they would ever feel themselves to be wholly British, whether they wouldn't be better off trying to get to America, or whether (if they were Jewish) they should be Zionists and support the emerging state of Israel. When you have lost everything, you can at least enjoy the fact that, since you have few ties, all options appear open.

For foreign exiles with serious cultural aspirations, post-war Britain could have seemed a somewhat sour place, a self-regarding residuum of complacency and complaint. Claus Moser, brought up in a world in which art and culture were central, grabbed with gratitude whatever was on offer – the occasional good concert or opera, or the arrival of the BBC Third Programme – but felt that such things were but islands. The British, he came to feel, were essentially philistines to whom art and culture were at best the icing on the cake; Claus longed to recover a world, like the *Mitteleuropa* of his childhood, in which they *were* the cake. He liked to quote Isaiah Berlin who thought British philistinism could in part be traced back to the public school system in which the governing elite had been raised. At these schools, said Berlin, art and culture were what you did on a rainy Wednesday afternoon when sports were cancelled and you had to stay indoors.

To most in the wider community, it seemed, art meant little more than routine obeisance to the patriotism of Shakespeare or the countryside of Constable: atavistic garments in which the

British liked to wrap themselves for comfort during the chilly years of post-war austerity. Along with this nostalgia for an imagined past came a new middle-class respectability. 'There'll always be an England,' people sang soulfully around the VE bonfires, even as the open-hearted neighbourliness of wartime gave way to the closed doors of post-war suburbia. Radical thinking, Modernist innovation, artistic challenges to the accepted order – these had been suspect before the war and remained so in the years following victory. At Covent Garden, the ballet danced old favourites like *The Sleeping Beauty* and *Nutcracker*, and the opera performed *Carmen* and *Meistersinger*. The Amadeus Quartet played Mozart and Beethoven at their inaugural concert, not Bartók and Berg. Kurt Jooss returned to Germany, disappointed in the bland reception his work was receiving in post-war Britain.

It may seem paradoxical that a radical, reforming Labour government presided over a culture in many ways obstinately conservative, that firebrands of planned egalitarianism like Aneurin Bevan coexisted with such earnest raisers of the national brow as T. S. Eliot or the BBC Third Programme. Voices of cultural dissent were heard from both right and left, including some from the émigré community. Hayek continued to pour forth periodic Jeremiads, lambasting the Socialism of Attlee as but a step or two short of that of Stalin. The Dada artist Kurt Schwitters, on the other hand, or the apostle of free dance Rudolf Laban, eked out a lean existence in the northern provinces preaching doctrines that were generally too radical for the audiences they tried to address. Their time, and that of Hayek, would come later. For the time being, a comfortable consensus prevailed which embraced the 'contemporary' but avoided the 'modern'. If brow levels were to be raised, then at least let everybody have equal opportunities to partake of the higher things in life.

To some, such a formula seemed designed to do precisely the opposite – to lower everybody's brow to an agreed common denominator. '[I]n our headlong rush to educate everybody, we are lowering our standards,' wrote Eliot in his *Notes Towards the Definition of Culture*, published in 1948 (the year he was awarded the Nobel Prize for Literature). The prophet of *The Waste Land* went on to fulminate that we were 'destroying our ancient edifices' in order to make space on which 'the barbarian nomads of the future will encamp in their mechanised caravans'. It was an alarming vision, one that was shared by many who did not otherwise buy into Eliot's particular brand of cultural elitism. In the same year as Eliot published his *Notes*, F. R. Leavis, as curmudgeonly a Little Englander as Eliot was a cosmopolitan Modernist, produced *The Great Tradition*. Here, as in the pages of his magazine *Scrutiny*, Leavis urged the tight-belted view that the English tradition was borne by a canon of outstanding literary texts, that these should be assiduously studied and restudied – and that little attention need be given to (i.e. squandered on) their wider historical or biographical context.

The aesthetic vision of Leavis was meaner and narrower than Eliot's, yet they shared a genuine fear that, as art became more widely diffused, quality was in jeopardy. The canon of the past offered more than the mechanised pulp of tomorrow. It was a view with which many agreed, and several of the most accomplished writers of the time chose to pay their own acid-edged homage to a disappearing past as they evoked class-ridden, pre-war, imperial England. Thus Evelyn Waugh wrote *Brideshead Revisited* and Anthony Powell began his sequence *A Dance to the Music of Time*.

To the émigré writer, neither of these two visions – not the egalitarian belief in social improvement that inspired those setting up the post-war infrastructure, nor the cultural conservatism of Eliot or Leavis – provided a natural habitat. The cheery optimism of the social reformers and the gloomy atavism of Eliot and Leavis were in some ways poles apart. Yet both perspectives looked inward. To Alfred Kerr or Elias Canetti, creative spirits who had outstared the face of catastrophe and survived, much that preoccupied post-war Britain seemed insular to a degree. What did Little Englanders know who only England knew? As the refugees struggled to extract meaning from the epochal history through which they had lived and the situation of exile in which they now found themselves, how could they write about country house weekends or review the latest Noël Coward comedy of manners?

The problems were compounded by the fact that a number of refugee writers (Canetti and Kerr among them) had built up important reputations on the Continent but were scarcely known in their country of adoption. Struggling with inadequate English and preoccupied with issues most people in Britain did not particularly want to read about, few émigré writers were able to make an impact. Erich Fried, an Austrian exile whose English was good enough to understand and translate into German the subtleties of *Under Milk Wood* and *A Midsummer Night's Dream*, preferred to write his own essays, stories and poetry in his native language. When Hilde Spiel or Robert Neumann published in English, their work received only limited attention outside the refugee community.

Yet there were other winds blowing through the intellectual life of post-war Britain that worked to the benefit of the émigré writer. The first was the rise of the Cold War. After the initial euphoria of victory in 1945, everybody looked forward to an era of European peace and stability. Within a couple of years such hopes looked distinctly fragile. The wartime alliance fell apart and gave way to rivalry between the Soviet Union and the USA, the rise of NATO and the Warsaw Pact, and a radical redrawing of the geopolitical map of Europe. Germany, theoretically governed by the four victorious powers, was in practice split into two separate and mutually antagonistic states, one 'Western' and capitalist, the other 'Eastern' and Communist. The old capital, Berlin (itself divided, though not yet by its infamous wall), once the proud centre of Europe, was now on the peripheries of its eastern and western zones. It was of immense strategic significance to both camps. But despite all the funding and encouragement that each side poured upon the city's showcase artists (the Berlin Philharmonic Orchestra in the West, Brecht's Berliner Ensemble or the operatic productions of Walter Felsenstein in the East), the broken capital at the edge of everybody's map was no longer the cultural powerhouse of earlier days. Much the same was true of other erstwhile centres of Central European culture and learning: Leipzig,

Dresden, Vienna, Prague and Budapest. All were now provincial cities, culturally marginalised, proud of a magnificent history but relegated, it seemed, from centre stage to sideshow. London, by contrast, was pushed back into the limelight. Britain was the one nation in the whole of Central and Western Europe that had fought Hitler and won and, as such, had immense prestige. No other nation held its head so high. Tired and ragged, Britain emerged from the war to the unaccustomed plaudits of the world.

The prominence of Britain was further emphasised by the changing geopolitical priorities of the Cold War. As the epochal events of post-war European history were unfurled in rapid succession – the Marshall Plan, the Berlin airlift, the establishment of NATO and of the Federal Republic of (West) Germany – London found itself at the very centre of affairs between the United States and continental Europe, the essential stepping stone, the arbiter, the broker. The 'Special Relationship' between the USA and the UK was probably always more a figment of British than American imagination. But it reached its apogee during these years as powerful and educated Americans valued their British contacts and felt comfortable in a nation with whom (as they said) they shared a common history, language and traditions. London was where Eisenhower had had his headquarters, Britain the land from which the liberation of the Continent had been planned and executed. In the wake of victory, and powered by the shared imperatives of the Cold War, people from the two nations continued to work closely together during the post-war years – and London's significance as a major international capital was further boosted.

By the later 1940s, therefore, a number of bright young men and women, born and raised at the heart of European culture, found themselves living in another part of the world which, as a result of a convoluted series of twists no novelist would have invented, looked capable of assuming similar prominence. The British might be insular, smug, self-regarding, unreflective. Their bourgeois stolidity and their capacity to take succour from the past might be easily parodied by the émigrés in their midst. But no Austrian, Italian, German or Spaniard could draw comfort from the essential continuity between past, present and future as the British appeared to do. If the British lacked fire in the belly, many refugees acknowledged that a little island of stability, of cultural continuity, was no bad thing in a world that had experienced such turbulence, and London a privileged vantage point from which to pick up the threads of civilisation that Hitler had so nearly destroyed for ever.

Arthur Koestler was in some ways the archetypal émigré, almost to the point of caricature. Brilliant, forceful, opinionated, Koestler spent his life on the move – from one domicile, country, woman, ideology to the next, constantly seeking stable, permanent solutions to intractable questions. Born in Budapest to assimilated Jewish parents who moved to Vienna when he was a boy, Koestler visited Palestine as a neophyte Zionist in the 1920s and travelled deep into the USSR as a committed Communist early in the following decade. His skills as a scientific and political journalist landed him stints in Berlin and Paris. In 1936 he went to Spain, reported (in the British newspaper the *News Chronicle*) that Franco was receiving help from the Germans – and was jailed in Seville (and nearly executed) by the Nationalists. Here he drafted (in German) a novel, *Darkness at Noon*, that portrayed the fierce dilemmas of a Communist ideologue accustomed to suppress every vestige of truth and humanity in the interests of a party which he believes in and which turns on him. Koestler wrote from the heart and from personal experience. How far can the end justify the means? Is the adoption of violence and falsehood acceptable if it helps achieve agreed aims? What pressures bring a man to confess to political crimes he has not committed? These were issues – graphically dramatised in the novel – that profoundly disturbed Koestler as he struggled to reconcile his fading Marxism with the transparent barbarism of Stalin's show trials.

In France at the outbreak of war, Koestler was imprisoned again, this time by nervous authorities who weren't quite sure what to make of him. He was released, fled south to avoid the German occupation, joined the Foreign Legion and, after further adventures, managed to get a flight from neutral Lisbon to Bristol in November 1940. From Bristol Koestler was accompanied by the British police (more genial than those he had encountered in France but equally uncomprehending) to Pentonville prison in London. Thus, he missed the publication, by Jonathan Cape, of *Darkness at Noon*.

After his release from internment, the restless little engine that was Arthur Koestler joined the Pioneer Corps, gave educational lectures to the troops, wrote scripts (by now in English) for the BBC and the Ministry of Information, produced books and articles, and tried desperately to communicate to the innocent British the true nature of the horror they were fighting. A natural polemicist who (in the words of Weidenfeld) 'liked intellectual cockfights with people he deemed his intellectual equals', Koestler spent the war years and after sparring with others on the intellectual left such as Crossman and Orwell, men whose persuasive skills, like his own, were honed by the exigencies of war.

His search for transcendent truth unquenched, Koestler revisited Palestine and wrote *Thieves in the Night*, which again reflected in graphic form on the use of abhorrent means in pursuit of supposedly legitimate ends. When the state of Israel was established Koestler, by now a former Zionist as he was a former Communist, announced that there was no longer any point in being a Jew if you chose – as he did – to live in the diaspora. Shorn of his Communism and now of his Zionism, no longer Hungarian or Austrian, German or French, Koestler sought new panaceas to advocate, new causes to fight for. And against. He found what he needed in the Cold War.

Armed with the single-mindedness of the disillusioned believer, Koestler became a ferocious anti-Communist, producing a torrent of speeches and articles in which he urged greater unity among the nations of Western Europe as a bulwark against the evils of the Soviet Union. He argued that the old conceptual divisions between 'left' and 'right', 'Socialism' and 'capitalism', were now of little account and had been replaced by a much greater confrontation: that between 'total tyranny' and 'relative freedom'. Thus the Attlee government might have introduced various benign reforms. But the more important point, to Koestler, was that their brand of Socialism was in danger of reinforcing rather than transcending British insularity (a concern that echoed the old Soviet debate about the acceptability or otherwise of 'Socialism in one country'), and he lost no opportunity to advocate international co-operation among the free nations of the West. Greater internationalism had to be the wave of the future, he said. What was vital was to harness the processes of history to the benefit of mankind – or humanity would be destroyed.*

Koestler's argument was one that many wanted to hear (and was not dissimilar to that of others at the time, e.g. Orwell in his novel *Nineteen Eighty-Four*). The fact that Koestler had experienced the evils of both Communist and Nazi totalitarianism at first hand bestowed added authority to his message, while his hectoring tone and richly rhetorical phrase-making lent a sense of urgency. When an organisation called the 'Congress for Cultural Freedom' (later revealed to be a creature of the CIA) brought together a collection of celebrated Western intellectuals in West Berlin in 1950, Koestler was called upon to draft its manifesto.

In later life Koestler continued to gravitate towards controversial causes. He was a prominent opponent of hanging and proponent of the right to suicide.† He argued that most Jews were descendants not of Abraham but of a Caucasian people whose leader had converted to Judaism in the eighth century, while his interest in the intangible nature of scientific discovery led him to examine the very nature of creation and the role of drugs, coincidence, the supra-rational and the paranormal in the sciences.

---

* Listening to Koestler's broadcasts, it is hard not to feel that he almost relished his warnings of imminent doom. In 1946 he expatiated engagingly on the properties of arsenic and suggested we are all suffering from moral arsenic poisoning, while in 1953, talking about the popularity of science fiction, Koestler hypothesised that the human race might be due for extinction as a biological misfit, like the pterodactyl. In 1972 he argued that, for the first time, mankind 'has to come to terms with the idea of his mortality as a species'. And yet you're an optimist, asked his interviewer? Yes indeed, answered this urbane prophet of apocalypse, distinguishing carefully between 'warnings of doom' and the 'preaching of gloom'. Three years later Koestler imagined the bleak letter a cosmic insurance company might write to earthlings after having made an assessment of their chances of survival.
† Koestler and his wife died in a suicide pact in 1983.

If there was any overall theme running through this dazzling diversity, it was the recurrent attempt to seek explanations of the inexplicable, impose order upon the random and the inchoate, carve new meanings from the apparently shapeless material of experience. Koestler (like another refugee from Central Europe, Albert Einstein) spent many years seeking a unified theory that would hold together the various truths upon which he thought he had alighted.

Koestler often found himself positing dual explanations, paradoxes, thesis and antithesis. He recognised this tendency towards dualism as going back to a moment in adolescence when he was bewildered by the sheer infinity of the cosmos, the idea that an arrow shot into blue space would travel in a straight line for ever. The universe was, of course, limitless – and yet at the same time it couldn't be. Many years later, in something of the same spirit, Koestler defined the act of creation as resulting (like jokes) from the 'bisociation' of two planes of thought; the old conflict between Socialism and capitalism, he said, had been transcended by a new one between totalitarianism and freedom; the role of the artist was not to solve but to expose, yet the intellectual evades his duty if not also a man of action. Books and articles were given antithetical titles like *Arrival and Departure, The Yogi and the Commissar, Insight and Outlook.* In his final decades it seemed as though Koestler were attempting to scale a new level of certainty, one allowing for the principles of relativity and uncertainty, for the transient, the hybrid and the inconsistent.

Arthur Koestler attracted an army of admirers, mostly people who shared his views and did not know about his compulsive sexual predatoriness and drunkenness (he was equally loathed by those who did not – and did!). The multifaceted nature of many of his explanations was redolent to his followers of the dialectic of Hegel; to his critics, this was a man wishing both to have and to eat his cake. Britain's finest émigré writer in English since Conrad, Koestler's personal magnetism and indefatigable intellectual energy ensured his was a voice that would be heard. If his books did not sell in his adopted country as well as he would have wished, he felt that this was in some ways to the credit of the British, a nation 'sceptical about Utopias, rejecting all blueprints, enamoured of its leisurely muddle, incurious about the future, devoted to its past'. Infuriated by British insouciance as to the true nature of Nazism and Communism, he nonetheless warmed to a nation he regarded as a refuge for 'bruised veterans of the totalitarian age'. Forever the foreigner, Koestler said he felt 'British to the bone'; a typically deracinated European intellectual, he became a patriotic Englishman – especially whenever he went 'abroad' (i.e. everywhere he had lived before for any length of time). In his last years he contributed to the fund to restore the local village church. There are those who would maintain that you can't get much more English than that.

CHAPTER FIFTEEN

Making Contact

Koestler was one of several émigré writers who came to love England while irritated by it, grateful for the freedom it offered, despairing of its provincialism. Coming, as they did, from lands where ideas were supposed to be taken seriously, many refugees were alarmed, and then incredulous, at the uncensored views freely expressed in the British media, at political meetings or from the soap boxes at Speakers Corner in Hyde Park. Koestler (like his fellow Hungarians Pressburger and Mikes) directed finely honed intellectual arrows at the insularity of the British, while revelling in the fact that he was permitted to do so. Even the British climate, for centuries the standard butt of foreign scorn, came to be regarded with affection as some used it to symbolise the virtues of the national character: unpredictable, impenetrable and (above all) unextreme. When Pressburger wished to create an aura of gentle, misty mystery (*I Know Where I'm Going*), he did not place his characters in the Alps or Andes but in the Western Isles of Scotland.

Many of the refugees came to savour the English language, becoming connoisseurs of its idiosyncracies, experiencing a fresh response to words and phrases that few native speakers could ever recover. This involved hard work. Koestler described how he would struggle to invent an arresting metaphor, only to discover that it had long been discarded as cliché. The poet Michael Hamburger became a master translator, from German into English, and tried for a while to write in both languages. But he worried at first 'whether the language I had adopted would adopt me' and feared he would succumb to 'the exaggerated correctness that betrays the foreigner'. The linguistic sensitivity of the exile could also prove highly entertaining. One of Gerard Hoffnung's most famous monologues included the inadvertent misuse of the English language by an Austrian hotelier replying to a request for information. In every room, he would announce with gusto, there are 'French widows' – adding, 'We are very good in bath – and in bed!' Fritz Spiegl, long the principal flautist in the Liverpool Philharmonic Orchestra, invented a celebrated second career for himself as affectionate scourge of the use and misuse of English.

For those who succeeded in mastering the language, especially creative writers who arrived young and learned English in their youth, the fulfilments could be considerable. Judith Kerr's semi-autobiographical novels introduced countless adolescent readers to the experience of exile, while her best-selling children's book, *The Tiger Who Came for Tea*, must have evoked a frisson of exquisite fear in all who read it and tried to imagine the unannounced arrival of a threatening, omnipotent 'guest'. Eva Figes's sensitive memoir of her own childhood and exile featured her personal 'Little Eden' of Cirencester; in her novel *The Tenancy*, a chronicle of inexorable neighbourly decline and degradation, Figes portrays a mysterious 'foreign' couple, the Wolfs, who have apparently escaped a terrible fate abroad but turn out to be the strongest, wisest people on the block.* Thomas Wiseman, in *The Quick and the Dead* (which opens in a Caligari-type fairground), plots the intersecting lives of two Viennese men, one a natural Nazi and the other a Jew, against the background of Hitlerism and war, while the devastation caused by the war provides the background to his later novel *Children of the Ruins*.

Few Hitler émigrés proved to be consistently successful novelists, however, nor did they make an especially noteworthy direct impact upon the development of post-war British drama

---

* Eva Figes, who was born in Berlin, said she thought of her writing as being 'more Modernistic' than that of many British-born writers 'in the sense that when I began to write I looked to Europe because it seemed to me that that was where the excitement was as far as fiction was concerned'. Her early novel, *Winter Journey*, was inspired by the Schubert song cycle, which she had known and loved since childhood.

or poetry. But the indirect influence was considerable. Many British writers incorporated the character of the refugee into their writings, among them Philip Larkin, Angus Wilson and Margaret Drabble. Iris Murdoch acknowledged the profound intellectual debt she owed to Canetti* and dedicated her early novel *The Flight from the Enchanter* to him. Martin Esslin introduced Central European writers such as Brecht to BBC audiences, while Michael Hamburger's translations brought the poetry of Hölderlin to a readership that had scarcely even known of his existence.

The greatest collective impact of the émigrés upon post-war British letters, however, was probably in their role as publishers. Horovitz, Foges, the Neuraths, Deutsch, Maschler (father and son), Weidenfeld, Maxwell, Elek, Hamlyn, Owen and others helped transform the literary and intellectual life of post-war Britain. When they arrived in Britain, publishing was still largely the domain of conservative family firms, the literary counterpart of gentlemen's clubs, producing elegant hardback volumes to grace the shelves of the *haute bourgeoisie*. Half a century later, few independent firms remained, while publishing routinely included mass-market colour reproduction, packaging and part-works, trade and paperback originals, international co-publishing deals, broadcasting and exhibition tie-ins.

The changes were by no means all due to refugee publishers. Back in the 1930s a handful of creative mavericks were already disconcerting the profession – Allen Lane, who had introduced Penguin paperbacks, for example, and the resolutely left-wing Victor Gollancz. The war itself brought further changes. Paper rationing was introduced, with each established firm's allow-

---

* Iris Murdoch's *affaire* with the mesmeric Canetti was recalled over half a century later by her husband, John Bayley, in some wonderfully acidic passages in an otherwise benevolent memoir of Iris. Canetti is referred to with mock reverence as the *Dichter*, the 'master-spirit of literature' and 'the Mage' – and with no reverence at all as the 'godmonster of Hampstead'. Canetti was evidently a man of such profound and mystical sensibilities that he could not stoop to having actual opinions about anybody else's literary work. 'Mystery', Bayley concludes with consummate cattishness, 'remains the hallmark of the Mage.' For more about Murdoch's relationship with Canetti (and her affair with the émigré writer Franz Steiner) see Peter J. Conradi, *Iris Murdoch: A Life*.

ance assessed at forty per cent of the amount used in the last year of peace. That effectively prevented existing publishers from expanding while opening the field to resourceful newcomers. Many publishers suffered grievous losses from the bombing raids. In a single night in November 1940, George Allen and Unwin lost 1,400,000 books; by the end of the year Longman's, Collins, Hutchinson and Eyre and Spottiswoode had all been hit and another 20 million volumes incinerated. As Andrew Sinclair noted wryly, literature was put to the torch in a way Hitler had never achieved in Nazi Germany.

To some extent the gap was filled by a plethora of magazines, many of which were founded before the war but achieved great popularity during and immediately afterwards. These ranged from serious literary showcases such as John Lehmann's *Penguin New Writing*, Connolly's *Horizon* and the Leavis flagship *Scrutiny*, to popular publications like Stefan Lorant's *Picture Post* and that enticing pocket-sized mix of the rarefied and the risqué, *Lilliput*. After the war many of these gradually faded in popularity* while the traditional British publishers got back to what they assumed would be business as usual. But the publishing business was rapidly being transformed beyond anything the pre-war fraternity could have imagined.

The doyen of the old school was Sir Stanley Unwin, chairman of his own firm and also for many years of the International Publishers Association. A patriarchal *littérateur* who lived in style in Hampstead, Unwin was on easy terms with the great figures of the day and liked to have himself photographed cosying up to Lloyd George or striding across the Heath with Ramsay MacDonald. A man of liberal instincts, an indefatigable traveller proud of his publishing contacts throughout the world, Unwin was appalled by the advent of the Nazis and was quick to express his views to friends in Germany. When he visited Vienna in the mid-1930s, one of the publishers he called upon was the Phaidon Press, run by Béla Horovitz. Phaidon was a publisher of books on culture and history, and was beginning to

---

* *Penguin New Writing* closed in 1949, *Horizon* in 1950, *Scrutiny* in 1953, *Picture Post* in 1957.

produce co-editions with the New York branch of Oxford University Press. Unwin was impressed by the books Horovitz published and also by his entrepreneurial business methods. But he knew everything would come tumbling down if Hitler marched in, and found that Horovitz had been preparing for just such an eventuality. Unwin and Horovitz reached an agreement whereby Unwin would buy all of Phaidon's stock so that, technically, the company was no longer in the hands of non-Aryans but a subsidiary of the British publishers George Allen and Unwin. It was a prescient and generous gesture on Unwin's part and was to help save the life of Horovitz and his family and colleagues, and bring Phaidon Press to London.

Béla Horovitz was born in Budapest in 1898 to a family that retained the values of traditional Judaism, while embracing the modern culture of the West. The family moved (around the same time as the Koestlers) to Vienna where Béla was brought up in the final years of Empire. Like Hayek, he was just old enough to see action in World War One and, in its immediate aftermath, entered the University of Vienna to study for a degree in law and business.

These were dark and dispiriting days throughout the defeated nations of Central Europe, with revolution and death in the air in Berlin, Budapest and Vienna, a time for reflection, for action. All traditional certainties were on hold as earnest young men and women tried to comprehend, and obtain their own purchase on, the rapid passage of history. Inflexible ideologues of left and right sprouted like dragons' teeth. Korda and Biro worked for the Kun government in Budapest; in Vienna, Karl Popper toyed with Marxism and watched troops shooting parliamentarians. Those with aesthetic sensibilities burned the midnight oil creating new movements and manifestos. Intellectual life was in ferment as devotees of alternative schools of thought sought to identify and indict those they believed responsible for recent catastrophes.

All this Béla Horovitz saw, heard – and discussed with fellow students, including an old comrade from the *Gymnasium*, a highly engaging poet called Ludwig Goldscheider. Horovitz and Goldscheider sensed a world in which the frenzied obsession with the problems of the immediate future was in danger of edging out valuable lessons from the past. Raised with a love of classical culture, which they sensed was in peril of eclipse, the two young men became possessed by a desire to bring the beauty and wisdom of Plato, Shakespeare, Goethe, Schiller and the great German historians to a wide general public. While still a student, Horovitz founded the Phaidon Press* which, with help from Goldscheider, gradually established itself as an important new Viennese imprint bringing out inexpensive but elegant editions of classical authors.

By the early 1930s, the two men were augmenting their list with what was to become Phaidon's hallmark: large-format art books. At the time, it was costly and technically difficult to reproduce works of art in book form, and few people apart from a handful of wealthy travellers and art connoisseurs could have claimed real familiarity with the works of Van Gogh, Velasquez or El Greco. The mixture of Horovitz's flair and business skills and Goldscheider's painstaking aesthetic sensitivity enabled the pair to create something new in publishing. Phaidon even started to make money, especially once Horovitz had begun to pioneer international editions.

The day the Nazis marched into Austria, Horovitz was in London and his wife in Switzerland. By a minor miracle of complex telephonic and telegraphic communication, the rest of the family all managed to get out of Vienna and, via various routes, meet in Antwerp. 'Phaidon Editions' were now published in London by George Allen and Unwin, so not only were Horovitz and his family (and the Goldscheiders) granted permission to come to Britain, but all the files and effects in Phaidon's Vienna offices were packed and shipped to Unwin's premises in London's Museum Street, much to the impotent fury of the Nazis.

For a while Béla Horovitz and his family lived in Lyndhurst Road in Hampstead. Then, to escape the blitz, they moved briefly to Oxford. From here Horovitz continued to run

---

* The name was intended as a homage to Plato's *Phaedo* and to the Enlightenment Jewish scholar Moses Mendelssohn whose *Phaedon* (1767) had proclaimed the immortality of the soul.

Phaidon (which Unwin continued to distribute), publishing, among other things, the catalogue of the drawings in the Royal Collection which required this 'friendly enemy alien' to make regular visits to Windsor Castle. It was in Oxford, as we have seen, that Horovitz asked Ernst Gombrich to write what became *The Story of Art*.

Béla Horovitz was not the only émigré publisher at work in Britain during the war. Wolfgang Foges was a Viennese journalist and magazine editor whose work brought him periodically to London. In 1934 he settled in Britain and founded Adprint, an advertising and printing company that initially made its money in Christmas cards and the like. Foges was ambitious, and helped pioneer what came to be called book packaging. During the war he engaged a number of other émigrés, among them an Austrian publisher named Walter Neurath who worked as his production manager. When Neurath came to Britain as a refugee he (and his then wife, Marianne) found protection at the home of Captain David Margesson, Chief Whip in the Chamberlain government and from 1940 to 1942 Churchill's Secretary of War. Margesson's American wife opened their country seat in Northamptonshire not only to the Neuraths but also to a woman from the Ballets Jooss – and to the adolescent Fritz Spiegl, who had English lessons from Lytton Strachey's sister, became aware of music for the first time and learned the 'facts of life' from the Margessons' son Frank. When the Margesson marriage broke up, Frank and his mother returned to America – with important consequences for Walter Neurath.

Neurath, who had studied art history at the University of Vienna and had contacts in the art world, found British culture to be extraordinarily verbal, that is, non-visual. Art to the British, he used to say, was a dirty word; why, at the University of Vienna there were two professors of art history while at the University of London there were none. Neurath was convinced that the balance could be shifted by the production of well-illustrated books that were carefully marketed. As Foges's production manager, Neurath was responsible for a number of Adprint's most successful series, notably a mass-market part-work, 'Britain in Pictures', which integrated illustrations and text, and was published by Collins.

Working alongside Neurath on the 'Britain in Pictures' series was a dynamic young woman from Berlin named Eva Feuchtwang whose husband was son of the chief rabbi of Vienna. Eva had been brought up by her mother and stepfather (neither of them Jewish); her stepfather had been a lawyer for UFA and as a girl Eva had hung around the film studios and was sometimes used as an extra. Having stormed out of school at the age of fourteen in solidarity with some other girls she (supported by her mother) felt had been unfairly expelled, Eva worked her way through a succession of jobs in rare books and antiques.

In 1938, Eva and Wilhelm Feuchtwang (her second husband), and their infant son Stefan, fled from Berlin just hours before the Gestapo came to pick them up. After a brief sojourn in the Netherlands, they fetched up in Britain and were living, almost penniless, in a flat in Kilburn when war broke out. Wilhelm, like so many others, was interned. Eva held her baby in her arms one night and looked forlornly out of the window as the air raid sirens began to moan. Stefan raised a smile on his mother's sad face by pointing his chubby little fingers at the clear, cold, dangerous sky and saying, almost joyfully, 'Look, the moon is singing!'

One of Wilhelm's fellow internees on the Isle of Man was Walter Neurath and when Neurath was released he helped secure work for Eva at Adprint. It was the beginning of a personal and professional partnership that led to the creation in 1949 of the publishers Thames and Hudson.

The company was evidently conceived on a romantic holiday in Cagnes. Walter and Eva were both still married to other people, but their dreams included starting a publishing house together.* Walter's idea was that they would publish books about visual subjects of universal interest – art, architecture, photography – in which (as in the 'Britain in Pictures' series) text and artwork were integrated and complementary. They would undertake international co-publishing ventures so that their books could be made available at reasonable cost in several

---

* Walter and Eva Neurath married in 1953

countries. It was decided at the outset that the new company would straddle the Atlantic. It was to be named after the rivers of London and New York. Walter approached Mrs Margesson for advice and finance, and she helped set up the American branch of the company. Her son Frank came to work with Walter and Eva in London. They had established their new firm in a tiny office at the top of 244 High Holborn. It was a courageous move, an attempt to create something out of nothing in a nation still bleeding from the effects of war.

'Courageous?' Eva Neurath, aged ninety-one, turned on me when I used the word. 'What is "courageous" when you have faced Hitler?' You must remember, she said, that it was a very exciting period, especially for those who had suffered and survived. 'The war had, of course, caused the total breakdown of everything we valued. But when it ended, we all had the feeling that now was the time to start again.'

George Weidenfeld felt the same way. Britain had experienced something of a cultural resurgence during the war and London had become the great cosmopolitan capital of the civilised world. As the war approached its end, Weidenfeld conceived the idea of starting a magazine 'that would capture and perpetuate this European spirit of wartime London'. Not a man to be cowed by the size of his ambition (or the cascade of other magazines pouring off the presses at the time), Weidenfeld decided his creation would combine the virtues of the *New Yorker*, *Fortune*, *New Republic* and *New Statesman*, contain regular essays by the great minds of the day and be published simultaneously in several languages in all the major capitals of Europe. He put together a network of talented and influential friends, many of them garnered through his work with the BBC, and early in 1944 registered his new company with the avowed intention of producing London's latest and finest literary magazine. It was to be called *Contact*.

Contact quickly ran into difficulties. Promises of sponsorship came and went, backers withdrew and the government's paper controller was said to be particularly harsh on new magazines. Weidenfeld loved every moment, bouncing back from each setback. It was decided to fool the paper controller by making the magazine look like a book that carried advertisements and, for good measure, to produce a few *bona fide* books as well. The initial book – the first Weidenfeld ever published – was a volume called *New Deal for Coal*, which had already been rejected by Gollancz. The author, an ambitious young don-turned-politician, was soon summoned to join the Attlee government. His name was Harold Wilson.

Before long, Weidenfeld invited Nigel Nicolson (son of Harold Nicolson and Vita Sackville-West) to join him as Assistant Editor. On the face of it they were an unlikely pairing. 'My taste and nature', wrote Nigel Nicolson, 'were fastidious; George's were adventurous.' For *Contact* Weidenfeld commissioned articles from Bertrand Russell, Ernst Gombrich, Arthur Koestler and the Italian philosopher Benedetto Croce, and had the effrontery to reject a piece from George Orwell. He brought in Richard Crossman, Kenneth Clark and the radical economist Ernst Schumacher as associates, and gave employment to bright young assistants including the cartoonist Gerard Hoffnung and (a few years later) Lord Pakenham's daughter Antonia (the historian and biographer Lady Antonia Fraser). Where Weidenfeld had the expansive and expensive instincts of an 'excitable flamboyant Austrian émigré' (his own words), Nicolson felt his role was to give *Contact* a more sober look. The magazine, he said, 'should dress like a lady, not as a tart'. Neither man had any business training, but while Weidenfeld claimed to regard this shortcoming as regrettable, he sensed that Nicolson – the personification of the English *amateur* – was secretly proud of the fact.

The absence of business experience caused near catastrophe as *Contact* sailed close to bankruptcy. Nicolson worried, but had not reckoned with Weidenfeld's inexhaustible networking. Not for nothing had his partner, the most gregarious of men, called his magazine *Contact*.* One day late in 1947, Weidenfeld was lunching with Israel Sieff of Marks and Spencer. Sieff said

---

* Many years later, Weidenfeld was to call his autobiography *Remembering My Good Friends*.

he admired *Contact* but that it would never make any money. 'You'd better turn to other things,' he said to Weidenfeld. 'I've an idea for you.'

> Without further ado he motioned me out of the room [Weidenfeld wrote]. We descended in the lift, climbed into his Bentley and drove to the Marble Arch store where crowds of people were milling around buying Christmas presents. We made our way to a counter covered with garishly presented children's classics which had been imported from America. 'They're selling like hot cakes,' Sieff explained . . . He turned to me and said, 'Why don't you do books like that for us?'

This suggestion proved to be Weidenfeld's salvation. Before long he was busy producing new editions of all the old favourites. The list – popular but characteristically cosmo-politan – included *Treasure Island*, *Black Beauty*, *Heidi*, *Grimms' Fairy Tales* and Erich Kästner's *Emil and the Detectives*. Books now took centre stage and could no longer be regarded as a sideline with which to prop up a magazine. In 1949 the partners officially launched themselves as a new publishing house. It was to be called Weidenfeld and Nicolson.

How were the new publishers received by the old? Weidenfeld sensed that the existing publishing fraternity was largely dismissive, many heads of houses giving his new firm a year or two at most. Some (he singled out Victor Gollancz, Frederick Warburg and Hamish Hamilton) were overtly hostile. Others were kinder. Allen Lane of Penguin wrote to congratulate Weidenfeld on his first list, Jonathan Cape granted the new-comer the rights to Erich Kästner, while the avuncular Stanley Unwin did his duty as chairman of the Publishers Association, took George and Nigel out to lunch and counselled them about the kinds of subject that would not sell (Latin America) and those that would (anything on Mary Queen of Scots).*

*

---

* Mary Queen of Scots was the subject of Antonia Fraser's first important book and the one that propelled her to fame as an historian. It was published by W & N in 1969.

For many émigrés the most important publisher in Britain was David Astor, who owned and edited the Sunday newspaper, the *Observer*. For all his legendary American lineage, wealth, and Eton–Oxford education, Astor was a man of liberal, internationalist instincts, 'probably the only real idealist to edit or own a major British newspaper this century,' wrote his biographer. For over thirty years, from the early 1940s when Astor began to have effective responsibility for the paper, he gathered around him a stable of outstanding journalists – men and women who were interested in ideas more than news, interpretation rather than reportage, people who could argue, think – and write. In the early days, quality newspapers did not always give their writers bylines, and Astor used this tradition of anonymity to protect the identity of his regular contributors and give them a greater degree of editorial latitude. Isaac Deutscher, a Marxist émigré from Poland who worked for *The Economist* and later became famous as biographer of Stalin and Trotsky, was the *Observer*'s roving European correspondent writing under the pen-name Peregrine. Sebastian Haffner (whose name was itself a pseudonym: Sebastian for Bach, Haffner for Mozart) wrote incisive commentaries as 'Student of Europe' or 'Liberator'. In addition to his regular contributors, Astor commissioned pieces from many of the more international-minded figures of the time such as Koestler, Orwell and Crossman. Later, when Ernst Schumacher, an old friend and periodic contributor, was struggling to publicise his ideas about the world economy, it was Astor who gave him an outlet; Schumacher's 1965 *Observer* article generated an enormous response, which helped lead to the foundation of the Intermediate Technology Development Group and to Schumacher's book *Small Is Beautiful*. When William Clark (later Eden's Press Secretary and then Press Head at the World Bank) joined Astor's *Observer* and attended his first editorial meeting, he found that 'more than half of the editorial group was German or Central European'.

The *Observer* under David Astor was the foremost organ of international-minded liberal thinking in Britain, essential reading for anyone with more than a provincial, Little England view of the post-war world. Haunted by what he regarded as the failure of the British press in the 1930s to awaken people to the realities of Fascist Europe, Astor defined his guiding ethic as 'trying to do the opposite of what Hitler would have done'. Whether campaigning against the nationalism of de Gaulle or the brutal acquisitiveness of Stalin, or rehearsing the arguments for and against British intervention in the Greek civil war, the paper was forthright, opinionated, controversial. Above all, it was internationalist.

PART FIVE

TOWARDS A NEW SYNTHESIS

CHAPTER SIXTEEN

Metropolitan and Micropolitan

David Astor's *Observer* was, said an admiring George Weidenfeld, 'without a doubt the flagship of a new European spirit'. It was a spirit in which Weidenfeld himself manifestly sailed and we have charted the course of several fellow mariners. But what of the rest of the fleet?

If you had embarked upon an odyssey through the cultural waters of Britain in the late 1940s and early 1950s, you would have been unlikely to encounter surging waves of cosmopolitanism. On the contrary, the strongest currents were probably still those of nation and empire, and of a proud yet cosy insularity. The West End theatre continued to thrive on Fry and Rattigan, the cinema on Michael Balcon's Ealing comedies, publishing on the latest works of Compton Mackenzie and Priestley. Indeed, as Britain emerged from the privations of war and austerity, patted itself on the back with a celebratory Festival and brought back the seventy-seven-year-old Winston Churchill to run its affairs, many sensed a reinforcement of English traditionalism. The historian Arthur Marwick concluded that intellectual and artistic endeavour were:

> inward-looking, seemingly unconcerned with the great issues which racked continental intellectuals: existentialism and social commitment, the challenge to Marxist faith presented by Stalinist tyranny, the possibilities of a Catholicism attuned to the needs of the modern world. The many British literary works which bring in the Second

World War seem somehow to treat it as a little local affair, without epochal significance.

Marwick was undoubtedly right. Yet to those who could read the runes a number of contrary tendencies were also becoming perceptible. Oxford philosophers might have been more pre-occupied with logic and language than the exigencies of existentialism, as Marwick suggests, but many among the younger generation caught what Koestler dubbed 'French flu', considered themselves to be radically 'engaged' as Sartre and de Beauvoir required, flocked to performances by Jean-Louis Barrault and Edwige Feuillère and affected the dark, emaciated look popularised on the Left Bank by the chanteuse Juliette Greco. To those who probed deeper, an interest in Sartre led to the works of Heidegger and Jaspers, and thence to the very nature and purpose of existence. The 'challenge to Marxist faith presented by Stalinist tyranny' was regularly addressed, not only by foreign exiles such as Deutscher and Koestler but also by that quintessentially English writer George Orwell, whose novels *Animal Farm* and *Nineteen Eighty-Four* were among the most widely read of the era. Graham Greene, meanwhile, tried to define and refine 'the possibilities of a Catholicism attuned to the needs of the modern world'.

A discerning argonaut might thus have found some evidence of the 'European spirit' of which Weidenfeld spoke. Yet the lodestar by which most still navigated was that of Middle England. Rudolf Bing may have brought Bruno Walter and Carl Ebert to Edinburgh in 1947, but Britten and Pears used the first Aldeburgh Festival a year later as a celebration of East Anglia, with an exhibition of Constable, lectures on Crabbe and Fitzgerald, and performances of Britten's own *Albert Herring*. If André Deutsch published the memoirs of von Papen and George Weidenfeld those of Schacht, Mussolini and Tito, what most people wanted were Churchill's. Nikolaus Pevsner called upon all the training in architectural history he had accumulated in Leipzig and Dresden as he embarked on his monumental survey of the buildings of England, but his readers used the Penguin volumes as aids to domestic tourism. Kurt Schwitters tried to promote Dada and John Heartfield photomontage, two playful forms of art largely ignored by a British public which, like Sir Alfred Munnings, President of the Royal Academy, wanted paintings of horses that *looked* like horses and was only just learning to digest Moore and Sutherland.* When the BBC replaced Sir Adrian Boult as Chief Conductor of the BBC Symphony Orchestra in 1950, the Head of Music noted that 'to appoint a non-resident foreigner would be a matter of such criticism that I should find it difficult to advise the Governors to accept the responsibility for the appointment'. They played safe and opted for Sir Malcolm Sargent.

Perhaps there were several cultures jostling for position, which intersected like the rings of the Olympic Games. Britten may have been the most archetypally English of composers, but he was influenced by Mahler and Berg, promoted by Hans Keller, published by Erwin Stein and was soon to invite Russians and Germans to his Festival and incorporate the Indonesian gamelan into his compositions. Film goers may have flocked to *Passport to Pimlico* and *The Ladykillers*, but the movie that everyone remembered as bringing colour back into their lives was a Powell–Pressburger fable about a girl with a fatal compulsion to dance, *The Red Shoes*, which starred Moira Shearer and the suave Anton Walbrook with sumptuous Oscar-winning designs by Hein Heckroth. Post-war architecture had to be harnessed to the production of homes, hospitals, schools and offices, but many of those tapped for such essentially domestic tasks had names like Berger, Biel, Bor, Goldfinger and Lubetkin, and were steeped in the Modernist styles of Central Europe, while others of similar background (Pevsner, Moro, Korn) were given high-profile posts teaching the next generation.

These two broad themes, which we might loosely call the international and the domestic, the cross-cultural and the provincial – what Kenneth Clark dubbed the metropolitan and the micropolitan – can be seen as having run in parallel throughout the post-war years, intersecting at times, mostly oblivious of one

---

* Schwitters died in 1948. Heartfield, a Communist, left England in 1956 to live in East Berlin.

another. Of the two, the more dominant was the rather cosy, middle-class, insular, largely retrospective English culture that gained succour from a victorious and vindicated past. This was the vision celebrated in the BBC's *Brains Trust*, the poetry of John Betjeman, the paintings of Sutherland and Piper, the history books of Arthur Bryant and G. M. Trevelyan. It was a world in which most people accepted the social order and believed in King and Country. Families sat together round the wireless set and took meals together. People respected bishops and generals, and relished little more radical than the latest ball-point pen or carpet sweeper.

In the early 1950s two events were to provide a popular apotheosis of this view of life, supplying spectacular platforms for much that was best and most attractive in an essentially domestic culture. Between them they produced the summit, cul-mination – and, in effect, the beginning of the end – of wartime Little Englandism, turning points that helped trigger the new world in which the Hitler émigrés were to play so striking a part.

The Festival of Britain was a conscious echo of the Great Exhibition a hundred years earlier. Where the 1851 exhibition was a celebration of early-Victorian England's solid achieve-ments in the arts and sciences, the 1951 Festival was meant to be a tonic to a nation that had faced privation and war, and emerged victorious – 'the people giving themselves a pat on the back', in the words of Herbert Morrison, the government Minister in charge.

Detailed planning was done by a group under the leadership of Gerald Barry (Editor of the *News Chronicle*) and his Chief Architect Hugh Casson. The Festival had many sites, but its principal locations were in London: the 'Pleasure Gardens' at Battersea (where the twenty-five-year-old Joseph Horovitz could be seen conducting the orchestra) and the main exhibition centre between Waterloo Bridge and County Hall on the south bank of the Thames. Stylistically, the Festival was self-consciously 'contemporary', for Barry and Casson had recruited a host of architects, artists and designers, MARS products many of them, whose gods (said Andrew Sinclair) were Gropius and

Corbusier, whom Festival work 'released from adapting Nissen huts, hangars, pillboxes and prefabs'. Young, ambitious, they could not have been an easy group to manage. Each was assigned a specific project. 'It was like casting a film,' Casson recalled, 'in which everybody had to be a star and given the best lines.' They all spoke the same language, Casson added, 'but each with enough variety of intonation to make it interesting'. Literally so, perhaps, for the team included a number of European émigrés. Stefan Buzas helped design 'The Land', while the flora and fauna of Britain in 'The Country' were brilliantly highlighted by F. H. K. Henrion's great fantasy tree. Ernö Goldfinger designed some of the Festival kiosks, Heinz Reifenberg was largely responsible for the Festival's Power and Production Pavilion and Bronek Katz for Homes and Gardens.

The Festival spaces were awash with murals, sculptures and paintings, every kind of art and artifice. Moore, Epstein and Hepworth all exhibited new work; Mitzi Cunliffe sculpted a group symbolising the origins of the 'Land' and the 'People', while John Piper created a mural for the 'Homes and Gardens' exhibition. Here, too, émigré artists were well represented. The sculptor Peter Peri, famous for his 'little people' of concrete, displayed an open-air mural group called *Sunbathers*, while Josef Herman, also normally more at home with the small scale, contributed six vast panels portraying Welsh coal miners.

The main structures of the Festival all showed the hand of European Modernism. Thus Buzas and Günther Hoffstead contributed to the exhibition designs in the Dome of Discovery, while structural engineering of the Skylon was by Felix Samuely (who had contributed mightily during the war to the design of air raid shelters, and whose handiwork was also evident at the Festival in the Transport Pavilion). As for the most famous of all the Festival structures, the auditorium of the Royal Festival Hall, this was in large part the work of another refugee, the architect Peter Moro.

Moro was born in Heidelberg in 1911 to a Catholic family with Italian, Slovenian and Viennese roots. He studied in Stuttgart and Berlin, whence he was dismissed by the Nazis in 1934 for failing to tell them that he had a Jewish grandmother.

For a while, he studied in Zurich and then, realising that life in Germany would be intolerable, made for England with the promise of a job with Gropius. This did not materialise, but Moro was soon taken on by Lubetkin who was to have a profound influence upon him. Art shows us what we want, Lubetkin would say; science shows us how to get it.

After the outbreak of war and a period of internment, Moro made ends meet by teaching architecture at the Regent Street Polytechnic when, in 1948, he was suddenly invited by the overall architect of the Royal Festival Hall, Leslie Martin, to take charge of the detailed design. The Royal Festival Hall was the first large-scale, permanent public building in post-war Britain. Leslie Martin and the chief architect of the London County Council, Robert Matthew, were both wedded to Modernist design. Hence, perhaps, the appointment of Moro. Martin explained that, because the site was so restricted, the auditorium of the new hall was to be cantilevered above and within extensive foyer spaces. Moro's job was to design the details of this strikingly original 'egg-on-stilts' concept. Everything had to function in its own right, while helping to lighten the texture of a building topped by a vast concrete concert hall – from the carpets, lighting, and the ubiquitous wood and glass to the split-level floors, stairways and the great curtain window overlooking the Thames. There would be little or no applied decoration. This wasn't the Modern style. Besides, time was limited: the building had to be ready when the King inaugurated the Festival in May 1951. Materials were restricted, too, in the post-war austerity. A steel-frame building, for example, was out of the question. But that was no reason why essentially functional features – acoustic devices and the like – should not be as decorative as time and money permitted. I remember being captivated by the 'Dunlopillo' cushioning that somehow rendered the squeaky trains just outside the hall inaudible from within. As for the outer walls of the auditorium, these Moro decided would be faced with Derbyshire fossil stone.

When the building was nearing completion, Moro showed its plans, and later the hall itself, to a procession of the world's leading architects. 'Have you ever designed a concert hall before?' enquired Frank Lloyd Wright. 'No? Well, it won't work.' Gropius visited and apparently had little to say beyond asking about changes of air. Corbusier was more forthcoming. 'Those boxes of yours are a joke,' he said to the startled Moro – and added with a smile, 'but they're a very good joke!' Everyone noticed the boxes, those flyaway open drawers that seemed to want to project their occupants to the very heart of the music (and which were rapidly copied across Europe). They were a great success with the public which, having no sour grapes to suck or axes to grind, took to the hall from the start.

The Royal Festival Hall established Peter Moro as one of Britain's leading experts on theatre and auditorium design, and he went on to create or renovate theatres in Nottingham, Hull, Bristol, Plymouth and Swansea. For Moro, the Festival of Britain provided a triumphant turning point in his professional life. A number of other émigrés, however, had hoped to contribute to the Festival but, in one way or another, found themselves rejected. Stephen Hearst, fresh out of Oxford, applied for the plum job co-ordinating the arts that Huw Wheldon was to get (they later worked together in BBC Television). Karl Rankl and Berthold Goldschmidt both entered operas for a Festival of Britain award and were pronounced prizewinners, but neither received the promised performances. Rankl's was *Deirdre of the Sorrows* based on Yeats, while Goldschmidt's, to a libretto by his BBC colleague Martin Esslin, was derived from Shelley's *The Cenci*. Esslin recalled that submissions for the Festival award had to be under cover of a pseudonym and that the two other prizewinners turned out to be Arthur Benjamin and Alan Bush. 'The authorities were aghast. They'd picked a bunch of foreigners and Communists – not at all what the Festival of Britain was supposed to be about!' None of the winning operas was performed at the time.*

The painter Lucian Freud was more fortunate. Freud – grandson of Sigmund and son of the architect Ernst – was born in Berlin in 1922 and brought to England in 1933. He was sent

---

*Goldschmidt's *Beatrice Cenci* was finally heard in concert form in 1988 while Rankl's opera has never been performed.

to Dartington and Bryanston, both of them conspicuously pro-gressive schools, but he was evidently something of a loner and spent more of his time riding horses (and drawing them) than attending classes. After a year at the Central School of Arts and Crafts, and two at the smaller East Anglian School of Drawing and Painting, Freud, now twenty, ran away to sea, but was soon invalided out. For a while he drifted in and out of the bohemian world of wartime and post-war Soho where he rapidly acquired a formidable reputation for his precocious artistry. In particular, people admired the unblinking, almost surly honesty of his canvases, his directness of expression and utter lack of sentimentality.

Freud's *Interior in Paddington* was given one of five Festival of Britain awards offered by the Arts Council. One of his first paintings to receive important public recognition, it portrays an anxious, bespectacled young man, thick-lipped and cleft-chinned, one fist involuntarily clenched, standing next to a drooping pot palm. The style suggests affinities with the *Neue Sachlichkeit* and, in particular, Otto Dix. Robert Hughes later noted that Freud's 'shabby, pale, tight-wound fellow with an unlit cigarette who wears his raincoat indoors . . . looks familiar from middle-European painting of the 1920s'. Freud, unlike the opera composers, *was* permitted to display his wares at the Festival.

The Festival of Britain embodied an aesthetic – 'contemporary' if not quite 'Modern' – that helped fuel the explosion of cultural self-confidence Britain was to experience a decade or two later. From the slimline Antelope chairs and cigar-shaped Skylon to the Dome of Discovery, Victor Pasmore's murals and the whimsical railway designed by *Punch* cartoonist Rowland Emmett that was a hit with visitors to Battersea, what was being celebrated was no longer imperial pomp or the victory of blood, sweat and tears, but a sleek, gleaming, quasi-Bauhaus vision of a mass-produced future. That future was clean, light, colourful, touched by fantasy, a world of Biro pens, plastic cruet sets and fold-away alarm clocks. The British may have reached Modernism later than the Continent and it may have arrived in a peculiarly diluted form. Nikolaus Pevsner upbraided his adopted country for its characteristic lack of bold planning, pointing out that the Festival of Britain came twenty-one years after Asplund's Exhibition in Stockholm. Yet the British approach had its advantages, he acknowledged. 'Initial mistakes are avoided, and a certain more human, more leisurely mellowness can be introduced.'

A few months after the end of the Festival of Britain, King George VI, who had opened it, died at the age of fifty-six. His daughter, who had been on a tour of Africa, flew back to London, welcomed at the airport by the Prime Minister, Winston Churchill. It was a sombre moment, an historic conjunction, some commentators liked to think, between the old and the new, past and future. Yet even as the BBC's Richard Dimbleby, observing the late King's coffin, intoned that 'the sunset of his death tinged the whole world's sky', people warmed to the twenty-six-year-old Princess now transformed into a queen and began to speak in hushed tones of entering a 'New Elizabethan Age'. The apotheosis of the new era, and of its youthful monarch, occurred on 2 June 1953, the date of her coronation.

For a proud Englishman, 1953 was to prove a year of miracles. It was the one in which Britain's greatest jockey (Gordon Richards) won the Derby, its greatest footballer (Stanley Matthews) inspired his team to victory in the Cup Final and – *miraculo miraculi* – its cricketers defeated the old enemy Australia and regained the Ashes. The central event in this sequence of triumphs was the Coronation and for weeks beforehand the newspapers reported on every detail: who was invited, what the young Queen would wear, the processional route, where to stand to get the best view on the day. And then, on the very eve of the Coronation, the press had an extraordinarily symbolic triumph to report: 'we' (in fact, a New Zealander and a Nepali, members of a British-led expedition) had 'conquered' the world's highest peak, Mount Everest. God, it seemed, was smiling on Britain.

On the day of the Coronation itself, God let it rain. But that did not prevent 2 million people gathering in London to see the processions to and from Westminster Abbey* while over 20 millions watched the whole thing live on television. More homes acquired their first TV set in the run-up to the Coronation than at any time before or since and it was the first event that more people in Britain watched on television than listened to on the radio. It was therefore arguably the first coronation in history when the monarch was crowned, as the rubric required, 'in the sight of the people'.

Like the Festival of Britain, the Coronation flowed with symbolism for those inclined to seek it. John Masefield, the ageing Poet Laureate, looked to the newly-crowned monarch to 're-establish standards shaken' and '[s]et the enfettered spirit free'. People spoke glowingly of the young Queen, of a new link in the unbroken chain of history, the spiritual links to the Kingdom of Heaven, an act of national communion – not a cliché was wasted as the population, swept up by the euphoria, held Coronation parties and bought souvenir medallions, mugs and magazines.

Many of those who hailed the New Elizabethan Age hoped the era might herald an artistic renaissance, reproduce the proud spirit of Tallis and Byrd, Marlowe and Shakespeare, and perhaps revive the courtly spirit of Raleigh and Drake. As the great and the good laid down their collective cloaks before Cecil Beaton's portrait of the young Queen, revelled in the vigorous patriotism of Walton's *Orb and Sceptre* march or ogled Fonteyn and Nerina in Ashton's *Homage to the Queen* at Covent Garden, their romantic aspirations might have seemed capable of fulfilment. But not for long. There was to be music and drama aplenty. But little that was designed to reassure the scions of the new Elizabethan Establishment.

Part of the Coronation celebrations included the première of a new opera about Queen Elizabeth I by Benjamin Britten. Britten had been widely acknowledged as the country's leading

---

* As in the Moscow May Day parade in Soviet times, would-be witnesses had to stake out positions at dawn or earlier before the security people blocked off the entrances.

composer ever since the first night of *Peter Grimes* in 1945, though canny judges of musical prowess had spotted his talent long before. The publishers Boosey and Hawkes had signed him up in the 1930s. B & H proved canny in other ways too (we have already noted them as prime movers in the resuscitation of Covent Garden as an opera theatre). After the *Anschluss* they gave employment to a number of émigrés from the Viennese music publishing house Universal Edition, thereby acquiring the rights and royalties to the work of some of the major composers of the century. Ernst Roth joined Boosey and Hawkes – who as a result published the later works of Richard Strauss, Bartók, Stravinsky and Kodály.

Another of the UE émigrés to work for Boosey and Hawkes was the musicologist and Schoenberg pupil Erwin Stein. Stein first met Britten in 1934 when the young English composer was visiting Vienna. Britten, not yet twenty-one, had hoped to meet Alban Berg, a composer commended by his teacher Frank Bridge, and perhaps have lessons with him. Britten had heard and admired Berg's *Lyric Suite* and was disappointed to find that Berg was out of town (and devastated to hear of his premature death a few months later). But he had other contacts. A letter of introduction to Universal Edition led to a meeting with Erwin Stein, whom the young Englishman found 'very nice', though nothing specific came of it.

Four years later, after the *Anschluss*, Stein, followed by his wife and eleven-year-old daughter Marion, left Vienna for London, where Leslie Boosey had offered him a job with B & H. One of the first composers Boosey pointed Stein's way was Britten. Britten and Stein struck up a friendship, cemented, no doubt, by their mutual admiration for the music of Mahler. When Britten and Pears returned permanently to England in 1942 from a sojourn in America, it was to Stein that Britten regularly turned to discuss the development of his career.

Britten and Stein might be seen as having embodied the two wings of musical life in post-war Britain: the resurgence of self-conscious Englishness pioneered by Vaughan Williams and the great Central European tradition that still infused much British music-making. Yet such a polarisation would be to oversimplify. Both men yearned to touch the tradition represented by the other. Britten, most English of composers, one might almost say provincial in personal inclination, was deeply imbued with the Mid-European tradition of Mahler and his successors, and tried to emulate Berg by marrying uncompromising musical discipline to warm and accessible lyricism. 'My struggle', he said, 'was to develop a consciously controlled professional technique. It was a struggle away from everything Vaughan Williams seemed to stand for.'

For his part Erwin Stein, a Jewish refugee who continued to bear the intense cultural baggage of his Viennese past, also managed to enter the aesthetic world of his adopted country. Lord Harewood, a cousin of the Queen who married Marion Stein in 1949, recalled that his father-in-law identified himself totally with England. Stein spoke and wrote in idiomatic English. When he talked about 'our' music, said Harewood, he meant English music. 'Erwin', stated Britten's friend and later editor Donald Mitchell, 'provided Ben with that experience of Vienna that he had been denied earlier when his plans to study with Berg had been scotched.'

If Peter Pears was Britten's musical alter ego, Stein was his father confessor, the one figure with whom Britten would talk about the technical details of his compositional struggles and one of the few who could question something Britten was attempting without putting the friendship at risk. Marion recalled the excitement of Britten turning up at the house with a score on which he was working, playing it to her father and the two men talking long into the night about details. While the composer was completing *Peter Grimes* in early 1945, Stein took the full score, as it was being written, and reduced it so that the soloists could be given their parts to learn even as later scenes were still being written. Harewood remembered Britten and Stein working closely together throughout the gestation of *Billy Budd* (an opera initially commissioned for the Festival of Britain). Stein wondered whether Britten would be able to find sufficient contrast in an opera with only male voices. 'I think you can trust me for that,' was Britten's confident riposte.

Erwin Stein was not the only European refugee to champion

Britten. Hans Keller was born in Vienna just after the end of the
First World War. His father, a well-known Vienna architect
(who died in 1938), loved music and played standard orchestral
classics with his son as piano duets. After the *Anschluss* Hans
had a series of desperately harrowing experiences at the hands
of the Nazis and finally escaped to England where he had a
married sister. For a while he and his mother lived near the sister
in Herne Hill in south London. Later they all moved to the Lake
District where Hans played second violin in a string quartet
formed by a man he had known from his Vienna days, the
doctor (and Schoenberg friend) Oskar Adler.

After the war Keller rapidly built a reputation as a brilliant,
quirky musicologist, a man of forceful views and unshakeable
prejudices who had such power of language and personality –
not to say love and knowledge of his subject – that he was
difficult to gainsay. When Keller would 'submit' (one of his
favourite words) that Gershwin was a greater composer than
Webern or laud the merits of Franz Schmidt above those of
Debussy, he would back up his breathtakingly heterodox case
with powerful arguments, mesmerically expressed. A master of
paradox, a mix of arrogance and impishness, Keller would play
with language, whether in print or speech, holding audiences
and interlocutors paralysed. William Glock said his pronouncements at their best had 'almost the authority of proverbs'. Keller
relished flaunting his powers. Why not? This was a man who
had been within a hair's breadth of torture and death at the
hand of the Nazis; when he escaped, he swore he would never
again be in a bad mood, an oath he was clearly determined to
fulfil.

Behind the bombast and the bravado lay a personality of
intense seriousness, the mind of a teacher, a moralist, a
missionary. Keller was profoundly influenced by the Freudian
school of psychoanalysis and not averse to using what he
regarded as psychiatric insights in his writings about music.
While still in his twenties, Keller made a name for himself as a
percipient writer on music who actually listened to performances he reviewed and whose critiques, packed with scholarly
detail and Freudian provocation, leaped off the page. In 1947 he

was sent to cover the first Edinburgh Festival. So was Milein Cosman, who was there to sketch some of the participants. Milein, later Hans's wife, remembered being struck by how slim Hans was, with his high brow, long face, bright eyes and thick moustache. Einstein without food, perhaps. 'He looked like a very thin Indian who had forgotten his turban,' Milein recalled. 'I remember thinking "I'd really like to draw that man!"'

Never one to dilute the impact of his opinions by unnecessary qualification, Keller could be an implacable foe but an intensely loyal supporter (of a football team as of a composer). He was an early admirer of Britten. Keller, so he used to tell people, had once gone to Sadler's Wells expecting to hear *Così fan tutte* and when the orchestra launched into something else, utterly unfamiliar, he realised with a pang that he had come on the wrong night and was disappointed. But not for long. They were playing *Peter Grimes*. Keller sat up, transfixed by what he was hearing.

In 1949, Keller and the music critic Donald Mitchell became co-editors of the journal *Music Survey* and in 1950 they devoted a special edition to Britten. A couple of years later the material was expanded and augmented to become a book. Keller's admiration for Britten was at times, perhaps, overstated. He saluted Britten as a worthy companion of Mozart and, with a characteristically Kellerian twist, called him 'the greatest of all living composers whose music I understand'. If this sounds (for Keller) anodyne, he also analysed Britten's pacifism and asserted that what lies behind such attitudes was 'strong and heavily repressed sadism'.

The volume caused a combination of pride and consternation among the Britten circle, and considerable controversy among the musical cognoscenti. Its principal effect was to raise Britten's profile still further. Erwin Stein was one of the contributors. Around this time, he and Harewood thought Britten would be the ideal Music Director at Covent Garden. Karl Rankl had got the thing going. Now it needed a musician of major stature. Britten was home-grown, an internationally recognised composer – and, as it happened, an outstanding pianist and conductor. His presence would ensure high-quality performances of his own works, something that would surely commend itself to Stein's employers. Harewood, who worked at Covent Garden, put the idea to David Webster and the Board, but nothing came of it. Walton, a member of the Board, was opposed; he regarded Britten as a rival and was not averse to inventing a homosexual conspiracy in the musical world that kept 'normal' people – i.e. himself – from achieving greater success. Leslie Boosey was also on the Covent Garden Board. He worried that Britten would become too tied up with performance and administration. No. Britten's job was to compose, and Stein's to help and encourage him.

In early 1952, shortly after King George VI died, George and Marion Harewood were with Britten and Pears in Austria where they fell to discussing what was meant by 'national' expression in opera and which were the 'national' operas of various countries. *The Bartered Bride* was archetypally Czech, *Manon* French, *Boris* Russian, *Aida* Italian and so on. But what was the English equivalent? 'You'd better write one, Ben!' But what would such an opera be like? What would it be about? Some hours later, by Harewood's account, they had homed in on the period of Queen Elizabeth I – the perfect subject, all agreed, for the following year's Coronation.

Gloriana concerns the infatuation of the ageing Elizabeth for the dashing young Essex, and the inexorable events that impel her to order his execution. The score contains some of Britten's most lyrical passages and includes elements of clever Tudor-style pastiche, including a ravishing lute serenade. But the pillars of the New Elizabethan age who attended the opera's première six days after the Coronation had evidently expected some simple-minded celebratory pageant. 'Boriana,' they guffawed to one another during the intervals, and 'Yawniana'. As an adjunct to the obligatory evening dress and decorations, they and their ladies were wearing white gloves, which further muffled the polite applause. They pronounced the work lacking in whistl-able tunes, while some of the more sophisticated music critics found too many of them. Britten was muttered to have verged on *lèse-majesté*, or at least a serious lapse of taste, in choosing to portray not the young Elizabeth I at the time of her accession but the pathetic old buffoon of forty years later.

Britten, deeply hurt, admitted to Harewood that he had 'received a broadside from Peter'.* Should he not in future stick to the public that wanted him, the loyal Aldeburgh friends, and not get mixed up with promoting something that was none of his concern? In the years that followed Britten seemed to retreat from the influence of those, like Erwin Stein and the Harewoods, who had been encouraging him to assume a 'metropolitan' rather than a 'micropolitan' stance. Instead, he turned to the composition of chamber-scale works, which he could control and perform in his own, safe East Anglian environment.

The lukewarm reception of *Gloriana* spread a message that radiated far beyond its influence on Britten alone. A Conservative government was well entrenched and talked of allying culture more closely to commerce. Proposals were progressing for a television channel financed by advertising. Was elite, effete art like *Gloriana* the sort of thing to which huge dollops of taxpayers' money should be devoted? Many thought not. Thus, the principle of state funding of the arts, only recently established, tottered for a while on its precarious pedestal.

Erwin Stein died in 1958. The following year Hans Keller joined the BBC at the request of the new Controller of Music, William Glock, where he went on to become one of Britten's most powerful advocates inside the Corporation. In 1959, too, the marriage of George and Marion Harewood began to unravel. Britten remained close to them both and in 1963, when Marion (later Mrs Jeremy Thorpe) co-founded the Leeds International Piano Competition with Fanny Waterman, he composed, at Marion's request, a piano piece to mark the occasion. After Erwin Stein's death, Britten's relationship with Boosey and Hawkes gradually cooled. It was always important to him to have a sympathetic editor and in 1964 he finally split with B & H and became the first important composer of the new music publishing branch of Faber and Faber. Here his editor was Donald Mitchell.

---

* Pears had expressed doubts from the start about *Gloriana*.

CHAPTER SEVENTEEN

The Angry, the Radical and the Modern

Between (roughly) the Coronation in June 1953 and the Suez crisis of October 1956, a wave of artistic regeneration swept away much of the comfortable post-war consensus and in its place created a vogue for anger and alienation, the cruel and the absurd, the 'anti-hero' and the outsider.* The Coronation itself, highlight of an emblematic year, symbolised for many the end of the old world and the beginning of the new. It was certainly an important year for George Weidenfeld (by then married to a member of the Sieff family) who always recalled the second of June not so much on account of the Coronation as because it was the day on which his daughter Laura was born. In 1953 the Weidenfeld and Nicolson list included the memoirs of Tito (Vladimir Dedijer's *Tito Speaks*), Isaiah Berlin's seminal essay *The Hedgehog and the Fox*, Rose Macaulay's *Pleasure of Ruins* and ('much to Hamish Hamilton's anger') two anthologies by Cyril Connolly. It was also the year in which Weidenfeld brought Antonia Pakenham on to his staff.

At Covent Garden the *Gloriana* débâcle was followed in September by a visit from the Bavarian State Opera of Munich, the first by a German company since 1936. The opening night hit the headlines because the German national anthem was played before 'God Save the Queen'.

In 1953, too, the novelist John Wain published an angry yet amusing book, *Hurry on Down*, which chronicled the adventures of a young man in revolt who worked his way *down*

---

* Colin Wilson's cult book *The Outsider* was written in 1956.

the class system. A year later came Kingsley Amis's *Lucky Jim*, portraying the touching absurdities of provincial academic life, and William Golding's *Lord of the Flies*, a parable of innocent children reduced in a state of nature to savage barbarity. Nineteen fifty-four was also the year that saw the heralding of a major new literary talent with the publication of Iris Murdoch's *Under the Net* (in which one of the principal characters, scion of a German immigrant family, puts money into the British film industry to give it 'a leg up' and produces films preceded by 'the familiar shot of City Spires'). Meanwhile, David Astor had installed the twenty-seven-year-old firebrand Kenneth Tynan as *Observer* Drama Critic – just in time for Tynan to hail Ionesco's *The Lesson* and Beckett's *Waiting for Godot* (1955), the debut season of the English Stage Company at the Royal Court Theatre and, in 1956, John Osborne's *Look Back in Anger** and the visit to London of Brecht's Berliner Ensemble.

For the most daring theatre in Britain during these years you probably had to go to a run-down building in London's East End. Joan Littlewood's 'Theatre Workshop' had its roots in pre-war Manchester where she and Ewan MacColl had run a radical performing group on a prayer and a shoestring, paying the bills courtesy of occasional BBC broadcasts. After a series of moves, their company came to London. They found a home in the derelict Theatre Royal in Stratford East where they made a major impact with their raw and forceful productions of contemporary drama. Littlewood thought of Theatre Workshop as a quasi-political unit – a commune, perhaps, or a cadre – whose sense of shared purpose, reinforced by intensive rehearsal, would regularly issue in theatre that contained a message for the times. Her work was avowedly subversive, an attempt to establish theatre for 'the people' in which speech, song, movement and simple visual effects would forge a sense of camaraderie between audience and performers. Theatre Workshop productions would move in harmony with the tides of emotion they portrayed.

---

* Royalty, said one of John Osborne's characters a mere three years after the Coronation, was 'the gold filling in a mouthful of decay'.

Movement was a central part of Littlewood's philosophy. As a girl of twenty she had walked out of RADA, finding its snobberies a 'waste of time' – but not before she had encountered a class on 'Central-European Movement'. Fräulein Fligg's movement class was a revelation. Here, at last, was 'action . . . It was great. I'd never felt so alive.' More important, it brought her for the first time into contact with the ideas of Rudolf Laban. For many years Littlewood devoured all she could find about Laban, discovering that he had been 'a Dadaist, a dancer, crystallographer, topologist, architect, composer, designer, choreographer' and had even earned his living at one time as a street cartoonist. Despairing of meeting him, she consoled herself with the thought that 'at least our system of movement was derived from his'.

After the war, when Laban was living in Manchester, Littlewood got to know him and she and her colleagues began attending his sessions. Laban had come north during the war at the behest of a management consultant who got him to apply his theories of movement to various industrial and engineering firms. In one he found women doing heavy lifting jobs normally undertaken in peacetime by men. Laban showed them how, with a swinging movement of the whole body, they could ease their burden while at the same time becoming more efficient. All this was meat and drink to Joan Littlewood. Whenever she sensed one or two of her actors were losing the faith, she would pack them off to Laban for a fortnight, whence they would return limping but converted.

Laban was a true revolutionary, the leading dance theorist of the twentieth century, a tireless seeker after universal truths. Nobody else in dance history paralleled the range of his interests: not only his own dancing, choreography and system of dance notation, but also his theories of movement in space and his application of these techniques and principles for educational purposes, industrial efficiency and personal therapy. To Laban, there were profound links between all his interests and activities. Like a religious teacher, he sought a path to universal spiritual fulfilment, a perfect balance between mind, body and soul. Nothing was too mighty or too lowly for his attention. The former crystallographer would sketch neo-cubist designs illustrating the complementarity of bodies in movement, the ex-choreographer of the Berlin opera advise Mars confectionary on how to apply his theories of 'lilt in labour' to the wrapping of chocolate bars.

Laban's own spirits were profoundly challenged by the trauma of his exile to Britain, where he endured a recurrent struggle against poverty, uncomprehending authorities and persistent ill health. Lisa Ullmann, Laban's muse, apostle and companion during these years, helped keep the flame alive but, many thought, guarded him too assiduously and diverted him from his main task. Joan Littlewood wrote that Ullmann 'sidetracked [Laban] into education' when he should have been working in the theatre. 'But of course the theatre didn't know anything about him. In fact, we were the only company in the country who regarded movement training as a necessary part of the preparation of a play.'

After a lifetime spent in restless search of a permanent base, Laban was able to move in 1953 to a property in Surrey donated by Bill Elmhirst, son of Dorothy and Leonard. Here he set up his final academy and, with encouragement from Ullmann and younger disciples such as Sylvia Bodmer,* Valerie Dunlop and Marion North, continued his teaching, writing, lecturing and occasional choreography. The old spark was still there, the magnetism, the messianic determination to use movement as a bridge to personal fulfilment. But Laban's health and energy were fading. He died in 1958, the very year in which Joan Littlewood's Theatre Workshop mounted two of its greatest triumphs: Brendan Behan's *The Hostage* and Shelagh Delaney's *A Taste of Honey*.

Laban (like Littlewood) sought elusive truths: theatre was far more than merely a form of art or entertainment, and he spent his life stretching out beyond accepted boundaries in an attempt to harness art to deeper purposes. His quest was ultimately a

---

* Mother of the distinguished geneticist Sir Walter Bodmer who went on to become Director of Research at the Imperial Cancer Research Fund and Principal of Hertford College, Oxford – and a Director of the Laban Centre in London.

spiritual one.* To him, as to Joan Littlewood, what happened in the studio or workshop was paramount. Each provided an important chapter in the history of their art – and both suffered subsequent eclipse as some of their ideas became common currency. In the 1960s and 1970s, when British theatre-goers could enjoy an efflorescence of publicly funded entertainment, a plethora of 'alternative' dance groups and 'agitprop' or 'working-class' theatre companies and venues sprang up across the land. 'Radical' became 'chic' as avant-garde directors integrated words, music and movement, and invoked influences as diverse as Brecht's Berliner Ensemble, Japanese Noh plays and the latest psychotherapeutic ideas from California. The name of Laban was rarely invoked. Yet his spirit was ubiquitous.

Another quiet revolution was going on in the 1950s. This one was so quiet that it hardly looked or sounded like a revolution at all. A softly-spoken, bespectacled German-born professor of art and architectural history was invited by BBC Radio to deliver its prestigious Reith Lectures. The year was 1955, the very year in which the arrival of ITV presented the BBC with the most severe challenge in its history. The professor chose as his subject 'The Englishness of English Art'.

Nikolaus Pevsner had always been something of an Anglophile. Born in Leipzig in 1902 and educated at the best universities in Germany, he first visited England on a research trip in 1930. Like many German intellectuals at the time, Pevsner was captivated by the spirit of 'Modernism' – the clean lines, industrial efficiency and social conscience preached by the Bauhaus. He was also interested in how 'national character' was manifested in art. By the time of his first trip to Britain, Pevsner was a lecturer in art history at the University of Göttingen. Already expert in post-Renaissance Italy, he came to London to widen his knowledge of the art of England. If Caravaggio, Bernini or Tiepolo had embodied the spirit of their particular time and place, how far was the spirit of eighteenth-century

---

* Littlewood's was primarily political and led her to develop the all-embracing but ultimately impractical idea of a 'Fun Palace', an informal 'university of the streets', which would bring theatre out of the theatre, as it were, and provide a bridge to the wider community.

England captured in the works of Robert Adam, Constable, Reynolds or Capability Brown, or that of the nineteenth in Turner or William Morris?

Morris became something of a hero to Pevsner, a linchpin helping to bridge his two central concerns. On the one hand nothing could be more English than the romantic rurality that underpinned so much of Morris's inspiration. There was a perceptible continuity from Reynolds's *Strawberry Girl* and Constable's *Hay Wain* to the bow-lipped beauties and leafy bowers of Morris. But as one of the great father figures of the Arts and Crafts Movement, Morris could also be interpreted as a precursor of British Modernism. Just as the Viennese *Werkstätte* had paved the way for the Bauhaus, so the English Arts and Crafts Movement had helped lead to a fruitful marriage between art and machine. Things in Britain had developed differently from in *Mitteleuropa*, of course. Pevsner would hardly have failed to notice, for example, that English styles continued to be imbued by a cosy pastoralism deeply at odds with the sleek international efficiency of Modernism. But this was doubtless the workings of 'national character'. Like the art of every nation, that of England embodied various inconsistencies or polarities: the quasi-permanent 'national character' and the changing 'spirit of the age',* the traditional and the modern, the rural and the industrial, the insular and the international. It was the dialectic between these that gave English art its peculiar character.

When Pevsner began developing these ideas in 1930 he could hardly have guessed how important English art and architecture were soon to become to him. Pevsner's parents were Jewish, and although he and his (half-Jewish) wife Lola were Lutherans they quickly realised there was no future for them in Hitler's Germany. Pevsner came to England, found temporary work in Birmingham, and by 1936 had brought Lola and the children to London and their new permanent home on the edges of

---

* The 'spirit of the age' or *Zeitgeist* was a concept much cited by followers of Hegel and the German metaphysical tradition but distrusted by rationalists such as Popper and Gombrich (see pp. 186, 198, 200).

Hampstead Garden Suburb (in an enclave where all three of Pevsner's children and their families continued to live). Self-disciplined and industrious, Pevsner worked by day for the furniture designer Gordon Russell (later Director of the Design Council and himself a follower of Morris), and at night completed his book *Pioneers of the Modern Movement* plus a stream of articles for the influential *Architectural Review*.

The outbreak of war struck Pevsner with great ferocity. His daughter Uta was trapped in Germany and he grieved over his divided family. The following year he was interned in Huyton and on his release had to do menial work clearing bomb debris in order to pay the family bills. It was a demeaning and distressing time for a man of considerable achievement approaching forty. Pevsner seems to have accepted his privations with stoical understanding. But he must have been mightily relieved when J. M. Richards, Editor of the *Architectural Review*, had to go off on war work and asked him to take his place for the duration. Pevsner was even more pleased when, as a result of a chance encounter while doing fire-watching stints, he was offered a part-time teaching post at Birkbeck College, London, which eventually led to a professorship. At the same time another book appeared, Pevsner's authoritative (and frequently reissued) *Outline of European Architecture*. In addition he found time to work for Allen Lane, father of English paperbacks and creator of Penguin Books, as Chief Commissioning Editor for King Penguins. Thus, as the war approached its end, Nikolaus Pevsner was rapidly becoming one of the most influential figures in the cultural life of his adopted country. He was particularly admired for his expertise on architecture – past and present, international and British – at what proved to be a defining moment. For the nation was about to embark on its most massive rebuilding programme since the time of Wren.

One day towards the end of the war, Nikolaus Pevsner and Allen Lane were sitting in the garden of Lane's home in the rural outskirts of London. 'You have done the King Penguins now and we are going on with them,' Lane said. 'But if you had your way,' he asked, almost casually, 'what else would you do?' Pevsner, surprised by the question, had a ready answer. There and then he outlined two projects: a multi-volume 'Pelican History of Art', which he would edit, and a series of books he would write himself about all the most important buildings in the country. On the face of it this was an absurdly ambitious, almost capricious response. But these were heady times. Once the war was over, anything was feasible. Lane was caught up in the general euphoria. 'OK,' he said in effect. 'You're on!'

For the next thirty years the indefatigable Pevsner dovetailed regular viewing-and-writing trips to every county of England with his multifarious other commitments: books and articles, teaching and lecturing (including the visiting Slade Professorship at Cambridge) and the many committees and conferences he attended and addressed. He was also a skilled broadcaster. When the BBC invitation came to deliver the Reith Lectures, he recognised a rare chance to step back from his labours and give the nation an interim report. He decided to call his lectures 'The Englishness of English Art' and to take further his idea of the 'polarities' that lay beneath a nation's character and therefore its art.

What were the essential characteristics of the English? Like many émigrés, Pevsner was highly sensitive to the subtleties of his adopted language, and sought clues in the sounds and syntax of the vernacular he heard around him. Popular usage, he noted, aspired towards the short and spare ('prams and perms, mikes and bikes, macs and vacs'), the understatement, the distrust of rhetoric. Language was always changing and evolving, but climate was more stable and Pevsner cited Britain's moist and misty weather, so evident in the painting of Constable or Turner, as a further indicator or determinant of national character. In their medieval churches the English opted for long, straight lines, flat walls and architectural rectangularity. Their painters tended to prefer the small-scale to the overblown, water-colours to oils. English portraiture, said Pevsner when considering Reynolds, 'speaks in a low voice' and 'conceals more than it reveals'. The English, he thought, are democratic and tolerant. They like moderation and dislike revolutions.

In addition to 'national character', there is the 'spirit of the age', a more movable feast. Thus Hogarth, for all his down-to-earth English love of everyday life and distrust of allegory, had links to the rococo style or Age of Reason philosophy of continental Europe, while a new spirit was in the ascendant by the time of Blake, whose work had parallels with that of contemporaries like Runge and David.

The peculiar qualities of English art, therefore, have origins that dig deep into history and climate, and are reflected in their language and politics. They might derive, too, Pevsner suggested (in an argument that sounds odd in the mouth of a Jewish refugee), in the racial origins of the people, the Celtic love of curves larded by a dose of Anglo-Saxon and Norman practicality. But art and artists also respond to whatever is currently the dominant (and international) *Zeitgeist*, an influence that, by definition, changes from one age to another and is not confined to the work of any single nation.

Pevsner was aware that his quest – an attempt to encompass in a single large-scale theory a wide variety of art and artists – was beset by contradictions. These were the 'polarities' that he emphasised as central to his argument. No interpretation of the art of a great nation, he acknowledged, could be unidimensional. Indeed, he made a special feature of the polarity between what he called the 'rational' and the 'irrational' in English art. On the one hand there was the practical, down-to-earth, detached, utilitarian and narrative tradition that responded to life as observed (e.g. the Perpendicular style in church architecture, the Elizabethan house, the paintings of Constable, Paxton's Crystal Palace). Opposed to this was a different tradition: that of the undulating, the unpredictable, the curvilinear, the dreamy, the visionary and apocalyptic (the Decorated style in architecture, the paintings of Fuseli, Blake and the later Turner).

Pevsner's attempt to pin down the 'Englishness of English Art' was, ultimately, doomed to failure. The prodigious range of his scholarship rendered generalisation hazardous, constantly forcing him to acknowledge exceptions to whatever rule he was expounding. Furthermore, his use of concepts of Hegelian abstraction was particularly ill-applied to the art of a nation that, by his own account, tended to distrust theory and allegory, and gravitate instead towards the informal and the practical. Yet the Reith Lectures were the one real opportunity Pevsner had to bring together his thoughts about the art and architecture of his adopted country.

Nobody listening to his talks or reading the (expanded and illustrated) texts as published could miss the drift. What did England offer? 'A decent home, a temperate climate, and a moderate nation.' These did not make for great art. 'There is no Bach, no Beethoven, no Brahms' in England, 'no Michelangelo, no Titian, no Rembrandt, no Dürer or Grünewald'. Indeed, the quality of English painting and much else had been in decline for the past century or more, said Pevsner. While admiring Britain's moderate and democratic culture, he regretted its penchant for the conservative and the picturesque in art, and made fun of the country house landscaping of Buckingham Palace, for example, and what he called scathingly the 'fancy-dress ball' aspect of Victorian architecture. Surely Britain can do better, you sense Pevsner saying, as politely and Englishly as he can. This nation, after all, was once 'the unchallenged pioneer of innovation, in technology, industry, and commerce'. What was needed, he said, was 'the replanning of city centres to make them efficient as well as agreeable places to work in, and the planning of new balanced towns, satellite towns, New Towns, which are towns and not garden suburbs'. London should lead the way, just as it did in Wren's day. As examples of the kind of planning he had in mind, Pevsner cited the Holford project for the precinct of St Paul's and the new scheme for the Barbican area, both of which were then coming off the drawing board.

Later generations would criticise these as concrete jungles, unattractive agglomerations that obliterated the historic beauty of St Paul's Cathedral and St Giles Cripplegate, just as many of the 'carefully placed skyscrapers' or tower blocks Pevsner liked to advocate would become a byword for social dysfunction. Pevsner, however, cannot be held responsible for all the anomalies and aberrations of British architecture in the 1950s and 1960s. He was an historian not an architect, an academic

---

* Hugh Casson remembered his first meeting with Pevsner. 'On the dot he appeared [looking] like a kindly postmistress – pink cheeks, gold spectacles, sweet smile, brisk, authoritative manner.' Alec Clifton-Taylor wrote that Pevsner was reserved, even shy: 'one does not forget how easily he blushed' (*Architectural Review*, October 1983).

not an advocate. Nor was Pevsner by temperament a sermoniser or rhetorician.* But when Pevsner spoke, Britain listened. Indeed, as his county guides poured off the Penguin presses at the rate of one every few months, he became for many *the* voice of English architecture.

At the conclusion of his Reith Lectures Pevsner complimented the British on their architectural tradition and expressed the view that 'England seems predestined to play a leading part in modern architecture'. Yet, said the professor, shaking his head more in sorrow than in anger, the creation of the Modern style in the early part of the century did not take place in England and its acceptance in England was much slower than in America, France and Germany. He berated the British for their inordinate dependence upon committees and their 'lack of sufficiently bold planning'. But he was able to end with a few words of hope. The British, he reminded his audience, had always benefited from their ability to welcome creative people from abroad and absorb them and their works into the national fabric; he cited as examples Holbein, Van Dyck, Rossetti and Whistler, just four among countless people whose foreign roots came to flower in English soil. More broadly, he suggested that England 'has . . . profited just as much from the un-Englishness of [her] immigrants as they have profited from the Englishing they underwent'. Pevsner's pre-eminent example was Prince Albert. But it is hard not to believe that he also had himself in mind. For, as the American architect Philip Johnson wrote shortly after Pevsner's death, 'His Englishness was quintessential, but his Europeanness incontestable.'

Pevsner was not the monster of Modernism he has sometimes been portrayed. His writings show great breadth not only of learning but also of aesthetic sympathy. The scourge of sentimental pastoralism valued, too, the genuinely picturesque, the critic of wedding-cake grandeur was also a champion of quality Victoriana. And if he was one of those who brought the message of the Modern to England, he was neither the only one to do so nor the first. We have noted how Gropius was given a warm reception by like-minded architects and designers such as

Maxwell Fry, Wells Coates and the MARS group. By the mid-to-late 1930s, indeed, a veritable community of émigré artists, loosely linked by friendship with Herbert Read, was living in and around the Hampstead area. Among them at one time or another were Gropius himself as well as Breuer, Moholy-Nagy, Naum Gabo and Mondrian, all of whom sojourned in London for a while. The architect and designer Ernst Freud (and his sons Lucian and Clement) came to live nearby. All, like Pevsner, had been touched by the Modern movement. In addition, the Read circle included Paul Nash, Henry Moore, Barbara Hepworth, Ben Nicholson, Edward Burra, Wells Coates and Tristram Hillier (briefly formalised as 'Unit One'). 'We regarded ourselves', wrote Hillier of Unit One, 'as the spearhead . . . of Contemporary European painting and sculpture, which at that time had scarcely penetrated England.' The interaction between these émigré and native-born artists was to have a crucial impact upon the subsequent development of art and architecture in Britain. It was here, Read wrote later, that 'the foundations were laid for the art that was to develop in England during the next twenty-five years'. This was where – and when – 'what was to be done for the future of art in England had been done'. Quite simply, Read concluded, 'English art had come of age. Within the next decade it was to become, what it had not been for a century, an art of international significance.'

The artistic impact of the exiles took time to bear fruit. Several of the most celebrated stayed in Britain for only a few years. By the time Kokoschka and Schwitters arrived, Gropius and Moholy-Nagy had already left. And even if most of the émigrés might loosely be said to have been apostles of continental Modernism, they hardly preached a united artistic credo. Gabo and Moholy-Nagy, for example, bore the influence of Eastern European Constructivism while the work of Kokoschka continued to suggest his Expressionist roots. The witty photomontage of Heartfield was driven by his fearless political radicalism, while his fellow Dada artist Schwitters was resigned for a while to doing naturalistic portraits or landscapes if that was what people wanted. In any case, artists of the stature of Moore, Hepworth, Nash and Nicholson drank from a wide variety of sources, some of them (especially in Moore's case) non-European.

In 1938 Read mounted an exhibition of twentieth-century German art at London's New Burlington Gallery. It was intended as a defiant response to the exhibition of 'Degenerate Art' held in Munich the previous year and celebrated many of the artists pilloried by Hitler, including a number by then living and working in Britain. Sympathy for the victims of Nazism was one thing; serious interest another. The exhibition was not a great success. To a public long inured to the idea that paintings were either modern and French or old and Italian, the display proved bewildering. Few works were sold and the critic Raymond Mortimer wrote in the *New Statesman*, 'If Hitler doesn't like these pictures, it's the best thing I've heard about Hitler.'

Dealers and gallery owners and curators, such as Jack Bilbo (in London) and Hans Hess (in Leicester and later York), gave whatever prominence they could to the work of their fellow émigrés, as did London's Marlborough Gallery, which was founded by Austrian refugees after the war. But it was not until 1986 that a major retrospective exhibition of 'Art in Exile in Britain 1933–45' was held at the Camden Arts Centre in Hampstead's Arkwright Road. By that time most of the artists exhibited were living elsewhere or had died.

Many left respected reputations; for some, fame had a rich late flowering. Schwitters was a case in point. After escaping to England from Nazi-occupied Norway in June 1940, he was subjected to a long period of internment on the Isle of Man, where he passed the time painting portraits of fellow inmates. He was released into a world that hardly knew of him. In December 1944 the indomitable Herbert Read helped arrange an exhibition of Schwitters's work at Jack Bilbo's Modern Art Gallery, which sold a few works. But Schwitters was sick, felt unappreciated and was earning very little, and the following year he moved to the Lake District. Here he was visited by Laban, and the two men discussed putting on a ballet together, but nothing came of it. Schwitters found some contentment painting naturalistic landscapes, while also starting work on a final (and never completed) *Merzbarn*, the name he gave to his unique brand of bricolage-building-cum-sculpture. He died in 1948 and some time passed before a new generation of artists began to rediscover the daddy of Dada who had lived among them. The absurd and witty juxtapositions of words, objects and images that were Schwitters's trademark are evident in the emergence of 'Pop' art. Indeed, it was one of the pioneers of Pop, Richard Hamilton, who, with Arts Council support, rescued the semi-derelict *Merzbarn* and transported it to Newcastle where it remains to this day.

Kokoschka was always more celebrated than Schwitters. This was partly, no doubt, because of Kokoschka's personal flamboyance. As a young man in Vienna he had conducted a passionate love affair with Alma Mahler while she was still married to Gropius (and had later commissioned a life-size doll of the lady which he exhibited in public). Also, his society portraits and cityscapes were more easily comprehensible than the playful 'Merzmontages' of Schwitters. In Britain, Kokoschka became virtually the official mouthpiece of the cultural community in exile throughout the war and afterwards. Widely admired for his craftsmanship and his sense of colour, this most peripatetic of émigré artists was forever receiving portrait commissions from all over the world. Yet artistically he remained a somewhat isolated figure. 'Your eyes should reach out like long arms and caress the sitter,' he told a young English painter who came to him for instruction. But few British artists followed Kokoschka's habit of applying his penetrating gaze to the psychological truth that lay beneath the surface appearance via the application of rough textures (rather as Lucian Freud was beginning to do). In Britain, from Lely to Gainsborough to Augustus John and Roger Fry, the accepted style had been to portray smooth features rather than unmask the sitter, and it was not until 1962 that the Tate Gallery mounted a substantial exhibition of Kokoschka's work. By then the painter was in his mid-seventies and living in Switzerland. He visited London for the exhibition and greatly enjoyed seeing crowds (wrote the ubiquitous Herbert Read) 'such as on previous occasions have paid tribute only to Van Gogh and Picasso'.

Did the artists in exile have a collective impact upon the

development of art and sculpture in Britain? By and large, it was probably as individuals rather than part of a 'School' that most made their mark. Thus Milein Cosman created vibrant sketches of musicians at work and Marie-Louise von Motesiczky (a Beckmann pupil) painted portraits of her mother and of fellow refugees such as Canetti. Hans Feibusch found work painting large-scale murals, most notably for churches. The Polish-born Jankel Adler brought something of the Expressionist legacy to the young Scottish painters, Robert Colquhoun and Robert MacBryde, whom he encountered during the war. Another Pole, Josef Herman, who had come to Britain after a sojourn in Belgium, called upon his background in a vanished culture to depict with stark dignity the twilight world of another, his portrayals of Welsh coalminers combining something of the expressiveness of Chagall and Ensor with the elegiac vision of Lowry.

Some commentators have identified a deeper legacy. It is hard not to see something of the geometrical precision of Mondrian in the early work of Ben Nicholson (who, with Hepworth, had first been introduced to the Dutch master by Moholy-Nagy in Paris in 1934). Similarly, many have detected the influence of Gabo on Moore's decision to 'open up the closed form and reveal the space within it', on the Festival Hall architect Leslie Martin and on the revelation of inner structure in the work of St Ives artists who had worked with him such as Peter Lanyon. Perhaps. In one field, however, the impact of the exiles and the 'International style' they brought with them from continental Europe was paramount. That field was architecture.

Berthold Lubetkin (like Naum Gabo) was a Russian émigré who had lived in Berlin and Paris before moving to Britain in 1931. He soon realised there would be no future for him on the Continent and put down roots in London where he formed a partnership, Tecton, whose very name was intended to suggest gleaming, machine-made, high-efficiency Modernism. Early Tecton achievements included the Gorilla House and, most famously, the Penguin Pool at London Zoo.

The latter is an aggressively non-naturalistic structure built of reinforced concrete with an exquisitely curved, cantilevered, double-helix penguin walkway. Engineered by Ove Arup and Felix Samuely, it became not only the best-known building at the zoo but a pioneering icon of British Modernism. Lubetkin's great block of modern flats, High Point in Highgate, similarly set a standard for sleek Modernism, characterised by a concrete grid of walls and rectilinear windows. As in the more or less contemporaneous Lawn Road flats by Wells Coates and Isokon, the overall effect resulted from the mechanical rigidity of long, unbroken lines subtly softened by curved balconies and a welcoming entrance hall. When High Point II was added a few years later, Lubetkin included great frame windows and, at the entrance, the witty absurdity of a pair of caryatids placed on unstably sloping ground.

One of Lubetkin's young colleagues was Denys Lasdun. Lasdun, a pupil of Wells Coates, became an active member of Tecton (and latterly a partner) until its dissolution in 1948. Lubetkin's influence is evident in much of Lasdun's mature work, notably in the stark style of the University of East Anglia outside Norwich and in the horizontal 'brutalism' of London's National Theatre.

Lubetkin's was not the only voice in Britain proclaiming architectural Modernism, nor Lasdun the only accommodating pupil. Several émigré architects, planners and designers found sympathetic colleagues with whom they went into partnership: Gropius with Maxwell Fry, Breuer (and later Eugene Rosenberg) with F. R. S. Yorke, and Erich Mendelsohn, one of the most celebrated architects in pre-Hitler Berlin, with the Russian émigré Serge Chermayeff. Mendelsohn and Chermayeff were responsible for another of the great pioneering models of Modernism in Britain, the de la Warr pavilion at Bexhill-on-Sea. One of Rosenberg's first jobs when he arrived in Britain was as a colleague of William Holford in the Department of Civic Design at Liverpool University.

After the war, with a Labour government committed to massive rebuilding, Rosenberg (still with Yorke) designed a number of schools and hospitals, a factory in Gateshead, a high-rise apartment block in Stevenage, a new terminal for Gatwick

Airport. Another émigré architect, Walter Bor, worked after the war for the London County Council where he rose to overall charge of the reconstruction of the Stepney area in the East End. Lubetkin, admired for the dramatic Finsbury health centre completed just before the war, worked on a series of housing estates for Finsbury and became for a while architect-in-charge of the proposed Peterlee New Town. The Hungarian-born Ernö Goldfinger, after a series of schools and offices, went on to mastermind a huge Ministry of Health complex at London's Elephant and Castle.

A *tour d'horizon* of the architectural legacy of the émigrés in Britain in the 1940s and 1950s leaves a recurrent image of bold rectilinearity, long uninterrupted lines, horizontal roofs and a commitment to clear and firm external structure (often like the box-upon-box effect of the decks of a liner). These schools, hospitals, factories, office blocks and housing estates pro-claimed the integration of function and form, frankly revealing the materials from which they had been built, such as reinforced concrete, rather than disguising them behind gratuitous decoration.

If all this gives an impression of austerity, of architectural 'brutalism', it must be remembered that the post-war building boom was initiated during a period of prefabs, food rationing and utility clothing. Lavish, sumptuous architecture would have been unthinkable. But so was building derived from the traditional, picturesque English tradition of *rus in urbe*. What was needed was practical planning that could answer the urgent needs of large urban populations. In the circumstances it was perhaps fortunate that so much civic (and some private) development was in the hands of people rooted in a tried aesthetic. The ideas of Le Corbusier and of German Modernism, in outline so contrary to the traditional tastes of Middle England, helped provide a firm intellectual scaffolding precisely as Britain sought to rebuild the fabric of its civic life. Thus the Modernist architecture of the exiles, reinforced by the advocacy of commentators like Nikolaus Pevsner, gave post-war Britain much of the physical character by which it can still be recognised to this day.

CHAPTER EIGHTEEN

Media and Messengers

By the 1960s the cultural face of Britain had been substantially altered by the infusion of talent, drive and ideas from people whose personal roots were once in Middle Europe. Many important figures had departed by then. Glyndebourne (which had reopened in 1950) was no longer in the artistic hands of Busch and Ebert, nor Edinburgh in those of Bing; Bing was one of several who had re-established themselves across the Atlantic. Some had returned to Austria or Germany* (West or East, according to political taste), while others had re-emigrated to Israel, Australia or elsewhere; the architect Harry Seidler, for example, arriving in Britain from Vienna after the *Anschluss*, went on to work with Gropius and Breuer in the USA and Oscar Niemeyer in Brazil, before moving to Sydney in 1948 where he set up one of Australia's most successful practices. Others, including survivors of the death camps, had arrived in Britain after the war. Thus the Hitler exiles (it is worth reiterating) did not constitute a single, homogeneous block of immigration living and working in Britain at a single time, nor did they have a monothematic impact upon Britain.

Nevertheless, as suggested in the introductory chapter, a snapshot of British cultural life at some point in the 1960s or thereabouts would have revealed many of the émigrés at the

---

* Perhaps the most famous to return permanently to Germany after the war was Max Born, who went back in 1954. Born was criticised for this, not least by Einstein (who had been one of the first to urge him to leave). But Born, a natural conciliator, felt he wanted to contribute to the post-war 'healing' process and help rebuild the sciences in the land in which his own gifts had initially been nurtured.

height of their powers and influence. People like Pevsner and Gombrich, who had arrived insecure and not a little anxious thirty years earlier, were among the revered deans of the nation's cultural life, while many younger arrivals, such as the film director Karel Reisz and the three émigré members of the Amadeus Quartet, were now at the forefront of their professions. Weidenfeld, having managed to avoid prosecution for obscenity with the publication of Nabokov's *Lolita* in 1959, had a best-seller on his hands and used his firm's celebrity (and wealth) to produce a torrent of original work, including (in 1962) *The Age of Revolution*, the first of Eric Hobsbawm's tetralogy on the history of modern Europe.

Not only were these and others masters of their respective crafts. Many were also breaking through the invisible barriers that traditionally prevented purveyors of 'high' culture from reaching a wide 'popular' audience. Gombrich had done this with *The Story of Art*, Pevsner with his 'Buildings of England' series. Everybody with even a passing interest in the arts knew of the Amadeus Quartet and of Klemperer and Solti, and of the volcanic wit (and perhaps the premature deaths) of Gerard Hoffnung and Vicky. The walls of exclusivity were under assault as the arts became 'democratised' and the expansion of the press and television brought in new audiences. Serious Sunday newspapers began to introduce 'colour' magazines or supplements, while *The Times* broke long precedent by placing news rather than small ads on its front page. 'Auntie' BBC, meanwhile, rebounding from the shock of commercial television (introduced in 1955), hitched up her skirts and reached out for newer, younger audiences with satire and pop music. These were crucible years for serious arts programmes on television. If millions came to know of Georg Solti, it was not from his Covent Garden performances or even his LPs; it was because they had seen Humphrey Burton's television film of the conductor recording Wagner's *Ring*.

In 1964 the BBC launched its second television channel. The idea was that, while BBC1 would aim to reach large audiences with mainstream programming, BBC2 would avowedly pursue the unusual, the artistic, the experimental and what a later generation would call the investigative. This was balm to the ears of Huw Wheldon, pioneer of television arts and famous as the inspirational editor-presenter of BBC TV's first regular arts programme, *Monitor*. Wheldon, with his jutting chin, beaky nose, bushy eyebrows and mesmeric Welsh-accented oratory, was a familiar and popular performer, a passionate advocate – on the air and within the councils of the BBC – of TV that communicated a serious appreciation of the arts to the widest possible audience. During the 1960s he rose rapidly up the Corporation hierarchy, sweeping along in his coat-tails a coterie of exceptionally talented producers and film makers, many of whom went on to have starry careers, among them John Schlesinger, Humphrey Burton, Michael Gill, Jonathan Miller, Patrick Garland, Ken Russell and Stephen Hearst. Schlesinger left the BBC early to direct for the big screen, while Miller became the nation's pet polymath. Russell produced a succession of TV portraits of composers that graduated from the elegant and elegiac (Elgar) to the caricature (Delius) to the near-obscene (Strauss) before he too left to direct for the cinema. Burton demoted himself from executive responsibility, pioneered arts programmes on ITV and went on to pursue his career as one of Britain's leading producers of music documentaries. Hearst became Head of Arts Features, before moving to radio as Controller of Radio Three.

Hearst remembered the 1960s and early 1970s as the 'heroic age' of arts and culture on television. Certainly it was exhilarating working for BBC2 in its first decade, especially in an arts department, as programmes came to be made in colour (and viewers gradually shifted from monochrome to colour TV sets, thereby paying a higher licence fee and boosting the BBC's finances). It was an era of landmark programmes. Hearst was Head of Arts Features at the time of Kenneth Clark's art history series *Civilisation* and Alistair Cooke's *America* (both directed by Michael Gill). Such projects proved it was possible to bring serious scholarship to audiences of millions. Traditional distinctions became blurred between something called art or culture and something else called popular entertainment, and there were signs of a new accommodation between the two.

Nor was this meeting of 'high' and 'popular' culture restricted to the media. Terence Conran, claiming inspiration from the Bauhaus, began to produce eye-catching babyware, kitchenware and furniture, aiming to make these available at affordable prices to a mass market. It was a laudable vision, an attempt to provide for the needs of all classes of society by harnessing the finest and latest designs. Why should the colourful, the exuberant and the expressive be restrained? Why shouldn't everybody be able to enjoy the best? That was the mantra as Joan Littlewood talked of her 'Fun Palace', Paul Hamlyn mass-marketed LPs of the classics under the title 'Music for Pleasure', Peter Blake and David Hockney painted colourfully 'naïve' portraits of their friends and psychedelic posters became collectors' items.

It was in the cinema that this new accommodation between 'art' and 'entertainment' was probably most successful. Rather to the surprise of those who had pronounced the obsequies of the movie industry, British films enjoyed an artistic renaissance in the 1960s. Directors such as John Schlesinger and Karel Reisz produced hard-hitting social dramas that appealed to large audiences. Was there any significance in the fact that Reisz was an émigré from Central Europe (and Schlesinger the son of one)? Not on the face of it. Reisz, after his arrival in Britain as a lad and his Quaker schooling, grew up to think of himself as an archetypal young Englishman, independent-minded, a little rebellious and steeped in the fashionable radicalism of the time. The films he went to see as a youngster were not *Caligari* or *Metropolis* but popular Ealing comedies and American blockbusters. None of his own films looks or sounds like a UFA-influenced film. On the contrary, Reisz helped set a standard for tough-minded, indigenous British film making whose roots were, if anywhere, in the British documentary movement.

Yet as Reisz looked back, he acknowledged that his personal history undoubtedly had an influence upon his work. Not, perhaps, stylistically so much as in subject matter. Again and again, the subjects to which he felt drawn tended to spotlight the outsider, the individual who breaks the mould (heroically, pathetically or pathologically) while also craving acceptance.

From his early collaborations with Lindsay Anderson (*We Are the Lambeth Boys*, *This Sporting Life*) through his string of personal triumphs – *Saturday Night and Sunday Morning* (1960), *Night Must Fall* (1964), *Morgan: a Suitable Case for Treatment* (1966), *Isadora* (1968), *The Gambler* (1974), *Sweet Dreams* (1985) and *The French Lieutenant's Woman* (1981) – this haunting dilemma of the insider-outsider recurs like a leitmotif. These are films containing powerful, raw passion, the emotions of someone who is here, yet not securely here.

Reisz incorporated a sharp critical edge into his art – like Schlesinger, Lindsay Anderson and Tony Richardson (and the 'Angry Young Men' of literature and the stage). The advent of widespread affluence, these artists seemed to be saying, may have solved some material problems but had brought in its train new social and psychological ones. Sex and money might have become cheap, but personal fulfilment was not so easily obtained. 'To be thus is nothing; but to be safely thus.' It was a message that found an eager audience among millions of film goers in a world threatened by nuclear destruction.

It was another insider-outsider – the British-based American director, Stanley Kubrick – who created the film that, more than any other, came to epitomise the lunatic uncertainty of a world under threat of annihilation: *Dr Strangelove or How I Learned to Stop Worrying and Love the Bomb*. *Dr Strangelove* climaxed in a crisis meeting in the Pentagon War Room when America is threatened by nuclear attack. Peter Sellers played three roles. As an insanely rational émigré rocket scientist (partly modelled on Werner von Braun, or perhaps Henry Kissinger), he gives the President (also Sellers) a series of gleefully objective assessments of various forms of atomic response. The giant War Room, with its vast, sloping walls and stark shadows, remained for all who saw the film the abiding image of power under threat. Ronald Reagan is said to have asked, on becoming President, if he could be shown the War Room at the Pentagon because he had been so impressed by it in the film *Dr Strangelove*. There is no record of how his officials broke the news that it had been a fictional re-creation.

The person who designed *Dr Strangelove*, and many of the

most visually memorable films from the 1960s to the 1990s, was born Klaus-Hugo Adam in Berlin in 1921. Ken Adam was especially adept at suggesting the vast, the exotic and the dangerous. He was the production designer of *The Ipcress File* and *Sleuth* – and a string of the most celebrated James Bond films.

The Bond movies, like *Dr Strangelove*, were typical of the new cultural synthesis, combining art and entertainment, and appealing to large audiences across the traditional boundaries. In an era in which real-life derring-do was largely a thing of the past, audiences, it seems, could not have enough of a formula which portrayed a British agent at his omnicompetent best and guaranteed excitement, glamour, danger and survival. The early Bond films loosely followed the storyline of one of the Ian Fleming novels. But they soon acquired a trajectory of their own led not by the detail of their plots but by the sheer visual bravado they displayed. In addition to spectacular locations, scantily-clad girls and breathtaking technological wizardry, a James Bond movie required an evil antagonist who comes within a whisker of achieving his malevolent designs and is finally toppled from his lair by the energetic resourcefulness of our hero. Jack the Giant Killer? David and Goliath? It is an old myth. It is also, of course, the mythologised story of Hitler, in his eagle's nest in Berchtesgaden, or holed up in his bunker in Berlin, plotting the end of the world as we know it, but destroyed in the final frame by the forces of decency.

Ken Adam's father, an entrepreneurial person with a streak of bravado to his personality, had studied in England as a young man. He had been one of the few German Jews to be decorated as a cavalry officer in the Great War. After the war he settled down with his brothers to manage their large, prestigious sports goods store in the heart of Berlin, fitting out some of the great athletes and adventurers, skiers and flyers of the time. Everybody visited 'S. ADAM' on the corner of Leipzigerstrasse and Friedrichstrasse. There was talk of rebuilding the entire complex and designs were drawn up by Mies van der Rohe.* Young

---

*An illustration of the Mies van der Rohe building is on display in Berlin's new Jewish Museum, beneath a large poster advertising the store.

Klaus was always hanging around the shop. When he was nine he had tea with Amundsen.

As an adolescent in the early 1930s Klaus, like the children of many of Berlin's elite, attended the French *Gymnasium*. Here he got to know the son of Max Reinhardt and fell into the habit of going to the cinema and theatre (often going backstage) and was particularly keen on the satirical cabaret that flourished in Berlin during those dangerous days. With the advent of the Nazis, S. ADAM was boycotted and the business went into liquidation. In 1934 the family decided to leave Germany. Klaus and his younger brother were sent to school in Edinburgh to learn English, joining the rest of the family a few months later in London. Klaus, now a teenager, went to St Paul's School where his childhood love of drawing was encouraged by a sympathetic art master. An avid cinema goer, Klaus at fifteen had already conceived the ambition to design for the movies.

Klaus's father died in 1936 but his mother had opened a guest house in Hampstead, which paid the bills. Every night, twenty or thirty people would sit around Mrs Adam's tables – artists, historians, psychiatrists, writers, lawyers. One of the people Klaus met was a Hungarian painter who had found work as a cameraman for London Films. He took the lad to Denham one day, showed him some monumental sets they were filming and managed to introduce him to the man who had designed them: Vincent Korda. 'If you want to design for the films,' Korda told him, 'you should take a course in architecture.' Klaus took the advice and, for a while, enrolled for evening classes at the Bartlett School of Architecture, while articled by day to an architectural firm. When war broke out he was exempted from internment on the grounds that he was designing air raid shelters. After a stint in the Pioneer Corps, Adam was recruited into the RAF and went on to become the only fighter pilot without British naturalisation. For a while Klaus Adam was known as Keith Howard, but before long (he never could remember how or when it happened) he became 'Ken'. It was as Ken Adam that the boy born in Berlin became a flying hero in the land which defeated Hitler. His father would have been proud of him.

Soon after the war, Adam found work as assistant art director on a number of films and built up a name for his particularly bold, colourful designs. His big break came in 1959 with *Around the World in Eighty Days* (his supervisor at MGM was Alfred Junge). This was Hollywood's most spectacular attempt to counteract what it saw as the growing popularity of television, and it made Adam's name. From then on, if you wanted a colourful evocation of another time or place, a burst of imaginative technological innovation plus a big dollop of visual humour, Ken Adam was the designer to go for. Did your filmscript have scenes set in the secret Pentagon War Room (*Dr Strangelove*) or Fort Knox (*Goldfinger*), or require an extravagantly customised car (*Goldfinger*, *Chitty Chitty Bang Bang*), yacht (*Thunderball*) or speedboat (*Moonraker*) – or a fleet of nuclear bombs or space rockets? You could rely on Ken to dream up a stylised creation far more memorable than the real thing. Was your villain's vast headquarters concealed inside an extinct volcano (*You Only Live Twice*), the interior of a submarine supertanker (*The Spy Who Loved Me*) or a city in space (*Moonraker*)? Just the thing for Ken Adam to design – and if necessary to destroy in a series of spectacular terminal explosions.

When London's Serpentine Gallery mounted a Ken Adam exhibition in 1999, many thought they saw the influence of German Expressionism in his work. A master of artifice, his designs are consistently architectural, with big, bold lines sweeping their angular way across the screen. Light and shade are liberally applied, with giant shadow projections suggesting danger. Curved, converging walls suggest the claustrophobia of *Caligari* while the vast hidden cities of militantly choreographed evil evoke memories of *Metropolis*. As for the great period pieces (*Barry Lyndon*, *The Madness of King George*, both of which won Oscars for their design) – these, thought some, were in the tradition of the great Korda classics, *Henry VIII* and *Rembrandt*, reaching through them to such early German classics as Lubitsch's *Madame DuBarry*.

Adam was bemused that critics looked to his continental past for insights into his art. He did not deny these influences but was inclined to add a few matter-of-fact qualifications. As a boy in Berlin he was the kid who enjoyed sketching and making models. His mother was an excellent water colourist, while his father loved gadgets and was always intrigued by the latest motor car, speedboat or bi-plane. What about all those great, diagonal lines and curved corridors and ceilings, and the vastiose cities of evil in the sky and beneath the earth and seas? Didn't they derive from the imagery of the UFA silents and their successors and imitators? Perhaps. But Adam did not, in fact, see most of the famous German Expressionist movies until he lived in England. The strong, bold lines of his drawing, he thought, probably had more to do with the fact that he liked to sketch in black and white with a thick felt pen.

No artist can be sure of the sources that have worked upon his or her imagination, and Ken Adam's work undoubtedly reflects a variety of influences, many of them purely personal. But as one watches one film after another portraying, in witty and extravagant fashion, the forces of global destruction, it is impossible not to remember that they were designed by someone whose young adolescence had been passed in the megalomaniac lunacy of Hitler's Berlin and who owed his life to the fact that his family left for England when it was still possible to do so. Is Largo Hitler? And Blofeld? And Stromberg? Of course not. They are creatures of fantasy, and Adam, a hired hand, designed what he was commissioned to design. But Ken Adam was never 'merely' the designer on these films; he was always integral to the production team from the start, playing a major part as ideas for plot, design and screenplay were developed in harness. Listen to the last speech of Drax in Adam's final James Bond film, *Moonraker*, and it is hard not to believe that Ken Adam got a special frisson of pleasure destroying him. Drax controls a vast city in outer space, invisible to terrestrial radar, to which he has transported pairs of beautiful people from earth. In triumph he stands upon a great platform and addresses the assembled multitude. First (he says) there was a dream:

Now there is reality. Here, in the untainted cradle of the heavens, will be created a new Super Race, a race of perfect physical specimens. You have been selected as its progenitors. Like gods, your offspring will return to earth and shape it in their image. You have all served in humble capacities in my terrestrial empire. Your seed, like yourselves, will pay deference to the ultimate dynasty which I alone have created. From their first day on earth, they will be able to look up and know that there is law and order in the heavens.

In 1972 Stephen Hearst surprised his television colleagues by announcing that he was going in for the post of Controller, Radio Three. Challenged by the defection of listeners to the newer medium of TV, BBC radio (which still had a monopoly of the airwaves) had been brooding over its counterattack. In 1967 the Corporation had launched Radios 1, 2, 3* and 4, and announced its intention to set up a series of local radio stations. The purpose, it seemed, was to create definable stations whose output had a degree of regularity and predictability so as to build up loyalty and regular listening habits. The policy, clarified in a controversial policy document ('Broadcasting in the Seventies') three years later, made perfect managerial sense. To some, it also spelled the end of the Reithian principle of 'education by stealth'.

Since 1959 the Controller of Music had been William Glock, a pupil of Schnabel and proponent of the modern. Glock was in charge of all the music broadcast on the Third Programme and also of the annual Promenade Concerts. Within weeks of his BBC appointment Glock recruited the redoubtable Hans Keller to assist and advise. Each had a sharp, analytical mind, loved Mozart and Haydn, and was committed to the encouragement of the modern and the contemporary. The British avant garde was to be encouraged (Glock brought Alexander Goehr in to the BBC as a music producer) while music in the more elegiac, insular English style would tend to be treated with benign neglect.

---

* The title 'Third Programme' was retained as part of a 'Third Network', which also included the (daytime) Music Programme and various sport and further education programmes. The title was finally abolished, to be replaced by 'Radio Three', in 1970.

Glock and Keller were utterly different in personal style. Nor did their tastes overlap entirely. Glock, with his cool, crystalline intelligence and icy blue eyes, approached twentieth-century music through the sound world of Stravinsky; Keller, expressive, witty and acerbic, via Schoenberg.* Glock thought Keller's advocacy of Gershwin and Britten overenthusiastic. Keller, a streak of devilry behind his every move, once included a hoax piece of prerecorded nonsense ('Mobile for tape and percussion, by Piotr Zak') in a broadcast concert of contemporary chamber music – just to see what the critics would make of it. Keller irritated Glock; everyone who had regular dealings with Keller found him insufferable at times. But Keller was a persuasive advocate and Glock was impressed by his 'rare ability to seize on relationships over a whole panorama of works'. It was the BBC's mission, Keller insisted, to broadcast music of the highest quality, however difficult, performed to the highest standards – and to persuade people to listen. Not to hear, but to *listen*, Keller would repeat.

Keller fiercely opposed the ideas embodied in 'Broadcasting in the Seventies', fearing the onset of 'generic broadcasting'. A master of paradox, he argued wittily but with transparent integrity that, as a music lover, he was opposed to increasing the musical output of the Third Programme (or Radio 3) at the expense of serious speech. An all-music network, he said, would debase music, turning it into 'aural wallpaper' (just as an all-speech Radio 4 would debase the value of its talks, documentaries and drama). In February 1970 *The Times* published a letter signed (contrary to the terms of their contract) by 134 members of BBC staff objecting to 'Broadcasting in the Seventies' and what they saw as 'the abandonment of creative, mixed planning in favour of a schematic division into categories'. Keller was not only (of course) one of the signatories of the letter. He was also one of its principal progenitors.

While Keller was injecting sparkle and controversy into the BBC's Music Division, something similar was happening over

---

* The composer Joseph Horovitz recalled joking to Keller that Schoenberg 'wrote no tunes' – whereupon Keller immediately riposted by *whistling* one of his hero's most intractable twelve-tone themes.

the way in the Drama Department, headed by another Viennese émigré, Martin Esslin. Esslin, most of whose BBC work had been in Bush House, had relatively little prior experience of radio drama when he arrived, but he had established his reputation as a rigorous critic with brilliant books to his credit on Brecht and on the Theatre of the Absurd. Esslin's predecessor, Val Gielgud (brother of John), more at home in the English theatrical tradition, had brought Esslin into the department to deal with such difficult customers as Beckett and Pinter; Esslin's appointment as Head in 1963 signalled a major step towards theatrical (including European) Modernism.

By 1972, the BBC's Controllers of Music (Glock) and of Radio 3* (the novelist Howard Newby) had moved on. Glock was succeeded by Robert Ponsonby, Newby by Stephen Hearst. When Hearst applied to become Controller of Radio 3, Esslin was his principal rival. Hearst got the job (in part because he was more prepared to acknowledge the importance of audience size for a network that spent over £40 million) and, for much of the 1970s, Radio 3 discussions on the subtler depths of British culture would regularly be led with awesome fluency and familiarity by that formidable trio of Viennese émigrés Stephen Hearst, Martin Esslin and Hans Keller.

Stephen Hearst became a forceful, proactive controller of the nation's premier cultural network. If he was not familiar with a name or a topic that came up in discussion he would ask; if he knew but disapproved he could crush. The tension between Hearst and Keller was palpable. When Keller proposed a Radio 3 series on psychiatry, a subject that to him was all-embracing, Hearst, who knew a thing or two about the subject (his wife was a psychotherapist), was scathing. Keller, always game for a scrap, went away to regroup and returned to the next meeting even more belligerently confident of his case. Hearst, aroused, was even more vehement in his veto.

Some said Hearst was still a television executive at heart, constantly pouring out ideas for the momentous, the dramatic, the spectacular and the expensive. Others said that this

---

* The two posts were later combined under John Drummond.

mercurial, attractive man was not really an executive at all but still fundamentally a producer. 'You probably think we're a bunch of Establishment old fogies,' he would say to a startled young colleague in the canteen queue. 'If so, I want you to come up with a series of programmes in which the brightest people – no matter who or where they are – argue the most heterodox views you or they can think of. On any subject.' It was Hearst, more aware than most of the poor sound quality given out by most TV sets, who pioneered the idea of joint opera relays on radio and television. This, like many of his initiatives, involved endless fights – with the Musicians Union and/or the financial bosses inside the BBC. Things came to a head in 1978 over a studio production (the last undertaken by the BBC) of Verdi's *Macbeth*, to which Radio Three contributed the (to it) large sum of £15,000. By the end of the allotted sessions, all but a few bars of the opera were 'in the can'. To record the final few seconds, however, the MU insisted on a further session fee for all its members. Hearst was incandescent, went to the Director-General, had to pay – and resigned as Controller.*

People used to joke at the apparent absurdity that the upholders of cultural standards within the 'British' Broadcasting Corporation included people like Hearst, Esslin and Keller.† Their contribution must not be exaggerated and was certainly not greater than that of (say) Wheldon, Gielgud, Newby or Glock. Nor did any of them overtly or consciously think of themselves as a conduit for 'alien' or 'European' ideas. On the contrary, their presence at the heart of British broadcasting is a reflection on the seriousness and broadmindedness of the people

---

* Hearst stayed on in the BBC for some years in various advisory capacities.

† There were many other émigrés, too, in influential BBC posts in the 1960s and 1970s. Paul Fox moved from Current Affairs to become Controller of BBC1 (1967–73) before moving to Yorkshire Television. Peter Adam, having survived childhood in Hitler's Germany, came to the BBC after sojourns in Paris and New York and used his multicultural background to produce a stream of TV portraits of artists and intellectuals (Nureyev, Henze, Visconti, Hannah Arendt, Lotte Lenya). In radio, the Russian-born, German-raised Anna Kallin (who had worked with Mann and Toynbee, and been close to Kokoschka) continued to weave cultural trails long after official retirement. Herbert Read's protégée Leonie Cohn consistently made architecture 'visible' on radio, while from 1973 to 1987 the head of radio talks and documentaries was a 1956-vintage Hungarian refugee, George Fischer (father of the novelist Tibor Fischer).

who recruited and promoted them. By giving top jobs to such émigrés, you might well get more Schoenberg or Ionesco. But you would also get a fresh appraisal of traditional British culture from people viewing it from a broad, humane and cosmopolitan perspective from which all could benefit.

Hans Keller died in 1985, but Stephen Hearst and Martin Esslin continued to be active cultural entrepreneurs into old age, Hearst as a writer and television producer, Esslin with visiting professorships as far afield as California and Vienna. Karel Reisz continued to work in films until the 1990s. Ken Adam designed seven James Bond films from *Dr No* (1962) to *Moonraker* (1979). His credits in the 1980s and 1990s included *Addams Family Values* and *The Madness of King George*. At the turn of the century Adam, a youthful seventy-eight, was commuting to Berlin, where he was advising on a futuristic millennium exhibition in the Martin Gropius Haus. When I last saw him, he had recently celebrated his eightieth birthday and had just done the designs for the film of Ronald Harwood's *Taking Sides* (about Furtwängler).

CHAPTER NINETEEN

Diminishing Returns

Fritz Schumacher's background hardly gave promise of a guru-in-waiting. The son of a brilliant but cold-blooded economics professor, he was born Ernst Friedrich Schumacher in 1911 in Bonn and raised in Berlin. During the severe privations following 1918, the family took in paying guests (including one of Professor Schumacher's students, a sparkling young Hungarian named Thomas Balogh). Fritz, like most Germans of his generation growing up in the shadow of the Great War, resented what he understood to be the complete lack of understanding for Germany's fate shown by the victors – a view reinforced when he got to know those complacent victors on their home ground. He spent a couple of years (1930–2) in England, under the benevolent eye of the Warden of New College, Oxford, H. A. L. Fisher. Oxford improved his English and kept him away from his father. He made a number of friends, among them David Astor and a young compatriot named Adam von Trott. But the more Schumacher got to know the British, the more he became a patriotic German, going out of his way to explain, and almost to justify, the rising prominence of the Nazi party back home. Five years later, having seen the reality of Nazism, the young economist – much against the pleading of his young wife – decided to accept an invitation to work in London.

The war years took the Schumachers to the depths of despair. Fritz was interned, and then worked for a time as a farm labourer. Throughout, he felt shredded by the fate of his country. Perhaps, he thought, he should have stayed in Germany, like his brother-in-law the physicist Werner Heisenberg, and pursued his intellectual work with as much integrity as possible. But wouldn't that have been giving tacit support to Hitler? Maybe he should have emulated his friend Adam von Trott, who stayed in order to fight the regime from within. That, thought Schumacher despairingly, was no option either. Germany was like a glass of water with sediment at the bottom; the Nazis had stirred up the dirt so that the entire contents were now contaminated. In 1941 Schumacher heard that his young brother, a bright, attractive lad seduced by the glossy paraphernalia of Nazism, had volunteered for the Eastern Front and been killed in action.

In 1942 Schumacher (leaving his wife and children behind on a farm) went back to Oxford – one of a number of refugee intellectuals on the staff of the Institute of Statistics (where one of his colleagues was Thomas Balogh). For a while he found solace in Marxism while also revelling in contacts with celebrities of the moderate left, among them Keynes, Beveridge and Stafford Cripps. But none of this removed the pall of perplexity he suffered. Schumacher felt he was seeking answers to questions that others, and maybe he himself, could not even formulate. In 1944 he heard that von Trott had suffered an unspeakable death for his part in the plot against Hitler.

Schumacher's sense of despair deepened when, after the war, he returned to Germany with the British Control Commission and came face to face with the ruin of his former homeland, which it was his job to help rebuild. He visited the Ruhr coalfields and realised that the linchpin of any recovery programme was the efficient distribution of energy, but it was hard to see how German industry could ever be properly restarted. On all sides, Schumacher encountered reminders of his former life. He revisited his own family, trying to hold back tears of mixed emotion; the new mayor of Hamburg was also his father-in-law. Everyone Schumacher met – his British colleagues as much as the Germans with whom he had dealings – seemed to regard him as alien, one of 'them'. Perhaps they were right. He was no longer a German patriot. How could he be? Nor would he ever be fully British. Perhaps the answer lay in the wider European regeneration of which some spoke, building on the achievements of the Marshall Plan, the first steps of which were to be the establishment in 1952 of the European Coal and Steel Community. Energy policy became Schumacher's obsession. From 1950 he was economic adviser to Britain's National Coal Board, a post he was to hold for twenty years. Coal, one of the industries nationalised by the Attlee government, lay at the basis of economic revival Schumacher felt – and fed directly into his growing internationalism.

This former German nationalist was beginning to think globally. He was also struggling to break out from traditional, linear thinking that preached permanent growth as the only criterion of economic success. Was big always, necessarily, better? Where did macroeconomics and microeconomics meet? Fuel and food were, of course, essential and doubtless the big corporate enterprises that provided them needed to grow and make a profit. But what every individual ultimately aspired to, thought Schumacher, was a sense of personal 'wholeness' – the integration of the needs of mind, body and soul. Proud of being as much a doer as a thinker, Schumacher found much fulfilment tilling his garden, providing his family with nourishing home-grown produce. Like Gandhi, he tried his hand at the practical things about the home: sewing, weaving, shoemaking and carpentry. Why set up huge corporations to do things *for* people? he asked. Surely it was better to find out what individuals were doing already and help them to do it better.

All this flew directly in the face of conventional economic thinking. But Schumacher, once regarded as a somewhat arrogant rationalist, now joked that he had become an 'anti-intellectual intellectual'. Most intellectuals, he felt (people like his father, perhaps, or Dr Strangelove – or maybe Schumacher had in mind his *bête noire* at the Coal Board, a brilliant émigré of earlier vintage, Jacob Bronowski*), coldly analysed problems into their component parts and worked out desiccated solutions. Real solutions could only be the product of creative, lateral

---

* Jacob Bronowski, born in Poland in 1908 and educated for a while in Germany, came to Britain, speaking virtually no English, at the age of twelve. By the time Schumacher knew him, Bronowski was Director of Research at the Coal Board, a man of immense erudition and charm widely known as a superb communicator who produced not only learned scientific and mathematical papers but also radio plays and books about poetry (particularly Blake). Bronowski is probably best remembered for his television series *The Ascent of Man*.

thinking, new paradigms, new syntheses. Moving ever further from the intellectual world of his father and of Oxford, Schumacher began to flirt (like Koestler) with ideas derived from the paranormal and joined the Society for Psychical Research. He read the works of oriental mystics. He visited Burma, found people living in harmony with nature, making use of renewable resources and enjoying the fruits of their own labour, and he returned a confirmed Buddhist.

Over the years that followed, Schumacher gradually refined his ideas until, in 1965, his old friend David Astor printed in the *Observer* Schumacher's landmark article arguing the benefits of 'Intermediate Technology'. Schumacher soon became something of a celebrity in circles concerned with global development. A few years later he finally left the Coal Board and in 1973 published his book *Small Is Beautiful: A Study of Economics as if People Mattered*. 'One of the most fateful errors of our age', Schumacher began starkly, 'is the belief that "the problem of production" has been solved.' In fact, we are living off capital and the world is on a collision course. In a series of essays, most of which had appeared earlier, he explored possible solutions: Buddhist economics, the introduction of intermediate technology, an end to 'the idolatry of large size'.

By the time he died in 1977, Fritz Schumacher had become the spokesman for a generation. Many played a part in the intellectual shift away from uncontrolled economic elephantiasis: Rachel Carson, Paul Ehrlich, Barbara Ward, Barry Commoner, Ralph Nader and the Club of Rome all warned of the dangerous mismatch between human needs and the use and abuse of available resources. It was the genius of Schumacher to crystallise the problem and give it a name, an organisation and a rallying cry.

Schumacher's intellectual (and, one might say, spiritual) journey was a tortuous one, beset by contradictions. A rational sceptic who went on to embrace the psychic and the paranormal, a proud patriot whose thinking became internationalist and then global, Schumacher preached brotherhood and family values ('economics as if people mattered') but was evidently a somewhat distant and selfish husband. Like Koestler, he embraced a dizzying array of ideologies during his lifetime, among them orthodox Christianity, reasoned agnosticism, Marxism, atheism, democratic Socialism, Buddhism and, shortly before his death, Roman Catholicism.

It would be easy to dismiss such ideological promiscuity as the mental meanderings of a dislocated personality – a son desperate to outdo the achievements of a brilliant and judgemental father, a refugee ultimately at home everywhere and nowhere. Such factors undoubtedly played a part; plenty of honourable people are driven by neurotic needs to search for elusive truths. But the intellectual trajectory of Fritz Schumacher cannot be fully explained as merely the product of a maladjusted psyche. For he not only sought. He found.

He did so, furthermore, by applying the intellectual principles acquired in his youth to his later experience of the real world, and then (in true Popperian style) adjusting them accordingly. Like many Germans of his generation, Schumacher was driven by a quest for 'wholeness', for a way of life (for the individual as for the wider community) that would link physical, emotional and spiritual needs. But the transcendental romanticism of the young patriot who loved to hike in the great German forests was far removed from the global visionary of sixty years later. Particularly altered was Schumacher's interpretation of history. In a 1968 lecture (reprinted in *Small Is Beautiful*), he outlined the belief prevalent in the Germany of his youth that, over time, successful political or economic units would inexorably become fewer in number and larger in size. That which was truly beautiful was of necessity big. Wasn't this, after all, the lesson of the Bismarckian Reich (and, he might have added, the unspoken yearning of so many during the years leading up to Hitler)? Yet the reality on which Schumacher reflected in the post-war years belied so simple a formula. Big was good in certain ways and could lead to economies of scale. Yet what he observed was not a diminution but a proliferation of smaller units: nation states, businesses, social and cultural groupings. In practice, he concluded, we needed both bigness and smallness, collective control and individual freedom, unity and diversity. Schumacher mentioned the Coal Board, one of the biggest concerns in

Western Europe, citing the way his benign boss, Lord Robens, had striven to create, within a necessarily huge structure, a series of quasi-autonomous local units each with its own drive and sense of achievement. Few leaders had that kind of vision, he lamented. 'Today, we suffer from an almost universal idolatry of giantism. It is therefore necessary to insist on the virtues of smallness – where this applies.'

Schumacher's was far from the only voice to preach against bigness. The old belief in liberal state funding of health, welfare and the arts started to fade by the mid-1970s as the political culture shifted sharply towards the more abrasive belief in the economics of the marketplace. During a decade in which taxes, inflation and unemployment all rose, many began to question the wisdom of government continuing to raise and spend large amounts of public money. Why not reduce taxes, devolve power and equip people to decide for themselves what they wanted to do with their disposable income? Nor should culture be given special treatment. Nobody wished to abolish theatre, opera or concerts. But the arts had taken some pretty bizarre directions in recent years. Why not treat them as a commodity, *comme les autres*?*

During the 1970s, as these quasi-political arguments against bigness and centralisation gained ground, some of the nation's great temples of culture found their support faltering as tastes and priorities shifted. Why should so many BBC programmes come from the metropolis, critics began to ask? At Covent Garden, in the first year of Claus Moser's chairmanship, the Royal Opera mounted a landmark production of *Peter Grimes* praised not for the extravagance of its sets but for their economy. Meanwhile, as the National and Royal Shakespeare companies encountered problems with their new homes,† a host of tiny companies sprang up, followed by a plethora of new venues – pubs and clubs, community centres, arts 'labs',

---

* Such arguments were rehearsed by an emerging cohort of intellectuals of the 'New Right' whose self-confidence was doubtless boosted by the award of the 1974 Nobel Prize for Economics to the ageing and ailing Friedrich von Hayek.
† The National Theatre finally opened, after long delays, in 1976, the Barbican (home of the RSC) in 1982.

'workshops' and the like – to accommodate them. In London (according to the theatre historian Dominic Shellard) 'there were approximately half a dozen such venues in 1968 [while] by the late seventies there were over a hundred'. By the time Margaret Thatcher led the Conservatives back to power, in 1979, small, if not invariably beautiful, had become stylish.*

Many of the Hitler exiles were outstanding businessmen and industrialists, heads of hospitals, university departments and finance houses, men and women of talent and drive, much admired (and sometimes feared) by colleagues though rarely known to a wider public. In the cultural world, too, the province of this book, the promoter or manager was normally far less familiar to the general public than his product. There were notable exceptions: people went to Korda films because it was he who had produced them, while Robert Maxwell constantly featured in his own newspapers. Generally, however, it is the film star or diva the public crave to know about, not the agent who manages, the editor or writer who promotes him or her, or the person who runs the studio, opera house or record company for which he or she performs. Art lovers may know the work of Freud or Auerbach and their contemporaries; but few remember the early visibility provided for émigré artists by the galleries of Jack Bilbo (born Hugo Baruch), Hans Hess or Harry Fischer. The finest amateur chorus in Britain from the mid-1960s was the New Philharmonia and audiences flocked to hear its landmark performances under Klemperer and Giulini; but the NPC would have run into the ground after its founder Walter Legge disbanded it had not the Viennese-born Charles Spencer, one of its members, agreed to take it on and run it as a business. Hundreds of thousands of youngsters had their first experience of performances at the Royal Opera House courtesy of an annual cheap-seat scheme financed by Paul Hamlyn; probably no more than a tiny fraction knew that Lord Hamlyn (brother

---

* This remained true. Trevor Nunn, Director of the National Theatre, when challenged on the absence of new plays at the NT making big statements, complained: 'I have approached many writers on the subject of the big play, and it's extraordinary how many of them are saying, "I want to go small"' (*The Guardian*, 4 May 2000).

of the poet and translator Michael Hamburger) was born in Berlin and had made his wealth as one of Britain's most prolific publishing moguls. Britain's opera lovers rightly revere the memory of Solti; but they should leave a space in their affections for Lord Moser.

Claus Moser's boyhood ambition was to become a concert pianist. But he soon recognised that he only had the makings of a passingly good one, so professionally he pursued other interests. A man of great charm and intelligence, one of nature's networkers and a compulsive bridge-builder, Moser was able to use his base as an academic statistician as a launch pad for a series of prestigious appointments in the world of the arts and education. In 1961 he was recruited by his senior LSE colleague Lionel (by then Lord) Robbins to mastermind the all-important statistics for Robbins's Committee on Higher Education. It was Robbins who proposed that Moser join the Board of the Royal Opera House (of which he was already a member). In 1967 Harold Wilson invited Moser to become Director of the Government's Central Statistical Office, one of the more senior and sensitive jobs in the Civil Service. Moser felt obliged to tell the Prime Minister that he had once been turned down for an attachment to the Statistical Office on the grounds that he had been born in Germany. Wilson waved the problem aside with typical aplomb. 'You may be disqualified from being a member,' he said breezily, 'but you're not disqualified from being its Head!' As the nation's top statistician, Moser presided over the birth of the CSO's popular annual publication, *Social Trends* (whose first editor and founding mother was Muriel Nissel, wife of Siegmund).

Moser went on to join a score of committees, advising on the governance of the Royal Academy of Music, the Royal Shakespeare Company, the BBC's music output, Paul Hamlyn's Octopus Press, *The Economist*, an arts trust here, a philanthropic organisation there. In 1974, by now Sir Claus, he became Chairman of the Covent Garden Board, a body that included not only Robbins but Isaiah Berlin, Noel Annan, Arnold Goodman, John Pope-Hennessy, Denis Forman and latterly Alexander Goehr and Jeremy Isaacs, all under the forceful Secretaryship of Robert Armstrong. These were 'strong and colourful personalities', wrote Moser's Chief Executive, the patient and headmasterly John Tooley, 'cultured men and women who were rarely slow to express their opinions'. Moser himself is described by Tooley as having a 'strong emotional streak in his make-up [which] could occasionally get the better of him'. Moser loved being at the hub of the musical world and continued to chair the Covent Garden Board until 1987, presiding over a golden period (especially in opera where regular guest singers included Caballé, Sutherland, Pavarotti, Milnes, Vickers and Domingo). But his annual reports frequently bewailed the stringent funding the British – as opposed to the French, Germans or Italians – gave to the arts. If the nation wanted world-class opera, he argued, it must provide the where-withal to support it. In Britain, he complained, culture was still regarded as no more than the thin icing on the cake. He was criticised in the press and in Parliament for his lack of gratitude.

During Moser's last few years at Covent Garden, another former refugee, Sir John Burgh, was Director-General of Britain's principal organ of cultural diplomacy, the British Council. Burgh was born in Vienna in 1925 of Jewish parents. His father died of leukaemia when John (in those days Hans) was eleven, and shortly after the *Anschluss* he and his sister and mother fled to England. John, briefly a Christian convert, was educated by Quakers and, after war work in a series of factories, became a student at the LSE (where Moser was by then a junior lecturer). Inspired by the 'good society' ethos preached by the Attlee government and at the LSE by Laski, Burgh entered the civil service. Here his natural brilliance concealed his unusual background; to colleagues, Burgh passed as a true-born Englishman (even when leading a tour group of them to Austria in the early 1950s). An able and ambitious young man, he rose up the Whitehall hierarchy, going on to say 'Yes Minister' to half-a-dozen Secretaries of State before joining the British Council in 1980.

Margaret Thatcher, an implacable opponent of state-subsidised culture, had recently become Prime Minister. When Burgh, a civil servant, was appointed to head the British

Council, it was widely believed to presage the rubber stamping of swingeing budget cuts. But Burgh was different. At last, he felt, he could doff the mask of civil service anonymity and pronounce his commitment to a cause in which he profoundly believed. To John Burgh, the most influential figures in any society are not its politicians or generals but its artists. 'I measure a society in good part', he liked to say, 'by the weight it gives to the importance of culture.'

Was this the Viennese coming out in him, the lad whose parents had played string quartets? Throughout his early career, this consummate civil servant had tried hard to shed his background. Yet to those who knew him well, the child was always the father of the man. Periodically frustrated by the smooth objectivity required in Whitehall, Burgh had placed his civil service career in some jeopardy by taking time off in the early 1970s to work with Mark Bonham-Carter at the Community Relations Commission, a body concerned with race relations and immigration. 'I felt, in some way, that I ought to do something to help, that I had a debt I ought to repay,' he said, looking back. And Burgh always retained the love of music and theatre he had imbibed from his parents. He joined one of the civil service choirs, met Robert Armstrong and, through him, spent a decade serving on the Covent Garden opera and finance boards. For all his archetypal Englishness, Burgh was constantly nagged by the sense that culture was more widely valued and certainly better funded on the Continent than in Britain. Like Moser, he simply could not understand why the British Establishment was so mealy-mouthed towards the arts.

When Burgh came to the British Council, therefore, he was far from the Civil Service yes-man some had anticipated. From the start he fought (in close alliance with colleagues in the BBC's World Service) to retain a decent cultural budget from a sceptical government, arguing the merits of culture as a legitimate and highly cost-effective arm of diplomacy. He relished the struggle, got the government to moderate its planned depredations, and was immensely proud to represent Britain and British cultural accomplishments around the world. He was even able to give Council policy a discreet tweak every now and then in the direction of music and the theatre. When the English National Opera returned seriously out of pocket from an American tour, Burgh had no hesitation in diverting that year's surplus to help pay off the debt, rather than do the proper thing and let the money revert to the Treasury. All this represented a breathtaking apotheosis for a man with his bureaucratic background. It was crowned by his appointment, on his retirement from the British Council, as President of Trinity College, Oxford.

Claus Moser, too, became head of an Oxford college. Like John Burgh, Moser was a man of wide-ranging interests (including banking, where he followed in his father's footsteps and became for a while a director of Rothschild's). But his natural habitat probably lay at the intersection between beauty and brains, the arts and academe, and during his last years as ROH Chairman he re-entered the world of higher education, becoming Warden of Wadham. Here Moser launched into yet another career, this time as scourge of the educational Establishment. Thirty years after C. P. Snow at Cambridge had bemoaned the estrangement between the 'two cultures', the arts and sciences, Claus Moser, as President of the British Association for the Advancement of Science, took the argument further, pleading for new links to be forged between the arts, sciences and social sciences. Britain, he also declared in a widely reported speech, was one of the least adequately educated of all the advanced nations. Every child, he said, should be offered some understanding of the methodology of the sciences and the social sciences, something that girls, in particular, were too often denied. Scientists and social scientists should be trained to communicate their work to the general public more effectively, just as those specialising in the arts and humanities should be given greater access to the sciences. All this, of course, would cost money. But, Moser argued (as he had at Covent Garden), such an investment would be more than justified by the results. Moser was a man accustomed to being listened to. Not long after these speeches, Tony Blair announced that his new government would have three principal objectives: 'Education, education and education!'

Moser had to leave Wadham at seventy, but was not the

retiring kind. Committees, good works and the occasional piano concert for charity or friends all continued to occupy his time. There was the Oxford Playhouse committee to attend, a report on the nation's literacy and numeracy to complete. Above all, Moser was Chairman of the British Museum Development Trust, which required him to oversee the raising of some £100 million towards the Museum's redevelopment, its most ambitious since it opened a century-and-a-half earlier. Even serious heart bypass surgery at the age of seventy-six scarcely staunched the workload. When I visited Moser during his convalescence he gave me a thorough rundown of the way the heart works, the symptoms and causes of malfunction and the various prophylactic steps he advised me to take to keep mine ticking successfully. A month later he was back at his British Museum office in the morning, then off to have lunch with Michael Kaiser, at the time the top man at Covent Garden, thence to Oxford where he had a theatre engagement that evening followed by a dinner . . .

Over the course of a fifty-year career (culminating in a peerage in 2001) Claus Moser became a one-man bridge spanning several normally separate islands of excellence – statistics, government service, banking, education, museums and the performing arts. In the range and particular directions of his activities he was unique. But in his desire to help engender in Britain something of the properly funded cultural excellence he had seen around him as a boy, Moser, like Burgh, was typical of the Hitler exile community. 'I think we provided the arts with two interrelated things over and above our numbers,' Moser said, looking back. 'The first was audiences, and the second was money.' There were not many émigré performers at Covent Garden during his time there, he recalled; a few instrumentalists and conductors, and maybe a handful of singers. 'But it was we who were the backbone of the audiences.'

The émigrés, by bringing with them the Mid-European tradition of going regularly to plays, operas, concerts and museums, helped enable the arts to thrive in the precarious decade or two after the war. If the Amadeus Quartet had played to half-empty houses, who knows whether they would have survived? Covent Garden in Moser's day was regularly patronised (and to some extent subsidised) by people who had acquired the habit in pre-Nazi Berlin or Vienna. It was in the final year of Moser's Chairmanship that his friend Paul Hamlyn, having made a fortune marketing popular books and records, initiated his series of subsidised annual Covent Garden performances for first-time visitors to the opera and ballet.

Moser and Burgh, like Korda and Weidenfeld, were among the great facilitators, men whose special talent consisted in enabling the words or images or music of others to reach a wider audience. This was the special genius of Stefan Lorant, creator of *Picture Post*, of opera impresarios Rudolf Bing and Peter Diamand (both of whom also directed the Edinburgh Festival) and of Victor Hochhauser who brought the Bolshoi asnd Kirov companies to London, and of the media executives Paul Fox and Stephen Hearst. Some of the entrepreneurs were performers manqué: Bing trained as a singer, Moser as a pianist, while Korda consistently exaggerated his skills as a film director. Conversely, history tells of many unhappy opera or dance companies, orchestras, theatrical troupes, museums or galleries that withered in the hands of talented artists who misguidedly assumed the role of manager. The two kinds of skill are not, of course, mutually exclusive.* But they tend to attract different types of personality and talent, and each is heavily dependent upon the other. Where would Korda have been without his film stars, Weidenfeld without his writers, Moser without his singers and dancers? Yet the symbiotic need is, if anything, even greater on the other side of the divide. For, without the great enablers, the great performers would have no one to perform to.

When the émigrés arrived in Britain, 'the arts' had meant a number of more or less agreed forms of creation or re-creation with, at their core, a canon of great works. Gombrich may have professed that there was no such thing as 'Art' but, in practice,

---

* Bing's predecessor as General Manager of the New York Metropolitan Opera *was* a singer, the Canadian tenor Edward Johnson. In our own time, Plácido Domingo became Artistic Director of the Washington and Los Angeles opera companies towards the end of his singing career (preparatory, some surmised, to taking over the same role at the New York Met).

he and his readers knew exactly what a book called *The Story of Art* would deal with and what it would not. When Rudolf Bing launched the Edinburgh Festival or the Amadeus Quartet their performing career, they did so secure in the knowledge that there was a broad consensus of expectation among those they hoped to attract. There was dissent about details, of course. Pevsner might praise a building others detested, Schwitters deride Picasso or Keller over-praise Gershwin. All, however, shared a vision of what was meant by art, or the arts, and of what the true artist was aspiring to do.

By the last years of the twentieth century much of this consensus had eroded. No single taste or style dominated; words like 'culture', 'art' or 'music' were blown this way and that, routinely rebranded by the shifting exigencies of media, marketing and political correctness. Was an unmade bed strewn with bodily fluids a work of 'art'? Yes, if its creator (Tracey Emin) and the authorities at the Tate Gallery who shortlisted it for the 1999 Turner Prize said it was. Were the violinist Vanessa-Mae or the singer Andrea Bocelli 'legendary performers'? Of course, if only because their promoters had made them so. Did a newspaper report on the Notting Hill Carnival or the tangled private life of a TV soap starlet belong in the 'culture' section? Yes, if the editor so deemed. 'Don't you like music?' asked a fellow drinker when a pub patron asked if the volume of the computerised rock beat could please be reduced.

This was no longer the Britain in which the Hitler émigrés had flourished. To many of those who survived, the optimism and expansionism of the post-war decades seemed to have given way to a value-free, democratised 'Post-Modern' culture in which what they had regarded as 'excellence' was now derided as 'elitism'. As opera companies hid inside 'leisure centres' and museums replaced valued objects with hi-tech interactivity, people talked darkly of the culture being 'dumbed down'. In an age of best-sellers, viewing figures and record charts, it often seemed that quantitative criteria had superseded qualitative ones. It was an attitude that came to haunt many of the surviving émigrés as the twentieth century gave way to the twenty-first.

In some ways, the cultural influence of the Hitler refugees might be said to have paralleled that of some of the nation's cultural institutions. Thus, a great arc of 'rise and fall' can be seen as having defined not only the impact of the émigrés but also the historical trajectory of the Arts Council, the British Council, the Royal Opera and Ballet, the Philharmonia and London Philharmonic Orchestras and the BBC's Third Programme, World Service and BBC2 – indeed, the very idea of the Welfare State itself. All were arguably at their zenith in the 1960s and into the 1970s, as were Britain's record industry, independent publishing houses and university culture. Ten or fifteen years later much of this was changing. All publicly funded institutions were under pressure, including those concerned with art and culture, most independent publishers were being routinely swallowed up by large business conglomerates and every college of advanced technology could call itself a university.

The 'rise and fall' argument is attractive but a tad too simple. Thames and Hudson remained a family firm. Hayek rejoiced in Thatcher's adoption of his economic theories. More public money was going to opera in real terms at the end of Thatcher's premiership than at the end of Attlee's.

Yet it is also true that the Britain at the end of the twentieth century was very different from that in which most of the refugees had arrived sixty-odd years before. Cultural priorities had undergone profound change in that time and many of the survivors felt distinctly out of sympathy with the spirit of the age in which they spent their declining years. As they looked back, some tried to assess the 'rise and fall' of their own lives and work. Was their work in vain? Was their legacy being swept away by the onrush of history? What was the nature, the quality and the impact of their cultural achievements and how would they be remembered?

PART SIX

CULTURE CONCLUDED

CHAPTER TWENTY

History Resurgent

The Second World War lasted longer than the First, killed not only soldiers but civilians, led the world to confront an unprecedented abyss of evil, took on the aspect of an epic moral crusade and returned to haunt the collective consciousness a full half-century after its conclusion. Its sheer magnitude caused the memory of the First to be somewhat superseded. Yet the Second War appears to have had less direct impact upon British cultural history than the First. A decade after the First World War, Virginia Woolf and D. H. Lawrence were portraying the lingering pain and dark scars left by the wounds of war, while Eliot pronounced sourly on how the world would end. A decade after the Second, Larkin, Wain and Amis were writing of the petty comforts and frustrations of small-town provincialism, while Osborne's Jimmy Porter railed against nothing more potent than the absence of any causes worth fighting for. When Britten, a committed pacifist, created his searing *War Requiem* it was to the poetry of the First World War that he turned for inspiration, not that arising from the Second.

Perhaps the sheer scale and horror of the conflict recently concluded had been intimidating; Theodor Adorno was frequently (slightly mis-) quoted as saying that, after Auschwitz, there could be no poetry.

However, while the Second World War might not have provided the artistic subject matter as frequently as the First, its long-term effects were arguably greater. First, as we have seen, much of the cultural infrastructure of modern Britain – the Arts Council and the Royal Ballet and Opera – these and much else arose in response to initiatives inspired in wartime. But the greatest effect of the war on Britain's artistic and cultural life lay in the talent that Hitlerism had caused to be transplanted across the Channel from Central Europe.

Most of the men and women featured in this book were victims of the war. Some, as it turned out, might also be regarded as beneficiaries insofar as their transplantation presented them with unanticipated opportunities. Virtually all were precisely the kind of people who would have got into severe trouble with the Nazis had they stayed: expressive, questing personalities, independent-minded, inclined to dissent, interested in alternative arguments – the kind of people who have always found it difficult to flourish in an authoritarian or strictly hierarchical environment. It is hard to imagine Kokoschka as a compliant court painter for long,* Koestler a party hack or Weidenfeld a career diplomat, or to envisage Solti or Popper settling down under the Third Reich to an indefinite period of 'internal exile'. These were not among nature's cosy conformists.

Did the émigrés have anything in common that enabled them to escape and survive the Hitlerian holocaust while so many more perished? Luck in most cases: a scholarship or a job in England that materialised at just the right time, a cousin in Cambridge or an uncle in Birmingham offering hospitality and protection. Hayek, Goehr and Gombrich, for example, came to London for work and stayed as refugees. Money helped. If you were from an educated, well-connected, upper-middle-class family, like the Mosers of Berlin, the head of the household would doubtless think strategically, nurse the right contacts, know how to apply for the correct documents and be able to pay whatever was required to get out while it was still possible to do so. Many also displayed considerable intellectual and emotional resourcefulness. It is impossible to overestimate the sheer grit and determination of a youngster, often bereft of parents and

---

* Never a man to toe the bourgeois line, Kokoschka continued into old age to kick against convention. At ninety, he was thundering against the fashionable egalitarianism of the day. Others, he said in a recorded interview (in the BBC Archives), want everything to be equal. But I – the old man almost shrieked – 'I *can't* be equal!'

speaking a foreign language, growing up in a strange land and going on to become a prominent publisher, professor, philosopher or film maker. George Weidenfeld, said his partner Nigel Nicolson, 'had greater resilience than me, an acuter mind, more daring. His character had been forged in a hotter furnace.' In some cases the inner resourcefulness was tested almost to the limits. The story of Hans Keller's escape from the Nazis in 1939, not to mention Anita Lasker's harrowing account of her survival in the death camps, suggests personalities of exceptional resilience.

Of the roughly 55,000 Hitler émigrés who made their permanent home in Britain, a handful were to make a powerful impact upon the country that had given them refuge – in business and industry, and in the arts, sciences and liberal professions. It is on this latter group, a small fraction of a small fraction, that this book has concentrated. What determined that these men and women in particular would go on to become prominent architects, musicians, publishers, film makers and scientists?

The energy and adaptability of many shine out. They were able to benefit, too, from institutions that helped welcome them to Britain, the Jewish Refugee Committee, the Academic Assistance Council and the rest, which helped find them homes, sorted out legal and linguistic tangles and pointed them towards prospects of work. Many refugees were later to speak with gratitude of the way they were helped by various Christian bodies, as well as nonconformist groups such as the Quakers and Plymouth Brethren, while a warm hand of friendship was extended to exiled intellectuals by the International PEN club and self-help groups like the Artists' International Association and Artists' Refugee Committee and the FDKB.

Certain skills were more portable than others. The tradition of the Jewish violinist goes back centuries and has been immortalised by Chagall (and the musical *Fiddler on the Roof*). Many of the world's most noteworthy string players and teachers since the mid-nineteenth century have been of Jewish extraction: the list stretches, like the progeny of Banquo, from Joachim, Auer, Elman, Heifetz, Kreisler, Zimbalist, Piatigorsky,

Feuermann and Huberman to Flesch, Rostal, Milstein, Menuhin, the Oistrakhs, Perlman, Zukerman, Mintz, Kremer and Vengerov and doubtless beyond. There are probably many reasons for this extraordinary lineage. But one factor, in a people proverbially on the move (and discouraged by the Decalogue from the graphic and plastic arts), was that an instrument provided a passport. When Emeric Pressburger fetched up in Berlin, it was his violin that provided him with a temporary income. When Albi Rosenthal was taken off for internment, he took his most valued possession – his violin. Anita Lasker's salvation from death at Auschwitz was provided by her cello.

The germ of the Amadeus Quartet was sown when Hans Schidlof, interned at Prees Heath (before being removed to Bury in Lancashire and eventually the Isle of Man), heard a fellow prisoner playing Mozart. Schidlof introduced himself with the words: 'I, too, play the violin!'

'You do?' replied the affable Norbert Brainin, handing him his instrument. 'Go on, then – play!'

More portable than the piano or harp, not dependent on language, capable in the right hands of a wealth of appealing expressiveness, the violin has long been the signature instrument of the peripatetic musician, the Romany gypsy fiddler, Viennese *Schrammel* merchant or fairground entertainer. Music, in general, is a skill that easily crosses boundaries of geography, politics and language. Thus, many of the Hitler exiles who had musical skills found ways of restarting their lives in Britain, some of them going on to careers of great distinction. We have noted the early contribution of Walter Goehr, Walter Bergmann and Karl Haas to the revival of interest in Early Music, and the influential presence of refugee musicians at Morley College, the BBC, and in Boosey and Hawkes and other music publishers during and after the war. There was scarcely a musical ensemble in the country that did not include, and was not sometimes conducted by, an exile from Middle Europe. Musical scholarship benefited, too. Otto Erich Deutsch completed his authoritative catalogue of the works of Schubert while in exile in Cambridge. Cambridge also housed the priceless collection of musical manuscripts belonging to Paul Hirsch, among them first editions of Bach and Handel (including the full score of *Messiah*), Corelli and Beethoven, shipped over from Germany in the 1930s (and now kept in the British Library). In Oxford, Egon Wellesz pursued his studies of Byzantine and early Christian church music, while his friend and protégé Albi Rosenthal, his interests shifting from art to music, became one of the world's leading collectors of musical manuscripts. It was Rosenthal who acquired the Stravinsky archive for the Paul Sacher foundation (though he liked to say that his greatest love was playing first violin in the Oxford orchestra for over thirty years).

Britain's musical life was possibly the greatest single beneficiary of the Hitler exiles who settled there. But other skills and specialities, too, discovered fertile soil. Many of the scientists who found work in Britain went on, as we have seen, to have distinguished careers. This is partly a reflection on the high quality of science in pre-Nazi Central Europe, and also on the tireless work by Tess Simpson and others in helping so many to transplant to Britain. But it is also due to the fact that the sciences, like music, speak an international language. There was no essential difference between the problems investigated by Einstein and Born in Berlin and those preoccupying their new colleagues in Princeton and Edinburgh. Krebs and Peierls may have noted an unfamiliar informality about British academic life, or felt that grading exam papers, while a greater chore, was also a fairer way of allocating undergraduate degrees than by oral exam. But the essential interests and values in which they had been raised were completely shared by the new scientific communities into which they and others like them were welcomed. As a result, comments the biochemist Hermann Blaschko (in an interview in the Archives of the Imperial War Museum), Britain played a supremely important role as a 'shelter' for German science at a time when it was being systematically eliminated in its home territory. Britain (and America) was where it was 'salvaged'. The pharmacologist Gustav Born was one of many who emphasised to me that Hitler's brutal suppression of the sciences and the consequent emigration of so many outstanding scientists (including his father Max Born) had the unintended effect of bringing the best of German science to the whole world. The impetus of having to start again, in a foreign country and a foreign language, acted as a stimulus. Indeed, many émigrés did more important work in exile than they might have done had their lives not been disrupted by Nazism. But much credit, Gustav Born insisted, must go to the British scientists who accepted and assimilated the newcomers with such generosity of spirit.

This was not, perhaps, quite so true in newer, more controversial fields such as psychoanalysis, where the small existing profession evidently viewed with some qualms the arrival of the 'Viennese'. Yet most émigré psychoanalysts were welcomed by the British Psycho-Analytic Society and Freud's protégé Ernest Jones. Sigmund Freud himself came in old age to London and lived out the end of his days in exile. The house in Maresfield Gardens which provided the old man with his final home was occupied by his daughter Anna Freud and is now a museum, complete with home movies and an exact re-creation of Freud's consulting room. Up the road is the Anna Freud Centre while, a couple of hundred yards away, is the Tavistock Clinic, which in part perpetuates their work.

If psychoanalysis came to flourish in exile in London, it was not only because figures like Freud and Ernest Jones (and, since the 1920s, Melanie Klein) lived there and provided a magnet. The subject matter itself was especially well-adapted to exile. The psychoanalytic approach probes the mental residues of childhood that continue, subconsciously, to influence the adult. It is premised on a theory of loss, a form of therapy designed to help people survive in a new world where they are bereft of their primary emotional influences – exiled forever, as it were, from the half-remembered Eden of infancy. As such, psychoanalysis is in some ways almost a paradigm of the refugee experience, of the emotional odyssey of the émigré, and was clasped and disseminated by members of the émigré community in Britain, America and elsewhere. Thus the ideas of Freud and his followers, far from being eliminated by the painful experience of emigration, might be said to have flourished in exile.

How influential the ideas of Freud and his British-based

followers were after the war on the wider cultural life of Britain is harder to pin down. Laurence Olivier went to see Ernest Jones to learn how the idea of the 'Oedipus Complex' threw light on the relationship between Hamlet and Gertrude, while play-wrights such as Beckett and Pinter recurrently fastened on to the subconscious motivations of their characters. Adrian Stokes, Richard Wollheim and others applied psychoanalytic concepts to aesthetics and the visual arts, expanding their subject by examining the response of the viewer. In time, the language of psychiatry entered the popular vocabulary as people began to talk of someone having a 'guilt complex' or an active 'libido', while the writings of Anthony Storr (especially on the relation-ship between psychology and music) and the broadcasts of Anthony Clare (*In the Psychiatrist's Chair*) reached a wide audience. A new generation of feminists, if sometimes taking fierce issue with what they saw as Freud's 'sexism', picked up many of his concepts and ran with them. Biographers and historians, too, made fruitful use of psychiatric concepts (a whole genre of 'psychohistory' became fashionable for a while); the émigré musicologist Mosco Carner wrote an influential book about Puccini, applying psychoanalytic insights to the composer's work and showing how some of Puccini's creations arose from his own unconscious needs. Literary critics diverted attention from the text to the subconscious agenda of the author. Some cultural historians, indeed, came to regard psychiatric insights as lying at the very heart of Modernism.

However, much of this infusion of post-Freudianism into the British intellectual bloodstream probably entered via New York rather than Swiss Cottage. Psychiatry and psychotherapy, after all, with their encouragement of the expressive, free-associative articulation of intimate thoughts and feelings, had initially found a less ready reception among the tightly buttoned British middle classes than with their counterparts across the Atlantic. While Anna Freud's continuing work on child development, for example, or the therapeutic and scholarly work of the Tavistock Clinic and Institute, may have been admired by those who knew of them, it was in the United States that psychoanalytic concepts took deepest root (and Anna Freud became something of a celebrity). Freud's original vision may have been diluted (some would argue distorted and betrayed) by a variety of new psycho-therapeutic techniques and fads. But it was in America, after all, not Britain, that Erik Erikson pioneered psychohistory with books on Luther and Gandhi, Erich Fromm wrote *The Art of Loving* and *The Fear of Freedom*, Wilhelm Reich apostrophised the mysteries of the orgasm and Herbert Marcuse sought links between Freud and Marx in *Eros and Civilization* and *One Dimensional Man*. If young sophisticates in late-twentieth-century Britain used and abused Freudian phraseology, they may have derived their inspiration indirectly from writings such as these – or, more probably, from the film scripts of Woody Allen.

The emotional adaptability required of the exile was paralleled among many by remarkable cultural dexterity. A number – impelled, perhaps, by a desire to link their old world to their new – became teachers: people possessed of a mission, carriers of a scared flame they wished to pass on. Kurt Hahn's vision of the integration of intellectual, physical and moral education led not only to the foundation of Gordonstoun (at which both Prince Philip and Prince Charles were educated), Atlantic College at St Donat's Castle and a host of schools worldwide, but also to the Outward Bound and Duke of Edinburgh Award schemes. Hahn was probably the most influential of the pedagogic exiles. But any comprehensive survey of the life and work of the Hitler émigrés would note the work of countless teachers up and down the land – of mathematics, the natural sciences, history, languages, dance and (especially perhaps) music. Several rose to become heads of schools and colleges.* Laban's pupil Marion North became Principal of the Laban Centre, a thriving dance conservatoire in south London, whose alumni included Matthew Bourne, the dancer and choreographer who created Adventures in Motion Pictures and its most famous production, the (almost) all-male *Swan Lake*. Hans and Katie Freyhan settled in Bedford where

---

* Heads of Oxbridge colleges included not only Sir Claus (later Lord) Moser and Sir John Burgh, but also, in Oxford, Sir Walter Bodmer (Hertford) and in Cambridge, the biochemist Sir Hans Kornberg (Christ's) and the mathematician Sir Hermann Bondi (Churchill).

they found work as music teachers in local schools; their son Peter grew up to become a cellist in the BBC Symphony Orchestra. Helene Isepp, once a singer, gave lessons to pupils who included not only Janet Baker and Heather Harper but also Hilde Beal, later Covent Garden's German-language coach – and a singer who went on to become one of Britain's leading singing teachers in her own right, Esther Salaman. The composer Hans Gál taught music at Edinburgh University while his erstwhile colleague Hans Redlich, biographer of Alban Berg, became Professor of Music at the University of Manchester.

The members of the Amadeus Quartet always enjoyed training young quartets. The Chilingirian was one that benefited from their help. After the death of Peter Schidlof in 1987 and the sudden, enforced end of a forty-year career at the top, his surviving colleagues flowered as teachers. Did they try to infuse their young charges with their own much-vaunted 'Viennese style'? Nissel laughed at the suggestion. 'Most Viennese are as unmusical as most people anywhere else!' Apart from which, the last thing a good teacher wants to do is create a clone of himself.* To Brainin, too, the point was to help young musicians to bring whatever are their own particular gifts to their music-making. A jovial seventy-eight, he spoke with infectious warmth about the latest talent to come his way – the ConTempo Quartet, for example, a Romanian ensemble he and his colleagues helped coach. Nissel agreed about the quality of the ConTempo, adding the Belcea and also the Armonico Quartet from Japan. 'We're teaching our grandchildren, as it were,' Nissel beamed, fourteen years into an almost full-time teaching career that continued to take him all over the world. 'I simply

---

* In October 2001, I visited Vienna with Nissel. We spent an evening at one of the *Heurigen* in the rural edges of town, sampling simple food and new, local wines, to the accompaniment of *Schrammel* musicians who struck up the tunes of old Vienna on a combination of fiddle, accordion and guitar. Nissel found it impossible not to sing along. The music was romantic, slushy, kitschy even, he admitted, and produced by its trio of old pros with more sugar than a pantryful of *Sachertorte*. Yet Nissel also felt that, in its very irregularities, this music contained something of a traditional Viennese 'lilt' (rather like the slightly premature second beat of the Viennese waltz). Here, perhaps, in practices going back as far as the time of Schubert if not earlier, lay the seeds of what – in the infinitely refined hands of Nissel and his colleagues – developed into the supposedly 'Viennese' style of the Amadeus Quartet.

love teaching!' – and his young charges spoke with equal warmth about their master.

Some skills and specialisms did not take so easily to the foreign soil in which they found themselves. People who were professionally dependent upon their native language – actors and writers, for example – tended to feel disadvantaged, especially if they left their homeland at a more advanced age when the mastery of a new language seemed an insuperable burden. Those who did make a successful career in these professions were either very young when they arrived and well able to master English (e.g. Andrew Sachs), or else (like the actors Anton Walbrook and Conrad Veidt or the writers George Mikes and Arthur Koestler) tended to use their foreignness as part of the package they were able to sell. Many refugees were trained in medicine and law. But these were not easily portable professions and required retraining – a fact that only serves to highlight the achievement of David Daube, Otto Kahn-Freund and Hersch Lauterpacht, each of whom left outstanding contributions to the study and/or practice of international jurisprudence.

In general, the greatest impact of the exiles was probably in the newer, more cross-disciplinary fields (art history, psychology, sociology, criminology, nuclear physics, biochemistry) and the most rapidly changing professions (film, photography, architecture, broadcasting) rather than in those long established. A new field or institution is likely to be in a greater state of flux than one of long standing, more receptive to ideas from outside, more open-minded, less of a closed shop. It was probably easier for Korda or Pressburger to work in film (and Esslin in broadcasting) than in the theatre, for Wolf Suschitzky to get his photographs published in Stefan Lorant's *Picture Post* than in *Illustrated London News*.

Perhaps the most conspicuous example of a traditional intellectual discipline in which the émigrés *did* make an important impact was history. When they arrived, the study of history, in Britain as elsewhere, tended to concentrate on the nation state and its (mostly male) leaders. It was not due to the émigrés alone that these priorities shifted over the following half-century. Some, indeed, continued to gravitate towards national history as perceived from the top down, while the pioneers of the 'new' English history, such as E. P. Thompson, Christopher Hill and Raphael Samuel, learned their craft largely in Britain with perhaps the French *Annales* school as their most important foreign frame of reference. But the presence of the Central Europeans brought a range of vital new perspectives to British historiography and contributed to a resurgence of interest in the subject. Some were experts on ancient Greece and Rome or oriental history, others on medieval Europe, many on the history of the German-speaking world. Most had several languages at their disposal and a preparedness to cross boundaries of time, place and discipline. Ullmann swept with bold originality across centuries of medieval ecclesiastical history. Francis Carsten and Peter Pulzer wrote about both British and German political movements while John Grenville assayed world history. 'A non-British background', said Grenville, doubtless speaking for many of his fellows, 'made me look at national history from the point of view of an insider as well as from that of an outsider with an acute sense that the individuality of any country is only revealed by comparison.'

On the face of it no two historians could have been more different than Eric Hobsbawm and Geoffrey Elton. Where Hobsbawm bestrode the world, Elton researched ever more deeply into the administrative interstices of Tudor England. Hobsbawm's Marxism, furthermore, was in the sharpest contrast to the dogged English conservatism in which Elton came to garb himself, a difference in outlook that subtly informed every page penned by these two outstanding scholars. Yet both also brought something of their Central European background to their work – a cultural legacy that, in each case, went on to influence countless pupils and followers.

Hobsbawm, by his early forties, was widely known as an inspiring teacher (at Birkbeck College, London), one of the founding fathers of the journal *Past and Present*, a noted essayist and pamphleteer, and a fanatical jazz enthusiast. But it was only now that he began to produce important books with the powerfully emblematic titles that were to become one of his trademarks: *Primitive Rebels* (1959), *The Age of Revolution* (1962), *Labouring Men* (1964). Like an athlete who finds his stride, he scarcely faltered for the next forty years, pouring out a profusion of books and essays as though compensating for a slow start. Whether writing about the Industrial or French Revolution, bandits or the bourgeoisie, Count Basie or Count Bismarck, Wellington or Ellington, Vienna, Venice or Venezuela, Hobsbawm's erudition was dazzling and his breadth of allusion encyclopaedic. His magnum opus was a four-volume history of the world over the past two centuries. Throughout, class and class-consciousness (and conflict) are a powerful and recurrent presence, while the traditional 'Great Men' of history are held firmly in place by an author not much enamoured of biography or the insights of psychology. There was a predilection in much of Hobsbawm's writing for patrician phrasemaking that could sometimes tend to obscure rather than reveal the texture of life as experienced by those he describes. But his sense of the sweep and structure of the drama as a whole was unrivalled.

The final volume of Hobsbawm's tetralogy, *The Age of Extremes*, essentially a chronicle of the tumultuous world of his own lifetime, begins in what Hobsbawm called the 'twilight zone' of his own childhood. Is the historian better equipped than others to understand a period of which one has personal memories? Hobsbawm recognised the value of individual experience as data, but was also fully aware of the distorting mirror this can provide. 'In the 1930s,' he said, 'we on the Left were campaigning against Fascism and I remember being convinced we were mobilising the people against war. But, with the benefit of historical perspective, I can see we were a total failure, merely rallying people already sympathetic to our cause.'

Personal experience can impede historical vision in another way too: it's not only a question of what you have lived through – but also where. 'Imagine, for example, that you were an Argentine or Brazilian trying to write the history of modern times. You'd live in a continent that had experienced no serious war in the twentieth century, in which both world wars impinged largely as distant news items – but where global economic fluctuations had immediate and dramatic consequences. That's the kind of perspective from which a Latin American historian has to try and emancipate himself.'

New topics required fresh approaches. Originally primarily an economic historian, Hobsbawm came increasingly to incorporate cultural and artistic issues into his purview. Thus, in a lecture in memory of Walter Neurath, founder of the art books publisher Thames and Hudson, Hobsbawm considered the struggle of the visual arts in the twentieth century to create a credible avant-garde, a struggle that had been spectacularly lost, he argued (somewhat provocatively, considering the audience and the occasion), by the art of painting.

Even more remarkable was a lecture to mark the Columbus Quincentenary in 1992. On this occasion Hobsbawm was probably expected to consider the effect of the Old World on the New. But he reversed things and addressed the impact of America on the rest of the world arguing, startlingly, that 'the major contribution of the Americas . . . has been to distribute across the globe a cornucopia of wild and cultivated . . . plants, without which the modern world as we know it would not be conceivable'. The potato, chocolate, tobacco, cocaine – these and other plants, unknown to Europeans before Columbus, changed the wider world far more profoundly than all the gold or silver mined by the Conquistadors. This, argued Hobsbawm, with truly global sweep, was the real significance of 1492.

Did Hobsbawm's Marxism skew his history? No more so, probably, than the work of anyone guided by an overall vision – and you surely can't write about several hundred years of world history without one. In any case, he suggested that Marx remained 'the essential base of any adequate study of history because – so far – he alone has attempted to formulate a methodological approach to history as a whole'.

Intellectually, Hobsbawm belonged everywhere and nowhere. Geoffrey Elton, by contrast, homed in on his new *Heimat* as his principal subject of study. But he, too, did so from a perspective no native-born historian could fully share. Elton, son of a distinguished German classicist (who spent his last years as a lecturer at Bedford College), was most famous for his work on the Tudors but also wrote books on Europe at the time of the Reformation. To Elton, Tudor England was best understood as the fountainhead of the emerging liberal bureaucracy from which Britain had benefited ever since. With his continental background and influenced perhaps by the theories of Max Weber, he wrote and lectured with unconcealed enthusiasm about what he saw as the administrative institutions of Tudor government (and its great innovator Thomas Cromwell). Not for Elton the 'new' history with its insights from inductive sociology and psychology. The revolution of which he wrote was a conceptual one: the creation of an essentially benign bureaucracy. For twenty years Elton was the dominant figure in the whole field of Tudor studies. Not only did he master the minutiae of Tudor history – an astonishing feat for a refugee from Hitler's *Mitteleuropa* – but, by sheer industry and force of character, he all but obliterated those who tried to gainsay him. Admired and feared in equal measure, Elton would enthral an undergraduate audience (including myself) in the morning, enjoy a genial pub lunch* – then hasten back to Clare College to mow down the latest wrong-headed hack with a rebarbative review. In later years a certain intellectual stubbornness stole over him, a degree of intolerant conservatism, which inevitably produced its nemesis as Elton, proud recipient of a knighthood, found himself under fire from a younger generation of historians for what looked like increasingly outdated attitudes.

Elton's conservatism did not take overt political form. Indeed, politics as a profession (like the law, medicine, diplomacy and the army) recruited relatively few of the Central European émigrés.† But an underlying political agenda informed much that they undertook. The psychologist Marie Jahoda, who worked in both the USA and Britain, studied the kinds of

---

* Elton used to include 'beer' as one of his hobbies in *Who's Who*.

† Jaques Mendelsohn and Silvia Schulmann were brought up in Berlin by Communist parents. John Mendelson became a Labour MP, while Silvia married the Labour MP William (Lord) Rodgers, later one of the founders of the Social Democratic Party. Robert Maxwell, who made his name as a flamboyant and forceful publisher, founding Pergamon Press and latterly owning the Mirror Group, was a Labour MP from 1964 to 1970. Clement Freud, son of Ernst and brother of Lucian, was a Liberal MP from 1973 to 1987.

personality attracted to authoritarianism, anti-Semitism and racism. Hobsbawm surveyed history from a perspective permanently marked by the idealistic Marxism of his youth. Hayek inveighed against the dangers of state control, Koestler against Communism, Haffner and Deutscher against illiberal nationalism, Schumacher against the squandering of resources, Rotblat against nuclear weapons, Popper against the dangers of all types of transcendental theorising.

Did people listen and learn? Was the teaching, writing, inveighing and campaigning effective? How far were the messages proclaimed by the émigrés absorbed and accepted by those to whom they were directed? The evidence is rich but fragmentary. Rudolf Peierls's calculations, with their disturbing suggestion that the Germans might be capable of developing an atomic bomb, helped propel the British into their own wartime atomic programme, while Rotblat's campaigns helped lead eventually to a degree of nuclear disarmament. The 'Pelican History of Art' series, edited by Nikolaus Pevsner, was designed by Hans Schmoller (Allen Lane's chief typographer and later production head) whose sense of style had immense influence on the Penguin empire and its many imitations.* Britain's foremost 'Contemporary' designers, Robin and Lucienne Day, early protégés of Peter Moro,† went on to become responsible for e.g. the John Lewis 'house style'. The novelist Salman Rushdie regarded Canetti's *Auto-da-Fé* as one of the finest books he had ever read, while Peter Medawar, the Nobel Prize-winning biologist, acknowledged a profound intellectual debt to Popper. The writer Colin Dexter admitted that some of the personal qualities with which he invested his TV detective Inspector Morse were derived from his classics-and-opera-loving school-teacher Gerard Hoffnung, while the conductor Simon Rattle recalls buying Hoffnung's book of cartoons, *The Maestro*, at the

---

* Schmoller took over at Penguin from another refugee, Jan Tschichold. The covers of the 'Pelican History of Art' series had calligraphy by Elisabeth Friedlander and a Pelican motif drawn by Bernard Wolpe: altogether, as one commentator rightly notes, a 'very English, but also a very German series of books!'
† Robin Day was responsible, under Moro's guidance, for the plywood and steel seating at the Royal Festival Hall.

age of ten. London's Design Museum, the creation of Terence Conran, a proud inheritor of the Bauhaus tradition, is itself designed in the style of European modernism.* Works by Schubert are still known by their 'Deutsch' numbers and Monteverdi, revived by Walter Goehr, is now considered mainstream repertoire, while every art lover is familiar with German Expressionism, and the work of Schwitters and Kokoschka. The movies of Powell and Pressburger made a huge impact. Countless young girls developed the ambition to become ballet dancers having seen *The Red Shoes*, while the author and actor Stephen Fry, asked by a newspaper what movie he'd watch for a 'great night in', singled out *A Matter of Life and Death*. The *Times* opera critic and former editor of *Opera* magazine Rodney Milnes recalled his interest in opera being awakened when, as a young adolescent, he was taken to the Powell and Pressburger film *The Tales of Hoffmann*. Pressburger's grandson and biographer, Kevin Macdonald, became a film maker, winning an Oscar in 2000 for his documentary film *One Day in September*.

The impact of the émigrés, however, goes far beyond a mere catalogue of specific contributions and legacies and raises a series of deeper questions. What was the overall nature of their contribution and what influence did it have upon the wider British culture? In what ways was British intellectual and artistic life altered in ways it might not have been without the influx from Hitler's Middle Europe? How far has that impact been paralleled elsewhere, notably in the USA? How lasting has that impact proved to be, and how far has it been superseded by subsequent influences? It is time to try and draw the strings together.

---

* When Conran asked Prince Charles to open the Museum, the Prince (Conran told me in a BBC interview in 1998) politely turned him down saying he did not like all those flat roofs and rectangular windows.

CHAPTER TWENTY-ONE

Messianic Agnostics

The cultural contribution of the Hitler émigrés was, as we have seen, immensely varied. Yet certain broad themes stand out. For example, many seemed driven by a desire to cross, or transcend, traditional intellectual and cultural frontiers. This was not surprising, given their personal histories. Koestler, Laban, Schwitters, Solti, Szilard and Pressburger all spent half their lives moving from place to place, occupation to occupation, language to language, becoming truly cross-cultural figures. Much though each appreciated the country in which he finally settled, such people were unlikely to become cultural nationalists. Cultural nationalism, indeed, was the scourge from which they had escaped.

Many moved, too, from discipline to discipline, one intellectual pursuit to another, characteristically seeking links between them.* This certainly seems to have been true in the sciences. Max Perutz, initially trained in chemistry, went on through his work on haemoglobin to pioneer the study of molecular biology. Heinz Wolf was one of the first to forge links between biology and engineering, founding the Institute for

---

* Interestingly, several key figures in this book (perhaps taking a cue from Hegel) espoused theories that depended on forging links between apparently irreconcilable opposites. Koestler advanced his theory that creativity (like wit and humour) arose from the 'bisociation' of 'two mutually exclusive codes of rules', while Pevsner explained the 'Englishness of English Art' in terms of a series of 'polarities'. Keller argued that a good composer leads the listener to expect the music to go on in a certain way, only to contradict that expectation in the next note, phrase or theme while nonetheless relating it to the initial expectation in a novel way. Gropius enjoined those he worked with to reconcile the competing skills of the engineer and the architect, the designer and the industrialist.

Bioengineering at Brunel University. Joseph Rotblat, appalled by the use on civilians of the atomic bomb, moved from physics to medicine and became a tireless campaigner for nuclear disarmament, going on to win the Nobel Peace Prize in 1995 and, in his late eighties, a knighthood for services 'to international understanding'. Max Born, celebrated as a mathematician and physicist, thought of himself as primarily an empirical philosopher who was interested in trying to discover why things were the way they were.

But this inclination to seek connections was not limited to scientists. Canetti's *Crowds and Power* (John Bayley's sour resentments notwithstanding) is a breathtaking cross between history, anthropology, psychology and ethology, incorporating insights from Africa, Asia and the South Seas, as well as ancient Greece, Rome and Islam – by a poet and autobiographer whose previous magnum opus was a novel. Popper developed a philosophical system that, he felt, applied effortlessly to both the arts and the sciences (the 'Two Cultures' that Claus Moser, in a lifetime of public service, constantly strove to bridge). Kurt Schwitters, to the end of his years, continued to intertwine everything he experienced with his art – and to interweave the resulting collages with poetry and the written word. Koestler's biographer gave his book the subtitle *The Homeless Mind*.

In part, this is a modern version of an age-old image: the Wandering Jew, the figure always on the move, intellectually and emotionally, never securely at home, carrying his worldly goods (and perhaps a fiddle) on his back in search of a new, doubtless temporary, home or refuge. But it is more positive than that. Isaac Deutscher, in his essay 'The Non-Jewish Jew', writes of the great Jewish 'heretics' – people like Spinoza, Heine, Marx, Rosa Luxemburg, Trotsky, Freud – whose special strength was that they dwelt on the borders of various civilisations, religions and national cultures and were born and brought up on the borderlines of epochs. 'Their mind matured where the most diverse cultural influences crossed and fertilized each other. They lived on the margins or in the nooks and crannies of their respective nations. Each of them was in society and yet not in it, of it and yet not of it.' Was there anything specifically

Jewish about this? Many would say not. Immanuel Jakobovits, for example, vehemently denied that the ideas of Marx or Freud (or Einstein) arose in any way from their Jewish backgrounds. As an orthodox rabbi, Lord Jakobovits regarded the historical importance of such people as lying outside Jewish history and therefore neither influenced by nor contributing to it. Deutscher, like many deracinated intellectuals of Jewish background, would have demurred. The very fact that such people transcended their Jewishness, he argued, and reached out to cross boundaries of mind, place and even time, itself arose from deep within Jewish history and tradition. To Deutscher, travelling across constricting boundaries is precisely what had defined Jews from time immemorial.

It is also, of course, part of what defines the exile. One senses in the life and work of many of the Hitler émigrés, Jewish or not, a positive sense that, in the modern world, homelessness is a virtue, that the only true culture is one that crosses boundaries. Many, as we have seen, gravitated towards international or multicultural areas of interest. The journalist Hella Pick, filing from a series of foreign postings, consistently gave readers of Britain's most liberal newspaper, the *Guardian*, a broad international perspective on the stories of the day, later becoming the paper's Diplomatic Editor and a senior figure at the Royal Institute of International Affairs (Chatham House) as well as a familiar foreign affairs pundit on German and Austrian television. George Steiner, who was brought up trilingual in Paris and New York by Viennese émigré parents and later held academic chairs in Geneva and Cambridge, wrote with pride at having published 'on ancient Greek literature and on chess, on philosophy and the Russian novel, on linguistics and aesthetics' as well as a novel and countless review articles. Yet he sensed he was resented, especially in Britain, for being polyglot and a polymath, for not sticking to one field. To Steiner, 'cows have fields'; the only domain of the human mind should be 'passions in motion'. Anne Karpf, in a sensitive memoir of her relationship with her parents (both Holocaust survivors), wrote that, to them, places and people all seemed provisional, unsafe. Emotionally, the bags always remained packed.

The émigrés lived in lots of places: literally, but also figuratively. From his secure fastness at Lincoln College, Oxford, Egon Wellesz continued to study the musical forms of ancient Byzantium, while also lecturing about the music of the baroque and writing a string of post-Schoenbergian symphonies and chamber pieces. Eric Hobsbawm, most global of historians, would speak with ill-disguised disdain of scholars capable only of writing national history, a theme also implicit throughout the oeuvre of George Steiner. Laban struggled to find links between dance, therapy, industry and education, Gombrich to bring to the history of art insights from psychology and anthropology. Weidenfeld – a veritable personification of European civilisation (in the words of Conrad Black) – told me he always saw himself as 'somebody who bridges and straddles worlds and doesn't wholly identify with one'. Weidenfeld's friends would joke that, when George said 'we', you never quite knew whether he meant the British, the Europeans, the Jews or the world.

It was almost as though those who had been given refuge in Britain wished to repay their hosts by injecting into British insularity the exquisite elixir of cosmopolitanism. In particular, of course, they brought to Britain a version of the somewhat unfamiliar cultural world of pre-Hitlerian Middle Europe. The process began even as the Third Reich was still in power. Thus Ebert and Busch masterminded high-quality, small-scale Mozart at Glyndebourne, while Gropius and a handful of British admirers pioneered architectural Modernism and Jooss startled ballet audiences with the dramatic intensity of modern dance. After the war a widespread British inclination to retreat into the cosy comforts of insularity and provincialism was challenged by a counterblast of cosmopolitanism as the Amadeus Quartet gave their nonpareil performances of the Viennese classics, Weidenfeld began to publish French, German, Spanish and Italian authors, and Horovitz and the Neuraths, Pevsner and Gombrich brought into British homes the artistic legacy of Europe. During these years, too, Leo Baeck and Ignaz Maybaum replanted on British soil the seeds of German Reform Judaism, while Anna Freud, in her determined way, helped ensure that the work of her father would continue to flourish.

Many of the figures we have encountered were compulsive communicators whose presence was magnetic and whose message was hard to ignore. But whereas history's great communicators, from Jesus to Mao, have been driven by an ideological message, the émigrés from Hitler were more often impelled by a passionate desire to eschew ideology as such. George Steiner, a brilliant and mesmeric orator, could grip audiences (and readers) by raising such fundamental enigmas as the capacity of men to listen to Schubert in the evening and torture people to death the next morning. How, Steiner would ask, can this alternation between nobility and barbarism be explained? Such questions, he insisted, must constantly be raised. But that did not mean that they were susceptible to easy answers. The largest questions never are. For all his erudition, Steiner claimed to have 'conducted his emotional, intellectual and professional affairs in distrust of theory'. Some things are more powerful for being beyond simple explanation. The burning bush, he wrote, in a striking metaphor, 'burned brighter because its interpreter was not allowed too near'. Writing of the non-ideological Judaism of his father, Steiner dubbed it 'messianic agnosticism'. It is a felicitous phrase, well applied to much of Steiner's own teaching which, like that of Isaiah Berlin, was posited on a distrust of dogma, an instinctive disavowal of simple, unidimensional explanations.

The ideological agnosticism of many Central European émigrés was a badge worn with pride and we have encountered dozens of examples in these pages. Gombrich chose to begin his celebrated history of art with the words: 'There is really no such thing as art.' Popper's most memorable contribution to philosophical theory was the contention that there was no such thing as inductive truth, only provisional hypotheses, and that even these were not worth considering unless they could in principle be falsified by further data. Even those more wedded to ideology were often more persuasive as critics than as advocates. It is the fearless scepticism of Isaac Deutscher, or Hayek's forceful criticism of Fascism and Socialism that stays in the mind. Pevsner may have been regarded by some as a dogged defender of German Modernism (John Betjeman is said to have called him the 'Herr-Doktor Professor'), but his writings reveal an enthusiastic and humane polymath capable of a wide range of critical sympathies. Again and again, the popular image of the industrious, system-building German ideologue, the humourless latter-day Hegel, Marx or Wagner, is dissolved by a down-to-earth practicality, a pragmatic respect for facts over theory. Pevsner's 'Buildings of England' series continues to be valued more for the detail the volumes contained than for the gigantism of the task. Hobsbawm, an avowed Marxist, when asked how he planned his great four-volume history of Europe since the French Revolution, laughed and told me how he had merely written a succession of books, each separately commissioned, which he gradually realised might work as a set.

A degree of pragmatism is to be expected, perhaps, among people who had seen at first hand the most destructive excesses of an unbending ideology. Few who had experienced Nazism would find it easy to espouse any other equally all-embracing dogma, and many who came to settle in the UK singled out the stubbornly undogmatic character of the British as among their principal virtues. Koestler, after a lifetime spent embracing and dropping ideologies, wrote of the 'lotus-eating disposition' of the British, which may have led them to dislike his books but which he admitted to finding attractive. Their 'supreme gift of looking at reality through a soothing filter', he wrote, 'their contempt for systems and ideologies, is reflected in their dislike of the *roman à these*, the political and ideological novel, of anything didactic and discursive in art, of any form of literary sermonising'.

Yet Koestler remained to the day of his death a passionate sceptic, a compulsive communicator, an archetypal Ancient Mariner looking for new causes to espouse and new guests to buttonhole. Like Steiner's father, he may have been 'agnostic' but he was also 'messianic'. In Koestler's case his final cause, the right to suicide, was appropriately emblematic in that, while remaining convinced that the only thing we could know for certain about our own death was that we could have no idea what would follow it, he was positively messianic in his mission to give people the right to bring it about. The particular combination of causes Koestler espoused was unique. But his brand of missionary zeal was not.

The good musician or architect must be a passionate advocate; the teacher, publisher, film maker or broadcaster, similarly, must have a compulsion to communicate, or to nurture and direct this capacity in others. Thus Popper's diatribe against 'Historicism', Koestler's *Act of Creation*, a performance by the Amadeus Quartet or an opera with Solti at the helm were deeply felt exercises in intellectual and aesthetic advocacy. *The Red Shoes*, thought Pressburger, would revolutionise film, revealing for the first time how plot and design could revolve around a genuine artistic event; Weidenfeld believed that the successful publication of Nabokov's *Lolita* would signal a triumph of literary criteria over Britain's obscenity laws and transform publishing. Walter Neurath, his widow Eva told me, wanted to shock the British out of their lethargy, to induce a nation obsessed with language to develop a visual culture.* To such cultural crusaders, each book, building, performance or film was, at least for the moment, the most important there had ever been. If something was worth doing, it was worth doing 110 per cent.

For all their burning enthusiasm, there was also a shrewd professionalism to much that the émigrés achieved. Béla Horovitz published a string of magnificent books on the arts and – like André Deutsch – liked to make sure he was on top of every contract detail, delivery date and sales figure. Emeric Pressburger, again and again, was pressing the more temperamental Michael Powell to decide on casts, agree to budgets, stick to deadlines. Musicians such as Walter Goehr and Franz Reizenstein had no truck with pretension; if there was a job to be done – composing, arranging, accompanying, conducting – then it would get done, on time, to the highest possible standard. Intellectual disciplines, like psychology and sociology, were examined with greater rigour than before; the study of criminology had been a subbranch of medicine until Hermann Mannheim and, later, his

---

* The Berlin-born theatrical designer Ralph Koltai, asked why the designer often received less than his fair share of credit, thought it was because 'by nature, the British really find the visual arts somewhat suspect and are very much concerned with the spoken word'.

rival Leon Radzinowicz, thoroughly professionalised the subject.

Accompanying this tough professionalism, there was a degree of contempt for the 'amateur' tradition so beloved of the English, the Sunday painters, gentlemen publishers and 'do-good' social workers, the inclination towards compromise and 'muddling through'. To the émigrés, schooled in a harder world, ideas were to be taken seriously and pursued systematically. One recalls Carl Ebert's scepticism when John Christie first showed him his little theatre at Glyndebourne, and his lofty insistence that he and Busch be given total artistic authority. Or Weidenfeld's comment that, while he and his partner Nigel Nicolson both lacked business training, 'I considered it a regrettable shortcoming [while] Nigel was secretly proud of it.'

The amateur historian, growled Geoffrey Elton, 'shows a tendency to find the past, or parts of it, quaint', while the pro-fessional, quite incapable of this, 'lives in it as a contemporary ... equipped with immunity, hindsight and arrogant superiority'. To Nikolaus Pevsner, '[t]he amateur is altogether characteristic of England', a country that has produced 'a nice crop of amateur painters from maiden aunts to Prime Ministers'. What the amateur lacks, added Pevsner, trying to be generous towards a British attitude which he conspicuously did not share, 'is a violent compulsion towards a singleminded self-expression to which a lifetime must be devoted'.

Art history was one of the disciplines the émigrés helped to professionalise. When young students of art history such as Norbert Lynton* and Pamela Tudor-Craig studied at the Courtauld Institute (then at Portman Square) after the war, they learned a great deal from the urbane Anthony Blunt. But it was a gentlemanly, almost amateur style of scholarship in which aesthetic sensibility was valued more highly than formal academicism. Blunt would stand languidly against the jamb of the door, talking brilliantly from a minimum of notes, Lynton

---

* Norbert Lynton, best known as author of *The Story of Modern Art*, told me that virtually no twentieth-century art was taught – and no German art at all – when he was a student at the Courtauld.

recalled, where 'the Germans' at the Warburg (who also lectured to Courtauld students) would footnote their knowledge and parade their theories. Elly Miller (née Horovitz), who knew them all, summed up the difference thus: 'I always felt that the English art historians at that time loved art,' she said, 'whereas what the German art historians loved was scholarship!'

A decade or two later, students of art history learned to address the 'iconography' of works of art – that is, to study the *meaning*, as opposed to the form or the 'mere' aesthetics, as art history entered the syllabus of universities up and down the country. By the end of the century, Francis Haskell, arguably Britain's leading art historian of the post-Gombrich generation, was said to have learned his trade at a time when 'the main concerns of most art historians had been with connoisseurship, with the development of style and with the study of individual artists', and was praised for being one of the first to have 'explored the social context in which art was commissioned and created'.*

Music, too, became more professionalised. Georg Solti was appalled at what he saw as the lack of discipline at Covent Garden when he arrived as Musical Director in 1961. To Solti (recalled John Tooley), 'English ways were a mystery . . . [H]e could not understand how anything was ever achieved in what he clearly perceived as such a relaxed, even amateurish, manner.' Solti, who had been raised in Hungary and whose previous posts had been in Munich and Frankfurt, was accustomed to a hierarchical chain of command. He soon set about rectifying things at the Royal Opera House and, at first, made himself very unpopular. It was not long before he acquired his nickname, initially in the pages of the satirical magazine *Private Eye*, the 'Screaming Skull'. Hans Keller, another who insisted on taking ideas to their conclusion and whose forceful wit and intelligence amused and wounded far beyond the confines of Broadcasting House, was dubbed by the same magazine, with appalling bad taste, 'Hans Killer'.

Perhaps there was an inclination to expressiveness,

---

* See his obituary in *The Times*, 21 January 2000.

exuberance, overstatement among some of the émigrés.* There was also a touch of the grotesque, of tragi-comedy, almost of desperation among some. One thinks of the satirical drawings of Hoffnung and Vicky, the later essays of Koestler or the brutal, over-energised leadership style of Robert Maxwell (all of whom, incidentally, were to die untimely deaths). Vicky, the most talented political cartoonist since Low, was in many ways the personification of the tragic clown. In a radio interview in 1959 he talked about his Berlin background, his father's suicide, his boyhood prowess as a boxer (although he was diminutive and bespectacled) and his frustrated ambition to be a painter. In a mournful voice he acknowledged to his interviewers that he suffered from severe insomnia, constantly fearful that he might have no good ideas, and that he felt the pressures left no time for leisure pursuits such as his beloved chess. But he didn't complain. 'Although I feel mighty sorry for myself,' he said, 'I don't think I would like to be without this terrible, haunting feeling. It's part of the job.' Vicky committed suicide in 1966. Hoffnung, a hugely cheerier figure, was said by his friend John Amis to be a person who always 'tried to yank life out of the ordinary and put it one notch higher'. When you were going to visit him there would be a series of phone calls, follow-up notes with drawings, a funny letter or two, a further phone call suggesting that, for undisclosable reasons, you arrive half an hour earlier than planned – and, at the eventually appointed time, a massive 'Come IN. Come IN!'

The compulsion to communicate, to share, to control, perhaps to overstate: all this was understandable among people unaccustomed to British understatement and sang-froid – especially those who had stared into the maw of Hades and been

---

* 'The majority of English people find my painting too emotive, too direct,' said an artist interviewed by Marion Berghahn in *German–Jewish Refugees in England* (pp. 94–5). 'In German art in our century, expression and feeling comes into it a lot. Whereas mainstream art in Britain is more good taste and playing down feelings ... English art is refined understatement.' David Eversley, at one time chief planner at the Greater London Council, was hailed in his *Guardian* obituary (10 July 1995) as 'the most brilliantly original thinker that the British town planning movement has produced since the pioneer generation of Ebenezer Howard, Patrick Geddes and Raymond Unwin'. But this 'gifted but turbulent man' (*The Times*) was one who 'didn't bother to conceal his contempt for conventional planners, a disdain they returned with interest' (*Independent*).

granted a second lease of life. Did the Koestlers and Kellers abuse colleagues and audiences with the sheer exuberance of their genius? Sometimes perhaps. But such self-indulgence was surely understandable, if not entirely excusable, from those who had survived the very cusp of almost certain torture and death. These were people determined to enjoy, or at least employ, every faculty and facility, every experience available to them.

The émigrés may have stumbled, occasionally a little hamfistedly, into a genteel England for which their background and recent experience had hardly prepared them, but many became proud patriots, observing and celebrating their new homeland with wit and compassion. The idyll of rural England is nowhere more lovingly evoked than in Pressburger's *A Canterbury Tale* or the romantic mystery of the Scottish lakes than in his film *I Know Where I'm Going*. No British-born historian studied the Tudors more assiduously than Elton, while it was the Leipzig-born Pevsner who compiled the most comprehensive study ever undertaken of the buildings of England. One of the earliest and most persuasive advocates of the music of Tippett was Walter Goehr, while Britten was powerfully championed by Erwin Stein and Hans Keller.

Did the émigrés become born-again Anglophiles, so grateful to the nation that had given them refuge and succour that they were oblivious to its faults? Were they reluctant to voice criticisms about Britain and the British, aware all the time that they were guests, not natives? Gratitude and admiration, certainly, were fulsome among many Central European refugees. 'I became more royalist than the king!' joked Sir John Burgh, a thoroughgoing British patriot for all but the first thirteen years of his life. Koestler took cold baths in the morning to be like English public schoolboys, and regretted that BOAC was obliged to order American-made planes. When I asked Sir Ernst Gombrich whether he felt he and others from Middle Europe had helped enrich British cultural life when they arrived, his first instinct was to point to some of the home-grown giants of the time, such as Russell and Vaughan Williams. Martin Esslin, a young arrival keen to understand the ways of the English, learned to play cricket and struggled his weekly way through the

Spectator and *New Statesman* (and later joined the Garrick Club 'easily'); Stephen Hearst's reminiscence of BBC Television's Music and Arts Department in its heroic days was prefaced by the proud comment that it contained eight Oxbridge Firsts. 'If it is thought that I have painted an unduly favourable picture of the English,' wrote Elton in the preface to his survey of English history, '[i]t is because they so appeared to one who came to them from the outside.' His book, he says, 'tries to repay a debt of gratitude, but it does so after careful reflection and after personal experience of other peoples'.

The Anglophilia of the émigré had its waspish side too. Few could be more waspish than Elton, though his sharpest attacks were usually reserved for fellow historians. Others directed their sting towards the society around them. They may have been foreigners, aliens, guests; but they were also immune to the traditional British constraints of class and accent, and therefore felt freer than the native-born to speak their minds. Walter Laqueur was scathing about Britain's cultural life, or lack thereof; almost the only good thing he had to say about London in the early 1950s was that it was a convenient vantage point from which to watch events in Europe and beyond. Walter Neurath told friends that the English regarded 'Art' as a dirty word, while Hans Keller saw the cultural remit of the BBC being wasted from within.

Some used humour as a way of cutting through British veneer. Vicky, forever bearing the heavy social conscience of his Hungarian and Jewish forebears, was merciless towards what he saw as the cynicism and hypocrisy of political leaders while millions around the world starved. 'I'm only a Hungarian, so I don't understand economics,' he is said to have quipped slyly in reply to an exasperated reprimand from one of his victims, a British Chancellor of the Exchequer whose advisers included Messrs Balogh and Kaldor (or 'Buda' and 'Pest' as the tabloids dubbed them). More than any other cartoonist, Vicky brought an international dimension to his drawings, familiarising readers of the *Mirror* and the *Evening Standard* with the faces and doings of Adenauer and de Gaulle, and reminding them of the relationship between the rich world and the poor. 'You see, they're trying to find some underdeveloped areas,' an emaciated African mother explains vainly to her huddling tots as, in the dark skies above, multi-million-dollar space satellites rotate the earth to no apparent purpose.

The sting of George Mikes was only less lethal than Vicky's for being sugar-coated. But it could be just as sharp. 'On the Continent people have good food,' wrote Mikes in *How To Be an Alien*, 'in England people have good table manners.' And, even more cruelly, he devoted an entire chapter to the one sentence: 'Continental people have sex life; the English have hot-water bottles.'

There was a bitter-sweet quality to much refugee humour, a touch of the gallows, the traditional tragic clown: Pierrot with a Middle European accent. You couldn't help smiling at the assemblages of cuttings made by Schwitters; 'Watt's the use of living?' asked one of his last. Vicky's cartoons, for all their savagery, were often very funny, their harshness modified by the little self-portrait, balding and bespectacled, he would some-times place in the corner. The grotesqueries of Hoffnung, similarly – a pigtailed Valkyrie pouring all her voluminous puff into a Wagner tuba, a dozy harpist plucking the spokes of a penny-farthing – were sketched with the innocent cruelty of the child. If Sir Adrian Boult moved very little while conducting, why not portray him with spiders' webs forming around his baton or handcuffs on his wrists? The Hoffnung concerts at the Royal Festival Hall in 1956 and 1958 included a wicked cross-cutting of the Tchaikovsky and Grieg piano concertos and an insane collage of opera plots and themes ('Let's Fake an Opera'), both by Franz Reizenstein, and a brilliant set of variations by Joseph Horovitz, based on the styles of various famous composers, on the theme of a television commercial ('Sleep Sweeter, Bournvita').

Among Hoffnung's occasional collaborators was the musician Fritz Spiegl. Spiegl's wit, like Hoffnung's, was both musical and linguistic. Many refugees became intrigued by the uses and abuses of their adopted language; it was her mastery of economical prose that secured for Anne Bohm her job at the LSE, while personalities as different as Pressburger, Koestler and

Popper would approach the task of writing communicative English with painstaking conscientiousness. Hoffnung would mesmerise public audiences and Hans Keller BBC meetings with the mordant wit and precision of their rhetoric. Nikolaus Pevsner savoured the subtle nuances of English usage, while George Mikes pointed fondly to some of its absurdities and parodied the vacuousness of English 'conversation'. Geoffrey Elton fulminated against lazy or flatulent writing (what he denounced as 'mental indolence'); Esslin wrote with early insight about the language of Pinter while Alfred Alexander, the vivacious Vienna-born throat specialist to the opera stars of Covent Garden and a man equally at home in several languages and literatures, penned witty pieces about (for example) common misunderstandings of phrases from opera libretti.

Spiegl, typically, would pick up a loose verbal thread from the tabloid press or a BBC broadcast and weave from it a gently provocative essay. A frequent broadcaster (with his own column for many years in the BBC's journal *The Listener*), Spiegl was particularly perceptive about changing speech styles. When someone on the radio was said to 'head up' an organisation, Spiegl was led to expatiate on the colloquial usages of 'up' and 'down' ('cock-up', 'put-down'), and prepositions in general ('getting off with'). He had a deft way of describing his confusions. Spiegl recalled calling on a friend and being told 'He's not up yet' – and the next day 'He's not down yet': both meaning that he had slept 'in'. An indefatigable lexicographer, Spiegl published compilations on the subtleties of speaking Scouse, the vocabulary of football, and musical and medical terminology. Nothing was safe from the Spiegl scalpel: vocabulary, syntax, acronyms, pronunciation, accent, headlines, misprints, house and town names, the cult of Olde Englande-sounding titles for musical ensembles, the indiscriminate use of people's first (or 'Christian') names, the impossibility of taking seriously most words ending in '-ggle'. Intrigued by cliché, Spiegl would notice how people would say, conclusively, 'in a word' – and then use several. Why, he wondered, instead of saying 'Why did you do it?' do interviewers ask, 'Just what was your motivation?'

There is a whimsicality to much of Spiegl's writing, tinged by sadness, its tone that of a long-suffering but humane understanding of the foibles of mere mortals. He writes of the French and German phrases for various cricketing terms in the course of which, of course, the game itself becomes lovably absurd. He tells of the misguided Nazi attempt to 'purify' the German language of foreign influences. If English, by contrast, has been repeatedly mongrelised and is in consequence one of the harder languages for a foreigner to master, the hazards are worth it. 'We will arrive dead on time,' one of Spiegl's schoolteachers announced, to the lad's consternation.

Again and again, the humour of the refugee was that of the underdog, the gauche innocent confronting a world of heartless sophistication: the horn player with his finger stuck in the *embouchure*, the little man who 'doesn't understand economics', the alien learning how to drink tea, the embarrassment of the football commentator who said 'Welcome to Tel Aviv – a real Mecca for tourists'. When I got to know the members of the Amadeus Quartet, I was at first daunted by the depth and intensity of their music-making. But I soon learned that an hour or two in their company, especially around a well-endowed table, guaranteed a string of wisecracks. The guffaws would grow by the minute and the stories become spicier. And what were the jokes about? The man suffering from impotence, the psychiatric patient, the browbeaten employee, the prisoner in the dock, the foreigner misunderstanding an instruction. The pleasure of the humour was of the little man, the sufferer, having the pay-off line, the last laugh. 'Why do you Jews always answer a question by asking another?' demands the irascible bureaucrat. And gets the shrugged answer: 'Why not?'

Today, 'Jewish jokes' have entered the standard repertoire, while the cultural misapprehensions of the immigrant have given rise to popular comedy shows on radio and television (for example, the self-mocking Asian series *Goodness Gracious Me!*). Vicky's most famous creation, 'Supermac', a sardonic portrayal of the neo-Edwardian Prime Minister Harold Macmillan in Superman outfit, received its homage thirty years later in Steve Bell's *Guardian* cartoons of the hapless John

Major with his underpants tucked over his shirt-tails. George Mikes is long dead, but the industry in witty national stereo-typing continues (as revealed by the popular success of Bill Bryson) while Tom Stoppard – and Geoffrey Elton's lively nephew Ben – continue to produce work much of which is premised on the absurdities of mutual misunderstandings.

Some of the qualities discussed above – the compulsion to communicate and to cross conceptual boundaries, the pas-sionate scepticism allied to muscular professionalism, the sardonic wit – if not introduced into Britain by the Central European émigrés, were surely reinforced by their presence. Influence, however, goes two ways. If the ideas and work of the migrants had an impact upon home-grown British cultural life, the refugees in their turn were often influenced not only by the fact of exile but by the particular culture in which they found themselves. Thus the Amadeus Quartet played not only the Viennese classics but also composers such as Priaulx Rainier, Peter Racine Fricker and Benjamin Frankel, while their early fame and income were greatly boosted by performances on the BBC's fledgling Third Programme. If Pevsner helped alert British sensibilities to European Modernism, his own thinking, in turn, became deeply imbued with the English architectural tradition. Korda and Pressburger may have brought something of the fabricated magic of UFA to British film making, but both loved to immerse themselves in what they thought to be typically British themes. Hayek's *cri de coeur*, so unlike Schumacher's in most ways, was nonetheless – like his – a synthesis of the economics of inter-war *Mitteleuropa* and the new, freer per-spective each was able to imbibe from Britain. At the risk of invoking an oversimple Hegelianism, one might say that, in these examples and many others, the *thesis* of the culture of Middle Europe, encountering the *antithesis* of that of Britain, went on to create a new *synthesis* – new cultural insights enriched by the interaction between elements of both.

The work of Joseph Horovitz is a good example. Born in Vienna in 1926, the son of Béla Horovitz the creator of Phaidon Press, he came to Britain as a boy of eleven. Early promise as a painter ceded to his musical talent, and he took a degree in music at Oxford (where one of his teachers was Egon Wellesz) before going on to study composition at the Royal College of Music. Here, under the influence of the Principal, Sir George Dyson, and the composition classes of Gordon Jacob, Horovitz drank deep from the well of Vaughan Williams and the English revival. He followed this with a year in Paris under the redoubtable Nadia Boulanger ('she hoovered my music of redundant notes') before embarking on a busy and versatile career as pianist, conductor and, above all, composer. Where is Horovitz's musical centre of gravity? The Vienna of Johann Strauss, Mahler or Schoenberg? English pastoralism? Debussy? Stravinsky? The answer depends on what you listen to. In his early years Horovitz was probably best known as a composer (and conductor) of ballet; many consider *Alice in Wonderland*, which has been performed and danced all over the world, to be his finest score. Others call to mind the wit and bravado of the comic miniatures he wrote for Hoffnung, or the exuberant collaboration with Michael Flanders for children of all ages which they called *Captain Noah and his Floating Zoo*. Brass ensembles owe Horovitz a debt of gratitude for a fistful of original compositions, while the King's Singers have often included his compositions in their concerts. His television themes (e.g. for *Rumpole of the Bailey*) have been heard by millions.

'I want to write music that I would like to hear but which nobody has yet written,' Horovitz would say when asked to characterise his compositions. His most profound work is probably his fifth string quartet. Commissioned by Phaidon Press to honour the sixtieth birthday of their most successful author, Sir Ernst Gombrich, it was first performed on 1 June 1969 by the Amadeus Quartet in a concert given in Gombrich's honour at the Victoria and Albert Museum. It is a closely argued work based on a simple initial theme, reflecting the Vienna that composer, dedicatee and performers once knew and the horrors that forced them into exile. In the course of a fifteen-minute score, the opening theme takes on a more decadent, dangerous hue, while Horovitz goes on to quote a popular Viennese folk song in waltz time and, at one point, the Nazi marching song the 'Horst Wessel Lied' – all incorporated into the underlying musical structure of the piece.

While eschewing the strict serialism of Schoenberg, Horovitz is clearly comfortable in both the lyricism and the lush post-romanticism of the Vienna he left and the pastoralism of the England to which he came. He has composed a number of concertos, several of which (for instance, those for clarinet, oboe and euphonium) contain exquisitely elegiac slow movements. Listening to these you can never be sure if it is a vestige of old Vienna you are hearing or perhaps a subtle arrangement of something by Delius, Bax or Warlock. Ultimately, it is this cross-fertilisation of influences that gives Horovitz's music its characteristic voice.

As we have seen, many of the émigrés were keen to transcend limits, straddle cultural and intellectual boundaries. Some were fiercely ambitious to do so. Was there a contradiction here? Did they permit their vaulting ambition to o'erleap itself? Was proficient versatility experienced as a boon or a burden, a liberation or an inhibition? Some sensed that a facility to cross boundaries could be regarded as a disadvantage in a post-war Britain that liked to constrict, typecast and label. Thus, Joseph Horovitz felt that, because he was best known for his lighter compositions, the more serious end of his oeuvre did not receive proper recognition. Solti, widely admired as a conductor of Wagner and Strauss, resented the fact that critics didn't take his *Messiah* seriously yet spent his last months trying to penetrate the mysteries of Bach's *St John Passion*. His fellow conductor, Otto Klemperer (in the tradition of Mahler), thought of himself as a composer as well as a conductor, rather as Schoenberg was both composer and painter. Kokoschka created plays as well as paintings, while Koestler, Canetti and Steiner strove to enrich all branches of literature.

This aspiration to cross cultural and artistic boundaries was not, of course, exclusively a product of exile. Rather, it was one of the features of Middle European *Bildung* which many refugees carried into exile with them. If you were a conductor in

Mitteleuropa, of course you were also – perhaps primarily – a composer. That is how Rankl would like to have been remembered, and Furtwängler. A good writer, similarly, was capable of penning poems and plays, essays, articles and novels – whatever was most appropriate for the message. Kandinsky wrote about theories of aesthetics, linking art and music. But the impulse to be all-embracing was especially pronounced among the émigrés. Some (Koestler and Schumacher were typical, Einstein the most celebrated), like the alchemists of old, sought to achieve through the diversity of their strivings a deeper, unitary truth.

It was an admirable quest, yet ultimately fruitless. The messianic impulse to educate, communicate, share, link, bridge – all this led to a variety of outstanding achievements. But the same drives took many of the émigrés beyond the easy certainties of their youth, towards a heightened yet frustrated ambition, the pained agnosticism of old age in a strange land. 'The more I know, the more I know I don't know.' This is a familiar cry of the elderly, going back at least to Socrates. But it is a sentiment especially moving, perhaps, when uttered or implied by those whose lives and talents have been forcibly transplanted. It is as though the very process of exile has enhanced the ambition, thereby inevitably reducing its chances of achievement. 'I have scattered and, thus, wasted my strengths,' wrote George Steiner poignantly – a rebuke not only to himself for his aspirations to intellectual versatility but also against the British for their preternatural resistance to it. British anti-intellectualism, the mistrust of people deemed 'too clever by half', the impulse to fudge and compromise, all this was alien to Steiner and many another. Perhaps the émigrés tried too hard, took art and ideas too seriously. It was certainly how some came to be regarded. 'You've published a good many books, I gather, made quite a reputation for yourself as an intellectual,' said Michael Hamburger's old headmaster to the poet at a retirement dinner. A compliment? No. It was a gentle reproof, for he added, 'But we mustn't be priggish, must we?' Better, evidently, to be more agnostic and less messianic, rein in the ambition, do a proper job, 'fit in', stick to one subject. That's the British way.

CHAPTER TWENTY-TWO

Culture Concluded

The culture of Blair and Britpop, while still recognisably a linear descendant of that to which the Hitler émigrés had fled, reflected a radically altered world. When the émigrés had arrived, British tastes were scarcely yet inured to European Modernism with its serious-minded search for new forms; it was the stylistic novelty of the Festival of Britain, not its cosiness, that most struck visitors. Fifty years later the fashionable buzzword was 'post-modern', the deliberate abandonment of form, the embrace of the inchoate, the juxtaposition of the incongruent, the self-conscious stab of inappropriateness. A girl wearing a tight skirt and huge clompy boots, or a production of Wagner's *Ring* in which the king of the gods was portrayed as a lollipop man at a children's crossing, were said to be 'post-modern' (or 'PostModern'). Post-modernism implied a posed lack of emotional commitment, the avowed absence not only of agreed aesthetic form but also of any agreed hierarchy of aesthetic values. An (almost) all-male *Swan Lake* was regarded as post-modern. So was a painting of an infamous child murderer composed of children's handprints or a work of art consisting of parts of a dead animal in formaldehyde. Part of the point was to shock; the post-modern response was to remain resolutely unshocked.

But the leap from the Festival of Britain to the Millennium Dome is also emblematic of a transition in the way in which culture was managed and purveyed: from gentlemanly goodwill to people's park, from central funding to lottery funding, from provision by those assumed to know best to one in which cultural activity was highly professionalised and deemed successful in proportion to how people were prepared to buy or sponsor it.

Britain at the century's end was a land in which regional and local cultural endeavours had been greatly boosted. Grants were carefully distributed around the country so that Edinburgh and Cardiff were seen to benefit as well as London. The Royal Scottish Museum, the Lowry Centre in Salford, the Earth Centre in Huddersfield, new concert halls in Birmingham, Belfast and Manchester, Anthony Gormley's stark and striking roadside sculpture *The Angel of the North* – all bespoke a revival of regionalism unimaginable to those who had trekked around the country during the war at the behest of CEMA and ENSA.

If cultural provision was distributed more widely, the emergence of microelectronic technology ensured that its very nature had also shifted. Art exhibitions routinely included computer-generated works using fractal images and similar digitally created material. New museum displays, often livelier than the old, featured interactive exhibits and video links. Film makers learned to use digital editing to produce visual and audio effects that Alfred Junge and Emeric Pressburger could only have dreamed about, while a popular opera like *Carmen* or *Madame Butterfly* could be mounted with great success in a vast arena thanks to advances in amplification. By the turn of the century, music and film could be downloaded anywhere on the planet from the Internet.

People spoke of the increasing 'globalisation' of culture. From New York to New Zealand, Chile to China, youngsters (in particular) aspired to wear the same clothes, listen to the same music and e-mail each other in the same casual vernacular, while their busy, globe-trotting parents could watch the same TV programmes in hotel rooms across the world. But if the development of digital technology helped facilitate the development of a global, 'macro' culture, it also had an equal but opposite effect, leading to what became known as 'niche marketing'. In the past, newspaper proprietors or television executives, theatre and museum managers, like manufacturers of cars or baked beans, had all essentially aimed at the largest potential readership, audience, visitor or consumer numbers they thought they could attract. By 2000 art and culture, like every other commodity, were systematically 'marketed' to 'consumers' or 'customers', like mortgages by a bank. Computerised information could reveal with great precision exactly who might want to know about (and part with money to enjoy) a particular concert or exhibition. Each of us was a potential 'niche market'.

When the refugees from Hitler had arrived, people in Britain commonly thought of culture as national and class-based. Thus working-class families would 'typically' spend their limited disposable income at the cinema, the pub and the football terraces. The cinema also appealed to the large middle class, the shopkeepers, insurance salesmen, journalists, doctors and teachers and their families who aspired to live in the new suburbs, went for a 'hike' (or a 'spin' in the car) on Sunday, listened to the popular dance bands on the wireless and gramophone records, and improved themselves by borrowing books from the library. They formed the backbone of the audience at Henry Wood's Promenade Concerts or the plays and operas mounted by Lilian Baylis. Meanwhile, a small but conspicuous upper class was perceived to live in a world of 'public' schools, debutante balls, domestic servants, country house weekends and elegant town houses. These were the aristocrats of lineage and money, brain and beauty who would seek entertainment on the French Riviera or on board a cruise liner, or during the 'season' at Wimbledon and Lord's, as well as at Glyndebourne, Covent Garden and the West End theatre.

By 2000, this somewhat rigid class structure had been largely superseded by a more fluid, flexible social system in which people were invited, at every stage of life, to consider opting for a variety of constantly shifting 'lifestyles'. 'Culture' by the year 2000 was widely construed to include not just the arts but also the way you dressed, how you talked, the kind of job you did, the car you drove or the partner you lived with, the groups whose norms and behaviour you identified with. Where once the émigrés had smiled sardonically at the 'amateurism' of the English, everything, it seemed, by the new century was 'professionalised' – not just art history and the 'music business', but much else that had formerly depended on the talents of the largely untrained: social work, journalism and sports.

But perhaps the most conspicuous difference between the Britain to which the Hitler émigrés arrived and that of their old age resulted from later waves of immigration. Starting in the 1950s, partly in response to a British labour shortage, migrants from the 'New Commonwealth', especially at first from the Caribbean and then from the Indian subcontinent, came to Britain to live and work. Many of these workers settled and were joined by their families, while the black and Asian community in Britain continued to be augmented by periodic waves of further immigration. Numbers were never large and successive governments, stimulated by problems real and imagined, imposed a series of severe restrictions on immigration. But by the last decades of the twentieth century, most British cities contained sizeable black and Asian populations.

Thus, as the twentieth century merged with the twenty-first and a host of new cultural imperatives jostled for primacy, it may seem that the spirit of the Hitler exiles was finally submerged by a self-consciously multicultural, multi-regional Britain in which 'global' corporations competed for 'niche' markets. At which point, however, one further legacy of the émigré generation gradually became apparent: for by now, the children and grandchildren of the Hitler émigrés were beginning to make their own distinctive contribution.

It is a commonplace of migration studies that each generation makes its own accommodation to its 'hyphenated' background. The first arrivals, especially those who are already in mid-life or beyond, often have difficulty adjusting to the mores of the host society. Sometimes they try to reproduce around them a tiny replica of the society and culture they left behind, or else they learn to mimic what they take to be the accepted norms and behaviour of their new homeland. We have seen many examples of both reactions among the first generation of Hitler émigrés. They may once have thought themselves thoroughly assimilated into the German or Austrian society in which they were raised. Hitler proved them disastrously wrong. Yet, even once safely abroad, there was no way they could ever think themselves completely integrated into their new society. 'With the English but not of the English' was a perpetual refrain.

Not uncommonly, the second generation at first tries to distance itself from the 'old country', finding the accent, religion, cuisine and perhaps even the 'foreign' name of their parents faintly embarrassing. Yet as time passes, the discarded 'hyphen' returns, the ethnic origins become a matter of pride, the old culture a source to tap once more. Thus, as many of the original Hitler émigrés became elderly or died, it became noticeable that some of their children and grandchildren continued to uphold earlier values and traditions.

Many were themselves born abroad and brought to Britain as youngsters. Of the children of the publisher Béla Horovitz, for example, Elly and her husband continued to run Phaidon Press for a while before setting up their own imprint, Joseph established himself as a composer and Hannah as a music agent and entrepreneur. The art restorer Sebastian Isepp and his wife the singer and teacher Helene were parents of Martin Isepp, for many years Head of Music at Glyndebourne, while Erwin Stein's daughter Marion, muse to musicians, was co-founder of the Leeds International Piano competition. Nikolaus Pevsner's children worked in architecture and town planning (Uta), film (Thomas) and publishing (Dieter). Walter Goehr's son Alexander became not only one of Britain's most respected composers but BBC Reith Lecturer and Professor of Music at Cambridge, while the cellist Raphael Wallfisch was the son of the musicians Anita (Lasker) and Peter Wallfisch. The son of Judith Kerr and her husband Nigel Kneale (creator of TV's *Quatermass* series) is the novelist Matthew Kneale, whose *English Passengers* observes the destruction of the Australian Aborigines – partly through the persona of a young Aboriginal boy. The first Chairman of Britain's Food Standards Agency (established in 2000) was Sir John Krebs, zoologist son of the refugee biochemist and Nobel laureate Sir Hans Krebs.

The most famous (or prolific) dynasty was probably that of the Freud family. Sigmund's daughter Anna never married, devoting her life to protecting and nurturing the flower of her father's intellectual legacy – especially, and bitterly, against Melanie Klein who emphasised the primary importance of infancy rather than childhood in moulding our psychiatric profile. Anna Freud's clinic in Maresfield Road became not only a highly professional and successful centre for the study and practice of child therapy but also something of an ideological shrine to the spirit of her father. Sigmund's son, the architect and designer Ernst Freud, was father of the broadcaster and writer (and erstwhile MP) Clement Freud and the painter Lucian. Clement's children Emma and Matthew became well known in the 1990s, she as a journalist, he as a publicist. Of Lucian's children, Bella became a fashion designer while Esther, after a false start as an actress, gained fame as a novelist: the quasi-autobiographical *Hideous Kinky* was made into a movie starring Kate Winslet while *Gaglow* was about an out-of-work actress and her German ancestors.*

How far did the spirit of the fathers and mothers infuse the work and perspective of the next generation(s)? A number of the 'children', themselves émigrés, were old enough when they left Central Europe to retain something of the language and culture of their childhood – Lucian Freud and Joseph Horovitz, for example. Martin Isepp and Dieter Pevsner were younger, while Alexander Goehr was brought to Britain as a baby. Many of today's cultural figures who bear the names of prominent exiles were born in Britain: the publisher and writer Tom Rosenthal (whose father Erwin Rosenthal was an oriental historian), the historian Orlando Figes and his sister the writer Kate (children of the novelist Eva Figes), the cellist Raphael Wallfisch and a proliferation of younger Freuds.

It might be reasonable to seek influences from both Central European and British traditions in the paintings of Lucian Freud or the music of Joseph Horovitz, though their work obviously contains many other strands as well. As one examines the life

---

* Esther Freud is currently at work on a novel that takes as its inspiration a cache of love letters between her grandparents. Another of Lucian Freud's daughters, Susie Boyt, wrote a novel, *The Last Hope of Girls* (2001), about an unresolved relationship beween a girl and her famous, reclusive and enigmatic father.

and work of those still younger, the web becomes more tangled and it grows ever harder to isolate influences specifically deriving from Central Europe. Orlando Figes, born in Britain in 1959, acknowledges a debt to his mother ('a past master of the art of narrative who always gave me good advice on how to practise it') in the Preface to his magnum opus *A People's Tragedy*. But the book itself, a gripping description of the 'long' Russian Revolution (1891-1924) researched and written in the heady times following the demise of the USSR, appears to owe little to its author's personal lineage. It would be at best simplistic and at worst reductionist to see the work of the children of the original émigrés, especially those born in Britain and raised in English-speaking households, as products of the imperatives that drove their parents.

Yet such influences are perhaps not wholly absent. Orlando Figes writes with a broad, international sweep, at the same time grounding his narrative in a fistful of individual characters who recur throughout the story. Tom Rosenthal tells how his father applied for a chair in Cardiff soon after he emigrated to Britain. Erwin Rosenthal had all the qualifications but didn't get the post. Bewildered, he asked why not. 'Well, we can't have a Jew teaching Hebrew at professor level in Wales,' he was told evasively. 'Why not?' Erwin pressed. 'Because you'd be teaching the clergy!' Tom himself, for some years one of the mighty movers and shakers in the tough world of publishing, has written with sensitivity about his own Jewishness, and has inherited the multitudinous cultural passions (especially opera) so characteristic of his parents' generation. As a publisher, he almost inevitably gravitated towards companies with a cosmo-politan, artistic bent: Thames and Hudson, Secker and Warburg, André Deutsch. Today, his son Daniel writes cultural features for *The Times*.

Alexander Goehr, too, has in some ways held aloft the flame of the previous generation. The musician son of a musician father, Goehr imbibed Schoenbergian influences early, com-posing for some years in a rigorously serial fashion. But many of his later works were deeply imbued with the spirit of Monteverdi whose music his father had done so much to revive. Goehr's *The Death of Moses* of 1992, for example, employs a Monteverdian orchestra, as does his 1995 opera *Arianna* – essentially, a reworking, in twentieth-century musical idiom, of what Monteverdi's missing opera might have been, using a recording of the surviving 'Lament' as a central reference.

However, this gives too tidy a shape to a complex progression. For a start, Goehr was not much helped or encouraged by his father to become a composer.* Goehr senior gave young Sandy the impression that he and his émigré friends drank from a mystical fountain unavailable to grubby adolescents, but would use Sandy as occasional slave labour to help copy out scores. When Sandy coveted a particular corduroy jacket, Walter wouldn't let him have it on the grounds that it was affectedly 'arty'. Sandy, who learned to keep his love of music to himself, was sent off to boarding school. A bright boy, he studied the classics and even began to pick up his music again, writing musical settings of Catullus and Horace (and Eliot). When he told his father he wanted to study music seriously, Walter Goehr was dismissive. But he did show his son's compositions to Tippett, who was kind to the boy and thought he had talent.

Alexander Goehr grew up a rebel, embracing a kind of Marxist Zionism. Ever the outsider, he turned down a Classics scholarship to Oxford, going instead to live as part of a Zionist cadre in what he recalled as a grim part of Manchester. Here, between political sessions and work as a hospital ward orderly, he encountered Richard Hall, the Professor of Composition at the Royal Manchester College of Music. In Hall, Goehr for the first time found someone prepared to nurture his talent. In consequence he entered the college and gathered around him a cadre of a different kind: musicians such as Harrison Birtwistle, Peter Maxwell Davies, Elgar Howarth and John Ogdon who were to become recognised as among the most talented artists of

---

* Tom Maschler, similarly, told me he received little but scornful discouragement from his father, the publisher Kurt Maschler, when he drifted into his father's profession. In due course Tom rose to become Managing Director and then Chairman of Jonathan Cape, and one of the most forceful and innovative figures in British publishing.

their generation. Goehr left Manchester a confirmed serialist, But his tastes and interests were far wider than that might suggest. Hindemith was a great influence in the 1950s, while Goehr's musical odyssey included a year in Paris studying with Messiaen.*

The bond between father and son was never broken. Alexander Goehr retained warm memories of his father's performances of the Monteverdi *Vespers* with Morley College forces† and later, at the invitation of Hans Hess, at the York Festival. Walter Goehr's work on this and other Monteverdi scores, his son always maintained with pride, helped promote Monteverdi in a single generation from obscurity to mainstream. Like his father, Alexander Goehr was always inspired and challenged by exposure to older music as well as to the newest.‡ After Walter Goehr died in 1960, Alexander wrote his 'Little Symphony' as a tribute to his father and found himself adopting many of his father's attitudes, using his scores, sharing his tastes. Both promoted serious musical analysis, something of which the British musical profession (which both affected to despise) fought shy. Analysis, said the younger Goehr in words that would have made his father proud, should only have one single purpose: to explain why a particular work of art makes its specific effect. I think Walter Goehr would have been proud, too, of his son's appointment as Professor of Music at Cambridge. After all, establishments are always better subverted from within.

One way of isolating the impact of the exiles is to look for parallels elsewhere. Britain, after all, was not the only place in which émigrés from Hitler sought refuge. Many went initially to the countries on Germany's borders, only to be hounded further by the cruel claws of subsequent history. Some survived, by a combination of luck and judgement, in occupied Norway,

---

* This caused the high priest of Paris Schoenbergianism, Max Deutsch, to throw him out.
† Including one at the Festival of Britain in which Sandy himself sang.
‡ One of Goehr's most recent works is *Overture with Handelian Air* written for the 2001 Handel Festival in Halle, Handel's birthplace, and performed with an extended second movement at the Royal Albert Hall in the 2001 Proms.

(*Above*) The Amadeus String Quartet: Norbert Brainin, Siegmund Nissel, Peter Schidlof, Martin Lovett. Ink and wash sketch by Milein Cosman. (*Below*) Cartoon by JAK.

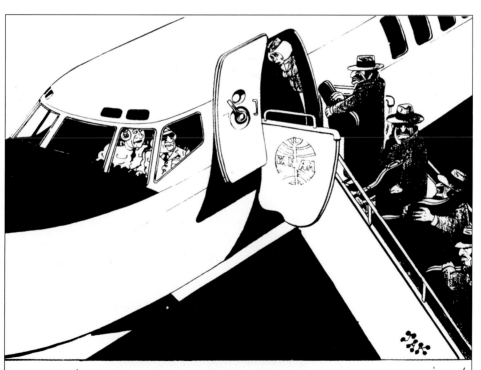

The Red Shoes.
This 1948 film by Michael Powell and Emeric Pressburger became an international success. It told of a girl (played by Moira Shearer) who dances herself to death, watched over by a stern but irresistible Diaghilev-like impresario (Anton Walbrook). The designs by Hein Heckroth won an Oscar.

Nikolaus Pevsner, engaged in research for the Pevsner Architectural Guides: *The Buildings of England.*

Karl Popper (*left*) with Friedrich von Hayek (*above*, 1982)
and Ernst Gombrich (*below*, 1986).

Two of the striking sketches by
Ken Adam for the 1979 James
Bond movie *Moonraker*.

George Weidenfeld in conversation with Teddy Kollek,
long-time Mayor of Jerusalem.

Georg Solti (1975).

Claus Moser at the piano.

Elias Canetti.
Portrait by Marie-Louise von Motesiczky.

Hans Keller with viola.
Sketched by his wife,
Milein Cosman.

In the corner of his cartoons, Vicky would sometimes include a sketch of himself - one of which he sent me when I asked for his autograph. Vicky's most celebrated invention was 'Supermac', the almost grotesque attribution of Superman qualities to the urbane, pseudo-Edwardian Harold Macmillan.
(*Evening Standard*, 6 November 1958)

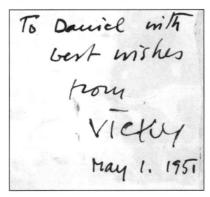

France or the Netherlands. A few managed to get to Singapore or Shanghai, to Canada, Australia, New Zealand and Latin America.* But it was only in Britain and the USA that substantial numbers were able to find permanent homes. How did the British and American stories compare?

British history used to be taught as the saga of an island race that, with the exceptions of the Romans and Normans long ago, successfully withstood periodic attempts at conquest. Nowadays historians are more inclined to emphasise the ethnic and social diversity of the British past: the blacks who escaped the shackles of slavery in the eighteenth century, the changing role of women and children, the part played by Huguenots, Irish, Eastern European Jews and Bengalis who successively settled in London's East End and then fanned out to all parts of the United Kingdom. Many famous foreigners lived in Britain, not only political refugees such as Mazzini, Kossuth, Marx and Napoleon III but such outstanding cultural figures as Holbein, Van Dyck, Rubens, Handel, Conrad and the founder of Manchester's great orchestra Sir Charles Hallé. These famous names represent but the visible tip of a huge iceberg, a host of people from all quarters of the world who sought and found a home in Britain. The truth is that British society, or English society, was probably neither as homogeneous nor quite as multicultural as it has been portrayed. The historical picture is, after all, partly inspired by the personal stance of the historian. If you are predisposed to look for black faces or Irish or German accents in British history, for pioneering women or trail-blazing developments that occurred far from London, you will find them. The diversity of British history is rich enough to provide grist for most mills.

But cross the Atlantic and you encounter an incomparably more diverse, decentralised society than anything in Europe. Other than a small number of people of Native American

---

* Tom Stoppard, born in Czechoslovakia, was taken to Singapore as an infant and thence to India before coming to Britain after the war. Hilde Beal's father, the artist Kurt Bialostotzky, managed to escape from Germany to Bolivia where he had a brother. The writer Stefan Zweig, after a disagreeable sojourn in Britain, re-emigrated to Brazil, where he subsequently committed suicide.

ancestry, all Americans and Canadians are of migrant stock. In the middle of the nineteenth century most had backgrounds that were either black African, or British, Irish, French, German and Scandinavian. By the middle of the twentieth, every North American city also contained communities originating in southern and eastern Europe, Latin America, Japan, China and elsewhere. These are not societies with immigrants; they are societies *of* immigrants and their descendants. They embrace multitudes; their very diversity defines them.

With the advent of Nazism, hundreds of thousands of people from Middle Europe, anxious to escape, pinned their ambitions on the USA where, as everybody knew, a welcoming statue of 'Liberty' in New York harbour offered sanctuary to the huddled masses of the world. But (as we saw in chapter 6) the Americans operated a strict quota system and the limited number of immigrants permitted from Germany was perennially over-subscribed. America thus proved far less amenable than the would-be émigrés had hoped. Nonetheless, some 130,000 refugees from Hitlerism did manage to settle, immediately or indirectly, in the United States, between 1933 when Hitler came to power and December 1941 when America entered the war. Among them were some of the most celebrated intellectual and cultural figures of the century. The universities created a haven for many: Einstein and the art historian Erwin Panofsky settled in Princeton, the political philosopher Leo Strauss in Chicago; the composer Paul Hindemith went to Yale, the architects Gropius and Mies van der Rohe to Harvard. Many gravitated initially to Black Mountain College in North Carolina or, later, to the New School for Social Research in New York City, each in its day a powerhouse of modern European culture and learning. Los Angeles, 3000 miles away, was a magnet for many émigrés with movie skills; how different the story of Hollywood would have been without the presence of directors such as Wilder, Lubitsch, Lang and Zinnemann. Bertolt Brecht settled in Los Angeles, too, as did such pillars of high culture as Schoenberg and Thomas Mann. Hannah Arendt and Herbert Marcuse went to the USA, and Otto Klemperer and Bruno Walter, Grosz and Moholy-Nagy, the philosopher Theodor

Adorno, the theologian Paul Tillich and the psychologists Bruno Bettelheim and Erich Fromm. Some of the leading atomic scientists on the Manhattan Project were Hitler exiles, such as Leo Szilard, Edward Teller and Hans Bethe. America provided a home for distinguished émigrés from Mussolini, too. Toscanini left Italy to live in the USA, while one of the best books about the cultural émigrés to America was by the widow of the great atomic physicist Enrico Fermi. Rarely, if ever, in American history can such an array of talent have arrived on its shores within so short a time.

What impact did the exiles have on American cultural history and – crucially for our purposes – how did that impact compare with that of their counterparts on Britain? In many ways the two stories run in parallel. Both countries had experience of immigration. But whereas, in the past, the newcomers were usually poor, persecuted souls fleeing from oppression or simply anxious to better themselves, many of the Hitler émigrés, by contrast, came from the wealthy upper middle classes, were deeply imbued with the culture of their homeland and were distressed at having to leave. This was a migration like no other.

It has sometimes been suggested that the two nations attracted a different type of émigré, that innovative, forward-looking figures gravitated towards the United States, while Britain became home for the more conservative. There is perhaps some justice in this. Of the pioneering practitioners of Modernism in art, architecture and design who came to Britain – Gropius, Moholy-Nagy, Mendelsohn, Breuer, Gabo, Mondrian – none stayed long and all landed up in the USA. Brecht and Eisler went to the States, as did most of those Marxist and Freudian thinkers trained in the radical Frankfurt tradition whom Beveridge had once tried to lure to the LSE. On the other hand, the behavioural psychologist Hans Eysenck, who stirred intellectual dovecotes with his controversial theories about race and intelligence, remained in Britain. Immanuel Jakobovits, most traditionally observant of Jewish leaders, moved from a high-profile post at New York's Fifth Avenue Synagogue to become British Chief Rabbi. If the glowering presence of Schoenberg among the swaying palms of Bel Air seems incongruous, try to imagine the correspondence that might have ensued had those nice, sensible men starting up the BBC's Third Programme felt obliged to turn down a new composition by the most revolutionary composer of the twentieth century. Or picture the reception that crusty old Popper might have received at the hands of the radical American students of the 1960s whose heroes were Herbert Marcuse and Erich Fromm.

The deeper truth is probably less schematic. Once Hitler had come to power, the point was to get out. Where to go was a secondary consideration, largely dependent upon the happenstance of a friend, a relative, a contact, the visa you could obtain, the ship you could board, the money or affidavit in your pocket, the job you were offered. It may be broadly true that American culture was better placed than British to draw out innovative thinking. But the exceptions to this thesis are so striking as to cast doubt upon its validity. Thus Leo Strauss, after a few years in Britain (and ten at the New School) presided over a neo-Arthurian court in Chicago dedicated to the intellectual defence of traditional, neo-Platonic ethical precepts, while neither Thomas nor Heinrich Mann was one to stretch the forms of literary acceptability. Hayek, prophet of economic conservatism, left Socialist Britain for capitalist America after the war, and was shortly followed by Rudolf Bing, lured by the glitter of the diamond horseshoe at the Metropolitan Opera. Conversely, nobody could label Hans Keller, Vicky, Isaac Deutscher, Kurt Schwitters, John Heartfield or Eric Hobsbawm cultural traditionalists.

If no simple political profile can encapsulate the migration from Middle Europe to the USA, however, the émigré impact in America was different from its British counterpart in two crucial respects. The USA is a far larger country than Britain, with a federal political system and many deliberately diffused centres of cultural gravity. Its central government is in one city, its finance centre in another, its film industry based in a third and its leading universities in a dozen others. America's newspapers are not national but city-based. The émigrés from Hitler who arrived in America settled throughout its length and breadth. Britain, by contrast, has always been dominated by its capital.

London, overwhelmingly larger than any other city in the country, is the seat of government, publishing, broadcasting and the arts, the irresistible magnet (despite recent attempts to redress the balance) for anyone with ambition. Once the exiles from Hitler had found their feet, it was inevitably in and around London (and the two ancient universities) that most were to settle. Thus the immigrants from Hitler's Middle Europe to the United States were far more scattered than their British counterparts and, to that extent, their impact, while in many individual cases outstanding, was collectively more diffused.

There is a further difference between the two migrations. In the United States, a society almost entirely composed of immigrants and their descendants, most citizens were to some degree 'hyphenated' Americans. In Britain there was a recognisable, stable society largely consisting of people whose ancestry was assumed to go back into the mists of history. Britain in the 1930s was therefore, at least by American standards, a fairly homogeneous society that, from time to time, had opened its doors to relatively small waves of immigrants. Thus, while generous-spirited Americans were delighted to receive Einstein, Gropius, Mann, Schoenberg and many less famous refugees from Hitlerism, the disembarkation of beleaguered or persecuted immigrants was merely the latest quayside scene in a national epic in which virtually all Americans had been bit players. In America, it has often been said, the immigrant ceases to be regarded as a 'foreigner' very quickly; in Britain – at least back in the 1930s – anyone with a Mid-European name and accent was marked for life. Therefore the arrival within a three- or four-year period of thousands of German-speaking refugees, many of them Jewish and most gravitating towards the southeast, constituted a conspicuous addition to a society which, at that time, contained very few 'hyphenates'. Hence the collective record of the Hitler exiles in Britain was appreciably more visible than that of their counterparts across the Atlantic.

The story does not end there, however. Any comprehensive history of British cultural life in the second half of the twentieth century would give considerable emphasis to influences from America: 'Pop' art, 'Minimalism' in painting and music, colourful clothing styles and the proliferation of popular television, and the democratisation and politicisation of the arts.

What part in all this was played by feedback to Britain from the Hitler exiles who went to the USA? It is easy enough to name names. Marcuse was almost as much an icon (and Edward Teller a devil figure) of the British student left as of the American. Brecht and Schoenberg profoundly influenced the direction of British theatrical and musical life. Some who had taken refuge in America enjoyed a later flowering in England. Klemperer, a mere comet in Los Angeles, became a star in London, while André Previn (who as a child had holidayed with fellow Berliner Gerhard Hoffnung) exchanged the glamour of Hollywood for the baton of the London Symphony Orchestra. The arrival of Kubrick, Losey and Carl Foreman in the wake of McCarthy brought to British film making something of the flair of an American film industry deeply imbued with the spirit of its émigré directors.

The feedback into British culture was, however, subtler and more complex than is suggested by such a litany. We have indicated that British familiarity with certain psychoanalytic terms and concepts probably owed less to the émigré psychiatrists who settled in the UK than to influences from New York. 'Oedipus, Schmoedipus – what does it matter so long as he loves his mother!' Such a joke, perfectly acceptable among urbane British intellectuals by the late twentieth century, probably has a complex pedigree leading from Freud's Vienna to the North America of Saul Bellow and Philip Roth (and Woody Allen) and thence back across the Atlantic.

Or consider the concepts of the social sciences. It has been said, only partly in jest, that 'structural-functional analysis', 'cognitive dissonance', 'input-output theory' or the 'aggregation and disaggregation' of public opinion must have derived from literal renderings of untranslatable German phraseology. Nobody born and bred on native English, surely, would willingly talk or write thus. Yet these 'German-American' phrases and the academic texts containing them had wide currency by the 1960s and 1970s, and for many became badges of honour.

The rapid growth of sociology, psychology, political science and philosophy in post-war America was greatly stimulated, some would say led, by the presence of such luminaries as Paul Lazarsfeld, Max Horkheimer, Theodor Adorno, Herbert Marcuse, Henry Kissinger and Hannah Arendt. Did they and others carry inelegant Teutonic multiforms into the language of American academe and, thereby, to Britain and beyond? Perhaps. They were, after all, struggling with complex concepts often derived from Mid-European models such as Hegel, Marx, Tönnies, Sombart, Max Weber and Freud. Yet they were all capable of speaking and writing idiomatic English. And it must be remembered that most specialist disciplines, especially those that are relatively new and trying to establish their credentials, have a tendency to develop their own jargon, partly because new words are needed for unfamiliar concepts and also, no doubt, to bestow a touch of exclusiveness upon its practitioners. In all this the social sciences were no exception. Within a couple of decades after the end of the war, as British academia heralded new universities and new disciplines, the latest concepts and vocabulary of the social sciences, hot from America, took firm root in British soil.

In some of the arts, too, it is possible to detect Central European influences apparently mediated by prior North American experience. Film and architecture, for example, are art forms in which national or personal styles can quickly become absorbed by wider influences. The Viennese architect Adolf Loos studied with Louis Sullivan in Chicago as a young man and went on to become a leading proponent of the new, undecorated style that Gropius and others brought to Britain. Mies van der Rohe emigrated from Germany to the USA, but his influence was enormous on British architects such as the Smithsons. The film director Alfred Hitchcock went to work as a young art director in Erich Pommer's UFA studios in Berlin in the mid-1920s. Here he watched Lubitsch, Lang and Murnau creating some of the great German classics. 'My models were forever after the German filmmakers of 1924 and 1925,' Hitchcock admitted and, of course, many of these later became among his most distinguished colleagues. 'They were trying very hard to express ideas in purely visual terms,' he explained. The visual precision the UFA exiles brought with them to Hollywood is palpable in Hitchcock's own work as he homes in on a haunting shadow, a bread knife, a clenched hand, a cracked pair of glasses reflecting a murder, a fairground roundabout – and, through his own successors and imitators, in the film making of our own day. Martin Scorsese regularly proclaimed his admiration for the films of Powell and Pressburger; we have quoted his acknowledgement of the influence of the cool ritualism of the duel scene in *Colonel Blimp* on his own movie *Raging Bull*. Here we catch a glimpse of the impact of UFA styles, via the subtlety of an Emeric Pressburger screenplay for an archetypally English movie, on a major home-grown American talent.

The very language spoken on the two sides of the Atlantic – and not just that of academia – shows the influence of the Hitler émigrés, and a subtle transatlantic interchange may have extended the process. The rich diversity of American English has, of course, been constantly irrigated by waves of immigrants, including the Hitler exiles. Indeed, since many of these were forceful communicators, it might be assumed that their impact was disproportionately large, and not only in the arcane jargon of psychiatry and the social sciences. There are many Germanisms in English English. Some probably arrived directly in Britain (with the late-nineteenth-century migration of Jews from Eastern Europe) in the form of Yiddish: *Schmaltz, Nosh, Schlepp, Oi veh*. Such forms doubtless received increased currency in Britain because of their prior acceptance into mainstream American English. Other German usages date back, perhaps, to the migration of German intellectuals to America in the wake of the 1848 revolutions, an argument developed by Fritz Spiegl in his reflections on the use of redundant prepositions ('to meet up with'). To Spiegl, such forms have a German feel to them, an example of what he calls the 'triangular traffic' – the influence of German on American and American on English. 'Print me up a dozen copies,' someone calls and Spiegl is minded of the German word *abdrucken*. Is he right? Did such Americanisation (or Americanization) of English English in the late twentieth century arise in part from the prior Germanisation of American English? And if so, who were responsible: the 'forty-eight-ers' or the Hitler exiles? The timing suggests the latter.

As people in Central Europe after the war tried to pick up the pieces and make a civilised existence once more, many émigrés found themselves invited back to settle in their former homelands. The enticements could be generous: a distinguished professorship, a fat salary, good opportunities for serious scholarly or artistic work (not to mention the political attractions of East Germany for those of Marxist bent). Some, as we have seen, went. The great majority did not. Of these, some could never contemplate again setting foot on soil drenched in the blood of their own friends and families. The American historian Peter Gay has written about his first visit to Germany after the war (in 1961) and his paranoia as he thought he saw murderous anti-Semitism in the eyes of the girl at the cash-exchange kiosk. But Gay is just one of many émigré intellectuals and artists who went on to make their personal peace with post-war Middle Europe.

Many felt that it was incumbent upon them, as bearers of all that had once been best in German culture, to help reinvigorate the new German world that was arising from the ruins of Hitlerism. Thus Johannes Bussmann, a bibliophile who settled in Cambridge, did a survey (commissioned by Robert Maxwell) of the needs of German university libraries after war, and spent the rest of his life helping to replenish their stocks.* George Weidenfeld, speaking at the fiftieth annual Frankfurt Book Fair in 1998 (he had attended every one), said that one of his chief motives for becoming a publisher had been to help build bridges

---

* His son Tom Bussmann, born in Berlin but brought to Britain as a baby, became a commercial film maker, living in London but doing most of his shoots in Germany and Austria. A man with a quick and quirky wit, Tom Bussmann often (and his daughter Jane occasionally) wrote the *Guardian*'s weekly 'Zeitgeist' column. Sir Peter Jonas, *Intendant* of the Bavarian State Opera in Munich, reflects on the irony that the city that once nurtured Hitler – in the country that his Jewish father fled because of Hitler – now nurtures him, an 'important' foreigner devoting himself to German culture. (See 'Opera Wars' by Jane Kramer, *New Yorker*, August 20 and 27, 2001.)

between the cultural orbit of Britain and that of the German-speaking world. Martin Esslin, after his years at the BBC, was regularly invited to lecture on European drama as a guest professor not only at Stanford but also at the University of Vienna. Ken Adam spent much of 1999 working on a Millennium Exhibition in Berlin ('Pictures and Images of the 21st Century'). As for the poet Michael Hamburger, when I visited him in his Suffolk home, he showed me with special pride the many volumes of his work in German translation; Hamburger received more recognition and awards for his writing in the land he had had to quit as a child than in the one in which he had spent most of his life.

The Amadeus Quartet, too, became celebrated in Germany and Austria, bringing high-quality music to audiences who yearned for it; for nearly forty years their principal record company was Deutsche Grammophon. In 1999 Norbert Brainin was decorated with the Vienna Cross of Merit. In his acceptance address, this doyen of the so-called 'Viennese style' made an elegant speech in which he pointed out that, of all the great string quartet composers associated with the city – Haydn, Mozart, Beethoven, Schubert, Brahms – only Schubert was actually Viennese. Be kind to the foreigners in your midst, pleaded Brainin to an audience whose new government included Jörg Haider's Freedom Party. It was just sixty years since Brainin himself had been forced to leave.

When the émigrés arrived, Britain, whatever its fissures and faults, was a nation 'at one with itself'. After the war this sense of national communality was, if anything, enhanced by the achievement of victory. The British had a clear sense of who they were and what they stood for. Their standing in the world was high. They were a people, a nation and a culture with whom anyone originating from elsewhere might be proud to identify.

Half a century later such certainties had eroded. In Britain, as elsewhere, it had become fashionable for people to emphasise not what united but what differentiated them. Region, religion, colour, ethnicity, sexual orientation or age bracket, often in the past subordinated to the interests of communality, were now asserted, with accompanying demands for appropriate respect and cultural provision. The old consensus of yesteryear broke down to be replaced by a fissiperous, fluid, post-modern 'culture of diversity'. Such was the emphasis on cultural diversity, indeed, that to speak of pyramids of 'excellence', as William Haley had once done, of one art or artist as having greater merit than another, was to invite opprobrium. As grant agencies allotted money here but withheld it there, they ran straight into unanswerable criticism and outrage. Nobody, not even the Secretary of State with responsibility for culture, dared define who and what would and would not be deserving of largesse.

In such a climate it was much harder for people – especially, perhaps, new arrivals – to have a clear image of 'Britain' or 'the British' against which to assess and identify themselves. There were as many Britains as there were Britons, and people frequently chose to identify themselves not with the nation or society as a whole but with one or other of its many subcultures. Millions purported to think of themselves as black or Asian, Welsh or Scottish, Northerners or Southerners, gay or lesbian. Novelists writing in English were as likely to be called Rushdie, Naipaul, Ondaatje, Ishiguro or Kureishi (or Zadie Smith) as Bainbridge, Drabble or Amis. Many who in the past might have felt themselves held back from pursuing artistic interests were now actively involved.

This was no longer the world in which Hitler émigrés had sought refuge and to which they had contributed so mightily. History had moved on. The story I have been recounting was largely over.

But its ramifications are not. Two issues have again bubbled up to the top of the media agenda: the recurrent controversies about Britain's relationship with the European Union and whether to join the single European currency; and the latest waves of migrants attempting, overtly or illicitly, to enter Britain. Both subjects are widely covered as political issues, gift-wrapped in seductively simple slogans. Would Britain gain or lose economically by joining the 'euro' and, if she does join, when would be the best time? And how can we ensure that only 'legitimate' (not 'bogus') 'asylum seekers' gain entry to Britain?

For centuries, ambivalence towards the Continent was a constant of fact of British political life. 'Culture', it was widely acknowledged, came from Europe. But political or economic intimacy with the Continent was another matter which many thought was better avoided. In the twentieth century, however, two great wars emanating from the Continent inextricably entwined British destinies with those of their continental neighbours. After the Second World War, statesmen struggling to create institutions that would make such conflicts impossible in the future proposed increasing the economic interdependence between the nations of Europe.

The Treaty of Rome inaugurating the Common Market was signed in 1958 and, after a couple of false starts, Britain was finally admitted in 1973. The European cause continued to divide people and parties, however, and each subsequent step 'towards a closer union' was fiercely resisted by some, citing the further erosion of national sovereignty they feared would follow. By the early twenty-first century, however, Britain was far more closely integrated into the affairs of continental Europe than would have been imaginable back in the 1930s when the Hitler émigrés arrived. Their presence in Britain thus coincided with the gradual emergence of a genuinely co-operative and increasingly united continent. Some of the exiles (e.g. George Weidenfeld) were passionate advocates of greater European integration, while others (e.g. the economist Peter Bauer and the materials scientist Robert Cahn) counselled against. All were living manifestations of the intellectual, cultural and personal links that had come to parallel the political and economic ones.

How far was this reflected in Britain's cultural life? Had the British by 2000 finally thrown off the mantle of cultural insularity in which they had so long been garbed? Some aspects of the popular culture remained resolutely insular. The main news stories continued to be domestic ones. Yet a glance at the newspapers or bookshop shelves also suggested a population keen to explore the more remote parts of the world, while journalists and broadcasters had increasing access to areas previously barred to them. Earlier generations might not have known much about the Armenian massacres, or even about the murder of European Jewry while these events were occurring. But the tragedies and turning points of the 1990s were on the nightly news on half a dozen different television networks. By 2000, people had access to more information about the wider world than had ever been available to their predecessors. On 11 September 2001, the whole world watched as hijacked planes slammed into the twin towers of the World Trade Center in New York, while the global coalition-building and 'War on Terrorism' that followed are nightly TV fare as I write.

Not only did the media give us a wider geographical purview as we tried to make sense of the world we inhabit. We were also offered a greater historical perspective. Much of it was doubtless superficial. The version of the past on TV or at many museums and historical sites often portrayed a past packed with vicarious excitements and dangers from which we were safely insulated. History was a foreign country, nothing to do with us. Ours was an era of the instant present, an age in which people were 'famous for fifteen minutes', where the models at Madame Tussaud's had a shorter life span than ever before.

When Britain spent three-quarters of a billion pounds on an exhibition to mark the turn of the twenty-first century, the result – the Millennium Dome at Greenwich – contained virtually no history. The calendrical page turned – and times and people past remained mute. Yet the munificence of millennium funding also helped build and equip museums and historical sites and exhibitions throughout the country, among them the new Holocaust Exhibition at the Imperial War Museum. Visitor numbers at 'heritage centres' exceeded expectations. Television mined gold with its costume dramas, antique road shows and time teams, and bookshops and public libraries reported a burgeoning of popularity for historical biography. In spring 2000 the national press noted that David Starkey's TV series about Elizabeth I had attracted more viewers than the popular comedian Ali G.

Had the people of Britain finally doffed the cultural and psychological insularity of centuries and acquired a profound sense of the essential continuity between past and present, and between themselves and their continental neighbours? Probably not. Looking back, George Weidenfeld told me that he detected a 'rise and fall' of cultural cosmopolitanism among Britain's intellectual elite. Having embraced their confrères around the world in the decades immediately after the war, they were in danger of reverting to a new cultural chauvinism. In the 1950s or 1960s, said Weidenfeld, any cross-section of Cambridge students could have come up with the names of ten or a dozen contemporary writers from France, Germany or Italy. Today, for all the globalisation of culture, you'd be lucky if they could name one or two. 'We don't translate enough books,' he lamented in his speech at the 1998 Frankfurt Book Fair. John Tusa sensed that, while the younger generation at the turn of the century 'knew' the wider world in a way their parents and grandparents could never have done, they were almost deliberately ignorant of Europe, or at least of its high culture. Anxious to avoid the supposed cultural imperialism of yesteryear, they would tend to bypass the work of 'Dead, White, European Males' and set out to 'empathise' instead with the art and music of Latin America, Africa and India. 'Europe' might mean sex, sunshine and sport, and/or a political shibboleth. But not culture, in the way it had half a century before.

Yet if the Goethe anniversary of 1999 went almost unnoticed in Britain and Molière at the Barbican was patronised as being interestingly sub-Shakespeare, popular attitudes were surely less insular by 2000 than in the 1930s as even preternatural Eurosceptics happily boarded the Eurostar to the continent, watched the quadrennial European soccer competition or annual Eurovision Song Contest, attended performances by the European Youth Orchestra and stayed in their friends' second homes in France or Italy. The idea of culture might have moved on as the old century gave way to the new. But most people in Britain had developed a greater awareness of their nation's place in the wider scheme of things than their grandparents could possibly have had back in the 1930s when the refugees from Nazism knocked at the door for admission.

Refugees are once again attempting to enter Britain, this time from Asia, Eastern Europe and the Balkans. Precise analogies are false, of course. The bedraggled beggars from Bosnia or Bucharest are not filling a labour shortage, as did the Caribbean arrivals in the 1950s, nor do most have the educational accomplishments of the Hitler émigrés. But who knows what they and their descendants might contribute to life in a thriving, multicultural Britain as the past and present yield to the unchartable future? If there is one thing about our new era of which we can be reasonably certain, it is that a rapidly growing world population, allied to increasingly cheap and accessible means of communication and transportation, will stimulate ever larger movements of people across national boundaries. As we gradually adjust to the migrations of the twenty-first century, we might do well to ponder once again the cultural enrichment from which Britain benefited thanks to the Hitler exiles it admitted back in the twentieth.

Notes

NB   Throughout the book, detailed references to (and quotations about) the life and work of men and women interviewed by the author are normally taken from those interviews unless otherwise documented. The notes that follow are for the most part references to the principal books consulted and the sources of direct quotations. For publication details of all core works, see Bibliography.

Introduction

Books abound on 'Swinging London' and the much-mythologised 1960s. Two that appeared soon after the event were Bernard Levin, *The Pendulum Years* and Christopher Booker, *The Neophiliacs*. For a more recent study, one with an international perspective, see Arthur Marwick, *The Sixties*.

The source of the Walter Cook quotation ('I collect the apples') is the Epilogue of Erwin Panofsky's *Meaning in the Visual Arts* which he entitles 'Impressions of a Transplanted European', p. 380. Panofsky first came to lecture at New York University in 1931, a distinguished visitor from the University of Hamburg. In 1933 he left Germany and became a full-time member of NYU's Fine Arts faculty (whose graduate division was to become the New York Institute of Fine Arts). When Panofsky was offered a post at the Princeton Institute for Advanced Study in 1935, he accepted on condition that he could continue to give lectures for Walter Cook's Institute in New York. Panofsky's autobiographical essay originally appeared as 'The History of Art', in 1953 in W. R. Crawford (ed.), *The Cultural Migration*.

Walter Cook was not the only one to thank Hitler for having inadvertently benefited others, including some of those he had wished to destroy. Ernest Jones, in his biography of Freud (p. 644), tells how the frail old father of psychoanalysis, on his first stroll into his garden after his arrival in London, looked over the lovely vista and threw up his arms saying, 'I am almost tempted to cry out *"Heil Hitler"*.'

For Georg Solti's memories of *Moses and Aaron* at Covent Garden ('one of the most difficult tasks I have ever undertaken'), see *Solti on Solti*, pp. 145–7.

The quotation from Judith Kerr's *When Hitler Stole Pink Rabbit* is from p. 241. For Sidney Pollard, see Peter Alter (ed.), *Out of the Third Reich: Refugee Historians in Post-war Britain*, p. 215. The Hannah Arendt quotation is from Mark M. Anderson (ed.), *Hitler's Exiles*, p. 253. George Tabori tells the story of the new citizen weeping over the loss of India in *The Anatomy of Exile*, p. 17.

The quotations from George Mikes can be found in *How To Be a Brit*, p. 20. This is an amalgamation of *How To Be an Alien* and its successor volumes, all originally published by André Deutsch. One of them, *How To Be Decadent*, originally published in 1977, was dedicated to Emeric Pressburger. The BBC interview with Mikes was for the Radio 4 programme *A Second Home*, broadcast on 8 September 1972. For Mikes, Pressburger and Koestler planning a 'pig-eating orgy', see Kevin Macdonald, *Emeric Pressburger: The Life and Death of a Screenwriter*, p. 409.

Part I   The Culture They Carried
Chapter 1   More German than the Germans
For Koestler's childhood, see David Cesarani, *Arthur Koestler: The Homeless Mind*; for his mother's cultural Germanness, see pp. 8, 12.

Steven Beller, in *Vienna and the Jews 1867–1938*, describes and analyses the cultural role of the Jews and is the principal source for the figures cited re Jewish academic achievement (see particularly Beller, chapters 3 and 4). The quotation about 'the towns of Bohemia and Moravia' and German as a synonym for

Western progress is from Beller, p. 144. Norman Davies, in *Europe: A History*, p. 849, says that, between 1848 and 1914, the population of Vienna grew five times as large, while its Jewish population increased by thirty-five times (from 5000 to 175,000) – that is, from one per cent of the total to nine per cent. In 1881–6, says Davies, Jews formed thirty-three per cent of the student body in Vienna, while in 1914, twenty-six per cent of law students and forty-one per cent of medical students. By 1936, he adds, sixty-two per cent of Viennese lawyers and forty-seven per cent of doctors were of Jewish origin.

The Vienna-born historian Peter Pulzer discussed the 'push' and 'pull' that led German and Austrian Jews towards the liberal and intellectual professions in his Fritz Thyssen Lecture, 'What Shall I Put in my Luggage? Thoughts on the Cultural Migration from Central Europe', delivered in Jerusalem in June 1999.

The relevance or otherwise of the Jewishness of many of the intellectual and cultural high achievers in pre-Nazi Central Europe continues to be controversial territory. In a 1996 seminar on '*Fin-de-siècle* Vienna and its Jewish Cultural Influences', organised by the Austrian Cultural Institute in London, Sir Ernst Gombrich took fierce issue with Steven Beller. Beller had shown that many leading figures in the Viennese cultural world were of Jewish origin (if not religious belief) and that, even in fields such as the visual arts where they were less prominent, many leading patrons were Jews. Gombrich, with considerable passion, cited prominent figures who were not Jewish and denied that the Jewishness of others was of relevance to what they achieved. The vexed question of who was and who wasn't a Jew clearly irritated Gombrich intensely, one that he said he would prefer to leave to the Gestapo. Some members of e.g. the Vienna Circle of philosophers or the Vienna School of Art History in which he had been nurtured might have been Jews, Gombrich acknowledged, 'but who cares?' The answer, he said pointedly, was that 'Hitler cared'. For more on the 'Jewishness' of many of the prominent Hitler émigrés see chapters 21 and 22, and accompanying notes, below.

Quotations from Fred Uhlman are from his autobiography, *The Making of an Englishman*, p. 60, and from his novella

Reunion , pp. 39–41. For Peter Gay on 'the gangsters who had taken control of the country', see *My German Question*, pp. 111–12.

Silvia Rodgers's impressions on visiting Poland are from her book *Red Saint, Pink Daughter*, p. 108.

Chapter 2   Scenes from Childhood
For Gombrich's childhood see E. H. Gombrich, *A Lifelong Interest*, pp. 13–49. An 'Autobiographical Sketch' is published in Richard Woodfield (ed.), *The Essential Gombrich*. Popper's childhood memories can be found in his *Unended Quest*; see in particular pp. 10–13 on his father and pp. 53–5 on his early love of music. For many refugees from Nazism music was to become an important link between the world of childhood and that of later adulthood. The Polish-born concert pianist Natalia Karpf, an Auschwitz survivor, told her daughter that, looking back, she saw her life as totally divided into two halves – with music providing the only continuity between the two (Anne Karpf, *The War After*, p. 151).

The development of German musicology up to and including the Nazi period is analysed in detail in Pamela M. Potter, *Most German of the Arts*.

For Gerard Hoffnung's childhood, see Annetta Hoffnung, *Gerard Hoffnung: His Biography*. Georg Solti recalls his mother's musical encouragement in *Solti on Solti*, p. 12. Anita Lasker tells how she went to Berlin to study cello with Leo Rostal in *Inherit the Truth*, pp. 19–20. Ida Haendel's story is recounted in *Woman with Violin*.

Weidenfeld tells of his father's love of Latin (and his imaginative bribing of his son) in *Remembering My Good Friends*, p. 27. Walter Laqueur's childhood is recalled in *Thursday's Child Has Far to Go*, Silvia Rodgers's in *Red Saint, Pink Daughter*.

Descriptions of school are from Fred Uhlman, *Reunion*, pp. 3–4 and (about 'Muscle Max') pp. 17–19, and Peter Gay, *My German Question*, pp. 63, 66. An amusing caricature of German school discipline can be seen in the 1930 film *The Blue Angel*.

For the *Wandervögel*, see Fred Uhlman, *The Making of an*

Englishman, pp. 75–7 and Walter Laqueur, *Thursday's Child Has Far to Go*, p. 79. Also Hermann Hesse, *Wanderings*; for the suppressed eroticism of wandering see p. 26.

The work and educational ideas of Kurt Hahn are described in H. Rohrs (ed.), *Kurt Hahn: A Life Span in Education and Politics*.

Silvia Rodgers writes of her problems with the Nazi salute in *Red Saint, Pink Daughter*, pp. 121–2.

Chapter 3   Dawn and Dusk

For summaries of the lives and careers of German (and Austrian) scientists who fled Nazism – and of some, like Heisenberg, who didn't – see Jean Medawar and David Pyke, *Hitler's Gift*. Fred Uhlman's student life is described in *The Making of an Englishman*; the quotation about student clubs is on p. 63.

Popper writes of the inaccessibility of his professors in *Unended Quest*, p. 40, and of his brief flirtation with Marxism and Socialism on pp. 33–6. Gombrich frequently spoke of his admiration for Schlosser. See, for example, Richard Woodfield (ed.), *The Essential Gombrich*, pp. 24–30, and E. H. Gombrich, *A Lifelong Interest*, pp. 37–41. Weidenfeld tells of his duel in *Remembering My Good Friends*, pp. 59–62. For his youthful membership of the Union of Social Democratic High-School Pupils, with its songs and salutes, see pp. 32–3.

For Korda's work under the Béla Kun regime, see Karol Kulik, *Alexander Korda*, pp. 25–6. Koestler's commitment to and subsequent rejection of Marxism is fully documented in David Cesarani, *Arthur Koestler: The Homeless Mind*. Silvia Rodgers contrasts her mother's opposition to the Social Democrats of Weimar Germany with her own commitment to the Social Democracy, British-style, of her husband Bill (Lord) Rodgers in *Red Saint, Pink Daughter*, p. 43.

Spender's evocation of German youth waiting for its leader is from Stephen Spender, *World Within World*, p. 116. For Walter Laqueur on the widespread rejection of democracy and desire for strong political leadership, see *Thursday's Child Has Far to Go*, p. 92.

Weidenfeld's Zionism is a recurrent theme in *Remembering*

My Good Friends; Koestler's changing attitudes towards Zionism are described in David Cesarani's *Arthur Koestler: The Homeless Mind*. For Fred Uhlman's early rejection of Zionism see *The Making of an Englishman*, pp. 65–6. Alfred Wiener's incredulousness on visiting Palestine is documented in Ben Barkow, *Alfred Wiener and the Making of the Holocaust Library*, chapter 2; the quotations are from p. 24. For material on Walter Zander I am indebted to his son Professor Michael Zander. Immanuel Jakobovits wrote of his attitude towards Zionism in '*If Only My People*'; the quotation is from p. 4.

For material about Ignaz Maybaum, I am grateful to his daughter Alisa Jaffa and his daughter-in-law Elisabeth Maybaum. Maybaum was one of a number of émigrés from Nazism to have become influential in post-war British 'Progressive' (i.e. Reform or Liberal) Judaism. Others included John Rayner, who arrived in Britain on the *Kindertransport* and became Rabbi of the St John's Wood Liberal Synagogue, and Rabbi Albert Friedlander, Dean of the Leo Baeck College, London. Leo Baeck himself lived in Britain for the last ten years of his life. Friedlander contributed a chapter about the impact of German-speaking émigrés upon British Progressive Judaism to Werner E. Mosse (ed.), *Second Chance*. Hugo Gryn, the Rabbi of the West London Reform Synagogue, arrived in Britain after the war, having survived Auschwitz. His story is told in *Chasing Shadows*. See also the references to, and quotations from, Hugo Gryn in Martin Gilbert's *The Boys*. A number of Christian theologians, too, became émigrés from Nazi Central Europe and made their homes in Britain, e.g. Ulrich Simon (Professor of Theology and Dean of King's College, London) and Canon Paul Oestreicher – both, interestingly, from what Hitler would have regarded as Jewish backgrounds. Oestreicher, who saw the horrors of *Kristallnacht* and initially found refuge in New Zealand before coming to England, writes of his childhood experiences and their impact on his faith in *The Double Cross*, pp. 30–4.

Good introductions to the art and culture of the inter-war years, especially of Weimar Germany, are contained in Peter Gay, *Weimar Culture* and Walter Laqueur, *Weimar: A Cultural*

History 1918–33. The classic work on the origin, nature and supposed influence of *Dr Caligari* and its successors is Siegfried Kracauer, *From Caligari to Hitler: A Psychological Study of the German Film.* See also S. S. Prawer, *Caligari's Children: The Film as Tale of Terror.* For an excellent summary of *Caligari* itself, see David Robinson, *Das Cabinet des Dr Caligari.*

The quotation about the gentlemen who usher in the next slaughter is from Hermann Hesse, *Steppenwolf,* p. 138. The anti-Bolshevik actress whom the cartoonist Vicky visited backstage was Adele Sandrock; see Russell Davies and Liz Ottaway, *Vicky,* p. 7.

For a brief but well-documented description of Nazi cultural policy (including the exhibition of 'Degenerate Art'), see Robert S. Wistrich, *Weekend in Munich: Art, Propaganda and Terror in the Third Reich,* chapter 4.

Many have tried to explain what prevented people, later doomed, from leaving when escape might still have been possible. No account is more touching than Giorgio Bassani's fictional portrait of the Finzi-Continis, an aristocratic Ferrarese Jewish family living out the twilight of their lives in their fading old estate as the tentacles of Mussolini gradually tighten around them. Italian Fascism may not have been as virulent, or as brutally efficient, as German. For the Finzi-Continis and their circle, the net closed slowly, almost imperceptibly: a tennis club withdraws membership, a library refuses entry. Throughout, the professional paterfamilias strives to maintain standards of culture and decency. At Passover, a Seder service is held with all the traditional forms properly observed; most around the table, says the narrator, were to be devoured in the German crematoria. The very gentility of life as evoked by Bassani in this most elegiac of novels reveals how unthinkable it would have been for the Finzi-Continis to consider living anywhere else.

Spender's equation of Hitlerism with the nightmares of Dostoevsky et al. is in *World Within World,* p. 190.

There is an extensive literature on those who remained in Nazi Germany and, for one reason or another, worked within the system. The topic has emerged on stage: Michael Frayn's play *Copenhagen* deals in part with Heisenberg's motives for staying (did he help or hinder Nazi efforts to produce an atomic bomb?), while Ronald Harwood's play *Taking Sides* considers the case of the conductor Wilhelm Furtwängler. Musicians, in particular, have been placed under the microscope. See Erik Levi's excellent *Music in the Third Reich*. Also such recent biographies as Richard Osborne, *Herbert von Karajan: A Life in Music* and Michael Kennedy, *Richard Strauss: Man, Music, Enigma*. For detailed consideration of musicology under the Third Reich, see Pamela M. Potter, *Most German of the Arts*.

Part II   Where They Carried It To
Chapter 4   Ars Britannica (or, No Modernism Please – We're English!)
The quotations from Stephen Spender about the Bloomsbury group are from *World Within World*, pp. 140, 141, 151 and 159.

For Noel Annan ('haunted by the disappearance of rural England'), see *Our Age*, p. 87. Forster's 'oh dear yes . . .' is from *Aspects of the Novel*, p. 40.

For the attitudes of Spender's friends, who deplored the time he spent in Germany instead of France, see *World Within World*, p. 142. 'The sense of political doom . . . defend a good cause from a bad one' is from pp. 249–50. Spender's time in Spain is described on pp. 210–265 *passim*. George Orwell wrote of his experiences in the Spanish Civil War in *Homage to Catalonia* (first published in 1938) and *Looking Back on the Spanish Civil War* (1953), later published as a pair by Penguin Books (1966, with frequent reprints).

The quotation from David Cannadine ('Instead of the Grand Tour . . .') is from *The Decline and Fall of the British Aristocracy* (Papermac ed., 1996), p. 384, in a section entitled 'The Allure of Far-off Places'.

I first heard the story of Ravel admonishing Vaughan Williams in 1994 from VW's friend Sir Thomas Armstrong. Armstrong, by then in his mid-nineties, retained a clear memory and a forthright tongue.

Forster's view of *Ulysses* is in *Aspects of the Novel*, pp. 113–14. Spender's initial dismissal of Modernism is from *World Within World*, pp. 108–9.

The Raymond Unwin speech is quoted by David Elliott ('Gropius in England') in Charlotte Benton (ed.), *A Different World: Emigré Architects in Britain, 1928–1958*, p. 108. Elliott's source was the *RIBA Journal* of 19 May 1934.

Frank Pick is quoted on Moholy-Nagy by Alan Powers in his introductory essay, 'The Search for a New Reality', in *Modern Britain, 1929–1939* (The Design Museum, London, 1999), p. 31; Powers quotes William Coldstream ('the thing really was to do what one wanted to do . . .') on p. 38.

For 'the English are great lovers of themselves' – and much more in the same vein – see *A Relation, or Rather a True Account, of the Island of England; with Sundry Particulars of the Customs of these People, and of the Royal Revenues under King Henry the Seventh, about the year 1500* (translated from the Italian, with Notes, by Charlotte Augusta Sneyd, 1847; printed for the Camden Society), pp. 20–1.

Erasmus's views on the British are from *Praise of Folly*, p. 68. Those of Pastor Moritz are in *Journeys of a German in England in 1782*, p. 186. Berta Geissmar's comment is from her book *The Baton and the Jackboot: Recollections of Musical Life*, p. 382.

Chapter 5 Early Arrivals
The description of Carl Ebert working with Berthold Gold-schmidt is from Peter Ebert's biography of his father, *In This Theatre of Man's Life*, p. 60; for Ebert's Berlin production of *Macbeth*, see pp. 70–4. Rudolf Bing writes about Ebert in *5000 Nights at the Opera*, p. 36. Bing and Peter Ebert both describe the creation of Glyndebourne. Fritz Busch writes of his early collaboration with Carl Ebert ('among the happiest experiences of my career') in his autobiography, *Pages from a Musician's Life*, pp. 189–91, and of his encounter with Göring on pp. 208–9. The book, first published (in German) in 1949, concludes with Busch's departure from Germany in 1933; he had intended to write a second volume of memoirs, to include his years at Glyndebourne, but was prevented from doing so by his sudden death in 1951. For more on the early years of Glyndebourne see Spike Hughes, *Glyndebourne: A History of*

the Festival Opera, Wilfrid Blunt, *John Christie of Glyndebourne* and John Jolliffe, *Glyndebourne*.

On Gropius and the Bauhaus, see Frank Whitford, *The Bauhaus*. See also the essay 'Gropius in England' by David Elliott in Charlotte Benton (ed.), *A Different World: Emigré Architects in Britain 1928–1958*. For my visit to Impington Village College on 9 July 1999 I am grateful to Jacqueline Kearns and Gerald Goldstone. For more on architecture see the latter part of chapter 17 below.

Dartington Hall, created by Dorothy and Leonard Elmhirst, welcomed a number of émigré artists, among them Gropius and Jooss. The Dartington story is told in Michael Young, *The Elmhirsts of Dartington: The Creation of an Utopian Community*.

The story of Aby Warburg and the Warburg Institute is told in a variety of sources, among them the various memoirs and autobiographical essays cited above by Gombrich. Dorothea McEwan tells the Warburg story in her well-documented chapter 'A Tale of One Institute and Two Cities' in Ian Wallace (ed.), *German-Speaking Exiles in Great Britain*. For more on the life and ideas of Aby Warburg, see E. H. Gombrich, *Aby Warburg: An Intellectual Biography* (Warburg Institute, 1970). Also, Ron Chernow, *The Warburgs: A Family Saga*. Kenneth Clark describes the impact upon him of Aby Warburg's lecture in *Another Part of the Wood*, pp. 189–90. Clark's report of the phone call from Saxl to Clark, and of the role of Arthur Lee in the transfer of the Warburg collection from Hamburg to London, is on pp. 207–8. Saxl's comment about Petrarch and Erasmus is quoted in Chernow, p. 407. I am grateful to Eckart Krause of the University of Hamburg, and to the staff of the 'KBW', for an enjoyable and informative visit to the Warburg house and institute in Hamburg on 18 June 1999.

Every serious book about the development of dance in Britain from the 1930s to the 1950s considers the work and influence of Jooss and Laban. For an excellent early study, see Fernau Hall, *Modern English Ballet*, in which Isadora Duncan's self-assessment is quoted on p. 69. From the same era is A. V. Coton, *The New Ballet: Kurt Jooss and His Work*. For more recent assessments of Jooss, see 'Choreography and Dance', Vol. 3, Part 2, edited by Suzanne Walther, and Andy Adamson and Clare Lidbury (eds), *Kurt Jooss: Sixty Years of The Green Table*. I am grateful to Jooss's daughter Anna Markard, and to Sir Peter Wright, for helping to point me in the right directions. For the life and work of Laban, see the books and articles of Valerie Preston-Dunlop, especially *Rudolf Laban: An Extraordinary Life*. Also: John Hodgson, *Mastering Movement*. See also the section in chapter 17 below.

For an outline of the life and work of Korda and Pressburger, see Karol Kulik, *Alexander Korda: The Man Who Could Work Miracles* and Kevin Macdonald, *Emeric Pressburger: The Life and Death of a Screenwriter*. See also chapter 10 below.

Chapter 6   Leaving Home

An early account of Jewish immigration from Nazi Central Europe to Britain by one who was actively involved is Norman Bentwich, *They Found Refuge*. See also A. J. Sherman, *Island Refuge: Britain and Refugees from the Third Reich, 1933–1939*. For the most recent substantial study, see Louise London, *Whitehall and the Jews 1933–48: British Immigration Policy and the Holocaust*. Also, the relevant sections in Kushner and Knox, *Refugees in an Age of Genocide*.

Peter Gay tells the story of his family's escape from Nazism in *My German Question*.

George Clare's eyewitness account of the *Anschluss* is from his *Last Waltz in Vienna: The Destruction of a Family 1842–1942*; the quotation about Vienna being like 'an aroused woman' is on p. 195. The story of the Children's Transports is told in the form of a structured montage of memories in Karen Gershon (ed.), *We Came as Children*; the quotations from children arriving at the Dutch border, eating and drinking and becoming boisterous, are from pp. 28–9. For a more discursive description, see Barry Turner, . . . *And the Policeman Smiled*. A moving documentary film about the Children's Transports was issued in 2000: *Into the Arms of Strangers: Stories of the Kindertransport*, directed by Mark Jonathan Harris (author, with Deborah Oppenheimer, of an accompanying book). Fritz Spiegl reproduces his schoolboy essay in his book *The Joy of Words*, p. 223.

It was not only children who were told to avoid talking German and to keep their voices down. 'Refrain from speaking German in the streets and in public . . . places such as restaurants,' said an instruction manual for refugees issued by the German-Jewish Aid Committee, pointing out that it was better to talk halting English than fluent German. 'Do not read German newspapers in public,' it instructed its readers – and (since 'the Englishman greatly dislikes ostentation') added the following, italicised for effect: '*do not talk in a loud voice*'.

The stories of Peter Schidlof and Siegmund Nissel are derived from my interviews with them, initially in connection with my book *The Amadeus Quartet*, plus follow-up conversations with Nissel in 1998. For more on the Amadeus Quartet, see the latter part of chapter 13 below.

Chapter 7   In a Strange Land

Kokoschka's reactions to the 'phlegm' of wartime Britain is quoted in Susanne Keegan, *The Eye of God: A Life of Oskar Kokoschka*, p. 203. For George Clare's, see *Last Waltz in Vienna: The Destruction of a Family 1842–1942*, p. 123. Weidenfeld's anecdote (about the Görings) is in *Remembering My Good Friends*, p. 96. Koestler's circuitous journey to England is in David Cesarani's *Arthur Koestler: The Homeless Mind*, pp. 168–171.

The night before Sigmund Freud arrived in England, he dreamed that he was landing in Pevensey – and had to explain to his son that this was where William the Conqueror had landed in 1066. As Freud's biographer Ernest Jones commented (p. 644), that did not sound like the dream of a depressed refugee!

Fred Uhlman's vision of what he thought England would be like is from *The Making of an Englishman*, pp. 196–201. Silvia Rodgers's impressions of the country to which she came as a refugee are from *Red Saint, Pink Daughter*, pp. 184 *et seq.* Sir Joseph Rotblat was interviewed on the BBC's *Desert Island Discs* in November 1998. The student recalling Popper was his successor as Professor of Philosophy at the London School of

Economics, John Watkins; see his contribution to Joan Abse (ed.), *My LSE*, especially pp. 79–80. Walter Laqueur recounts his social solecism in *Thursday's Child Has Far to Go*, p. 370. I am grateful to Henry Kuttner for a delightful and informative visit to the Belsize Square Synagogue and for material about its origins and early history. Michael Hamburger told me about his childhood in St John's Wood, which he has also written about in *String of Beginnings*, pp. 34–5. I heard about Bunce Court from various alumni, and from Hilde Beal who worked in its gardens; see also Zoe Josephs et al., *Survivors: Jewish Refugees in Birmingham, 1933–45*, pp. 71 *et seq*. I heard about Bernard Schlesinger from Michael Maybaum's widow Elisabeth, and read about him in the delightful *Voltaire's Coconuts* by his grandson, Ian Buruma. For a charming and evocative description of what it felt like being a Hitler refugee in Britain, see '*Where do you come from?*' by Carl F. Flesch (son of the violinist).

The archives of the Academic Assistance Council (AAC) and its successor the Society for the Protection of Science and Learning (SPSL) are held in Oxford, while many of those directly involved, including grateful recipients of help, have left memoirs. My account comes in part from the two books based on conversations with Tess Simpson compiled and edited by Ray M. Cooper, *Refugee Scholars*, and *Retrospective Sympathetic Affection*. Also, from Beveridge's memories of the AAC's foundation and early history in *Power and Influence*, pp. 234–8, and *A Defence of Free Learning*. Robbins's account of the founding of the AAC is from his *Autobiography of an Economist*, pp. 143–4. See also Ralf Dahrendorf, *LSE: A History of the London School of Economics and Political Science 1895–1995*, pp. 286–90.

Many of the émigré scientists left memoirs and autobiographies, notably Max Born's *My Life*, Hans Krebs's *Reminiscences and Reflections*, Otto Frisch's *What Little I Remember* and Rudolf Peierls's *Bird of Passage*; Peierls describes his encounter with Rutherford on p. 115. The quotation from Krebs about the civility of British academic life is from a 1961 lecture in memory of Gowland Hopkins; Krebs made similar comments in 1965, in a speech presenting the British Academy with a 'Thank You Britain' cheque for £90,000, raised by the Association of Jewish Refugees. A book that includes mini-biographies of many refugee scientists, including those such as Einstein who settled in the USA, is Jean Medawar and David Pyke, *Hitler's Gift: Scientists Who Fled Nazi Germany*. The Oral History Archives of the Imperial War Museum contain illuminating interviews with, among others, Blaschko, Katz, Krebs, Kurti, Peierls, Perutz and Rotblat.

One of the most vivid descriptions of internment is also by one of Britain's most celebrated émigré scientists: the essay (originally for the *New Yorker*) by the biochemist and Nobel laureate Max Perutz, most recently reproduced as 'Enemy Alien' in his collections *Is Science Necessary? Essays on Science and Scientists* and *I Wish I'd Made You Angrier Earlier*. The art historian Klaus Ernst Hinrichsen and the composer Hans Gál were among several distinguished internees who recorded interviews about the experience of internment for the Oral History Archives of the Imperial War Museum. The first important book on internment was François Lafitte, *The Internment of Aliens*. More recent studies include Peter and Leni Gillman, *Collar the Lot!* and Ronald Stent, *A Bespattered Page: The Internment of 'His Majesty's Most Loyal Enemy Aliens'*. Walter Zander is quoted by Fred Uhlman in *The Making of an Englishman*, pp. 226–7, while Uhlman's own description of the range of lectures available in internment is from pp. 232–3. The catalogue of scientific lectures at Hay in Australia is quoted in Michael Seyfert, 'His Majesty's Most Loyal Internees' in Gerhard Hirschfeld (ed.), *Exile in Great Britain*, p. 183. Michael Foot's *Evening Standard* article ('*Why Not Lock Up de Gaulle?*') was published on 17 July 1940. I am grateful to Florence Pevsner for her girlhood memories of life on the Isle of Man, and to Iris Burton, Audrey Ainsworth, Yvonne Cresswell and others who helped me to understand more about internment when I visited the Isle of Man in February 2001.

For the later wartime experiences of Koestler, see David Cesarani, *Arthur Koestler: The Homeless Mind*; for refugee historians (or historians-to-be), among them Carlebach,

Hennock and Koenigsberger, see Peter Alter (ed.), *Out of the Third Reich*. The cold encouragement of the former Viennese *hausfrau*, now a domestic servant, to play the family Bechstein, is quoted by Jillian Davidson, 'German-Jewish Women in England' in Werner Mosse (co-ordinating ed.), *Second Chance: Two Centuries of German-speaking Jews in the United Kingdom*, p. 540; the following article, 'An Alien Occupation – Jewish Refugees and Domestic Service in Britain, 1933–1948' by Tony Kushner in Mosse op. cit., pp. 553–78, gives more on refugee women as British domestic servants.

Part III Culture at War
Chapter 8 The Commissars Close Ranks
Kenneth Clark was one of the founding fathers of Britain's post-war cultural world – the environment within which so many of the Hitler émigrés were to flourish. In the second volume of his autobiography, *The Other Half*, Clark tells the story of the removal of the National Gallery paintings from London on pp. 1–8; his period in charge of film at the Ministry of Information on pp. 9-22; the War Artists scheme on pp. 22–4; the origins of CEMA on pp. 24–7; and the National Gallery concerts on pp. 27–30. For Tyrone Guthrie ('public taste was serious'), see *A Life in the Theatre*, p. 198.

Many memoirs include references to the day war was declared and Chamberlain's speech. The description of the Korda workforce listening in a coal bunker is from Michael Powell and is quoted in Karol Kulik, *Alexander Korda*, p. 232. Nigel Nicolson describes his youthful encounter with Nazism and the family listening to Chamberlain in Sissinghurst in his memoirs *Long Life*, pp. 79–81. Clark's memory of Chamberlain's 'tired old voice' is on the final page of his first volume of autobiography, *Another Part of the Wood*, p. 278. For David Webster's early career (including his presence in mid-Atlantic on 3 September 1939), see Montague Haltrecht, *The Quiet Showman*, pp. 32–54. The Unwin family adventures are recounted by Sir Stanley Unwin in *The Truth About a Publisher*, pp. 250–1.

The development of broadcasting in the 1930s and 1940s is the subject of a massive bibliography. The most authoritative treatment is in A. Briggs, *The History of Broadcasting in the United Kingdom*, vols II and III (OUP, 1965 and 1970). For the origins and early history of the BBC Symphony Orchestra, see Nicholas Kenyon, *The BBC Symphony Orchestra 1930–1980*, chapter 2. Also Sir Adrian Boult: *My Own Trumpet*, chapter 9. For a more general picture of British life and culture during the war, see Angus Calder, *The People's War: Britain 1939–1945*. Also, Norman Longmate, *How We Lived Then: A History of Everyday Life During the Second World War*.

The story of Powell and Pressburger's trip to Canada to research *49th Parallel* is told in Kevin Macdonald, *Emeric Pressburger: The Life and Death of a Screenwriter*, pp. 166–71.

The origins of CEMA and of its successor the Arts Council are dealt with in Andrew Sinclair, *Arts and Cultures* and – with engaging cynicism that occasionally verges on cruelty – in Richard Witts, *Artist Unknown*. Individual biographies include: Wilfrid Blunt, *John Christie of Glyndebourne*; Ursula Vaughan Williams, *R.V.W.: A Biography of Ralph Vaughan Williams*; Robert Skidelsky, *John Maynard Keynes* (3 vols). Vaughan Williams is quoted (as wanting 'to make opera the thing that everyone wants to go to') in Witts, p. 47. There is no adequate biography of Beecham; his autobiography, *A Mingled Chime*, only takes the story to the early 1920s. For Beecham's kindnesses to Berta Geissmar, see the latter half of her memoir *The Baton and the Jackboot*. The story of Lilian Baylis is recounted by many who knew and worked for her and the Vic-Wells companies. See, for instance, Tyrone Guthrie, *A Life in the Theatre*. The quotation from Rudolf Bing, pressing Christie not to engage Sadler's Wells singers, is from Spike Hughes, *Glyndebourne: A History of the Festival Opera*, p. 117.

Chapter 9   By the Waters of Isis and Cam
Part of the text of Martin Miller's 'Hitler' speech is reproduced in Lisa Appignanesi, *The Cabaret*, pp. 166–7. The story of émigré theatrical and cultural activities in the years preceding and during the war is the subject of Günter Berghaus (ed.), *Theatre and Film in Exile: German Artists in Britain, 1933–1945*. See, in particular, chapter 3, 'German Theatre and

Cabaret in London, 1939–45' by Hugh Robinson, who writes in some detail of the *Laterndl* etc. (and quotes the review by Goronwy Rees). Also chapter 5, ' "They Came to a Country"; German Theatre Practitioners in Exile in Great Britain, 1938–45' by Alan Clarke, which includes the quotations from Sybil Thorndike and Frederick Valk. Gunter Berghaus has also contributed a valuable chapter on émigré theatre to Werner E. Mosse (ed.), *Second Chance*. Fred Uhlman describes the foundation of the FDKB (and its early infiltration by Communists) in *The Making of an Englishman*, pp. 215–17. The quotation from Fritz Kortner ('anaemia of expression . . . theatre became paler and paler') is from Kortner's memoirs and is quoted by Marion Berghahn in *German-Jewish Refugees in England*, p. 105.

The BBC during the war is the subject of A. Briggs, *The History of Broadcasting in the United Kingdom,* vol. III, *The War of Words* (OUP, 1970); for German-language broadcasting, see especially pp. 429–32. Weidenfeld describes his wartime work with the Corporation in *Remembering My Good Friends*, chapter 5; Gombrich's account is in *A Lifelong Interest*, pp. 58–62 and in an essay reproduced in *Ideals and Idols* (Phaidon, 1979). While doing research for this chapter, I was able to talk to Lord Briggs, Lord Weidenfeld, Sir Ernst Gombrich and Martin Esslin about the wartime BBC, and my account reflects something of what I learned during those conversations.

Egon Wellesz was one of several former Schoenberg students (among them Karl Rankl and Peter Stadlen) to reside in Oxford for all or part of the war. Much of the section on Oxford and Cambridge during the war is based on interviews with those who were there. I have also consulted printed accounts, among them the biographies or autobiographical writings (listed in the Bibliography) of e.g. Chain, Michael Hamburger and Milein Cosman ('Oxford 1940': *Aquarius* 23/4, 1998: John Heath-Stubbs Eightieth Birthday Issue) on Oxford, and Robbins, Keynes and Perutz on Cambridge.

For the history of the LSE see Ralf Dahrendorf, *LSE: A History of the London School of Economics and Political Science, 1895–1995*. For a bite-sized summary of the life of

Hayek, see John Raybould (ed.), *Hayek: A Commemorative Album*. Galbraith's memory of the Robbins–Hayek seminars is quoted on p. 30. For Aubrey Jones's recollections of Hayek lecturing, see Joan Abse (ed.), *My LSE*, pp. 35–6. Robbins recalls Hayek in *Autobiography of an Economist*, pp. 127 *et seq*; the comment that Hayek 'lived at the frontiers of speculation' is on p. 128. The relationship between Hayek and Keynes – intellectually in conflict but personally courteous and even friendly – is described by Robert Skidelsky in his biography of Keynes. See especially vol. 2, *The Economist as Saviour*, pp. 454–9, from which my quotations are derived. Bruce Caldwell kindly cast a helpful critical eye over early drafts of my section on Hayek, here and in chapter 12 below.

I am grateful to Sue Himmelweit for material about her mother, Hilde Himmelweit; see also Hans Eysenck, *Rebel With a Cause: The Autobiography of Hans Eysenck*, p. 100. For Walter Ullmann, see his chapter in Peter Alter (ed.), *Out of the Third Reich: Refugee Historians in Post-war Britain*.

Chapter 10: The Freedom of the Foreigner
The life and work of Korda and Pressburger are described in two excellent biographies: Karol Kulik, *Alexander Korda: The Man Who Could Work Miracles* and Kevin Macdonald, *Emeric Pressburger: The Life and Death of a Screenwriter*. Macdonald, a grandson of Pressburger, won an Oscar in 1999 for his documentary film *One Day in September* about the murder of the Israeli athletes at the 1972 Olympic Games in Munich. For more on Korda see the books by Paul Tabori and Korda's nephew Michael.

Michael Powell's *A Life in Movies* contains much material about his relationship with Pressburger, as does Kevin Gough-Yates (ed.), *Michael Powell in Collaboration with Emeric Pressburger* (BFI, 1970). For an analysis of the films of Powell and Pressburger, see Ian Christie, *Arrows of Desire: The Films of Michael Powell and Emeric Pressburger*. The Foreword is by Martin Scorsese; it is here that Scorsese writes of the influence of the duel scene in *Blimp* on his own film *Raging Bull*. Ian Christie also edited the film script of *The Life and Death of*

Colonel Blimp, from which I have quoted. The best way to know about the films is of course to see them. Some of my most enjoyable hours while preparing this book were spent watching many of the films produced by Korda, The Archers and other film makers featured in this chapter, sometimes on television or video but more often courtesy of the British Film Institute and National Film Theatre.

The quotation about Emeric Pressburger by his daughter (Angela) is on p. 230 of Kevin Macdonald's biography. The Isherwood novel about the émigré film maker, loosely based on Berthold Viertel, is *Prater Violet*; the quotations are from pp. 29–30 and 42. Popper's comment about the standards required in writing good English is from *Unended Quest: An Intellectual Autobiography*, p. 114.

Chapter 11 'Somewhere in England'

For a general picture of British life and culture during the war, see Angus Calder, *The People's War: Britain 1939–1945*. Also, Norman Longmate, *How We Lived Then: A History of Everyday Life during the Second World War*. Kenneth Clark's comment about Sandy Macpherson is from *The Other Half*, p. 27. George Steiner's reflections on his multicultural youth are in *Errata: An Examined Life*; he mentions learning the Mowbray speech from *Richard II* on p. 13. Tippett wrote of his work at Morley College in his autobiography *Those Twentieth-Century Blues*, especially pp. 114–16. For the BBC Symphony Orchestra during the war, see Nicholas Kenyon, *The BBC Symphony Orchestra 1930–1980*, chapter 2. Also Sir Adrian Boult, *My Own Trumpet*, chapter 9.

For the wartime touring of the Vic-Wells companies, see Tyrone Guthrie, *A Life in the Theatre*, chapter 14. Also Ninette de Valois, *Come Dance With Me: A Memoir, 1898–1956*. Joan Cross's recollections of wartime are in Eric Crozier (ed.), *Opera in English*, pp. 18–24; a list of cities in which Sadler's Wells opera appeared is on p. 25. The critic Edwin Evans contributes a chapter; my quotations from Evans about Kurt Jooss are from p. 15. For more on Jooss, see A. V. Coton, *The New Ballet: Kurt Jooss and his Work*. Ida Haendel recounts the story of her

CEMA concert to the American troops in *Woman With Violin*, pp. 135–7. For a more general picture of the arts in wartime Britain, and of the work of CEMA and ENSA, see Andrew Sinclair, *Arts and Cultures* and Richard Witts, *Artist Unknown*. Walter Legge's widow Elisabeth Schwarzkopf (who was in Germany during the war) includes a section quoting Legge's memories of his wartime activities with ENSA in *On and Off the Record: A Memoir of Walter Legge*, pp. 60–2. Berta Geissmar writes of Beecham and the London Philharmonic in *The Baton and the Jackboot: Recollections of Musical Life*; the story about the LPO having to spend the night on the floor in ARP blankets is on p. 386.

Anyone interested in Vaughan Williams will want to start with the biography by his widow Ursula, *R.V.W.: A Biography of Ralph Vaughan Williams*. Ursula Vaughan Williams also contributed a preface to VW's own collection of writings, *National Music and Other Essays*. I am grateful to Claire Rauter for showing me the correspondence between Vaughan Williams and her husband Ferdinand Rauter. The Rauter–VW correspondence is quoted in Alain Frogley (ed.), *Vaughan Williams Studies*, chapter 4, 'Vaughan Williams, Germany, and the German tradition: a view from the letters' by Hugh Cobbe; chapter 7 by Jeffrey Richards deals with VW's wartime film music, including (in some detail) that for *49th Parallel*.

Part IV   Culture at Peace
Chapter 12   Three Wise Men
The transition from war to post-war is covered in many books. See, for example, the latter part of Angus Calder's *The People's War: Britain 1939–1945*, Paul Addison's *Now the War is Over* and Peter Hennessy's *Never Again: Britain: 1945–51*. An excellent introduction to the atmosphere of the era can be gleaned from the essays in Michael Sissons and Philip French (eds), *Age of Austerity 1945–1951*. Calder's comment about planning becoming a universal craze is from *The People's War*, p. 545, at the end of a section dealing with the Beveridge Report. My quotations from F. A. Hayek's *The Road to Serfdom* are from the Phoenix edition published by the University of Chicago

Press, with a new preface by Hayek, in 1976. The letter from Margaret Thatcher is reproduced in John Raybould (ed.), *Hayek: A Commemorative Album* (Adam Smith Institute, 1998), p. 101. Hayek's principal writings (in addition to *The Road to Serfdom*) include *The Constitution of Liberty*, the three-volume *Law, Legislation and Liberty* and *Economic Freedom*. His *Collected Works* are being systematically published (by Routledge in the UK and the University of Chicago Press in the USA). Volume 9 (*Contra Keynes and Cambridge Essays, Correspondence*) is edited by Bruce Caldwell, to whom I am grateful for constructive criticism of an early draft of my comments on Hayek.

Much of the biographical material about Karl Popper is from his 'intellectual autobiography' *Unended Quest*. Malachi Haim Hacohen, author of *Karl Popper – the Formative Years*, has studied earlier drafts of *Unended Quest* and shows how the published version, if not untruthful, was in some ways misleading and self-serving. Hacohen's book is particularly valuable on Popper's ambivalent relationship with the Vienna Circle, and he writes with great insight about Popper's relationship with Hayek. He also shows how world events and the onset of war redirected Popper's attention from natural to social science and from the philosophy of logic to political philosophy. 'Deprived of one *Heimat*,' writes Hacohen (p. 522), 'Popper created another: cosmopolitan philosophy.' Hacohen rightly holds Popper in the highest regard as a thinker of rare originality. But he is not blind to his hero's faults. Carnap, one of the leading philosophers in the Vienna Circle, helped promote Popper's work; but in later years, says Hacohen (p. 212), Popper 'showed him . . . that no good deed goes unpunished [and] pursued him mercilessly, winning one battle after another, pretending all along that truth alone, not rivalry, was at stake'.

Popper's notorious confrontation with Wittgenstein lies at the core of *Wittgenstein's Poker* by David Edmonds and John Eidinow. Something of Popper's personality and style of argument can be gleaned from an interview with Bryan Magee recorded in December 1970 for a BBC Radio series of conversations with philosophers. The recording has been preserved in the BBC Sound Archives; edited texts were published in Magee's *Modern British Philosophy*. The quotation from Sir Peter Medawar is from another BBC programme presented by Bryan Magee: a homage to *Popper at Seventy* broadcast in 1972. Magee's *Popper* provides a good introduction to the man and his work; for an excellent and more recent *tour d'horizon*, see the Phoenix paperback by Frederic Raphael. Popper's most influential works are *The Poverty of Historicism* and *The Open Society and its Enemies*. For an Englishman's view of the Vienna Circle, see A. J. Ayer, *Part of My Life*, pp. 128–34; the story of Ayer and Isaiah Berlin discussing 'Poor Popper' is on p. 194. John Watkins's and Kenneth Minogue's memories of Popper are from their respective chapters in Joan Abse (ed.), *My LSE*. Popper's influence on his students could be immense. Sir Terence Beckett, former Chairman of Ford and Director General of the Confederation of British Industries, told me how the principle of the falsifiability of hypotheses, which he learned from Popper, profoundly influenced his managerial style throughout his career in industry.

For Gombrich's personal reminiscences, see *A Lifelong Interest*. Also the autobiographical sketch from *Topics of Our Time* (Phaidon, 1991) included as the first chapter in Richard Woodfield (ed.), *The Essential Gombrich*. It is from these (and my own conversation with him) that I have chiefly quoted. I heard about the origins of *The Story of Art* from both Gombrich himself and from Elly Miller (née Horovitz) who, half a century before, had recommended that her father publish it. The book itself, still – as ever – in print, is available from Phaidon. A prolific writer of essays and reviews, Gombrich also produced a number of highly influential scholarly books, chief among them *Art and Illusion: A Study in the Psychology of Pictorial Representation* (Phaidon, 1960); his three 'Studies in the Art of the Renaissance': *Norm and Form* (Phaidon, 1966), *Symbolic Images* (Phaidon, 1972) and *The Heritage of Apelles* (Phaidon, 1976); and *The Sense of Order: A Study in the Psychology of Decorative Art* (Phaidon, 1979).

Chapter 13   The Wolf Gang

For the origins of the Royal Opera, see Harold Rosenthal, *Two Centuries of Opera at Covent Garden* and Frances Donaldson, *The Royal Opera House in the Twentieth Century*, both of which tend to see the ROH through a somewhat privileged, roseate glow. For a harder critical edge allied to the latest research, see Norman Lebrecht, *Covent Garden: The Untold Story*. On Webster, see Montague Haltrecht, *The Quiet Showman: Sir David Webster and the Royal Opera House*; Boosey and Hawkes's manifesto is quoted in Haltrecht, pp. 51–2. See also the final volume of Skidelsky's biography of Keynes, *passim*. For Beecham's broadsides against Rankl, see Haltrecht, pp. 107–9 and Lebrecht, pp. 107–10. Rankl's appointment was officially as 'Musical Director', a title that, by Solti's time, was commonly abbreviated to 'Music Director', the term in use since.

The history of the BBC Third Programme (later Radio Three) is recounted in Humphrey Carpenter, *The Envy of the World: Fifty Years of the BBC Third Programme and Radio 3*. The quotation from Haley is on p. 9. The complaint about 'third-rate poets' and 'Bloomsbury intellectuals' (by Austin Welland of the *Sunday Mercury*) is quoted on p. 51, while the laments about the low standards of British music-making are from pp. 18 and 19. The quotation from Mátyás Seiber is from pp. 94–5.

For the origins and early history of the Edinburgh Festival, see George Bruce, *Festival in the North: The Story of the Edinburgh Festival* and chapters 12 and 13 of Rudolf Bing, *5000 Nights at the Opera*. Bing recalls his first impressions of Edinburgh on pp. 93 and 110. For the all-important conversations between Bing and Henry Harvey Wood, see the latter's article in *The Scotsman*, 7 August 1947, quoted in Bruce, pp. 17–18, and Bing (who calls him Harry Harvey-Wood), pp. 112–13.

Material about the Amadeus Quartet is largely drawn from interviews and research originally undertaken for my own book, *The Amadeus Quartet: The Men and the Music*, plus subsequent interviews with Norbert Brainin, Siegmund Nissel and Susi Rózsa Lovett. See also Muriel Nissel's memoir, *Married to the Amadeus: Life with a String Quartet*.

Glock describes his 1947 tour of Europe and his Directorship of the Bryanston and Dartington Summer Schools in *Notes in Advance*, pp. 46–77.

Chapter 14   Bruised Veterans of the Totalitarian Age

There are many memoirs of the atmosphere in London during and just after the war. The 'Fitzrovia' of Dylan Thomas became legendary, a world Michael Hamburger knew well as a young man. Hamburger's recollections of the Soho of Lucian Freud and Tambimuttu are in *String of Beginnings, passim*. George Weidenfeld writes about his contacts with the various governments in exile in *Remembering My Good Friends*, pp. 106–14. Andrew Sinclair attempts a portrait of British literary life as a whole during these years in *War Like a Wasp: The Lost Decade of the 'Forties*. Two books that incorporate artistic and cultural life as a whole – and several further decades of history – are Bryan Appleyard's *The Pleasures of Peace* and Robert Hewison's *Culture and Consensus*. Both consider the cultural contributions and critiques of Eliot and Leavis.

Alfred Kerr is transparently disguised as the wise father in *When Hitler Stole Pink Rabbit* by his daughter Judith Kerr, and is evocatively described by Weidenfeld in *Remembering My Good Friends*, p. 106. For a longer English-language consideration of the life and work of Alfred Kerr after his arrival in exile, see the article by Deborah Vietor-Englander in William Abbey et al. (eds), *Between Two Languages: German-speaking Exiles in Great Britain, 1933-45*. In the following article, Richard Dove (one of the editors of the anthology) considers the problems faced by German-speaking novelists writing in English. Richard Dove's book *Journey of No Return* examines in detail the life and work of five German-language writers in exile: Alfred Kerr, Max Herrmann-Niesse, Karl Otten, Robert Neumann and Stefan Zweig. Each a writer of great talent, Dove concludes somewhat poignantly (p. 265) that none 'made any lasting mark on English literature'.

The definitive (and exhaustively documented) biography of Arthur Koestler is David Cesarani's *Arthur Kostler: The Homeless Mind* which includes a comprehensive Koestler bibliography. Weidenfeld's description of Koestler (who liked 'intellectual cockfights') is from *Remembering My Good Friends*, p. 152. Koestler left a great deal of autobiographical writing, notably *Arrow in the Blue* and *The Invisible Writing*, while a novel like *Darkness at Noon* is clearly driven by its author's searing personal experiences. Koestler's belief that the Attlee government reinforced British insularity and that the division between 'Socialism' and 'capitalism' was obsolete is most persuasively asserted in *The Trail of the Dinosaur*. For the hypothesis that the Jews were derived from the Khazars, see *The Thirteenth Tribe*, while Koestler's theories about creativity and 'bisociation' are developed in *The Act of Creation*. For Koestler's ambivalence about feeling British, see the epilogue to *The Invisible Writing*. It is here that he refers to the 'human climate' of England as 'particularly congenial and soothing – a kind of Davos for internally bruised veterans of the totalitarian age'. In an article in the *Observer* on 10 February 1963, Koestler acknowledges feeling patriotically British whenever he goes 'abroad'. But he uses the article to launch a fierce critique of his adopted nation for its insularity, and the article led to a collection of essays edited by Koestler entitled *Suicide of a Nation?* As Cesarani says, Koestler 'never let himself feel totally at ease even in England'.

Chapter 15 Making Contact
Koestler's despair in discovering that his original metaphor was the native-speaker's cliché is from the epilogue to *The Invisible Writing*. For Michael Hamburger's reflections on writing in both English and German, see *String of Beginnings*, pp. 291–2.

Eva Figes's view of her writing as 'more Modernistic' is from the BBC Radio 3 programme *Private Passions*, broadcast on 15 September 2000. Both Judith Kerr and Eva Figes are quoted on the ambivalent feeling each experienced as an émigré writer in English by Marion Berghahn in *German-Jewish Refugees in England,* pp. 98–100. In an article from the *Observer* (11 June 1978), Figes is quoted as saying that 'my novels have more in common with post-war writing in Europe than with anything being produced in England . . . After the Second World War life, as far as European writers were concerned, could never be the same again, and prose had to reflect that convulsive change. Only England, locked in her dream of past greatness, believed that everything would go on as before. But I am a European survivor, wrestling with a different reality.'

Novels containing characters who are refugees from Nazism (or Fascism) include Philip Larkin's *A Girl in Winter*, Angus Wilson's *No Laughing Matter*, Margaret Drabble's *The Radiant Way* and Iris Murdoch's *Under the Net*. John Bayley's tart comments about Canetti (the 'Mage') are in *Iris*, pp. 176–81.

Andrew Sinclair devotes considerable space to the state of publishing, the rise and fall of the little magazines etc. in Britain during and after the war, in *War Like a Wasp*. His comment about books being put to the torch is on p. 58. Sir Stanley Unwin's account of the relationship with Horovitz is in his autobiography, *The Truth About a Publisher*, pp. 223–7. The outlines of the Phaidon story are in Nigel Spivey's *Phaidon 1923–98*, while a collection of essays about Horovitz, Goldscheider and the Phaidon Press can be found in a special issue of *Visual Resources* (vol. XV, no. 3, 1999, Harwood Academic Publishers). My account of the origins of Phaidon is also based on extensive conversations with members of the Horovitz family. My accounts of the origins of Thames and Hudson and of Weidenfeld and Nicolson, similarly, are in part based on conversations with Eva Neurath and Lord Weidenfeld – as well as on Weidenfeld's autobiography, *Remembering My Good Friends*, especially chapter 6. Weidenfeld's description of himself as an 'excitable flamboyant Austrian émigré' is on p. 119, his comment about himself and Nicolson lacking business training on p. 125. The quotation about Israel Sieff is from Weidenfeld, pp. 137–8. For Nigel Nicolson's memories of the origins of W & N, see his memoir *Long Life*, chapter 7; the quotations are from p. 187. While working on this book, I learned much from conversations with others with experience in publishing, notably Dieter Pevsner, T. G. (Tom) Rosenthal and Thomas Maschler. I also spoke on the phone a number of times with André Deutsch who, in the event, proved too ill to see me and sadly died shortly thereafter. A portrait of André Deutsch by someone close to him for half a century is provided by Diana

Athill's memoir, *Stet*; see, particularly, her account of Deutsch's painful relationship with Tom Rosenthal, pp. 120–8. For more on émigré publishers, see the chapter by Uwe Westphal in Werner Mosse (co-ordinating ed.), *Second Chance*, pp. 195–208.

For David Astor, see his biography by Richard Cockett, *David Astor and the Observer*. Astor is described as 'probably the only real idealist to edit or own a . . . newspaper this century' on p. 135. William Clark's comment that 'more than half of the editorial group was German or Central European' is on p. 144, while Astor's guiding ethic as 'trying to do the opposite of what Hitler would have done' is quoted on p. 133. Astor had an important influence on the lives of many of those discussed in this book. See, for example, the frequent references to him in David Cesarani's biography of Koestler, or in the biography of Ernst Schumacher, *Alias Papa*, by Schumacher's daughter Barbara Wood.

Part V: Towards a New Synthesis
Chapter 16: Metropolitan and Micropolitan
Weidenfeld's comments on Astor's *Observer* are in *Remembering My Good Friends*, pp. 125–7. The quotation from Arthur Marwick is from *British Society Since 1945*, p. 101. Noel Annan agreed with Marwick about the insularity of British intellectual life after the war. British creative writers, thought Annan, 'were exhausted by the war'. Indeed, the war, he said in a lapidary statement, 'had cut Britain off from the continental experience – the experience of being occupied by the Nazis' (*Our Age*, p. 336).

For the BBC's appointment of Sir Malcolm Sargent, see Nicholas Kenyon, *The BBC Symphony Orchestra*; the quotation about the inadvisability of appointing a foreign Chief Conductor is on p. 228. Kenneth Clark's use of 'metropolitan' and 'micropolitan' was from a lecture delivered in Aldeburgh at the time of *Billy Budd* (see Harewood, *The Tongs and the Bones*, p. 132).

The best guide to the Festival of Britain is the official catalogue. Also the essays in Mary Banham and Bevis Hillier (eds), *A Tonic to the Nation: The Festival of Britain, 1951*, which accompanied the exhibition held at the Victoria and Albert Museum to mark the Festival's twenty-fifth anniversary; the quotations from Hugh Casson are from his contribution to the book. Andrew Sinclair's comment about the architects being released from working on Nissen huts is from *War Like a Wasp*, p. 272. For the contribution of some of the émigré designers and architects, see Charlotte Benton, *A Different World: Emigré Architects in Britain 1928–1958*. Benton writes helpfully about Peter Moro. An interview with Moro recorded in 1995 is kept in the Royal Festival Hall archives; see also his unpublished memoir, *A Sense of Proportion* (available in the RIBA Library). My descriptions of the Festival of Britain and the Coronation are coloured by my memories of both events (and of attending the Royal Festival Hall for the first time a month after it opened). For more on the Festival of Britain, see Michael Frayn's famous essay, describing the people who created the Festival as 'herbivores' (as opposed to 'carnivores' like Churchill) in Michael Sissons and Philip French (eds), *Age of Austerity 1945–1951*. Also Robert Hewison's *Culture and Consensus* (especially pp. 57–64) and the final chapter of Paul Addison's *Now the War is Over*. Robert Hughes writes of Lucian Freud's *Interior in Paddington* in *Lucian Freud: Paintings*, p. 15. Pevsner's bitter-sweet comments on the British penchant for being behind the times are in *The Englishness of English Art*, p. 196.

Much of the material in this chapter about Benjamin Britten is derived from, or confirmed by, Humphrey Carpenter's *Benjamin Britten: A Biography*. Carpenter describes Erwin Stein reducing the full score of *Peter Grimes* to vocal scores on p. 216, and goes on to quote Donald Mitchell on Stein's background and his importance to Britten. Marion (Stein) Thorpe was one of many who told me about her father's relationship with the composer. Lord Harewood writes touchingly of his former father-in-law in *The Tongs and the Bones*; see especially pp. 105–6 and (on Stein's involvement in the creation of *Billy Budd*), pp. 130–1. For the proposal, by Harewood and Stein, that Britten become Music Director of Covent Garden, see pp. 133–4.

Hans Keller's advocacy of Britten's work and subsequent friendship with the composer was described to me by (among others) his widow Milein Cosman. I knew Keller during his later years at the BBC and afterwards, though not as well as people like William Glock and Donald Mitchell who have written evocatively about him, or producers who worked alongside him at the BBC such as Misha Donat and Robert Layton. Donald Mitchell wrote movingly about his friend after Keller's death; 'Hans Keller (1919–1985)' and 'Remembering Hans Keller' are both included in his collection of essays *Cradles of the New* (pp. 457-60 and 461-80). Like all who knew Keller, I have the clearest memory of his voice, personality and *modus operandi*. He was always very kind to me, though it is easy to see how his temperament and style could have irritated some of his senior colleagues (such as Stephen Hearst). For an introduction to Keller's writing, see the essays in *Music, Closed Societies and Football*. Glock, in *Notes in Advance*, quotes Keller (p. 103) as saying that Gershwin was a better composer than Webern ('as though in purpose and ideals they inhabited the same universe!' he adds with some exasperation); on p. 104 Glock acknowledges that some of Keller's pronouncements had 'the authority of proverbs'. Carpenter writes of Keller's early advocacy of Britten, and of his collaboration with Donald Mitchell, on pp. 315–17 of his biography of Britten. Britten's final major composition, his third string quartet, was written for the Amadeus Quartet and dedicated to Hans Keller. For Keller's years at the BBC see chapter 18.

The story of *Gloriana* is told at some length by both Carpenter and Harewood. Harewood's report of the post-*Gloriana* 'broadside' Britten received from Pears is in *The Tongs and the Bones*, p. 138. Britten's departure from Boosey and Hawkes after the death of Stein (in part, ironically, because he was insufficiently nurtured by another Viennese refugee, Ernst Roth) is told in Carpenter, pp. 427–8.

Chapter 17   The Angry, the Radical and the Modern
Weidenfeld's memories of 1953 are in *Remembering My Good Friends*, especially pp. 234–5, 264. Many of the principal

literary and theatrical figures in the 1950s (e.g. Kingsley Amis, John Osborne, Peter Hall and Kenneth Tynan) have left letters, diaries and memoirs of this pivotal period. For the wider story of British theatre during these years, see John Elsom's *Post-war British Theatre* and, for a more recent study, Dominic Shellard's *British Theatre Since the War*. See also Richard Eyre's *Changing Stages*, written with Nicholas Wright to accompany a television series about British theatre in the twentieth century.

Much of the material about Joan Littlewood is derived from her own memoir, *Joan's Book*. Fräulein Fligg's movement class is described on pp. 68–9. Littlewood devotes a special appendix to Laban (pp. 771–5). The story of Laban showing people how to 'lift and swing' when loading a truck is on pp. 181–2. A recent biography of Laban, by one who knew and worked with him, is Valerie Preston-Dunlop's *Rudolf Laban: An Extraordinary Life*; this (like Preston-Dunlop's many journal articles) paints a sympathetic portrait of a gifted but pained man who – unlike most of the émigrés featured in this book – co-operated willingly for a while with the Nazis. See also John Hodgson, *Mastering Movement*. Laban's work is continued to this day at the Laban Centre, a dance academy in south London.

The best introduction to Nikolaus Pevsner is his own writings, especially perhaps his *Outline of European Architecture* and *Pioneers of the Modern Movement* (later revised and reissued as *Pioneers of Modern Design*). To the general public Pevsner is best known for the volumes in his 'Buildings of England' series (currently being updated and reissued). The story of how Allen Lane accepted this ambitious project is told in Pevsner's own words in Steve Hare (ed.), *Penguin Portrait: Allen Lane and the Penguin Editors, 1935–70*, p. 210.

The texts of Pevsner's 1955 Reith Lectures (as subsequently revised) are available in *The Englishness of English Art*. Here his comments on monosyllables ('macs and vacs' etc.) are on p. 17 and the moist British climate on pp. 18–19, 173–4 and 198–9. The predilection of English artists for small scale and water colours is on p. 169, the subdued characteristics of English portraiture (which 'speaks in a low voice') on p. 79. Pevsner introduces the distinction between the 'spirit of an age' and 'national character' on p. 21, illustrating the interaction between the two as applied to Hogarth and Blake on p. 193. For the Celtic love of curves and Pevsner's views about the relationship between English 'racial types' and English art see pp. 197-8. His central thesis, about the 'polarities' that lie at the core of Englishness, first appears on p. 24; the polarity between the 'rational' and 'irrational' in English art underlies much that Pevsner says throughout the book and is spelled out on pp. 199 *et seq.* 'No Bach, no Beethoven' is on p. 80, the decline of English painting on p. 205, Pevsner's views on Buckingham Palace on p. 179 and the 'fancy-dress ball' aspect of Victorian architecture on p. 50. England is described as the nation that was once 'the unchallenged pioneer of innovation' on p. 195; the recommendation that it should replan its city centres 'to make them efficient as well as agreeable' is on p. 186. The belief that 'England seems predestined to play a leading part in modern architecture' is on p. 194, while England's 'lack of sufficiently bold planning' is on p. 196. The examples of creative people with foreign roots flourishing in British soil are on p. 198.

Philip Johnson's assessment of Pevsner (like those quoted by Hugh Casson and Alec Clifton-Taylor) is from a symposium of tributes to Pevsner shortly after his death in the October 1983 edition of the *Architectural Review*. Colin MacInnes wrote an article on 'The Englishness of Dr Pevsner' (*Twentieth Century*, January 1960), in which he said that Pevsner preserved the rare and enriched dual vision of a 'thoroughly inside outsider'. Pevsner's 'Modernism' is contrasted (overmuch, I would say) with the more traditional English view of art and culture in Timothy Mowl, *Stylistic Cold Wars: Betjeman versus Pevsner*. The most forthright scourge of Pevsner has probably been David Watkin, whose *Morality and Architecture* was updated and reissued in 2001. Ian Buruma devotes a chapter to Pevsner in *Voltaire's Coconuts*. I am grateful to Pevsner's son Dieter Pevsner, and to Susie Harries, for some of the biographical detail I have included. For an attractive symposium about Pevsner (including material by MacInnes, Buruma and Dieter Pevsner) see Simon Bradley and Bridget Cherry, *The Buildings of England: A Celebration*.

Tristram Hillier's comments about the significance of 'Unit One' are from a 1978 letter he wrote to Charles Harrison, quoted in Peter Lasko's article in Werner Mosse (ed.), *Second Chance*, p. 258, footnote no. 13. The quotations from Herbert Read about 'Unit One' and his group of artists in and around Hampstead in the 1930s are from an article in *Apollo* (September 1962), reproduced in the catalogue to 'Art in Britain 1930–40', an exhibition held at the Marlborough Gallery in March–April 1965. For a view of Read's pivotal importance in helping the Modern movement (and émigré artists) towards respectability in Britain, see James King, *The Last Modern: A Life of Herbert Read*.

Hans Hess (1908–75) was raised in Erfurt in a home frequented by leading German artists of the post-World War One era. It was partly due to his influence (and to the bequest of another refugee, Rosa Schapire) that the Leicester Museum, where Hess worked from 1944 to 1947, consolidated its reputation for modern German art. Hess went on to become Curator of the York Art Gallery and Director of the York Festival, moving in 1967 to become Reader in the History of Art at the University of Sussex.

The catalogue of the 1986 'Art in Exile' exhibition at Arkwright Road provides information about many of the émigré artists.

Fred Uhlman gives a subtle and sympathetic description of Schwitters, whom he befriended when they were interned together, in *The Making of an Englishman*, pp. 234-9. Schwitters's portrait of Uhlman is reproduced on the back cover of Uhlman's *Reunion*. An exhibition of Schwitters's work at the Hatton Gallery, University of Newcastle, in April–May 1999 ('No Socks: Kurt Schwitters and the *Merzbarn*') was accompanied by a 'Newsletter' (BALTIC Newsletter no. 4) containing a number of authoritative articles about Schwitters's life and work. See also J. Elderfield, *Kurt Schwitters*. For Kokoschka, see Susanne Keegan's *The Eye of God: A Life of Oskar Kokoschka*. The young English painter who came to Kokoschka for instruction was Ishbel McWhirter (who quoted Kokoschka about eyes caressing the sitter in a BBC programme assessing Keegan's new biography of the painter). The Herbert Read comment is quoted in Keegan, p. 254.

A useful guide to the architecture and design of Lubetkin and others is provided by Charlotte Benton's *A Different World: Emigré Architects in Britain 1928–1958*. The introduction and development of Modernism in British architecture and design was the subject of the exhibition 'Modern Britain 1929–39' held at London's Design Museum in 1999; see the catalogue, edited by James Peto and Donna Loveday (commissioning ed. Alan Powers). For a detailed study of the work of Lubetkin, see J. Allan, *Berthold Lubetkin: Architecture and the Tradition of Progress*. Lubetkin's enigmatic and sometimes difficult personality (including his mid-career decision to quit architecture for farming, and his repression of his Jewish background) is chronicled in the memoir by his daughter, Louise Kehoe, *In This Dark House*.

Chapter 18   Media and Messengers
Much of the material in this chapter is based on interviews with some of the principal personalities discussed (notably Karel Reisz, Ken Adam, Stephen Hearst and Martin Esslin) and on my own knowledge and memories of film and broadcasting in the 1960s and 1970s. The best way of gaining insight into the work of Reisz and Adam, a form of research I greatly enjoyed and thoroughly recommend, is of course to see their films. The catalogue of the 1999 Serpentine Gallery (London) exhibition of the work of Ken Adam was entitled 'Moonraker, Strangelove and other celluloid dreams' and was edited by David Sylvester.

Humphrey Carpenter writes about Stephen Hearst's tenure as Controller of Radio 3 (and Hans Keller's presence at the BBC) in *The Envy of the World*, especially pp. 267–96 *passim*. For more on Keller, see *Hans Keller and the BBC*, a PhD thesis by Alison Mary Garnham (Goldsmiths College, University of London, 1999). This is a thoroughly documented and engaging survey written under the supervision of Keller expert Christopher Wintle and is to be published by Ashgate Publishing Ltd. Garnham is particularly good on Keller's preoccupation with a theory (the 'Unity of Contrasting themes') and a method (what

Keller called 'Functional Analysis') as ways of elucidating what lies at the heart of 'great' music. Both, she suggests, derive in part from Keller's interest in Freudian psychoanalysis and its concern with the adjustment between apparently irreconcilable forces. For Glock's memories of Keller, see chapter 16, above, and the accompanying notes. One of Martin Esslin's successors as BBC Radio's Head of Drama, John Tydeman, is quoted by Carpenter (p. 281) as saying that the Mid-European 'mafia' – Hearst, Esslin and Keller (and the Hungarian George Fischer) – were 'much greater supporters of British culture than the British were!' For 'Broadcasting in the Seventies' and the letter to *The Times* signed by Keller and others (including myself), see Carpenter pp. 252–8. Sir John Drummond, in *Tainted by Experience*, writes of BBC arts policy, programmes and personalities in characteristically forthright fashion, while Peter Adam's memories of making arts programmes for BBC Television are vividly evoked in his autobiography *Not Drowning But Waving*. Drummond writes (p. 177) with insight and affection about Hearst, his former boss in television and later his predecessor as Controller of Radio 3. Though the two men clearly did not agree about everything, Drummond admired Hearst's 'sense of aspiration', his insatiable and widespread enthusiasms – and the fact that he 'wrote and spoke the English language better than most of us'. Hearst, says Drummond, 'worried away at prejudice and ignorance'. He was 'a true internationalist' who recognised at the same time the value of what was distinctively British.

Chapter 19: Diminishing Returns
For the life of E. F. Schumacher see the biography by his daughter Barabara Wood, which she calls *Alias Papa*. The best source for Schumacher's ideas is *Small Is Beautiful*. Schumacher's 1968 lecture, outlining the belief in bigness that he imbibed in the Germany of his youth and his latter-day anxiety about the 'idolatry of giantism', is reproduced in *Small Is Beautiful* as chapter 5 ('A Question of Size'). Schumacher's ideas were the inspiration that led to the establishment of the Schumacher Society, Schumacher College (at Dartington Hall, Devon) and the Intermediate Technology Group.

The quotation from Dominic Shellard about the growing number of small-scale theatrical venues in London is from *British Theatre Since the War*, p. 148.

Sir John Tooley's comments about Claus Moser and the Covent Garden Board are from Tooley's book *In House*, p. 218. Much of the detailed material about Moser and Sir John Burgh is derived from my interviews with them and with people who have known and worked with them. A further link between Moser and Lord Hamlyn may be detected in the British Museum Reading Room where, since the reopening in 2000, the general public can wander freely and browse through the 12,000-volume Paul Hamlyn Library containing books touching on all aspects of the Museum's collections.

PART VI   Culture Concluded
Chapter 20   History Resurgent

Theodor Adorno wrote that 'to write poetry after Auschwitz is barbaric' (*Prisms*, MIT, 1981, p. 34). Nigel Nicolson's comments about Weidenfeld are from *Long Life*, p. 190. Hans Keller's description of his escape from the Nazis, originally a broadcast, is reproduced as the first chapter ('Vienna, 1938') in *Music, Closed Societies and Football*. For Anita Lasker-Wallfisch's account, see her book *Inherit the Truth 1939–1945* (also based on broadcasts). Albi Rosenthal writes about his life and work in *Obiter Scripta*.

The scientific migration from Hitler is described by Jean Medawar and David Pyke in *Hitler's Gift*.

There is no single book encapsulating the development of psychiatry and psychoanalysis in Britain after the war and, to my knowledge, none at all documenting its wider cultural influence. Psychoanalysis was, of course, well established in Britain before the arrival of the Hitler émigrés, its insights eagerly absorbed by some of the Bloomsbury set. Virginia Woolf's brother and sister-in-law Adrian and Karin Stephen, with James Strachey (brother of Lytton Strachey) and his wife, were instrumental in Melanie Klein's move to London. Ernest Jones's life of Freud concludes with Freud's arrival, and death, in London and the story is taken further in two studies of his daughter Anna, by Elizabeth Young-Bruehl and Rose Edgcumbe. Joseph Schwartz, in *Cassandra's Daughter*, has a chapter entitled 'Breakthrough in Britain' in which he outlines the Melanie Klein–Anna Freud controversy and the subsequent split in the profession into Kleinians, Anna Freudians and Independents. The Melanie Klein–Anna Freud controversy has been thoroughly documented by Pearl King and Riccardo Steiner. For some of the repercussions of the 'emigration' of psychoanalysis, especially to Britain, see Steiner's two books *It's a New Kind of Diaspora* and *Tradition, Change, Creativity*.

Freud in Exile, edited by Edward Timms and Naomi Segal, contains a number of valuable articles, including Timms's own elucidation of the special relevance of psychoanalysis to the experience of exile. In a revealing chapter in Werner Mosse (ed.), *Second Chance*, Mitchell Ash outlines the migration of Central European psychologists and psychoanalysts to Britian – and reminds us how few there were. For a dissident (behavioural, as opposed to psychoanalytic) perspective, see Hans Eysenck's somewhat combative autobiography, *Rebel With a Cause*.

Laurence Olivier recounts his visit to Ernest Jones in *Confessions of an Actor*, p. 109. On pp. 112–13, Olivier tells amusingly how he and director Tyrone Guthrie were impressed by Jones's idea that Iago, in *Othello*, was motivated by unconscious love for his leader – an interpretation they couldn't, however, get their nonchalant Iago, Ralph Richardson, to accept. Martin Esslin has written about both Beckett (see *The Theatre of the Absurd* – a phrase Esslin coined) and Pinter (in *The Peopled Wound*); the most recent study of Pinter is Michael Billington's *The Life and Work of Harold Pinter*. The critical works of Adrian Stokes were edited by Lawrence Gowing (three vols, Thames and Hudson, 1978); the best introduction to Stokes's writings is probably *The Image in Form* edited by Richard Wollheim. For Wollheim's own explorations of the relationship between art and the mind of the viewer, see *Painting as an Art*. Anthony Storr's books include *The Dynamics of Creation* and *Music and the Mind*. Key feminist texts produced in post-war Britain include Germaine Greer's *The Female Eunuch* and Juliet Mitchell's *Psychoanalysis and Feminism*.

For the work and educational ideas of Kurt Hahn, see H. Rohrs (ed.), Kurt Hahn: *A Life Span in Education and Politics*; see also chapter 3 above.

Matthew Bourne achieved further *réclame* in 2001 as the choreographer of the Royal National Theatre's production of *My Fair Lady*.

On émigré historians, see the autobiographical essays by many of them in Peter Alter (ed.), *Out of the Third Reich: Refugee Historians in Post-war Britain*; the quotation from John Grenville is on p. 69. I am indebted to Peter Pulzer for a stimulating and helpful conversation about the impact of the Hitler émigrés upon the study of history in post-war Britain. Pulzer suggested that the principal impact was probably in subject-matter (more German and comparative history, for example) rather than in style or approach.

The many books and articles by Eric Hobsbawm and Sir Geoffrey Elton speak for themselves. My comments on Hobsbawm are partly derived from a long conversation we had in 1998 and my subsequent article about him and his work published in the January 1999 edition of *History Today*. Hobsbawm's Columbus Quincentenary lecture is reproduced as the final chapter in an anthology of his essays collected under the title *Uncommon People*, while his Walter Neurath Lecture was published by Thames and Hudson in 1998 as *Behind the Times*. Noel Annan writes about Hobsbawm in *Our Age*, pp. 361-3.

As an undergraduate at Cambridge, I was gripped by the lectures and writings of Geoffrey Elton, and got to know him reasonably well in later years when he participated in several of my BBC programmes. Elton could be notoriously rebarbative towards professional colleagues and rivals, but kindness itself to those who were clearly neither. Part of what I have written about Elton was first published in a review of the work of David Starkey, one of Elton's Ph.D. students, in the January 2000 edition of *History Today*. For a further critique of Elton, see John Kenyon, *The History Men*, pp. 219-24; also, Noel Annan's *The Dons*, pp. 92-7. Elton's approach, says Kenyon, has sometimes been described as 'teutonic' (p. 219). Kenyon compares Elton in some ways to another, earlier émigré historian who specialised in English political history, Sir Lewis Namier. Both were natural conservatives, says Kenyon, suggesting how Elton's background led him to his belief that a strong state was the best guarantee of liberty (p. 223). For more on the Hitler émigrés and British historiography, see the chapter by Christhard Hoffmann in Werner Mosse (ed.), *Second Chance*, pp. 153–73. *Second Chance* also includes chapters about British Jews of German background who entered politics and the law.

For the work of Hans Schmoller et al. at Penguin Books, see the article by Justin Howes and Pauline Paucker, 'German Jews and the Graphic Arts' in the 1989 Leo Baeck Institute Year Book (published for the Institute by Secker and Warburg). Salman Rushdie spoke about the importance to him of Canetti's *Auto-da-Fé* in the BBC Radio 3 programme *What Books I Please* broadcast in November 1981. Colin Dexter recalled Hoffnung, and the influences upon Dexter's TV creation, the Wagner-loving Inspector Morse, in the BBC Radio 4 programme *Dear Teacher* broadcast in March 1994. Sir Simon Rattle wrote of his youthful enthusiasm for Hoffnung's cartoons in a Foreword to the reissue of *The Maestro* in 2000.

Chapter 21   Messianic Agnostics
Hans Keller's theory about the nature of good music was most clearly expounded in his lecture on 'Moon Music' delivered at the Aldeburgh Festival in 1971. Music, said Keller, is too often like the moon in that people can see whatever they want to see in it. 'Moonless' music – that which really communicates – is music that incorporates the tension between the expected and unexpected.

Isaac Deutscher's list of great Jewish 'heretics', and the quotation about living on the margins and in nooks and crannies, are from *The Non-Jewish Jew and Other Essays*, pp. 26–7. Lord Jakobovits told me his views about Marx, Freud and Einstein when we discussed some of the issues raised in this book in spring and summer 1999, shortly before his death. George Steiner writes of having published 'on ancient Greek literature . . . linguistics and aesthetics', of cows having fields and the importance of 'passions in motion' in *Errata: An Examined Life*, p. 155. Conrad Black's description of Weidenfeld as the 'personification of European civilisation' is from Nigel Nicolson's *Long Life*, p. 190. For Steiner's 'distrust of theory', see *Errata*, p. 5, while the burning bush metaphor appears on p. 22. The 'proud Judaism' of Steiner's father is described as 'messianic agnosticism' on p. 9. Isaiah Berlin's biographer, Michael Ignatieff, writes of Berlin's indefatigable liberalism, his 'moral pluralism' – and his inclination to quote Kant to the effect that 'out of the crooked timber of humanity no straight thing was ever made'.

Koestler's genial dismissal of the 'lotus-eating disposition' of the English and their 'contempt for ideologies' is from the epilogue to *The Invisible Writing*. His penchant for cold baths and his regret that BOAC ordered American-made planes are recounted in Cesarani's biography, pp. 566–7. Ralph Koltai's comment about the British finding the visual arts somewhat suspect is from his interview on the BBC's *Desert Island Discs*, broadcast in August 1998.

For Weidenfeld's (and Nicolson's) lack of business training, see *Remembering My Good Friends*, p. 125. Elton's strictures on amateurism are from *The Practice of History*, p. 30, Pevsner's from *The Englishness of English Art*, pp. 80. A summary of the impact of the Hitler émigré art historians is contained in the chapter by one of them, Peter Lasko – a former student at, and later Director of, the Courtauld Institute – in Werner Mosse (ed.), *Second Chance*. See also the excellent biography of Anthony Blunt by Miranda Carter.

For Sir John Tooley on Solti, see *In House*, chapter 2, specifically p. 26 for Solti's incomprehension at 'English ways'. The Vicky quotation is from the BBC's *Frankly Speaking*, broadcast on 12 February 1960. John Amis's memories of Hoffnung are from his book *Amiscellany*, chapter 9; the quotations are from p. 112. See also the biography of Hoffnung by his widow, Annetta. The Hoffnung concerts at the Royal Festival Hall are described by both John Amis and Annetta Hoffnung; my memory was further refreshed by conversations with Joseph

Horovitz and Fritz Spiegl, with Annetta Hoffnung, and by listening once again to the recordings.

Elton's reflective gratitude to the English is from the preface to *The English*. Laqueur's low opinion of British cultural life in the early 1950s ('a wasteland') is from *Thursday's Child Has Far to Go*, pp. 368–74. Many of Vicky's cartoons are reproduced in Russell Davies and Liz Ottaway's *Vicky* (including, on p. 127, 'You see, they're trying to find some underdeveloped areas'). George Mikes's satirical books about the British are collected in *How To Be a Brit*. For Mikes on food (as opposed to good table manners), see pp. 20–2; on sex and hot-water bottles, p. 35. His parody of English conversation (about the weather) is on pp. 26–8. Elton devotes Part III of *The Practice of History* – over sixty pages – to the writing of history; the 'mental indolence' to be avoided is on p. 130. I knew Alfred Alexander a little, and am grateful to his widow Kitty for letting me see his papers.

For Fritz Spiegl's ruminations on the use and abuse of the English language see *The Joy of Words*. His comments about prepositions are on pp. 29–30, the Olde Englande names for musical ensembles on pp. 121–2 and French and German versions of cricketing terms on pp. 142–3. Many who knew Erich Fried and his work have spoken with great warmth about both. Michael Hamburger wrote of Fried applying 'much of his prodigious energy to helping other refugee poets, circulating their work in typescript, arranging poetry readings for them, and generally acting as a catalyst' (*String of Beginnings*, p. 291). Fried's German translation of Dylan Thomas's *Under Milk Wood* for the BBC is the subject of Steven W. Lawrie's wide-ranging essay 'Crossing Borders through the Ether' in Edward Timms and Ritchie Robertson's *Austrian Exodus*. In Ian Wallace (ed.), *German-Spaking Exiles* Lawrie has a chapter about the importance of the German language to Fried as a link with the *Heimat* of his childhood; in a later chapter, Axel Goodbody compares Fried and Hamburger as poets and translators. For Lucie Rie and Hans Coper see the books (both beautifully illustrated) by Tony Birks. George Steiner's sense of having scattered and wasted his strengths is from *Errata*, p. 153.

Michael Hamburger tells of the put-down he experienced when visiting his old school in *String of Beginnings*, pp. 330–1.

Chapter 22   Culture Concluded

The 'post-modern' *Ring*, with Wotan as traffic warden, was produced by Richard Jones at the Royal Opera House in the mid-1990s; the (predominantly) male *Swan Lake* was by Matthew Bourne's company Adventures in Motion Pictures. The portrait of Myra Hindley, by Marcus Harvey, composed of children's handprints, was shown as part of the Royal Academy of Arts' 'Sensation' show in 1997.

An excellent insight into the shifting cultural politics of the late 1990s, allied to an eloquent plea for the maintenance of artistic excellence, is provided in John Tusa's *Art Matters*.

For a generational study of the Hitler émigrés, see Marion Berghahn's *German–Jewish Refugees in England*. Berghahn examines British refugees from Nazism and their patterns of assimilation before and after emigration. Based on (anonymous) interviews, her study assesses the 'Germanness' and 'Jewishness' (or ethnic identity) of the émigrés, and ends by considering the fusion of attitudes displayed by many of the children and grandchildren of the original refugees. For a distillation of Berghahn's research, see her chapters in *Exile in Great Britain*, edited by Gerhard Hirschfeld and in Sybille Quack (ed.), *Between Sorrow and Strength: Women Refugees of the Nazi Period*. Many have noted (and Berghahn documents) the apparent paradox that, whereas German Jews often thought of themselves as fully assimilated into the wider community prior to the advent of Hitler, some of the same people, as refugees, never became similarly integrated into British life, conspicuously (some observers felt stubbornly) retaining their 'Germanness'. 'We continue to harbour a constant conscious device to become more and more "English",' writes Carl F. Flesch, 'and to be accepted by others as such' ('*Where do you come from?*', p. 199). Yet, he adds a few pages later, 'we felt and often still feel more comfortable among ourselves – choosing, as a matter of course, to consult refugee doctors, lawyers and accountants whever possible' (pp. 206–7).

Diana Athill gives a colourful account of Tom Rosenthal's acquisition (and subsequent disposal) of the publishing firm of André Deutsch in *Stet*, pp. 120–8. Rosenthal wrote at length about his Jewishness in the *Daily Telegraph* on 16 May 1998 ('Weekend Telegraph', p. 3).

The story of the cultural émigrés from Nazism to the United States has been frequently told. Important English-language books on the subject (in addition to countless individual memoirs and biographies – and Christopher Hampton's play *Tales from Hollywood*) include Mark M. Anderson (ed.), *Hitler's Exiles: Personal Stories of the Flight from Nazi Germany to America*; Stephanie Barron (ed.), *Exiles+Emigres: The Flight of European Artists from Hitler*; Laura Fermi, *Illustrious Immigrants: The Intellectual Migration from Europe, 1930–41*; Donald Fleming and Bernard Bailyn (eds), *The Intellectual Migration*; Anthony Heilbut, *Exiled in Paradise*; H. Stuart Hughes, *The Sea Change: The Migration of Social Thought, 1930–1965*; Jarrell C. Jackman and Carla M. Borden (eds), *The Muses Flee Hitler: Cultural Transfer and Adaptation, 1930–1945*; Claus-Dieter Krohn, *Intellectuals in Exile* and Friedrich Stadler and Peter Weibel (eds), *The Cultural Exodus from Austria*. See also John Russell Taylor, *Strangers in Paradise: The Hollywood Emigrés 1933–1950*.

A recent book that attempts to incorporate both the British and American experience into the pages of a single short volume is *Hitler's Loss* by Tom Ambrose.

The *locus classicus* of the hypothesis that the radical figures migrated to the USA while the more conservative settled in Britain is Perry Anderson's 1968 article, 'Components of the National Culture', in the fiftieth edition of *New Left Review*. From his Marxist perspective Anderson observes that Britain, unlike other European nations, has no coherent and militant student movement; British culture is profoundly conservative. But he notes that the traditional cultural aristocracy of Britain has been replaced by foreigners from Central and Eastern Europe (he picks out Wittgenstein, Malinowski, Namier, Popper, Berlin, Gombrich, Eysenck and Melanie Klein, adding for good measure the names of Gellner, Elton, Balogh, Hayek, Plamenatz,

Lichtheim, Steiner, Wind and Wittkower). These and others fled instability (i.e. violent change), says Anderson, gravitating to England, which they saw as 'the antipode of everything that they rejected'. They thus formed what Anderson calls a 'White' emigration, a conservative group (many of them from 'the parish-pump positivism of interbellum Vienna') who valued 'tradition, continuity and orderly empire'. Once in Britain, they 'accentuated and crystallised' the pre-existing character of British culture but did not significantly alter it. Many, including Namier, Berlin, Popper and Gombrich, were rewarded with professorships and knighthoods while the only real radical among them, the Marxist historian Isaac Deutscher, was 'reviled and ignored' by British academia. Anderson says that a parallel 'Red' emigration, containing more Germans, avoided Britain and headed for America. Here he mentions, among others, the members of the Frankfurt School as well as Fromm, Reich, Brecht, Mann [sic] and – in a footnote – Mondrian, Gropius and Moholy-Nagy. Anderson goes on to examine each of a variety of intellectual disciplines, concluding a bleak survey with a summary: 'A White emigration rolled across the flat expanse of English intellectual life,' he says, 'capturing sector after sector, until this traditionally insular culture became dominated by expatriates, of heterogeneous calibre.' As I argue in the main text, there may be some *ex post facto* truth in Anderson's polarised categories; but in practice most refugees made for wherever they happened to have a friend or relative, or prospects of work.

The USA was not the only country other than Britain in which the Hitler émigrés left a mark. Their impact may have been greatest in Britain and the USA, the nations in which the largest numbers were to settle. But parallel stories can be traced elsewhere. Thus the post-war cultural and intellectual history of Australia and Canada (and even locations as diverse as New Zealand, Hong Kong, Shanghai and Brazil) reveals the presence of prominent refugees from Nazism, e.g. the architect Harry Seidler and the immunologist Sir Gustav Nossal, both leading public figures in Australia – and, working for periods in both Australia and Canada, the conductor George Tintner. All were born in Austria.

Alfred Hitchcock's apprentice years in Germany are described in Donald Spoto's biography, *The Dark Side of Genius*, pp. 66–71; the quotation is from p. 68. Fritz Spiegl's discussion of the 'triangular traffic' is from *The Joy of Words*, p. 29. Peter Gay writes about his first post-war visit to Germany in *My German Question*, pp. 1–7.

Robert Cahn, for many years Professor of Materials Science at the University of Sussex, told me he had become a passionate Eurosceptic. Having been 'spirited out' of Hitler's Germany to England (via Spain) as a boy, he developed a profound attachment to what he saw as the English concept of liberty. This, argued Cahn – with experience of unfathomable French bureaucracy to buttress his case – would be seriously jeopardised if 'my acquired birthright [were] sold by my governors in exchange for their influence in distant places'. See Cahn's essay in *Alien Thoughts* (Bruges Group Occasional Paper no. 34, 1999).

Bibliography

NB   The following bibliography does not (could not!) contain all the scholarly works of history, biography, fiction, philosophy, art history etc. published by or about the Hitler émigrés, any more than it includes all radio and television broadcasts, musical recordings or art works they produced. Rather, it concentrates on key texts, and other reasonably accessible books, especially those English-language sources from which I have quoted (normally in the editions I have consulted), that address or illustrate aspects of our central theme: the impact of the Hitler exiles and refugees on the subsequent cultural history of Britain.

Abbey, William et al. (eds), *Between Two Languages: German-speaking Exiles in Great Britain, 1933–45* (Verlag Hans-Dieter Heinz, Akademischer Verlag Stuttgart, 1995)

Abse, Joan (ed.), *My LSE* (Robson Books, 1977)

Adam, Peter, *Not Drowning But Waving: An Autobiography* (André Deutsch, 1995)

Adamson, Andy and Lidbury, Clare, *Kurt Jooss: 60 Years of The Green Table* (University of Birmingham, 1994)

Addison, Paul, *Now the War Is Over: A Social History of Britain, 1945–51* (BBC/Jonathan Cape, 1985)

Ades, Dawn, *Photomontage* (Thames and Hudson, 1996 edition)

Agassi, Joseph, *A Philosopher's Apprentice* (Rodopi, 1993)

Alderman, Geoffrey, *Modern British Jewry* (OUP, 1998)

Allan, J., *Berthold Lubetkin: Architecture and the Tradition of*

Progress (RIBA, 1992)

Allen, Mary, *A House Divided: The Diary of a Chief Executive of the Royal Opera House* (Simon and Schuster, 1999)

Alter, Peter (ed.), *Out of the Third Reich: Refugee Historians in Post-war Britain* (I. B. Tauris/The German Historical Institute, London, 1998)

Ambrose, Tom, *Hitler's Loss: What Britain and America Gained from Europe's Cultural Exiles* (Peter Owen, 2001)

Amis, John, *Amiscellany: My Life, My Music* (Faber and Faber, 1985)

Anderson, Mark M. (ed.), *Hitler's Exiles: Personal Stories of the Flight from Nazi Germany to America* (The New Press, New York, 1998)

Anderson, Perry, 'Components of the National Culture' (*New Left Review*, no. 50, July–August 1968, pp. 3–57)

Annan, Noel, *Our Age: The Generation that Made Post-War Britain* (HarperCollins, 1995)

——*The Dons: Mentors, Eccentrics and Geniuses* (HarperCollins, 2000)

Appignanesi, Lisa, *The Cabaret* (Studio Vista, 1975)

Appleyard, Bryan, *The Pleasures of Peace: Art and Imagination in Post-war Britain* (Faber and Faber, 1989)

Arkwright Arts Trust and Monica Bohm-Duchen, 'Art in Exile in Great Britain, 1939–45' (exhibition at Camden Arts Centre, Arkwright Road, 20 August–5 October 1986)

Athill, Diana, *Stet: A Memoir* (Granta, 2000)

Ayer, A. J., *Part of My Life* (Collins, 1977)

Bader, Alfred, *Adventures of a Chemist Collector* (Weidenfeld and Nicolson, 1995)

Banham, Mary and Hillier, Bevis (eds), *A Tonic to the Nation: The Festival of Britain, 1951* (Thames and Hudson, 1976)

Barkow, Ben, *Alfred Wiener and the Making of the Holocaust Library* (Vallentine Mitchell, 1997)

Barron, Stephanie (ed.), *Exiles+Emigres: The Flight of European Artists from Hitler* (Los Angeles County Museum of Art, 1997)

Bassani, Giorgio, *The Garden of the Finzi-Continis* (Quartet, 1992)

Bayley, John, *Iris: A Memoir of Iris Murdoch* (Duckworth, 1998)

Beecham, Sir Thomas, *A Mingled Chime: Leaves from an Autobiography* (Hutchinson, 1944)

Beller, Steven, *Vienna and the Jews: 1867–1938: A Cultural History* (CUP, 1989)

Benton, Charlotte, *A Different World: Emigré Architects in Britain 1928–1958* (Heinz Gallery, 1995)

Bentwich, Norman, *They Found Refuge: An Account of British Jewry's Work for Victims of Nazi Oppression* (Cresset Press, 1956)

Berghahn, Marion, *German-Jewish Refugees in England: The Ambiguities of Assimilation* (Macmillan, 1984)

Berghaus, Günter (ed.), *Theatre and Film in Exile: German Artists in Britain, 1933–1945* (Berg, 1989)

Beveridge, Lord, *Power and Influence: An Autobiography* (Hodder and Stoughton, 1953)

———*A Defence of Free Learning* (OUP, 1959)

Billington, Michael, *The Life and Work of Harold Pinter* (Faber and Faber, 1996)

Bing, Sir Rudolf, *5000 Nights at the Opera* (Doubleday, 1972)

Birks, Tony, *Hans Coper* (Marston House, 1991)

———*Lucie Rie* (Marston House, 1999)

Blunt, Wilfrid, *John Christie of Glyndebourne* (Geoffrey Bles, 1968)

Bogdanor, Vernon and Skidelsky, Robert (eds), *The Age of Affluence, 1951–1964* (Macmillan, 1970)

Booker, Christopher, *The Neophiliacs* (Collins, 1969)

Born, Gustav V. R., 'The Effect of the Scientific Environment in Britain on Refugee Scientists from Germany and their Effect on Science in Britain' in Rudolf Elvers (ed.), *Festschrift Albi Rosenthal* (Hans Schneider, 1984)

Born, Max, *My Life: Recollections of a Nobel Laureate* (Taylor and Francis, 1978)

———*The Born–Einstein Letters, 1916–1955* (Macmillan, 1971)

Boult, Sir Adrian, *My Own Trumpet* (Hamish Hamilton, 1973)

Bower, Tom, *Maxwell: The Final Verdict* (HarperCollins, 1996)

Bradbury, Malcolm, *The Modern British Novel* (Penguin, 1994)

Bradbury, Malcolm and McFarlane, James (eds), *Modernism: A Guide to European Literature 1890–1930* (Penguin, 1991)

Bradley, Simon and Cherry, Bridget (eds), *The Buildings of England: A Celebration Compiled to Mark Fifty Years of the Pevsner Architectural Guides* (The Penguin Collectors' Society for the Buildings Books Trust, 2001)

Briggs, Asa, *The History of Broadcasting in the United Kingdom* (5 vols, OUP)

Brinson, Charmian et al. (eds), *'England? Aber wo liegt es?': Deutsche und österreichische Emigranten in Grossbritannien, 1933–1945* (Institute of Germanic Studies, University of London, 1996)

Britt, David (ed.), *Modern Art: Impressionism to Post-Modernism* (Thames and Hudson, 1999 edition)

Bruce, George, *Festival in the North: The Story of the Edinburgh Festival* (Robert Hale, 1975)

Buruma, Ian, *Voltaire's Coconuts or Anglomania in Europe* (Weidenfeld and Nicolson, 1999)

Busch, Fritz, *Pages from a Musician's Life* (Hogarth Press, 1953)

Cabarga, Leslie, *Progressive German Graphics 1900–1937* (Chronicle Books, 1994)

Calder, Angus, *The People's War: Britain 1939–1945* (Jonathan Cape, 1969)

Calvocoressi, Peter, *The British Experience, 1945–75* (The Bodley Head, 1978)

Canetti, Elias, *Auto-da-Fé* (Bard Books edition, 1969)

——*Crowds and Power* (Penguin, 1973)

——*The Conscience of Words* (André Deutsch, 1986)

——*The Tongue Set Free: Remembrance of a European Childhood* (Continuum, 1979)

——*The Torch in My Ear* (Farrar, Straus and Giroux, 1982)

Carner, Mosco, *Puccini: A Critical Biography* (Duckworth, 1974 edition)

Carpenter, Humphrey, *Benjamin Britten: A Biography* (Faber and Faber, 1992)

——*The Envy of the World: Fifty Years of the BBC Third*

Programme and Radio 3 (Weidenfeld and Nicolson, 1996)

Carter, Miranda, *Anthony Blunt: His Lives* (Macmillan, 2001)

Cesarani, David (ed.), *The Making of Modern Anglo-Jewry* (Blackwell, 1990)

——*Arthur Koestler: The Homeless Mind* (Heinemann, 1998)

Cesarani, David and Fulbrook, Mary (eds), *Citizenship, Nationality and Migration in Europe* (Routledge, 1996)

Cesarani, David and Kushner, Tony (eds), *The Internment of Aliens in Twentieth-Century Britain* (Frank Cass, 1993)

Chappell, Connery, *Island of Barbed Wire* (Corgi, 1986)

Chernow, Ron, *The Warburgs: A Family Saga* (Chatto and Windus, 1993)

Christie, Ian, *Arrows of Desire: The Films of Michael Powell and Emeric Pressburger* (Faber and Faber, 1994)

Christie, Ian (ed.), *Michael Powell and Emeric Pressburger: The Life and Death of Colonel Blimp* (Faber and Faber, 1994)

Clare, George, *Last Waltz in Vienna: The Destruction of a Family 1842–1942* (Pan, 1982)

Clark, Kenneth, *Another Part of the Wood* (John Murray, 1974)

——*The Other Half: A Self-Portrait* (John Murray, 1977)

Clark, Ronald W., *The Life of Ernst Chain: Penicillin and Beyond* (Weidenfeld and Nicolson, 1985)

Cobbe, Hugh, 'Vaughan Williams, Germany and the German Tradition: a view from the letters' in Alain Frogley (ed.), *Vaughan Williams Studies* (CUP, 1996)

Cockett, Richard, *David Astor and the Observer* (André Deutsch, 1991)

Conrad, Peter, *Modern Times, Modern Places: Life & Art in the 20th Century* (Thames and Hudson, 1998)

Conradi, Peter J., *Iris Murdoch: A Life* (HarperCollins, 2001)

Cooper, R. M. (ed.), *Refugee Scholars: Conversations with Tess Simpson* (Moorland Books, 1992)

——*Retrospective Sympathetic Affection: A Tribute to the Academic Community* (Moorland Books, 1996)

Cosman, Milein, 'Oxford 1940' (*Aquarius* 23/4, 1998, John Heath-Stubbs Eightieth Birthday Issue)

Coton, A. V., *The New Ballet: Kurt Jooss and his Work* (Dennis Dobson, 1946)

Crawford, W. R. (ed.), *The Cultural Migration: The European Scholar in America* (University of Pennsylvania Press, 1953)

Crozier, Eric (ed.), *Opera in English* (John Lane, The Bodley Head, 1946)

Curran, James and Seaton, Jean, *Power Without Responsibility: The Press and Broadcasting in Britain* (Routledge, 1997)

Dahrendorf, Ralf, *LSE: A History of the London School of Economics and Political Science, 1895–1995* (OUP, 1995)

Davies, Norman, *Europe: A History* (OUP, 1996)

Davies, Russell, *Foreign Body: The Secret Life of Robert Maxwell* (Bloomsbury, 1996)

Davies, Russell and Ottaway, Liz, *Vicky* (Secker and Warburg, 1987)

Deutscher, Isaac, *The Non-Jewish Jew and Other Essays* (OUP, 1968)

Donaldson, Frances, *The Royal Opera House in the Twentieth Century* (Weidenfeld and Nicolson, 1988)

Dove, Richard, *Journey of No Return: Five German-Speaking Literary Exiles in Britain, 1933–1945* (Libris, 2000)

Drazin, Charles, *The Finest Years: British Cinema of the 1940s* (Deutsch, 1998)

Drogheda, Lord, *Double Harness: Memoirs by Lord Drogheda* (Weidenfeld and Nicolson, 1978)

Drummond, Sir John, *Tainted by Experience* (Faber, 2000)

Dube, Wolf-Dieter, *The Expressionists* (Thames and Hudson, 1996)

Ebert, Peter, *In This Theatre of Man's Life: The Biography of Carl Ebert* (The Book Guild Ltd, 1999)

Edgcumbe, Rose, *Anna Freud: A View of Development, Disturbance and Therapeutic Techniques* (Routledge, 2000)

Edmonds, David and Eidinow, John, *Wittgenstein's Poker: The Story of a Ten-Minute Argument Between Two Great Philosophers* (Faber, 2001)

Einstein, Albert, *The World As I See It* (Carol Publishing, 1995)

Elderfield, John, *Kurt Schwitters* (Thames and Hudson, 1985)

Elsom, John, *Post-war British Theatre* (Routledge and Kegan Paul, 1979)

Elton, G. R., *The Tudor Revolution in Government* (CUP, 1953)

———*England Under the Tudors* (Methuen, 1974)

———*The Practice of History* (Fontana, 1976 edition)

———*The English* (Blackwell, 1992)

Erasmus, *Praise of Folly* (Penguin edition, 1993)

Erikson, Erik, *Young Man Luther: A Study in Psychoanalysis and History* (Faber, 1959)

Esslin, Martin, *Brecht: The Man and his Work* (Doubleday, 1971)

———*The Theatre of the Absurd* (Penguin, 1980)

———*The Peopled Wound: Pinter: A Study of His Plays* (Eyre Methuen, 1973)

Eyre, Richard and Wright, Nicholas, *Changing Stages: A View of British Theatre in the Twentieth Century* (Bloomsbury, 2000)

Eysenck, H. J., *Know Your Own I.Q.* (Penguin, 1962)

———*Rebel With a Cause: The Autobiography of Hans Eysenck* (W. H. Allen & Co., 1990)

Farrer, David, *The Warburgs* (Michael Joseph, 1975)

Ferguson, Howard (ed.), *Myra Hess by Her Friends* (Hamish Hamilton, 1966)

Fermi, Laura, *Illustrious Immigrants: The Intellectual Migration from Europe, 1930–41* (University of Chicago Press, 1968)

Festival of Austrian-Jewish Culture, London (October–November 1996, catalogue, Jewish Music Heritage Trust/Austrian Cultural Institute, London 1996)

Figes, Eva, *Little Eden: A Child at War* (Faber and Faber, 1978)

———*The Tenancy* (Minerva, 1994)

———*Winter Journey* (Faber and Faber, 1967)

Figes, Orlando, *A People's Tragedy: The Russian Revolution 1891–1924* (Pimlico, 1997)

Fleming, Donald and Bailyn, Bernard (eds), *The Intellectual Migration: Europe and America, 1930–1960* (The Belknap Press of Harvard University Press, 1969)

Flesch, Carl, *The Memoirs of Carl Flesch* (Rockliff, 1957)

Flesch, Carl F., *'And do you also play the violin?'* (Toccata Press, 1990)

————'Where do you come from?': Hitler refugees in Great Britain then and now: The happy compromise! (Pen Press, 2001)

Ford, Boris (ed.), *Modern Britain: The Cambridge Cultural History*, vol. 9 (CUP, 1992)

Forster, E. M., *Aspects of the Novel* (Pelican edition, 1981)

————*A Passage to India* (Penguin, 1979 edition)

Frayling, Christopher et al., *Vision: 50 Years of British Creativity* (Thames and Hudson, 1999)

Freud, Esther, *Gaglow* (Hamish Hamilton, 1997)

Fried, Erich, *Children and Fools* (Serpent's Tail, 1992)

Frisch, Otto, *What Little I Remember* (CUP, 1979)

Frogley, Alain (ed.), *Vaughan Williams Studies* (CUP, 1996); especially chapter 4: 'Vaughan Williams, Germany, and the German tradition: a view from the letters' by Hugh Cobbe

Fromm, Erich, *The Art of Loving* (Allen and Unwin, 1957)

————*The Fear of Freedom* (Kegan Paul and Co., 1942)

Gay, Peter, *The Bourgeois Experience* (4 vols, various publishers, 1984–96)

————*Weimar Culture: The Outsider as Insider* (Penguin, 1968)

————*Freud, Jews and Other Germans: Masters and Victims in Modernist Culture* (OUP, New York, 1978)

————*My German Question* (Yale UP, 1998)

Geissmar, Berta, *The Baton and the Jackboot: Recollections of Musical Life* (Hamish Hamilton, 1944)

Gershon, Karen (ed.), *We Came as Children: A Collective Autobiography* (Gollancz, 1966)

Gilbert, Martin, *The Boys* (Weidenfeld and Nicolson, 1996)

Gillman, Peter and Leni, *'Collar the Lot!' How Britain Interned and Expelled its Wartime Refugees* (Quartet Books, 1980)

Glock, William, *Notes in Advance* (OUP, 1991)

Goehr, Alexander, *Finding the Key: Selected Writings of Alexander Goehr* (ed. Derrick Puffett, Faber and Faber, 1998)

Gombrich, E. H., *Art and Illusion: A Study in the Psychology of Pictorial Representation* (Phaidon, 1960)

————*The Story of Art* (Phaidon, 1950)

———*A Lifelong Interest: Conversations on Art and Science with Didier Eribon* (Thames and Hudson, 1993)

Greene, Graham, *The Third Man* (Penguin, 1977)

Greer, Germaine, *The Female Eunuch* (MacGibbon and Kee, 1970)

Grunfeld, Frederic V., *Prophets Without Honour: A Background to Freud, Kafka, Einstein and Their World* (Hutchinson, 1979)

Gryn, Hugo (with Naomi Gryn), *Chasing Shadows* (Viking, 2000)

Guillery, Peter, *The Buildings of London Zoo* (Royal Commission on the Historical Monuments of England, 1993)

Guthrie, Tyrone, *A Life in the Theatre* (Hamish Hamilton, 1960)

Hacohen, Malachi Haim, *Karl Popper – The Formative Years, 1902–45* (CUP, 2000)

Haendel, Ida, *Woman with Violin: An Autobiography* (Gollancz, 1970)

Haffner, Sebastian, *Germany: Jekyll and Hyde* (Secker and Warburg, 1940)

———*The Meaning of Hitler* (Weidenfeld and Nicolson, 1979)

Hall, Fernau, *Modern English Ballet* (Andrew Melrose, 1951)

Haltrecht, Montague, *The Quiet Showman: Sir David Webster and the Royal Opera House* (Collins, 1975)

Hamburger, Michael, *String of Beginnings* (Carcanet Press, 1973; Skoob Books, 1991)

———*Collected Poems, 1941–1994* (Anvil, 1995)

Hare, Steve (ed.), *Penguin Portrait: Allen Lane and the Penguin Editors, 1935–70* (Penguin, 1995)

Harewood, Earl of, *The Tongs and the Bones: The Memoirs of Lord Harewood* (Weidenfeld and Nicolson, 1981)

Harris, Mark Jonathan and Oppenheimer, Deborah, *Into the Arms of Strangers: Stories of the Kindertransport* (Bloomsbury, 2000)

Hartley, Keith et al. (eds), *The Romantic Spirit in German Art 1790–1990* (Scottish National Gallery of Modern Art, Edinburgh and Hayward Gallery, London, 1994)

Hayek, Friedrich A., *The Road to Serfdom* (University of Chicago Press, 1944; Routledge Classics, 2001)

————*The Constitution of Liberty* (Routledge and Kegan Paul, 1960)

————*Law, Legislation and Liberty* (Routledge and Kegan Paul/University of Chicago Press, 3 vols, 1973, 1976, 1979)

————*Economic Freedom* (Basil Blackwell, 1991)

Heilbut, Anthony, *Exiled in Paradise: German Refugee Artists and Intellectuals in America from the 1930s to the Present* (Viking, 1983)

Hennessy, Peter, *Never Again: Britain: 1945–51* (Cape, 1992)

Hesse, Hermann, *Wanderings* (Triad/Panther, 1985)

————*Steppenwolf* (Penguin, 1965)

Hewison, Robert, *The Heritage Industry: Britain in a Climate of Decline* (Methuen, 1987)

————*Culture and Consensus: England, art and politics since 1940* (Methuen, 1997)

Hirschfeld, Gerhard (ed.), *Exile in Great Britain: Refugees from Hitler's Germany* (Berg, for the German Historical Institute, London, 1984)

Hobsbawm, E. J., *Industry and Empire* (Pelican, 1969)

————*The Age of Revolution 1789–1848* (Sphere, 1973)

————*The Age of Capital 1848–1875* (Weidenfeld and Nicolson, 1975)

————*The Age of Empire 1875–1914* (Weidenfeld and Nicolson, 1987)

————*Age of Extremes: The Short Twentieth Century 1914–1991* (Abacus, 1995)

————*On History* (Abacus, 1998)

————*Uncommon People: Resistance, Rebellion and Jazz* (Weidenfeld and Nicolson, 1998)

Hoch, Paul K., 'No Utopia: Refugee Scholars in Britain' (*History Today*, November 1985)

Hodgson, John, *Mastering Movement: The Life and Work of Rudolf Laban* (Methuen, 2001)

Hodgson, John and Preston-Dunlop, Valerie, *Rudolf Laban: An Introduction to his Work and Influence* (Northcote House, 1990)

Hoffman, Eva, *Lost in Translation: A Life in a New Language* (Minerva, 1991)

Hoffnung, Annetta, *Gerard Hoffnung: His Biography* (Gordon Fraser, 1988)

Hoffnung, Gerard, *The Maestro*, *The Hoffnung Symphony Orchestra*, *The Hoffnung Music Festival* (Dobson/Putnam, mid-1950s). Republished 2001 by the Hoffnung Partnership, 44 Pilgrims Lane, London NW3 1SN

Hoggart, Richard, *The Uses of Literacy* (Chatto and Windus, 1957)

————*Speaking to Each Other; vol 1: About Society* (Chatto and Windus, 1970)

Hopkinson, Tom (ed.), *Picture Post, 1938–50* (Penguin, 1970)

Howard, Michael S., *Jonathan Cape, Publisher* (Cape, 1971)

Hughes, H. Stuart, *The Sea Change: The Migration of Social Thought, 1930–1965* (Harper and Row, 1975)

Hughes, Robert, *Lucian Freud: Paintings* (Thames and Hudson, 1989)

————*Frank Auerbach* (Thames and Hudson, 1992)

Hughes, Spike, *Glyndebourne: A History of the Festival Opera* (Methuen, 1965)

Ignatieff, Michael, *Isaiah Berlin: A Life* (Chatto and Windus, 1998)

Isaacs, Jeremy, *Never Mind the Moon: My Time at the Royal Opera House* (Bantam, 1999)

Isherwood, Christopher, *The Berlin Novels* (*Mr Norris Changes Trains* and *Goodbye to Berlin*, Minerva, 1992)

————*Prater Violet* (Minerva edition, 1991)

Jackman, Jarrell C. and Borden, Carla M. (eds), *The Muses Flee Hitler: Cultural Transfer and Adaptation, 1930–1945* (Smithsonian Institution, 1983)

Jacobs, Arthur, *Henry J. Wood: Maker of the Proms* (Methuen, 1994)

Zvi Jagendorf, *Wolfy and the Strudelbakers* (Dewi Lewis, 2001)

Jakobovits, Immanuel, *The Timely and the Timeless: Jews, Judaism and Society in a Storm-Tossed Decade* (Vallentine, Mitchell, 1977)

————*'If Only My People . . .' Zionism in My Life* (Weidenfeld and Nicolson, 1984)

Johnson, Paul, 'Hitler's Gift to Britain' (*Sunday Telegraph*, 29 January 1995)

Jolliffe, John, *Glyndebourne* (John Murray, 1999)

Jones, Ernest, *The Life and Work of Sigmund Freud* (edited and abridged by Lionel Trilling and Steven Marcus, Pelican, 1964)

Josephs, Zoe et al., *Survivors: Jewish Refugees in Birmingham, 1933–45* (Meridian Books, 1988)

Kafka, Franz, *The Trial* (Penguin, 1968)

Kapp, Yvonne and Mynatt, Margaret, *British Policy and the Refugees, 1933–41* (Frank Cass, 1977)

Karpf, Anne, *The War After* (Minerva, 1997)

Keegan, Susanne, *The Eye of God: A Life of Oskar Kokoschka* (Bloomsbury, 1999)

Kehoe, Louise, *In This Dark House: A Memoir* (Penguin, 1997)

Keller, Hans, *Music, Closed Societies and Football* (Toccata Press, 1986)

Kemp, Ian, *Tippett: The Composer and His Music* (Eulenberg, 1984)

Kennedy, Michael, *Richard Strauss: Man, Music, Enigma* (CUP, 1999)

Kenyon, John, *The History Men: The Historical Profession in England since the Renaissance* (Weidenfeld and Nicolson, 1993 edition)

Kenyon, Nicholas, *The BBC Symphony Orchestra 1930–1980* (BBC, 1981)

Kerr, Judith, *When Hitler Stole Pink Rabbit* (Collins Modern Classics, 1998)

——*The Other Way Round* (Collins, 1998)

——*A Small Person Far Away* (Collins, 1995)

——*The Tiger Who Came to Tea* (Collins, 1998)

King, James, *The Last Modern: A Life of Herbert Read* (Weidenfeld and Nicolson, 1990)

King, Pearl and Steiner, Riccardo, *The Freud–Klein Controversies, 1941–1945* (Routledge, 1992)

Kochan, Miriam, *Britain's Internees in the Second World War* (Macmillan, 1983)

Koestler, Arthur, *Darkness at Noon* (Penguin, 1964)

——*The Yogi and the Commissar* (Hutchinson, 1965)

————*The Invisible Writing* (Hutchinson, 1969)

————*The Act of Creation* (Hutchinson, 1964)

————*The Thirteenth Tribe; The Khazar Empire and its Heritage* (Hutchinson, 1976)

————*Arrow in the Blue* (Hutchinson, 1969)

Kokoschka, Oskar, *My Life* (Macmillan, NY, 1974)

Kolinsky, Eva and van der Will, Wilfried, *The Cambridge Companion to Modern German Culture* (CUP, 1998)

Korda, Michael, *Charmed Lives: A Family Romance* (Penguin, 1980)

Kracauer, Siegfried, *From Caligari to Hitler: A Psychological Study of the German Film* (Princeton University Press, 1947)

Kranzfelder, Ivo, *George Grosz, 1893–1959* (Benedikt Taschen, 1994)

Krebs, Hans, *Reminiscences and Reflections* (OUP, 1981)

Krohn, Claus-Dieter, *Intellectuals in Exile* (University of Massachusetts Press, 1993)

Kulik, Karol, *Alexander Korda: The Man Who Could Work Miracles* (Virgin, 1990)

Kushner, Tony, *The Persistence of Prejudice: Anti-Semitism in British Society During the Second World War* (Manchester University Press, 1989)

————*The Holocaust and the Liberal Imagination* (Blackwell, 1994)

Kushner, Tony and Knox, Katharine, *Refugees in an Age of Genocide: Global, National, and Local Perspectives during the Twentieth Century* (Frank Cass, 1999)

Lafitte, François, *The Internment of Aliens* (originally published by Penguin, 1940; republished 1988)

Laqueur, Walter, *Weimar: A Cultural History 1918–33* (Weidenfeld and Nicolson, 1974)

————*Thursday's Child Has Far To Go* (Scribner, 1992)

Lasker-Wallfisch, Anita, *Inherit the Truth 1939–1945* (de la Mare, 1996)

Lawford-Hinrichsen, Irene, *Music Publishing and Patronage: C. F. Peters, 1800 to the Holocaust* (Edition Press, 2000)

Lebrecht, Norman, *Covent Garden: The Untold Story:*

Dispatches from the English Culture War, 1945–2000 (Simon and Schuster, 2000)

Leo Baeck Institute, *Annual Year Books*

Levi, Erik, *Music in the Third Reich* (Macmillan, 1994)

Levin, Bernard, *The Pendulum Years* (Pan Books, 1972)

Lewis, Jeremy, *Cyril Connolly: A Life* (Pimlico, 1998)

Littlewood, Joan, *Joan's Book: Joan Littlewood's Peculiar History As She Tells It* (Methuen, 1944)

London, Louise, *Whitehall and the Jews 1933–48: British Immigration Policy and the Holocaust* (CUP, 2000)

Longmate, Norman, *How We Lived Then: A History of Everyday Life during the Second World War* (Arrow Books, 1973)

Lucie-Smith, Edward, *Lives of the Great 20th-Century Artists* (Thames and Hudson, 1999)

Lynton, Norbert, *The Story of Modern Art* (Phaidon, 1989 edition)

Macdonald, Kevin, *Emeric Pressburger: The Life and Death of a Screenwriter* (Faber and Faber, 1996)

Magee, Bryan, *Modern British Philosophy* (Paladin, 1973)

——*Popper* (Fontana, 1973)

Manchester, P. W., *Vic-Wells: A Ballet Progress* (Gollancz, 1942)

Mann, Thomas, *Selected Stories* (Penguin edition, 1993)

Marcuse, Herbert, *One-Dimensional Man: Studies in the Ideology of Advanced Industrial Society* (Routledge and Kegan Paul, 1964)

——*Eros and Civilization: A Philosophical Inquiry into Freud* (Routledge and Kegan Paul, 1956)

Marwick, Arthur, *British Society Since 1945* (Penguin, 1982)

——*The Sixties: Cultural Revolution in Britain, France, Italy, and the United States, c.1958–c.1974* (OUP, 1998)

Medawar, Jean and Pyke, David, *Hitler's Gift: Scientists Who Fled Nazi Germany* (Richard Cohen Books, 2000)

Mendes-Flohr, Paul, *German Jews: A Dual Identity* (Yale University Press, 1999)

Mikes, George, *How To Be a Brit* (Penguin, 1986)

Mitchell, Donald, *Cradles of the New: Writings on Music 1951–1991* (Faber and Faber, 1995)

433

Mitchell, Juliet, *Psychoanalysis and Feminism* (Penguin, 1975)

Moritz, Carl Philip, *Journeys of a German in England in 1782* (Jonathan Cape, 1965)

Mosse, Werner (co-ordinating ed.), *Second Chance: Two Centuries of German-speaking Jews in the United Kingdom* (J. C. B. Mohr (Paul Siebeck), Tübingen, 1991)

Mowl, Timothy, *Stylistic Cold Wars: Betjeman versus Pevsner* (John Murray, 2000)

Murdoch, Irish, *Under the Net* (Penguin, 1960)

——*The Flight from the Enchanter* (Penguin, 1962)

Myers, Rollo H., *Music Since 1939* (Longmans Green, 1947)

Nicolson, Nigel, *Long Life: Memoirs* (Phoenix, 1997)

Nicolson, Nigel (ed.), *Harold Nicolson: Diaries and Letters, 1945–62* (Fontana, 1971)

Nissel, Muriel, *Married to the Amadeus: Life with a String Quartet* (dlm, 1998)

Oestreicher, Paul, *The Double Cross* (Darton, Longman and Todd, 1986)

Olivier, Laurence, *Confessions of an Actor* (Coronet, 1984)

Osborne, Charles, *Giving It Away: Memoirs of an Uncivil Servant* (Secker and Warburg, 1986)

Osborne, Richard, *Herbert von Karajan: A Life in Music* (Pimlico, 1999)

Panofsky, Erwin, *Meaning in the Visual Arts: Papers in and on Art History* (Penguin, 1993 edition)

Parkes, James, *An Enemy of the People: Antisemitism* (Penguin, 1945)

Paucker, Arnold, 'Speaking English with an accent' in Charmian Brinson et al. (eds), *'England? Aber wo liegt es?': Deutsche und österreichische Emigranten in Grossbritannien, 1933–1945* (Institute of Germanic Studies, University of London, 1996)

Peierls, Sir Rudolf, *Bird of Passage: Recollections of a Physicist* (Princeton University Press, 1985)

Perutz, Max, *Is Science Necessary? Essays on Science and Scientists* (Barrie and Jenkins, 1989)

——*I Wish I'd Made You Angrier Earlier* (OUP, 1998)

Peto, James and Loveday, Donna, *Modern Britain 1929–1939* (Design Museum, 1999)

Pevsner, Nikolaus, *The Englishness of English Art* (Penguin, 1997)

——*The Sources of Modern Architecture and Design* (Thames and Hudson, 1968)

——*Pioneers of Modern Design: From William Morris to Walter Gropius* (Penguin, 1960)

——*An Outline of European Architecture* (Pelican, 1963)

Pick, Hella, *Simon Wiesenthal: A Life in Search of Justice* (Weidenfeld and Nicolson, 1996)

——*Guilty Victim: Austria from the Holocaust to Haider* (I. B. Tauris, 2000)

Popper, Karl, *The Poverty of Historicism* (Routledge, 1986 edition)

——*The Open Society and Its Enemies*, vols I and II (Routledge, 1995 edition)

——*Unended Quest: An Intellectual Autobiography* (Routledge, 1993)

Potter, Pamela M., *Most German of the Arts: Musicology and Society from the Weimar Republic to the End of Hitler's Reich* (Yale UP, 1998)

Powell, Michael, *A Life in Movies* (Heinemann, 1986)

Prawer, S. S., *Caligari's Children: The Film as Tale of Terror* (OUP, 1980)

Preston-Dunlop, Valerie, *Rudolf Laban: An Extraordinary Life* (Dance Books, 1998)

Priestley, J. B., *The Good Companions* (Penguin, 1964)

Pulzer, Peter, *The Rise of Political Anti-Semitism in Germany and Austria* (Harvard UP, 1988)

——*Jews and the German State: The Political History of a Minority 1848–1933* (Blackwell, 1992)

Quack, Sybille (ed.), *Between Sorrow and Strength: The Political History of a Minority 1848–1933* (German Historical Institute, Washington DC/CUP, 1995)

Raphael, Frederic, *Popper* (Phoenix, 1998)

Raybould, John (ed.), *Hayek: A Commemorative Album* (Adam Smith Institute, 1998)

Read, Herbert, *Contemporary British Art* (Penguin, 1964)

Redcliffe-Maud, Lord, *Support for the Arts in England and*

Wales (Gulbenkian Foundation, 1976)

Renier, G. J., *The English: Are They Human* (Benn, 1956 edition)

Rhode, Eric, *A History of Cinema from Its Origins to 1970* (Pelican, 1978)

Ritchie, J. M., *German Exiles: British Perspectives* (Peter Lang, NY, 1997)

Roberts, Peter, *The Old Vic Story: A Nation's Theatre, 1818–1976* (W. H. Allen, 1976)

Robbins, Lionel (Lord), *Autobiography of an Economist* (Macmillan, 1971)

Robinson, David, *Das Cabinet des Dr Caligari* (BFI, 1997)

Rodgers, Silvia, *Red Saint, Pink Daughter* (Carcanet, 1997)

Rohrs, H. (ed.), *Kurt Hahn: A Life Span in Education and Politics* (Routledge and Kegan Paul, 1970)

Rosenthal, Albi, *Obiter Scripta* (Offox Press, 2000)

Rosenthal, Harold, *Two Centuries of Opera at Covent Garden* (Putnam, 1958)

Roth, Ernst, *The Business of Music: Reflections of a Music Publisher* (Cassell, 1969)

Rustin, Michael, *The Good Society and the Inner World: Psychoanalysis, Politics and Culture* (Verso, 1991)

Schumacher, E. F., *Small Is Beautiful: A Study of Economics as if People Mattered* (Abacus, 1974)

Schwartz, Joseph, *Cassandra's Daughter: A History of Psychoanalysis in Europe and America* (Allen Lane, 1999)

Schwarzkopf, Elisabeth, *On and Off the Record: A Memoir of Walter Legge* (Faber and Faber, 1982)

Sebald, W. G., *Austerlitz* (Hamish Hamilton, 2001)

——*The Emigrant* (Harvill, 1996)

Sereny, Gitta, *The German Trauma: Experiences and Reflections, 1938–2000* (Allen Lane the Penguin Press, 2000)

Shellard, Dominic, *British Theatre Since the War* (Yale University Press, 1999)

Sherman, A. J., *Island Refuge: Britain and Refugees from the Third Reich, 1933–1939* (Elek, 1973)

Sinclair, Andrew, *War Like a Wasp: The Lost Decade of the 'Forties* (Hamish Hamilton, 1989)

————*Arts and Cultures: The History of the 50 Years of the Arts Council of Great Britain* (Sinclair-Stevenson, 1995)

Sissons, Michael and French, Philip (eds), *Age of Austerity 1945–1951* (OUP, 1986)

Skidelsky, Robert, *John Maynard Keynes: Hopes Betrayed, 1883–1920* (Macmillan, 1983)

————*John Maynard Keynes: The Economist as Saviour, 1920–1937* (Macmillan, 1992)

————*John Maynard Keynes: Fighting for Britain, 1937–1946* (Macmillan, 2000)

Snowman, Daniel, *The Amadeus Quartet: The Men and the Music* (Robson, 1981)

Solti, Sir Georg, *Solti on Solti* (Chatto and Windus, 1997)

Spalding, Frances, *British Art Since 1900* (Thames and Hudson, 1986)

Spender, Stephen, *World Within World* (Faber and Faber, 1977 edition)

Spiegl, Fritz, *The Joy of Words: 'A Bedside Book for English Lovers'* (Elm Tree Books, 1986)

————*Sick Notes* (The Parthenon Publishing Group, 1996)

————*Lives, Wives and Loves of the Great Composers* (Marion Boyars, 1997)

Spivey, Nigel, *Phaidon 1923–98* (Phaidon, 1999)

Spoto, Donald, *The Dark Side of Genius: The Life of Alfred Hitchcock* (Plexus, 1994)

Stadler, Friedrich and Weibel, Peter (eds), *The Cultural Exodus from Austria* (Springer Verlag, 1995)

Stansky, Peter and Abrahams, William, *London's Burning: Life, Death and Art in the Second World War* (Constable, 1995)

Steiner, George, *George Steiner: A Reader* (Penguin Books, 1984)

————*Errata: An Examined Life* (Phoenix, 1998)

Steiner, Riccardo, *'It's a New Kind of Diaspora': Explorations in the Sociopolitical and Cultural Context of Psychoanalysis* (Karnac Books, 2000)

————*Tradition, Change, Creativity: Repercussions of the New Diaspora on Aspects of British Psychoanalysis* (Karnac Books, 2000)

Stent, Ronald, *A Bespattered Page: The Internment of 'His Majesty's Most Loyal Enemy Aliens'* (Deutsch, 1980)

Storr, Anthony, *The Dynamics of Creation* (Secker, 1972)

———*Churchill's Black Dog* (Collins, 1989)

———*Music and the Mind* (HarperCollins, 1992)

Sylvester, David, *Moonraker, Strangelove and Other Celluloid Dreams: The Visionary Art of Ken Adam* (Serpentine Gallery, 1999)

Tabori, Paul, *Alexander Korda* (Oldbourne, 1959)

———*The Anatomy of Exile: A Semantic and Historical Study* (Harrap, 1972)

Taylor, John Russell, *Anger and After: A Guide to the New British Drama* (Penguin, 1963)

———*Strangers in Paradise: The Hollywood Emigrés 1933–1950* (Holt, Rinehart & Winston, 1983)

Tessler, Gloria, *Amélie: The Story of Lady Jakobovits* (Vallentine Mitchell, 1999)

Tewes, Henning and Wright, Jonathan (eds), *Liberalism, Anti-Semitism and Democracy: Essays in Honour of Peter Pulzer* (OUP, 2001)

Thompson, Denys (ed.), *Discrimination and Popular Culture* (Penguin, 1964)

Timms, Edward and Robertson, Ritchie (eds), *Austrian Exodus: The Creative Achievements of Refugees from National Socialism* (Edinburgh UP, 1995)

Timms, Edward and Segal, Naomi (eds), *Freud in Exile: Psychoanalysis and its Vicissitudes* (Yale UP, 1988)

Timms, Edward, 'In Freud's Shadow. The double exile of Wilhelm Stekel' in Charmian Brinson et al., op. cit.

Tippett, Michael, *Those Twentieth-Century Blues: An Autobiography* (Hutchinson, 1991)

Tooley, John, *In House: The Story of Covent Garden* (Faber and Faber, 1999)

Turner, Barry, *. . . And the Policeman Smiled* (Bloomsbury, 1990)

Tusa, John, *Conversations With the World* (BBC Books, 1990)

———*Art Matters: Reflecting on Culture* (Methuen, 1999)

Uhlman, Fred, *Reunion* (Harvill, 1997)

———*The Making of an Englishman* (Gollancz, 1960)

Unwin, Sir Stanley, *The Truth About a Publisher* (George Allen and Unwin, 1960)

Valois, Ninette de, *Come Dance With Me: A Memoir, 1898–1956* (Hamish Hamilton, 1959)

Vaughan Williams, Ralph, *National Music and Other Essays* (OUP, 1987 edition)

Vaughan Williams, Ursula, *R. V. W.: A Biography of Ralph Vaughan Williams* (OUP, 1964)

Vicky (with Introduction by James Cameron) (Allen Lane the Penguin Press, 1967)

Wallace, Ian (ed.), *German-Speaking Exiles in Great Britain* (Yearbook of the Research Centre for German and Austrian Exile Studies, London; Rodopi, 1999)

Walter, Bruno, *Theme and Variations: An Autobiography* (Hamish Hamilton, 1947)

Walther, Suzanne K., *The Dance Theatre of Kurt Jooss: Choreography and Dance*, vol. 3, part 2 (Harwood Academic Publishers, 1993)

Wasserstein, Bernard, *Britain and the Jews of Europe 1939–1945* (OUP, 1979)

———*Vanishing Diaspora: The Jews in Europe Since 1945* (Penguin, 1997)

Watkin, David, *Morality and Architecture Revisited* (John Murray, 2001)

Weidenfeld, George, *Remembering My Good Friends* (HarperCollins, 1995)

Whitford, Frank, *The Bauhaus* (Thames and Hudson, 1984)

———*Oskar Kokoschka: A Life* (Weidenfeld & Nicolson, 1986)

Wiseman, Thomas, *The Quick and the Dead* (Viking, 1969)

———*Children of the Ruins* (Cape, 1986)

Wistrich, Robert S., *Weekend in Munich: Art, Propaganda and Terror in the Third Reich* (Pavilion, 1995)

Witts, Richard, *Artist Unknown: An Alternative History of the Arts Council* (Little Brown, 1998)

Wollheim, Richard (ed.), *The Image in Form* (Penguin, 1972)

———*Painting as an Art* (Thames and Hudson, 1987)

Wood, Barbara, *Alias Papa: A Life of Fritz Schumacher* (OUP, 1985)

Woodfield, Richard (ed.), *The Essential Gombrich* (Phaidon, 1996)

Young, Michael, *The Elmhirsts of Dartington: The Creation of an Utopian Community* (Routledge and Kegan Paul, 1982)

Young-Bruehl, Elisabeth, *Anna Freud: A Biography* (Macmillan, 1989)

Zander, Walter, *Israel and the Holy Places of Christendom* (Weidenfeld and Nicolson, 1971)

Index

Plato: 195, 196, 198
Pleeth, William: 221
Plymouth Brethren: 101, 319
Poland, Polish: xxiv, 3, 4, 8, 87,
 88/f, 89, 134, 141, 176, 379
Pollard, Sidney: xx, 377
Pomeroy, Jay: 212
Pommer, Erich: 81, 367
Ponsonby, Robert: 297
Pontecorvo, Guido (and brothers
 Gillo and Bruno): 112/f
Pope-Hennessy, Sir John: 307
Popper, Sir Karl: xviii, xix, 12, 13,
 25, 27, 98, 165–6, 185, 191–8,
 200, 201, 203, 204, 242, 274/f,
 304, 318, 331, 334, 337, 339,
 346, 364, 379, 380, 387–8, 394,
 396–7, 417, 418
Portugal: 97, 233 (Lisbon)
Post-modernism: 313, 352
Pound, Ezra: 50, 55
Powell, Anthony: 230,
Powell, Michael: 84, 120, 127–8,
 155, 159, 160–7 passim, 169,
 171/f, 204, 255, 332, 339, 368,
 390, 391, 393
Prague: 4, 81, 155, 208, 232
Prawer, S.S.: 382
Preminger, Otto: 80
Pressburger, Emeric: xx, xxii, 81–4,
 85, 120, 121, 127–8, 155, 160–7,
 169, 171/f, 204, 238, 255, 320,
 326, 332, 333, 339, 343, 345,
 348, 353, 368, 377, 386, 391,
 393–4
Previn, André: 366
Priestley, J.B.: 57, 59, 123, 136,
 253
Primrose, William: 218
Princeton (university, Institute for
 Advanced Study): 321, 362, 376
Pritchard, Jack: 67, 86
Promenade Concerts: 170, 173,
 354, 360/f
Proust, Marcel: 50, 51, 76
Psychiatry; see Psychoanalysis
Psychical Reasearch, Society for:
 303

Psychoanalysis, Psychiatry,
 Psychology, Psychotherapy:
 152–3, 265, 273, 297, 322–4,
 363, 366, 409, 410–11; see also
 Freud, Sigmund
Publishing: 240–250; see also names
 of individual publishers and
 companies
Puccini, Giacomo: 323
Pulzer, Peter: 327, 378, 412
Punch: 260
Purcell, Henry: 94, 209

Quakers: 93, 100, 289, 308,
 319
Quant, Mary: xv
Queen's Hall (London): 170, 172,
 215

Radzinowicz, Sir Leon: 340
Rainier, Priaulx: 348
Raleigh, Sir Walter: 262
Rambert, Marie; Ballet Rambert:
 75, 176
Rameau, Jean Philippe: 216
Rank, Lord (J. Arthur): 121
Rankl, Karl: xvii, 208–213, 218,
 225, 259, 266, 351, 392, 398
Rathbone, Eleanor: 111
Rattigan, Sir Terence: 253
Rattle, Sir Simon: 331–2, 413
Rauter, Ferdinand: 180–1, 220,
 395
Ravel, Maurice: 55, 383
Rawicz and Landauer: 107
Rayner, John: 381
Read, Sir Herbert: 48, 53, 196,
 280–1, 282, 298/f, 407, 408
Reading (university): 107
Reagan, Ronald: 191, 290
Redlich, Hans: 325
Reed, Carol: 162
Rees, Goronwy: 136
Reich, Wilhelm: 324, 418
Reifenberg, Heinz J.: 257
Reinhardt, Max: 12, 15, 292
Reisz, Karel: 93, 287, 289–90, 299,
 408